2003 Edition

Tourism Market Trends

Asia and the Pacific

World Tourism Organization
Capitán Haya 42, 28020 Madrid, Spain
Tel: (+34) 915678100; Fax: (+34) 915713733
E-mail: omt@world-tourism.org
Web: www.world-tourism.org

Tourism Market Trends: Asia and the Pacific
2003 Edition

ISBN: 92-844-0648-X
Published by the World Tourism Organization

Printed by the World Tourism Organization
Madrid, Spain

Foreword

This report has been prepared by the WTO Market Intelligence and Promotion Section. Chapter I, *Main Features*, was drafted by Tourism Consultant Mr. Tim Bartlett, director of TRI Hospitality Consulting Spain. The WTO Regional Representation for Asia and the Pacific also made a valuable contribution.

Except where otherwise indicated, data used was collected by the WTO Secretariat from the official institutions of the countries and territories. Quantitative data has been reported by National Tourism Administrations (NTAs), National Tourism Organizations (NTOs), statistical offices or national banks and a few international organizations. The *Survey* sections for the various countries and territories included in Chapter III were contributed by the tourism institutions that replied to the corresponding questionnaire sent by the WTO Secretariat.

The World Tourism Organization wishes to express its sincere gratitude to all who have participated in the elaboration of this report for their valuable and decisive cooperation, in particular to the organizations and persons involved from the various countries and territories.

Explanation of symbols and conventions used

*	=	provisional figure or data
..	=	figure or data not (yet) available
0 or 0.0	=	rounded figure where the original figure is less than half of the unit chosen (-0 when rounding a negative figure)

(000)	=	thousand
mn	=	million (1,000,000)
bn	=	billion (1,000,000,000)

Due to rounding, some totals may not correspond exactly with the sum of the separate figures.

Table of Contents

The *Tourism Market Trends, 2003 Edition* series

Tourism Market Trends is WTO's regular series of reports whose objective is to present international tourism trends in the world as well as in each region, subregion and country. The full series consists of one volume providing an overview of the tourism trends in the world and five regional volumes highlighting the international tourism trends in each of the regions.

The structure of the series introduced in the 2001 edition, and further developed in the 2002 edition, has been maintained in the *Tourism Market Trends, 2003 Edition,* namely:

- The analysis of the evolution of international tourism worldwide and the accompanying aggregated data is presented in a separate volume *World Overview and Tourism Topics*. The second part of this volume is dedicated to a discussion of tourism topics of interest, which for this year are related to cultural tourism, the hotel industry and the impact of major events.
- Detailed information on the various regions of the world and on the individual countries and territories they are composed of is included in five regional volumes respectively covering Africa, Americas, Asia and the Pacific (integrating the WTO regions of East Asia and the Pacific and South Asia), Europe and the Middle East.
- Each regional volume opens with a first chapter *Main Features* containing an overview of the tourism development in the region based on the information provided by the National Tourism Administrations or National Tourism Organisations of the various countries in response to the survey conducted by the Market Intelligence and Promotion Section.
- Chapter II includes a more in-depth quantitative analysis of tourism trends in terms of tourism arrivals and receipts, as well as a breakdown of inbound by regions of origin, means of transport and purpose of visit. Concerning outbound tourism, data is also included on international tourism expenditure and outbound trips taken.
- Chapter III of the regional volumes includes results for the individual countries or territories of the region. For each country the following information is included (to the extent that data has been made available):
    - A Profile table including the following data series:
        - different categories of International Arrivals (inbound tourism);
        - Tourism accommodation: number of rooms and nights spent (inbound tourism and domestic tourism);
        - Trips abroad (outbound tourism);
        - Receipts and Expenditure for International Tourism;
        - various indicators of an economic or general nature.
    - The full response to the survey conducted by the WTO Secretariat for each individual country or territory that replied. The survey encompasses an evaluation of the past year (2002) as well as an outlook on the year 2003.
    - Detailed tables on arrivals and nights broken down by country of origin.
- Each of the six volumes is concluded with an annex comprising overview tables of data on international tourist arrivals and international tourism receipts for all countries for which data are available, methodological notes on concepts and definitions, sources of the data used, and sources of information.

The WTO Secretariat is constantly striving to extend and enhance the content of the Tourism Market Trends series. Some of the changes and additions introduced in the 2003 edition are:

- The evolution of International Tourism Receipts has been analysed in local currencies in order to eliminate the distortion caused by exchange rate fluctuations with the US dollar. The tables on International Tourism Receipts in the Annex are included in both US dollar and euro.
- In the survey section for the individual countries in Chapter III, except for the regular questions on tourism development, a set of questions has been included paying special attention to Cultural Tourism.

When using the reports the following considerations should be borne in mind:

- In accordance with the nature of the data provided by the countries and territories, the focus is on inbound tourism. When referring to outbound tourism trends, it should be taken into account that this information is largely derived from the same inbound-oriented data. The Secretariat covers outbound tourism in a separate series of reports, see the annex for more information.
- The emphasis in the analysis and the tables is on medium-term rather than on short-term development. For the short-term evolution of tourism WTO recently introduced the *WTO World Tourism Barometer*. The *WTO World Tourism Barometer* is published three times a year (January, June and October) and contains three permanent elements: an overview of short-term tourism data; a retrospective and prospective evaluation of tourism performance by the WTO Panel of Tourism Experts and selected economic data relevant for tourism; see the annex or the WTO website for more information.
- The reports generally reflect data as collected by the WTO Secretariat up to September 2003 (see the foot of each table). Data is often still provisional and can be updated or revised by the reporting countries in a later stage without further notice. When making references it is preferable always to attempt using the latest published data.
- In the world and (sub)regional aggregates (totals, subtotals), estimates are included to make allowance for the countries and territories with data still missing based upon data available for a part of the year or the general trend for the region. The data presented for the individual countries, however, reflect what has been reported for each country and does not include estimates of the WTO Secretariat.
- The Secretariat of the World Tourism Organization is aware of the limitations of the available statistical information on tourism. Despite the considerable progress made in recent decades, tourism statistics are often not uniform, because definitions and methods of data collection tend to differ. Every user of this information should bear in mind that the international comparability of statistical data is still not optimal.

The contents of this report are prepared under the responsibility of the WTO Market Intelligence and Promotion Section. Except where otherwise indicated, the quantitative and qualitative information in this report is based on data supplied by the official institutions of the various countries and territories.

The WTO Secretariat wishes to express its sincere gratitude for the reception given to this publication and for the cooperation it received in preparing this report. It welcomes the active involvement of countries, as well as their comments and suggestions on the design and contents of this series.

I

Main Features: Asia and the Pacific

I Main Features: Asia and the Pacific

2002 was a year of continuous growth for international tourism in the Asia and the Pacific region. Although the region was hit in the second semester by terrorist attacks of significant repercussion, these events have not deter the positive evolution of tourist arrivals. The most affected destinations reacted promptly, putting into practise special and effective marketing plans.

Asia: International Tourist Arrivals (ITA) and International Tourism Receipts (ITR)

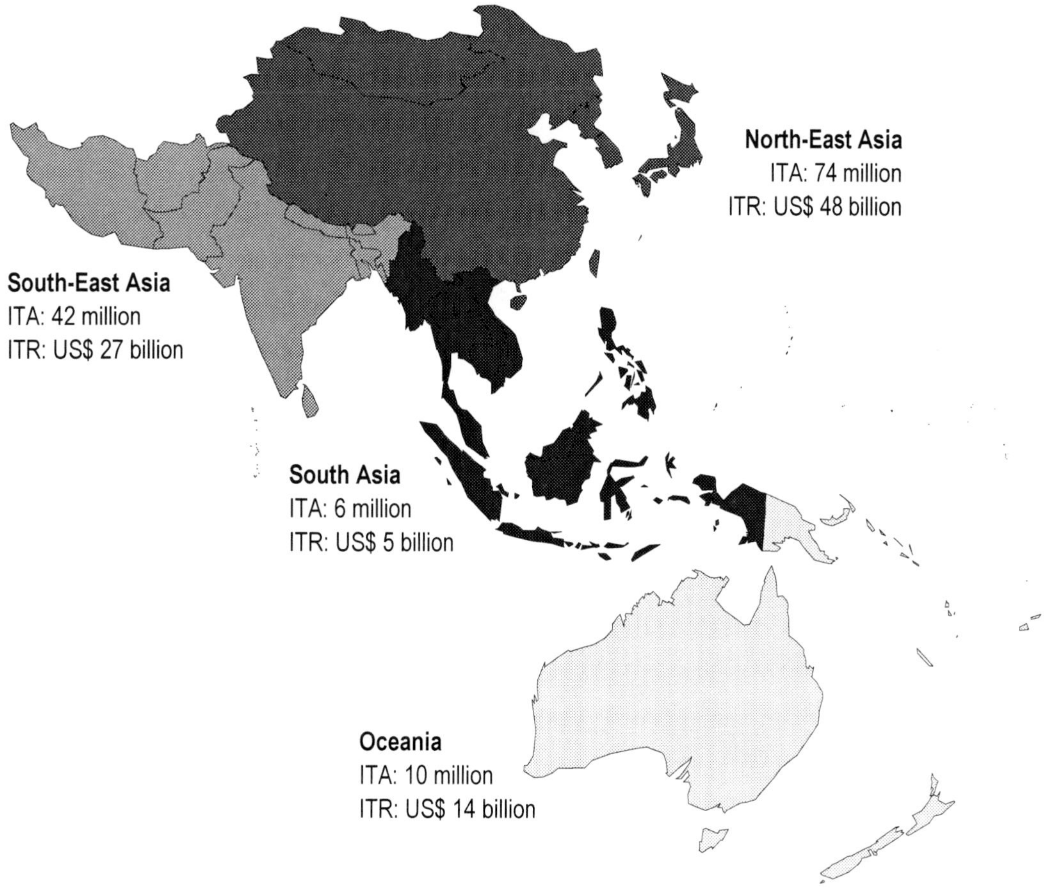

North and South-East Asia showed the best results in the region, while South Asia and Oceania returned to the positive track, though still very much below the regional performance. This positive result was due in particular to intraregional markets. Traditional generating markets for the region, like Japan, the United States and some European countries, had a limited growth, which was compensated by the traffic from regional emergent markets, in particular from China. Results in South Asia were also very much driven by the Indian generating market, which has gain momentum with the improvement of its economic and political situation. Alike in other subregions there was also a significant increase in arrivals from nationals residing abroad as well as in domestic tourism. The Pacific registered a somewhat dissimilar evolution as the generating markets of Japan, the US and Europe generated the biggest number of arrivals. Within the region Australia also positioned as an important source market.

Tourism development in the region, and in particular in many destinations in the Pacific, was constrained by world and regional air transport conjuncture. Nevertheless there was a clear capacity of reaction by national carriers which tended to occupy market shares left by other airlines. Access to destinations in the region was improved due to the high number of interventions envisaged to enhance infrastructures in all transportation systems, in terms of external access to countries, but also in terms of internal circulation. Travel advisories remained, however, as a negative note, restraining travel decisions to the region both by consumers and companies.

In terms of Tourism Policy there was a clear progress in the field of the legal and institutional framework towards a bigger liberalization. There was also an increased intervention in the area of investment. Actions undertaken by the National Tourism Administrations have been essential in the definition of development and / or recovery plans. These have mainly reflected priorities in the areas of liberalization, security, development of regional routes, creation of employment, human resources and public-private partnership.

There were also joint efforts to improve the quality of tourism products and the effectiveness of promotional activities, through a clear definition of markets and marketing instruments. Many destinations still in an early development stage have defined tourism as a national priority, stimulating development through the participation of local communities and criteria of sustainability.

Though most countries continued to use traditional promotional instruments, there was an increased employ of information technologies (IT) and particularly of Internet. There has been a frequent use of familiarization trips and such other activities aimed at the distribution circuits as well as at the media. A clear emphasis has been given to the promotion of cultural and nature tourism and in particular to the promotion of congresses and water activities. Marketing plans envisaged at very specific segments were implemented in the case of some countries such as the ones aimed at expatriated nationals or passengers in transit.

Overall Performance

Asia Pacific had a very good year with growth in arrivals of 8.4 per cent, a considerable improvement over its 2001 result of plus 5.1 per cent. East Asia and the Pacific (8.8%) performed better than South Asia (0.9%), which suffered several regional disturbances.

North-East Asia was the subregional star with 12.2 per cent growth. Not surprisingly mainland **China** made a good contribution to this with an 11 per cent increase, but there were extraordinary performances from China's special territories **Hong Kong** and **Macao** with increases of 20.7 per cent and 12.4 per cent respectively, and from **Mongolia** with an increase e of 19.4 per cent but on a very small base. **Japan** and the **Republic of Korea** both benefited from the Football World Cup which brought almost 50,000 supporters from overseas, of which 60 per cent were Europeans. However the Republic of Korea saw a decrease in arrivals in the first half of the year, due mainly to the impact of September 11th. There was a gradual recovery in the second half, and the very successful World Cup significantly boosted the country's image overseas. The tourism balance was however aggravated by a surge in Koreans travelling overseas. **Japan's** arrivals grew by 9.8 per cent to 5,239 million, mainly due to an increase in East Asian travellers showing a preference for short-haul trips following September 11th. The Yen was stable against the dollar in 2002 but consumer prices were down by 9 per cent, the fourth consecutive year of decrease. These factors depressed domestic travel but encouraged incoming.

South-East Asia grew at a rate of 5 per cent in 2002, significantly slower than the 8.7 per cent recorded in 2001. **Cambodian** arrivals grew at an impressive 30 per cent, but **Indonesia's** declined by 2.3 per cent due to the significant impact of the Bali terrorist attack in October. **Malaysia** grew at a steady 4 per cent, while **Myanmar** reached 6 per cent, being able to provide safe and secure access to the main tourist sites of Mandalay and Bagan throughout the year, even during the rainy season. **Thailand** grew faster at 7.3 per cent. In the **Philippines** the focused and aggressive marketing campaign *"Visit Philippines Year 2003"* achieved significant arrivals growth to that country of 7.6 per cent after several years of negative growth - the general shift away from long-haul markets helped to boost intraregional growth. **Singapore** also recovered from the 2001 negative results and grew by 4 per cent.

South Asia's increase in arrivals of 0.9 per cent was quite good considering the range of problems which the region suffered in 2002. Arrivals in **Bhutan** decreased to a total of 6 thousand (-6%) due to regional disturbances and to severe climactic conditions which created major problems for the single national airline and for surface travel. **India's** arrivals decreased from 2.5 million in 2001 to 2.4 million in 2002, a decline of 6.6 per cent following its 2001 decline of 4.2 per cent. Figures were consistently negative from September 2001 to September 2002 due to world tourism conditions plus heightened tensions on the India/Pakistan border. However there was a good recovery in the last three months – up 17 per cent, 16 per cent and 10 per cent respectively. The estimated growth rates for foreign exchange earnings in those months were even higher (+24%, +20%, and +14%). The Maoist insurgency damaged **Nepal's** image, but arrivals have been picking up since the cease-fire, especially from India, where economic conditions are improving. **Pakistan's** results were also hit by geopolitical, economic and security factors, and by severe weather. The bright spots in the subregion were the **Maldives**, which has a stable, tropical, upmarket and well-differentiated image, and **Sri Lanka**. These grew by 5.2 per cent and 16.7 per cent respectively, but it should be noted that Sri Lanka was bouncing back from a decline of 16 per cent in 2001.

Oceania's marginal 0.8 per cent growth reflects the decline in long-haul travel and the impact of distance from the main source markets. The collapse of Canada 3000 and Ansett hit Canadian and Australian traffic; directional traffic flows throughout the region were greatly affected. But performance varied widely from increases of 25 per cent in **Micronesia**, 18 per cent in **Kiribati**, 14 per cent in **Fiji**, 14 per cent in **Tonga**, 9 per cent in **Palau** and 7 per cent in **New Zealand** to decreases of 17 per cent in the **French Polynesia**, 9 per cent in **Guam**, 7 per cent in **Vanuatu**, and 2 per cent in the **Cook Islands**. **Tonga** attributes its large increase in arrivals and foreign exchange earnings wholly to successful promotion and marketing. **Vanuatu** was constrained by lack of air capacity. The **Cook Islands**, despite showing a small annual decline, bounced back in the last quarter with growth from all key markets stimulated by strong marketing campaigns. Tourism contributes 54 per cent of Gross Domestic Product (GDP). In the **Marshall Islands** tourist arrivals increased by 10.2 per cent. Geographical isolation is still a constraint. **Yap** received 53 per cent more arrivals than projected: some donated infrastructure development projects boosted traffic, especially from the Philippines and China. **New Caledonia** suffered from the bad international tourism climate and from economic weakness in Japan, but it still managed an increase in arrivals of 3.5 per cent to a total of 104 million. **Papua New Guinea** showed a small 0.4 per cent decline, due to domestic instability, the general election, and poor image perception. Tourism development over the last two years has been very slow, but the locals are becoming more interested in tourism and there has been some spin-off from decreases in other regions.

Arrivals to **Australia** declined marginally by 0.3 per cent (following minus 1.5% in 2001) but tourism expenditure rose by 6 per cent. Due to the uncertain world economic environment and regional security concerns following the Bali bombing in October there were significant drops in overnights for holidays (-10%) and for "visiting friends and relatives" (-7%), which were offset by increases in overseas students (21%), employment (10%) and business visitors (9%). Backpackers and people coming to Australia for the purposes of employment together account for only 16 per cent of visitors but over half (52%) of overnights and 45 per cent of total expenditure. Capital cities, particularly those significantly dependent on international visitors, fared worst; destinations within an easy drive from major population centres fared better. Tourism GDP and employment fell slightly. Three states were affected by bushfires at the end of the year; this was coupled with drought conditions in some areas. Rapid increases in the price of public liability insurance and difficulty in obtaining it was a top concern for many small tourism businesses, especially adventure and tour operators and the horse riding industry. Arrivals to **New Zealand** showed an increase of 7.1 per cent. This good performance was greatly assisted by two major showcase events: the release of the first part of the Lord of the Rings and the Americas Cup Yachting Regatta.

Source Markets

China recorded notable growth from its top 15 markets and more than 20 percent from near markets like Thailand, the Republic of Korea, Malaysia, and Philippines. It sees good future growth potential from Japan and Indonesia. **Japan's** good performance was mainly due to increases from China and the Republic of Korea. Arrivals from Hong Kong (China) and Taiwan (Province of China) were also better than expected. These four markets comprise 55 per cent of total arrivals. Major source markets for **Macao (China)** are Hong Kong (China), which accounts for 44 per cent of arrivals, China with 37 percent, and Taiwan (Province of China) with 13 per cent. Arrivals from China grew by 41 per cent to 4.2 million. Taiwan (Province of China) showed growth of 6 per cent, Japan of 1 per cent, and the United States of 4 per cent, but Hong Kong (China) declined by 1.8 per cent. **The Republic of Korea** benefited from the World Cup effect: the share of arrivals from Europe and the Americas, which had been on the decline, rose to 20 per cent from 18 per cent. Japan was the largest market and produced 43 per cent of inbound travellers compared with 46 per cent in 2001. The number of arrivals from Japan has declined for two consecutive years. Arrivals from China, which became the number two market in 2001 ahead of the United States, grew by 12 per cent in 2002. More visitors came from the major South-East Asian countries and from Hong Kong (China) for winter tourism products. **Taiwan's (Province of China)** main markets are Japan, the overseas Chinese, Hong Kong (China), South-East Asia, and MICE segments. Emerging markets and segments are China and cruises.

In **Malaysia** arrivals from China and India rose by 23 per cent and 28 per cent respectively. 57 per cent of arrivals in **Myanmar** were from Asia and 30 per cent from Europe. In **Philippines**, declines from the Unites States and Japan were compensated by the performance of growth markets like Singapore, Hong Kong (China) and the Republic of Korea. China moved up **Singapore's** market league from 5th to 3rd overtaking Malaysia and

Australia, while India rose from 9th to 7th, overtaking the United States and the Republic of Korea.

India's main markets are the United Kingdom with 390,762 arrivals, a share of 16.5 per cent; the United States with 333,382 arrivals and a 14 per cent share; and Sri Lanka with 107,729 arrivals and a 4.6 per cent share. Next come Canada with a 3.7 per cent share, France 3.5 per cent, Germany 2.8 per cent, Japan 2.5 per cent, Malaysia 2.3 per cent, and Nepal 2 per cent. Tourism to **Nepal** benefited from India's economic growth, but poor economic conditions in Japan, in the United States, and in other generating markets had a negative impact. The **Maldives** reported growth from France, Japan, the Netherlands, Switzerland, the United Kingdom and the United States. However the Italian market, which is the largest, declined by 0.7 per cent, and the German, which used to be number two, declined by 4.4 per cent. The Australian market fell by 21.3 per cent. **Pakistan** reported a sharp decline post September 11th from the United States, the United Kingdom and other European markets. Emerging markets with potential are Japan, the Republic of Korea, the Far and the Middle East, and a strong emerging segment is expatriate Pakistanis. Domestic tourism is rising, mainly from industrial cities like Karachi, Lahore, Faisalabad, Sialkot. Many Pakistani families go on holidays to the mountains during the summer.

The **Cook Islands** reported a low level of arrivals from European markets in the first three quarters. The Canadian and Australian markets were hit by airline collapses, but fortunately extra capacity from New Zealand compensated these losses - arrivals from New Zealand ended the year 23 per cent up. There were good increases in weddings, honeymoons, special interests, cultural and educational tours. **Guam** benefited from the growth in Korean outbound and increasing interest from China. Wedding groups remained a steady business. Japanese arrivals to the **Marshall Islands** dropped considerably, but an increase from North America demonstrated the destination's resilience. Japanese and American divers make up approximately 60 per cent of all holiday visitors. There were also indications of growth in sports fishing (big game and fly) and in the cultural market. Taiwan (Province of China) is emerging as a good general interest market. The Japanese market to **Papua New Guinea** increased due to the introduction of a direct flight. The American market also increased. **Samoa** reported that its Australian and New Zealand arrivals continued to grow, and that its German, British and American markets were strong. **Tonga** achieved a large increase from the United States. **Tuvalu** depends heavily on the MICE market, since it is mainly business travellers who can afford to visit. The aim in future is to concentrate more on the ecotourism sector. **Yap's** main market is the United States mainland, followed by Japan. In recent years arrivals from Europe have been increasing fast, especially for diving.

French Polynesia's principal markets are the United States, France and Japan. Its secondary markets are Italy, the United Kingdom, Germany, Spain, South America (principally Argentina, Brazil and Chile), Australia and New Zealand. There are also emerging markets with good potential in Northern Europe, Central Europe and Russia. The United States' market has declined partly due to general tourism trends but principally as a result of the cessation of Renaissance Cruises to French Polynesia. There has been a 20 per cent growth from Japan directly due to an increase in air capacity. New **Caledonia's** main markets were France with 29,964 arrivals; Japan with 27,702; Australia with 19,216; and New Zealand with 5,935. Most of **Vanuatu's** arrivals come from Australia and New Zealand. It is looking towards Japan for future growth.

Australia saw remarkable growth in the Chinese market in 2001 (plus 31%) and 2002 (plus 17%). However following the events of September 11th the outbound Japanese market shrunk by 33 per cent, leading to a 24 per cent decline in Japanese visitors to Australia in the four months to December 2001. An aggressive marketing campaign by the Australian Tourism Commission (ATC), coupled with slowly improving air capacity, steered the market back into growth of 6.2 per cent, a total of 715,500 arrivals by 2002. **New Zealand's** top 10 markets provided 78 per cent of inbound arrivals. There was strong growth from the Republic of Korea (26%); from China (44%); from Japan (16%); from the United Kingdom (12%); and from the United States (10%). The Australian market was weak, growing by just 0.3 per cent, and Germany declined by 7 per cent.

Tourism Products

Japan increased its focus on nature and greenery, for example featuring the hot springs which particularly attract Asian visitors, also special flowers of the north, salmon returning to their native rivers, and monkeys enjoying hot spring baths on winter snowfall days. Japan also re-evaluated its security and hygiene infrastructure. A massive range of projects is underway in **Macao (China)**. US$ 594 million in being spent on extending the Hotel Lisbon's gambling palace, on constructing Fisherman's Wharf and on reforming the Inner Harbour. Fisherman's wharf alone will cost US$ 119 million and will comprise Dynasty Wharf, encapsulating Chinese history and culture, an East meets West attraction with man-made volcano, and Legend Wharf. It will be completed in 2004. A major theme park is planned for the Inner Harbour and a new luxury hotel, destination casino resort and retail/entertainment complex (Wynn Macau) will open in 2004. Also under construction are: a luxury resort with casino, multi-purpose trade show and conference facilities; a Venetian style hotel casino joint venture, which will comprise a casino covering 100,000 square metres, three exhibition and convention centres able to accommodate 25,000 people, a hotel with more than 3000 rooms, an art museum, a hall for variety shows, and more than 10 restaurants; the A-Ma cultural village; TV City, which will be one of the largest production facilities in Asia, with 9 studios plus tourist attractions; Cultural Centre Plaza; the Macau Science Centre; and a Stadium and Dome for the 2005 East Asian Games. Historic Taipa Village is being enhanced and two new museums have been created - the Heritage Exhibition of a Traditional Pawnshop Business and the Sound of the Century Museum, which exhibits for example antique gramophones, radios and wooden telephones. The **Republic of Korea** has also been very active in product development, much of it stimulated by the holding of the FIFA World Cup and the Busan Asian Games. For the World Cup the Government secured a total of 178,000 rooms, including the designation of 135 thousand rooms in ten venues as recommended lodging facilities, to prepare for the transient demand surge. In addition from among the designated establishments, the Government named outstanding ones as World Inns, equipping them with internet reservations systems. Interpretation phones enabling three people to talk together were installed in accommodation facilities and taxis. The *"Before Babel Brigade"* (BBB) translation service provided interpretation by volunteers through mobiles. Emphasis was also placed on special *"Experience Korea"* products, for example herbal medicine and kimchi making. A Temple Stay Programme was offered at 33 temples nation-wide giving the opportunity for visitors to participate in everyday Buddhist activities. A trial overland tour to Mount Kumgang was carried out and efforts were made to develop better tourism utilisation of traditional events and pageantry, for example the Royal Guards Changing Ceremony and the Coronation Ceremony of King Sejong. **Taiwan (Province of China)** co-ordinated 12 major festivals in 2002.

Indonesia focused on achieving high spending through product diversification, for example MICE, eco and marine tourism, and cruises, and on encouraging regional spread through community based tourism. **Myanmar** promoted its festivals and ecotourism attractions, together with ballooning, pilgrimages and seminars. Potential tourism sites were developed in Myitkyina, Putao, Kawthaung, the Myeik Archipelago, Ngwe Saung Beach, and Mrauk-U. The **Philippines** created new affordable *"Wow Packages"* and, in collaboration with Singapore, *"VIPS Travel Packages"*. Product diversification continued with growing emphasis on nature and adventure, also health and spa tourism. **Singapore** majored on events, for example the Hari Raya Lightup, Chingay, the Singapore Arts Festival, the Caltex Masters, plus fashion and food events.

In **Bhutan** a new Dzongkhag (district) Haa was opened to tourists. The annual inspection of hotels and restaurants was conducted and hotels were classified to improve standards. The number of available rooms in **India** reached 80,936 in 2002. Over 20,500 of these are at three star level, over 15,400 at two star and over 15,000 at five star De Lux. Demand for hotel management and catering education programmes boomed: there are now 21 Institutes of Hotel Management and 9 Food Craft Institutes. The product offer is wide, ranging from nature, art, architecture, adventure, rural, wildlife into more unusual areas like Yoga and the Siddha, Ayurveda and Unani systems of dealing with physical and mental illnesses. There are 3,606 protected monuments, 89 National Parks and 483 wildlife sanctuaries. **Pakistan** has added new products, including more accommodation capacity, and prices are low. However there is a lack of proper planning for events and of evening entertainment. In **Nepal** hotel prices have dropped. 103 new peaks have been opened up for climbing and 5 new rivers for rafting. Bed capacity in the **Maldives** at the end of 2002 reached 18,827: 16,400 in the 87 island resorts, 670 in 8 hotels, 282 in 17 guesthouses, and 1,475 in 96 safari boats. Each island open for tourism has one resort with modern facilities. Proposals for a Yacht Marina were evaluated and the project was awarded. A new resort is being constructed on Villingili Island, which will commence operations at the end of 2003, initially with 500 beds. A programme to install recreational mooring buoys was launched; its aim is to minimise reef damage from safari boats anchoring at popular sites.

Several new upmarket boutique hotels opened in the **Cook Islands**, and one luxury resort on the island of Aitutaki. Some private home rentals also commenced operations while existing establishments focused on upgrading. New products included an ecotourism operation and a lagoon cruise. **Guam's** infrastructure was damaged by two devastating typhoons in 2002. Its general aim is to strengthen and improve the product. A new 32-room luxury establishment opened in the **Marshall Islands** and there were also extensions and renovations to existing facilities. Development is hampered by difficult access to funds for domestic investors. A new dive operator started up. Events such as fishing tournaments and sailing canoe races are maturing satisfactorily. **Papua New Guinea** developed new accommodation, tourism facilities, entertainment and cultural events. However the increase in import prices due to devaluation is inhibiting development. **Samoa** now has better infrastructure services in place, having for example improved road networks, telecommunications, water supply, education and health standards. The Teuila festival in September and Village Beautification Competitions are popular products. In **Tonga** new accommodation capacity is due to be constructed and the upgrading of current establishments is underway. Environmentally friendly products will be incorporated into promotion and marketing. **Tuvalu's** accommodation capacity consists of one hotel, four guesthouses and a conservation area run by native people. There is limited land available. The number of buoys in the lagoon was increased to cater for boat tourism. Many entertainment events were organised, for example beauty contests. New hotel rooms are being planned in **Yap**, also more entertainment and activities. Traditional sea navigation sailing is being revived.

In **French Polynesia** hotel capacity grew by 15 per cent. 412 new international hotel rooms are under construction for 2003, and around 140 new family rooms. Products were reinforced for the main segments – honeymoons and underwater swimming/diving. Green tourism is growing, so eco attractions and footpaths have been upgraded. Attractive events were maintained, for example Hawaiki Nui, Heiva, and Billagong Pro. Service quality was improved through training and the classification of accommodation is underway. Rules were changed to improve quays and encourage more nautical activities. A successful family stay product was developed for travellers in search of authenticity. **New Caledonia** saw the opening of the three star Ouré Lodge on the Ile des Pins and of the Casa de Sole Aparthotel in Nouméa (128 apartments). However three hotels closed for renovation. Assistance from the European Union (UE) helped achieve the establishment and upgrading of the **Vanuatu** Island Bungalows Association. Another successful Vanuatu product is the Efate Round Island Relay.

In **Australia** accommodation capacity decreased by a marginal 0.9 per cent as operators shed capacity. The Government continued to work co-operatively with the industry to help develop and encourage participation in voluntary tourism accreditation schemes, including one for tourism businesses and another to improve the standard of service provided by tour guides. An extra AU$ 8 million over three and a quarter years was allocated to the Regional Tourism Programme, which boosts the capacity of businesses to develop higher quality tourism products and services. The new Australian Tourism Data Warehouse aims to catalogue all tourism products electronically: by June 2002, 10,500 operators were featured. The Gay Games in November attracted approximately 30,000 competitors to Sydney. **New Zealand** has seen little innovation in product development over the last five years. The majority of new products have been luxury lodges in spectacular settings and nature tours. Mainstream accommodation capacity has increased considerably, but there has been little reinvestment, so quality has declined. The Government is funding through the tourist office the development of a national quality system which will be applied to all tourism experiences and services. This has been welcomed by the international travel trade. New Zealand has one of the lowest REVPARs (revenue per available room) in the world. This is increasing gradually, but not as fast as occupancy.

Access

China undertook major infrastructure improvements. 145 airports were expanded. Shanghai and the province of Hainan will apply visa exemptions for tourists. 22 ports will issue visas on arrival. With the inauguration in April 2002 of a second runway of 2,180 metres at Narita airport, short-haul flights between **Japan** and other Asian destinations, such as Taipei, Hong Kong (China), Seoul and major cities in mainland China, almost doubled. The border between **Macao (China)** and mainland China opened in 1979. The Macao Border Gate is under construction and will be finished in 2003. 4.8 million visitors entered Macao (China) here in 2002, an increase of 18.8 per cent. The Third Macao – Taipa bridge is under construction. In 2002 Air Macau inaugurated regular flights to Singapore and Malaysia. To encourage visits from China, 528 mainland tour operators have been approved under the Macao Tour Scheme. Moreover 76 agencies in Macao (China) have been admitted as ground receiving agents for this scheme. Further visa exemption was added for holders of Republic of Croatia passports entering Macao (China) with valid passports for a stay of up to 90 days. The Macao Government Tourist Office and Silkair signed a memo of understanding in May 2002 to jointly develop a Singapore-Macao route. In April 2002, Yangyang International Airport in the **Republic of Korea** opened. This should increase visitors to Gangwon province which is rich in tourism product, for example skiing and autumn foliage. As of April 2002, there were 259 routes (including freight) into the Republic of Korea and 1,073 international passenger flights a week – an increase of 20 routes and 142 flights compared with April 2001. **Taiwan (Province of China)** eased entry formalities for visitors from Hong Kong (China), Singapore, and Malaysia by offering landing visas and visa free entry. Flights between Taiwan (Province of China) and Japan increased from 168 weekly to 176, and between Taiwan (Province of China) and Hong Kong (China) from 121 weekly to 153.

Indonesia reported that its local transport systems between islands, cities, and countryside are often not good enough. **Malaysia** continued to improve entry procedures, for example by granting visas on arrival. **Myanmar** also made immigration improvements, allowing 28 day tourist visas to be extended by another 14 days, and introducing visas on arrival for charter flights, cruises and package groups. Two new airports were constructed in the **Philippines**: Santa Barbara in Iloilo Province (to international standard); and Laginlingan in Misamis Orientalo. Many regional airports and ports were improved and upgraded. However tourism growth is still inhibited by low frequencies and/or no flights to key cities in Europe and China. It is also inhibited by complicated visa processes in new markets like China and India due to the lack of tourism offices there and to strict visa policies. The Philippine Government is particularly concerned at the damage which can be done by sudden and misinformed travel advisories. In 2002 it worked with other Governments, for example the United States, Japan and China, to press for more carefully worded advisories.

Bhutan is served by a single airline, Druk Air, which has two planes with a capacity for 72 passengers each. In 2002 Druk Air initiated measures to procure bigger aircraft, probably Airbus 318s with capacity for 130. In the meantime they increased frequencies, especially to Bangkok which is an important entry point for Bhutan. Druk Air also operates via Rangoon. **India** launched its New Highways Development Project three years ago. This project comprises the 6,000 kilometre long Golden Quadrilateral (GQ) connecting the four metropolitan centres of Delhi, Mumbai, Cheney and Collate, and the 7,000 kilometre North-South, East-West corridors connecting Srinagar-Kanyakumari and Silichar-Porbandar respectively. The GQ has been awarded. It is expected to be substantially completed by December 2003 and the two corridors by 2007. It is proposed to upgrade the international airports at Delhi, Mumbai, Cheney and Collate to world class standards. 17 new inter city train services have been introduced. Singapore Airlines pulled out of **Nepal** and some international airlines reduced frequencies. However a MartinAir flight connecting Nepal to the Netherlands, replacing Transavia on that route, started operations in 2003. Improvements were made in visa and frontier formalities. In **Pakistan** terminals were built at Karachi and Lahore International Airports, and a plan is underway to upgrade Islamabad airport. New highways were constructed and major ongoing motorway projects include Lahore-Islamabad, Islamabad-Peshawar, Karachi-Gawadar, the Indus Highway and the Gawadar Port/Coastal Highway. However entry formalities remain rigid post September 11th.

Air travel to the **Cook Islands** was severely impacted by the collapse of Canada 3000 and of Ansett Australia. However New Zealand is a key gateway, and fortunately Air New Zealand increased its services to daily non-stop flights with B767 aircraft. Air New Zealand also put on three Los Angeles- Rarotonga services per week, one service via Tahiti and one from Fiji connecting with Auckland flights. Moreover Aloha Airlines launched services linking Vancouver and United States west coast cities to the Cook Islands via Honolulu. The **Cook Islands** maintain a visa-free policy for trusted visitors staying up to 31 days. Airline capacity to **Guam** was reduced due to low demand. International and domestic airfares to and within the **Marshall Islands** remained relatively high. A positive development was the addition of Air Kiribati flights, reconnecting the Nadi and Majuro hubs, once a week at present. Since 2000, there have been five weekly flights from Honolulu and three from Guam. The bottleneck via Guam for Asian visitors to Majuro remained a major constraint. Domestic capacity on Air Marshall Islands improved with the acquisition of a 36 seats Dash-8 aircraft. **Papua New Guinea** benefited from the introduction of new direct holiday flights, particularly Port Moresby to Narita in Japan. **Samoa** was able to maintain frequent flights to and from the major markets of Australia and New Zealand. Airfares remained very expensive because it was still only served by three airlines. Efforts were made to streamline entry formalities. **Tuvalu** suffered from limited and expensive air access, with all flights routed via Fiji. Continental Airlines is the main carrier to **Yap**, while domestic carrier Pacific Missionary Aviation gives access to the outer islands using small runways. Traditional sailing sea navigation is being revived and its potential explored, including the possibility of viable access to neighbouring sister states and to other Pacific countries. Access by sea is under the control of the Yap State Government.

Tahiti Faaa airport in **French Polynesia** is open 24 hours a day. 44 new airports have been opened throughout the islands. French Polynesia has suffered from the termination of Air Liban services and from cutbacks over the last two years by Air France, Qantas, Hawaiian Airlines, Lan Chile, and Corsair. The resulting shortage of air capacity from Europe has only been partly compensated by the spectacular development through Paris of its own airline Air Tahiti Nui, which has just bought two new Airbuses A340, and by an increase in capacity from Japan. Renaissance Cruises withdrew from French Polynesia at the end of 2001. However thanks to the efforts of the President, the cruise market has now begun to recover, notably with the start of Tahitian Princess services. There are now 8 cruise boats based in French Polynesia with a total of 804 cabins. **New Caledonia** maintained five Air France flights weekly from Tokyo; two Aircalin flights from Osaka; seven shared Aircalin/Qantas flights from Sydney and three from Brisbane; and four flights from New Zealand (two Aircalin and two Air New Zealand). The Pacific Princess, with capacity for 700 passengers, has stopped in New Caledonia since November 2002. **Vanuatu** upgraded Pekoa Airport in Santo (the country's second urban centre) to accommodate international carriers. It also upgraded the air terminal in the capital Port Vila to cater for larger aircraft. Air Vanuatu is short of capacity – so too is the only domestic airline.

Air **New Zealand** had financial difficulties in 2002, leading the Government to buy a majority share in it. In **Australia** the demise of Ansett Airlines was a major blow, but the sale of its Sydney terminal and the development of this as a common user facility helped facilitate expansion by other airlines. Qantas' new low cost international carrier, Australian Airlines, commenced operations to a range of Asian destinations from its base in Cairns. Virgin Blue continued to add to its domestic network. The Electronic Travel Authority (ETA) expanded in 2002, with residents from 34 countries able to apply for visas via the internet. Working holiday arrangements have been extended to 14 countries and the Department of Immigration and Multicultural and Indigenous Affairs (DIMIA) are currently negotiating similar arrangements with a number of countries including Belgium, Italy, France, Taiwan (Province of China), and Greece.

Tourism Policy

China's priorities are to strengthen tourism regulations; to improve order; to promote jobs; to invest in inland infrastructure; and to improve tourism information and communication systems. In **Japan** the importance of tourism has now been recognised by all levels of central and local Government and by economic federations. **Macao (China)** embarked upon more liberalisation of the gaming industry to attract international investors. It also enhanced co-operation with nearby Guandong and Hong Kong (China) to encourage regional tourism. It set up a MICE Research and Information Centre, and continued the Macao Tourism Awareness Campaign - *"Be my guest, feel at home"*. The **Republic of Korea's** First National Tourism Resources Development Plan ended in 2001, and the second was implemented in 2002. An Information Strategic Plan in the tourism sector was set up to respond to advances in digitalisation. The primary establishment of a Comprehensive Tourism Information System was achieved. The Foreign Investment Promotion Act and the Restriction of Preferential Taxation Act were amended to encourage foreign investment. The five key tasks of **Taiwan** (Province of China)'s *"Doubling of Tourist Arrivals Plan"* are: prepare package tour itineraries; develop new itineraries and attractions; establish a visitor services network; launch international advertising and promotion campaigns; and promote MICE.

In response to the Bali atrocity, the **Indonesian** Government launched a four phase recovery programme, with a Rescue Phase from October to December 2002; a Rehabilitation Phase from January to June 2003; a Normalisation Phase from July – December 2003; and an Expansion Phase from 2004 onwards. Emphasis was also placed on the development of competency-based training programmes. **Malaysia** focused on improving public/private partnerships; raising quality; encouraging local private investors; increasing local community participation in tourism activities; and developing domestic tourism. **Myanmar** introduced legislation to allow FIT's (Fully Independent Travellers) to change US$ 200 for foreign exchange certificates on arrival at Yangon. The third phase of the Tourism Manpower Training Programme and, under the initiative for ASEAN (Association of Southeast Asian Nations) integration, the Hospitality and Tourism Executive Programme for Myanmar were both implemented with Singapore Government support. The **Philippines** initiated area specific Master Plans and closer collaboration with local authorities to further regional spread. A domestic tourism advocacy programme and systems for assistance to tourists were implemented. The National Ecotourism Strategy was finalised. **Singapore** placed increased emphasis on tourism's contribution to the economy - the key tourism performance indicator will not be arrival numbers, but receipts and market share of total Asia and the Pacific receipts. The tourism organisation was realigned into strategic tourism business units reflecting purpose of visit, the aim being to enhance visitor experience. Since tourism is a multi-dimensional industry, there will be units looking into shared tourism clusters, and inter-agency collaboration to facilitate overall tourism sector development and to focus on improving service quality.

In **Bhutan** the Tourism Department initiated a feasibility study into the development of community-based tourism. The first phase has been completed. The establishment of a National Hotel and Tourism Management Training Institute is underway. Tourism has a high priority in the ninth five year plan, with particular emphasis on sustainable development. The

Master Plan is under review – guidelines and legislation are being developed. A series of meetings was held with stakeholders to discuss incentives, regulations, and human resource development. The Department provided training for front-line staff, for example cooks, guides, and receptionists. **India** announced a new tourism policy in May 2002. This will be Government led, private sector driven, and community welfare oriented, and will aim to position India as a global brand. Product development priorities will be: cultural tourism; beach and coastal tourism; cruise/river tourism; rural/village tourism; adventure tourism; ecotourism; cuisine; MICE; and festivals/shopping. There will be a new approach towards infrastructures and product development with seven key areas providing the thrust: 1. Swagat (Welcome); 2. Soochana (Information); 3. Suvidha (Facilitation); 4. Suraksha (Safety); 5. Sahyog (Co-operation); 6. Samrachna (Infrastructure Development); and 7. Safai (Cleanliness). **Pakistan** carried out a study for a Master Plan in collaboration with the World Tourism Organization (WTO) and the United Nations Development Programme (UNDP) in 1998-1999, but implementation of the recommendations has been slow. The **Maldives** continued the implementation of the second Tourism Master Plan (1996-2005) which focuses above all on human resources and the environment. A survey of some atolls was carried out to identify areas or islands suitable for resort development. A Shark-Watch programme was introduced to create awareness of the importance of sharks and the problems in protecting them.

In the **Cook Islands**, tourism has been concentrated on only two of the fifteen islands. The policy now is to develop tourism on other islands to stimulate economic growth. The emphasis will be on small scale, low-key developments. Human resource development and training was given a higher profile. A major Tourism Forum held in December 2002 called for an update of the Tourism Master Plan of 1992 and of the Island-Specific Strategic Development Plans of 1994 and 1995. The **Marshall Islands** gave priority to placing secure land on the market for both foreign and domestic investors, fostering the establishment of a Land Registry Authority. Tourism was identified by the National Training Labour Market survey as the number four human resource priority. A review of the tax structure was commenced. Greater attention was given to private sector development in the new Compact of Free Association with the United States. Special software was installed for broader tabulation of data from in-flight arrival forms. A long-term tourism Master Plan is expected no later than 2005. The Tourism Promotion Authority (TPA) is the lead agency in **Papua New Guinea**. Its Corporate Plan for 2002 to 2006 is based on: optimisation of impact within the context of limited resources; prioritisation of implementation strategies; and co-ordination and integration of focus and initiatives of both government and industry. Clear strategies have been developed with achievable measures. There is currently no National Tourism Master Plan, but TPA will take the lead in developing this in collaboration with government agencies and the private sector. The Government's Strategy for the Development of **Samoa** has identified tourism as one of its nine key priorities. A Trade and Investment Promotion Unit has been set up and transparent policies introduced to encourage foreign and local investment. Special duty concessions are offered for investors in hotels and other tourism operations. Samoa is in the process of joining the World Trade Organisation which will help open it up as an investment prospect. A hospitality and tourism course was set up at the Samoa Polytechnic. The Samoan Visitors Bureau had its name changed to the Samoan Tourism Authority (STA) as part of the development of the programme for a *"Focused Future of Tourism in Samoa"*. It has now formulated its *"Tourism Development Plan 2002-2006"*, identifying a new path forward for the STA and a new direction for the tourism industry as a whole. **Tonga** advocates active public participation in the tourism business, the encouragement of community participation, increased marketing and improved infrastructure.

In **Tuvalu** there has been no tourism planning during previous years but its development is now under study. The number of personnel in the tourism office will be increased; so too will the number of tourism training courses and workshops. More campaigns are planned to Keep Tuvalu Clean. The **Yap** State Legislature passed a resolution to broaden the assessment of potential products to be developed and marketed alongside existing attractions.

To encourage its young people to stay, **French Polynesia** is developing green/nature tourism to create employment. There are four priorities: to develop tourism infrastructure; to promote via tour operators in target markets, also using Public Relations and travel agent training; to create and maintain an international carrier – Air Tahiti Nui – to allow adaptation to demand and to insulate against world airline problems; and to improve the quality-price relationship using techniques like accommodation grading and staff training. A strict environment policy has been announced by the President of the Government. **New Caledonia** offered tax breaks for tourism investments and undertook a local tourism awareness campaign. **Vanuatu** concentrated on increasing facilities, improving quality, and promoting tourism development in the outer islands. It implemented the revised version of the Tourism Master Plan which was produced by the Commonwealth Secretariat in 2002.

In **Australia** the Minister for Small Business and Tourism released a consultative document to canvass the key issues for developing a medium to long term tourism strategy. Its five key themes are: evolution from a travel destination to a lifetime experience; product diversification; business yield/niche markets; profitability; and improved asset utilisation and co-ordination across the public and private sectors. Following September 11th and the collapse of Ansett Airlines, a National Tourism Issues Response Plan was developed setting out a process for delivering a coherent national response to minimise the impact of crises. The Plan was initiated for the Iraq War and extended to cover SARS (Severe Accurate Respiratory Syndrome). An Action Plan was formulated for the Japanese market to remove impediments to growth. A similar plan will be produced in 2003/4 for the market of the Republic of Korea. **New Zealand** implemented key recommendations in its Tourism Strategy 2010, including the re-branding of Qualmark to set in place a national quality framework for tourism products and services; the relaunch of the Visitor Information Network with the fern and i-site branding; the creation of the Business Builder CD-Rom; a new customer service training course for tourism employees; the consolidation of tourism statistics in one organisation (the Ministry of Tourism); and environmental management.

Marketing

China staged its International Tourism Market and initiated an exchange of tourism activities with Japan. In **Japan** a 2003 budget of almost US$ 9 million was approved for the *"Visit Japan Campaign"* which will cover five major markets - Republic of Korea, United States, China, Taiwan (Province of China) and Hong Kong (China). Japan also puts considerable emphasis on travel agent and media familiarisation visits. **Macao (China)** concentrated on its main source markets, especially Hong Kong (China), Taiwan (Province of China), Japan, Republic of Korea, Singapore, Malaysia, India and Thailand. 2002 was the second *"Visit **Korea** Year"* focusing on overseas promotion along with efforts to improve the infrastructure in order to heighten satisfaction levels inbound. The Busan Asian Games and above all the FIFA World Cup gave the Republic of Korea a major profile boost. Joint marketing activities were undertaken by World Cup venues, by the World Cup Organising Committee, and by the tourism sector. Between January and March *"2002 World Cup Special Tourism Promotion Teams"* were dispatched to 21 cities in 12 countries in Europe, North America, South America and Asia for publicity and promotion activities using the slogan *"Dynamic Korea, the Hub of Asia"*. Nineteen explanatory meetings were held with local journalists from 503 media outlets, and 20 Korean tourism trade fairs were held with 4,170 participants. Four World Cup commercials were made, tailored to each market, and aired on 42 major broadcasting systems, for example CNN, Eurosport, and STAR Sports, in 3 phases – before, during, and after the World Cup. A portal site in seven languages was developed and advertised though banners on the FIFA website. Promotion activities were carried out on key search engines, for example Yahoo, AOL and MSN. **Taiwan (Province of China)** concentrated its marketing campaigns on Japan, Hong Kong (China) and Malaysia. It also developed half day tours for transit passengers.

Indonesia was obliged to transform its marketing plan after the terrible attacks in Bali. Response activities included specific and intensive public relations; a peace mission and anti-terrorism campaign; the establishment of a communication centre; image campaign road shows visiting Europe, Asia, ASEAN countries and Australia; and redistribution of overall demand focusing on the regional and domestic markets. **Malaysia** developed more targeted promotion in traditional and new markets. **Myanmar** emphasised regional collaboration, working closely with ASEAN, PATA (Pacific Association of Travel Agents) and WTO. A *"Two countries – one destination"* promotion was developed with Thailand and a *"Four countries – one destination"* promotion with Cambodia, Laos and Thailand. A sister cities agreement between Bagan in Myanmar and Angkor Wat in Cambodia is being implemented. Approved Destination Status for Chinese citizens was achieved. The **Philippines** used positive and unique branding - "Wow Philippines – More Than The Usual", emphasising variety and colour. Most of the budget was spent overseas, including print and TV campaigns using CNN and the BBC. A series of major international sales missions were staged. Key target markets were Japan, Republic of Korea, Taiwan (Province of China), and China, plus the Philippines' traditional number one market – the United States. Australia will be considered for future growth. Overseas Filipino communities were targeted with the Tourism Volunteer 12 Programme. Sophisticated market segmentation was undertaken, and efforts were made to develop affordable packages. Specialised products were developed for the Chinese market and closer co-ordination took place with the Chinese Government regarding "zero tour fares and shopping scams". **Singapore's** new strategic focus was on Asian markets, including traditional ones like Indonesia and Malaysia, plus the aggressive targeting of new ones like China and India. More resources were dedicated to these markets, including the opening of new offices. Singapore also worked on the building of market segments for health and education services.

At the Outbound Travel Mart (OTM) held in India, **Bhutan** was declared and certified as the most promising new destination for regional tourists. In addition to its traditional marketing activities, **India** in 2002 placed special emphasis on countering negative publicity in the foreign media and restoring confidence amongst prospective visitors. It divided its markets into primary, secondary and tertiary, with total marketing support in primary markets including advertising, PR, consumer and trade shows; limited activity in secondary markets; and just servicing and some promotion in tertiary markets. An integrated electronic campaign on leading TV channels across the globe was undertaken centrally, supplemented by print advertising. In view of the global trend towards intraregional tourism, additional focus was given to aggressive promotion in East Asia and in the ASEAN countries. The Government-led Destination **Nepal** Campaign 2002-2003, along with the International Year of Ecotourism and the celebration of the Mount Everest Golden Jubilee, helped raised Nepal's image internationally. A special campaign was launched in North India to encourage border city traffic and a Sales Mission was organised in China. The Promotion and Publicity Department of the **Pakistan** Tourism Development Corporation has been converted into a fully fledged marketing department, but there is concern that Pakistan is not investing enough money in overseas promotion. Marketing efforts were focused on the Middle and Far East and in South Asia. The **Maldives'** principal aim is to create a distinctive image. In 2002 it invested in new European markets as well as traditional ones, for example by attending the Czech Republic Tourism Fair. In Japan its target segments are: working women; seniors; honeymooners; and special interest segments (for example water sports).

In the **Cook Islands** co-operative marketing initiatives between the Tourism Corporation and the private sector were strengthened. The main marketing thrust was Europe, North America, Australia, and New Zealand with emphasis on trade seminars, co-operative advertising with tour operators, trade and media familiarisation visits and the establishment of a Cook Islands Specialist Programme for selected travel agents. **Guam** promoted regional tourism through a *"Visit Magnificent Micronesia"* campaign. New tourism prospects include Korean visitors, military personnel and expatriates. Core targets are group travel, family travel from Japan, and young executive women. The over-riding aim is to brand Guam as a world class tourism destination. The **Marshall Islands** continued to focus on key niches, notably diving and sports fishing, and to a lesser extent in nautical tourism and World War II. The Marshall Islands attended specialised diving fairs worldwide and a general tourism fair in Taipei. Special campaigns focusing on cultural tours were conducted in nearby source markets, for example the Hawaiian Islands and the Kwajalein Atoll US military base. **Papua New Guinea** launched a new logo and slogan. It carried out aggressive campaigns in traditional, existing markets, and an awareness campaign in new markets, for example Russia and Scandinavia. **Samoa's** marketing campaign focused on New Zealand, Australia, and American Samoa, with the United States and Europe being targeted by web based marketing. Its key positioning is a unique destination with an authentic cultural and natural environment and not "touristy". There are no five star chain hotels and most tourism operations are owned and run by local Samoans. A customer survey was launched to obtain feedback. **Tonga's** priority was the active promotion of ecotourism and of quality products. **Tuvalu** also concentrated on ecotourism in order to preserve its environment naturally, culturally and economically. A Conservation area has been set up and successfully run for several years. Yacht and cruise tourists are particularly targeted, due to high airfares. **Yap** launched a new website.

French Polynesia's marketing was governed by five guiding principles: to promote the destination all year round to combat seasonality; to promote Tahiti as a separate and complete destination; to promote Huahine, Raiatea, Tahaa, Tikehau, Fakarava, Manihi and the Iles Marquises; to rationalise press activities; and to encourage the harmonisation of the hotel and airline seasons. A specialist travel agents programme was set up and a web strategy developed to move beyond information and feed customers to commercial booking sites and to special offers. Common procedures were developed for promotion and publicity – local professionals will be able to see clearly in which markets, when, and for what projects they will be able to link their budgets to tourism office budgets for joint advertising and brochures. **New Caledonia** strengthened its campaigns in Japan and worked on the development of MICE markets from Australia and New Zealand. **Vanuatu's** promotion budget for 2003 has been increased.

In **Australia** the ATC received an AU$ 24 million boost over five years to implement a business and leisure tourism market re-development package. A new AU$ 6 million TV campaign was launched in the United States promoting Australia as a realistic and affordable two week holiday destination. A marketing initiative was launched in Singapore. The Government provided an additional AU$ 8 million over four years to extend the existing *"See Australia"* marketing initiative, focusing on domestic tourism in regional and rural areas. **New Zealand** has developed significant understanding of its comparative international market share performance. This has led to increased investment in some markets, for example United States. Tourism New Zealand rolled out Phase 2 of the *"100% Pure New Zealand"* campaign with a new set of images. It also worked with the Discovery Channel to deliver New Zealand Week to audiences in over 11 countries. Successful efforts were made to increase the profile of Maori culture and to exert maximum leverage from the America's Cup and from the Lord of the Rings launch.

Prospects

China expects growth to continue, despite the major but short-lived setback of SARS. Its long-term target is 30 million international visitors and US$ 21.5 million in earnings. Major positives include joining the World Trade Organisation; the Beijing Olympics in 2008; and the World Expo in Shanghai in 2010. **Japan's** original forecast for 2003 was another 9.8 per cent increase, but SARS in its key generating markets between March and June has reduced expectations considerably. However a relatively fast recovery is predicted from China and from the Republic of Korea and a slower one from Hong Kong (China) and Taiwan (Province of China). The **Republic of Korea** also suffered a major impact from SARS both inbound and outbound. Figures started to decline in March 2003 and plummeted in April. The Republic of Korea has a high level of dependence on Asia both inbound (60%) and outbound (70%). It is predicting that inbound arrivals will decrease by 17 per cent in 2003 to a total of approximately 4.4 million. **Taiwan (Province of China)** however is still targeting an increase in 2003 to 3 million arrivals. It has designated 2004 as *"Taiwan Tourism Year"*. Taiwan's *"Doubling of Tourist Arrivals Plan"* aims by 2008 to boost yearly arrival figures to five million and to double the numbers of foreign visitors who come for tourism purposes from one million to two million.

Indonesia's forecast for 2003 is pessimistic. It expects only 3.6 to 3.8 million arrivals, compared with over 5 million in the previous three years. **Malaysia** is also predicting a major 20 to 30 per cent decline, but expects to reverse this in 2004 through aggressive promotion. Marketing activities and three festivals in January and February 2004 are leading **Myanmar** to predict a massive increase in arrivals that year to one million. The **Philippines** sees growth continuing in 2003, though the internal conflict in the south is a concern in these terrorism aware times. The budget allocation has been increased for 2003 and a major programme of marketing activities is being undertaken, including: Visit Philippines Year; Visit ASEAN Year; road shows to the Republic of Korea, Australia, North America and Japan; attendance at general and specialist fairs (for example diving); and the continuation of the *"Volunteer 12 Programme"* which uses expatriate Filipinos as sales ambassadors. Another cause for optimism looking forward is a range of successful MICE bids, for example the Asian Conference of Pediatric Infectious Diseases in 2006, the Asia Pacific Hospice Palliative Care Network in 2007, and the International Society of Tropical Pediatrics in 2008. **Singapore's** forecasts are currently being revised due to the impact of SARS.

Bhutan is forecasting an increase in tourist arrivals to 16 thousand by 2007. **India's** tourism budget has increased by 50 per cent from RS150.00 crores during 2001-2002 to RS225.00 crores during 2002-2003. The estimate for 2003-2004 is RS325.00 crores. It has ambitious marketing plans looking forward, and is aiming to ensure that the tourist becomes physically invigorated, mentally rejuvenated, culturally enriched, spiritually elevated and that he "feels India within him." **Nepal** is cautiously optimistic provided that the cease-fire holds and that world economies start to improve. It is working towards a Tourism Master Plan and possibly Tourism Satellite Account (STA) during 2003, and will put together a tourism recovery strategy. **Pakistan** expects a further decline in 2003 but, due to improvements in the relationship with India and in the security situation in Afghanistan, it is predicting recuperation in 2004 to pre September 11th levels. 2003 is the Year of the Nanga Parbat Mountain and 2004 is the Year of the K2 Mountain. The **Maldives'** plans include familiarisation trips from China, France, Germany, the Netherlands, India, Japan, Switzerland, Spain and the United Kingdom; global TV advertising, using for example the BBC, Star World, Discovery and Star Plus; and increased evaluation of marketing activities.

The **Cook Islands** are predicting average annual growth of 6 per cent over the next five years. **Guam** reports that 2003 results will be damaged by SARS and by Japan's economic downtown. The **Marshall Islands** expect a decrease of around 3 per cent in 2003 tourist arrivals, counteracted by growth in other arrivals, for example business and "visiting friends and relatives" (VFR). Continued increases are expected from North America. Growth in late 2003 could be significant due to promotion campaigns scheduled in September and October. **Papua New Guinea** expects growth over the next few years due to increased air capacity and the promotion of regular cultural events. It estimates an annual increase of 4 per cent in arrivals over five years and 3.7 per cent over ten, with numbers growing from 54 thousand in 2002 to 66 thousand in 2007 and 78 thousand in 2012. **Samoa** reports that European and American arrivals have now picked up again. A 5 to 10 per cent annual increase is predicted for the period 2002 to 2006, with arrival numbers growing from 89 thousand in 2002 to between 118 thousand and 157 thousand in 2006. **Tonga** is forecasting stable growth over the next three years, while **Yap** predicts 7,860 arrivals in 2003.

French Polynesia is expecting growth, mainly due to a recovery in the cruise market. **Vanuatu** is increasing its tourism promotion budget and activities with the aim of doubling its current total of 49 thousand visitors.

Total arrivals to **Australia** are expected to decrease by 5.3 per cent to 4.6 million in 2003, but to increase to 7.6 million by 2012 at an average rate of plus 4.6 per cent. SARS has caused a major reversal in Chinese traffic, which plunged almost 60 per cent in the June 2003 quarter. However prospects from China clearly remain excellent and the two Governments are finalising arrangements to expand Australia's Approved Destination Status for group leisure tourism to allow residents of six new Chinese regions to travel to Australia. Asia totals approximately 43 per cent of Australia's total inbound arrivals and was forecast to grow by 5.4 per cent in 2003. However, following SARS and the Iraq war this forecast was revised to minus 10 per cent. A strong rebound of 15.4 percent is forecast for 2004, bringing the total number of Asian arrivals to almost 2.2 million, marginally higher than in 2002. Growth up to 2012 is expected to be dominated by China at an average rate of 12.6 per cent per annum, while Japan will grow by just 2.7 per cent. The Tourism Forecasting Council expects domestic visitor nights to increase by 2 per cent per annum up to 2012. Outbound traffic in 2003 is forecast to be static, then to grow at an average rate of 2.7 per cent over the next ten years. The Rugby World Cup in October/November 2003 is expected to attract 40 thousand international spectators. This event will be viewed by 1.3 billion people in 130 countries. International arrivals to **New Zealand** are forecast to increase by an average 6 per cent per annum to 2008.

All in all, the picture is optimistic, but the short-term impact of SARS (on top of the Iraq situation) should not be underestimated. However a strong Asian rebound is predicted in the second half of 2003, driven by an 18 per cent year on year growth in Chinese outbound travel. The extraordinary motor which is China, combined with healthy overall intraregional demand and with the recovery which surely must begin soon in Japan, should ensure a bright future for this vast and varied region, which in 2002 took over the Americas' position as the second most visited region in the world. Every indication is that Asia and the Pacific will have little difficulty in maintaining this position.

Cultural Tourism

Although there are major built heritage sites in Asia Pacific, like Borobudur and Melaka, the prime focus in this region is on living culture. Key products include, for example: music, dance, food, festivals, handicrafts, educational tours, customs and traditions. The emphasis, unlike in Europe, is more ethnological than historical.

China has been placing major emphasis on gastronomy, the martial arts, traditional Chinese medicine, and educational experiences, for example learning the Chinese language or opera in Beijing. Promotion of cultural products is often carried out by tourism delegations visiting other countries. In **Taiwan (Province of China)** there are twelve major festivals, one each month in different cities, encompassing folk art, fine cuisine and scenic attractions. These festivals are promoted by attending overseas trade shows and organising overseas campaigns. Most overseas promotion campaigns have cultural/gastronomic performances, for example a tea ceremony, pearl milk tea, or Chinese Dim Sum. 40 per cent of international arrivals visit historic sites and attend festival events. **Japan's** definition of cultural tourism focuses on education, rather than history and the built heritage. Student school excursions are the biggest segment – almost 3.8 million domestic students participated in 2002, and 210 thousand students went overseas to neighbouring countries, especially to the Republic of Korea and to China. Popular special interest tours include: agriculture, especially rice transplantation and harvesting; a snowstorm experience; participation at local festival dances; fire-fly watching; fishing (watching from another boat) and whale watching. A few overseas visitors come to study or on culinary excursions, but, by Japan's definition, cultural tourism is of very minor importance as a part of total inbound. The **Republic of Korea** places more emphasis on culture, but again history is subservient to activities. Festivals play a major role. The Government is encouraging festivals based on traditional culture to become fully-fledged cultural tourism festivals. 29 were selected in 2002 including the Bullfighting Festival in Cheongdo, the World Taekwondo Festival, and the International Mask Dance Festival in Andong. Support for local festivals was reinforced - not only funding but also know-how was provided, for example marketing techniques. The Government is utilising the success in Japan, China, and South-East Asia of Korean TV dramas and movies, developing products related to actors, actresses and filming sites - first hand experience and participation are increasingly desired by customers. Traditional music, pageantry and ceremonies are also featured; so too is gastronomy, and in 2002 the first Seoul World Food Expo was held to publicise and commercialise Korean food. The Government's cultural goals include preservation and management, developing unique cultural resources by region, and the systematic transformation of cultural resources into tourism products. Examples are the project to create seven major cultural tourism regions and the ten year plan to develop the North Gyeongbuk Confucian Cultural Zone. Of the Government budget provided for tourism resource and product development in 2002, 45 per cent was allocated to the cultural sector including development of Confucian cultural tourism, festivals, and souvenirs. Korea National Tourism Organization survey in 2002 showed that 8.8 per cent of foreign tourists participated in cultural events and festivals, an increase of 1 per cent over 2000. When asked what they found most memorable, 35 per cent replied "the unique culture". **Macao (China)** offers a rich combination of Chinese and Portuguese heritage, so it is not surprising that it approaches cultural tourism more like a European destination. It is one of the oldest meeting points of East and West, dating back 400 years. Macao (China) has passed a law to defend the architectural, environmental and cultural heritage. There are fiscal incentives to preserve it, and 128 attractions are legally listed. Macao (China) has also set up a Cultural Institute, combining heritage, cultural activities, training, and research. In 2002 the Cultural Institute trained 58 Young Heritage Ambassadors and designed three cultural heritage walking tours.

In South-East Asia, a rich mixture of colonial heritage, ancient monuments, ethnic traditions, festivals and events is promoted. **Indonesia** has a major World Heritage Site – Borobudur – and more than 500 ethnic groups. Its main theme is mega diversity and it makes major effort to empower local communities. In June 2003 it held an event at the Borobudur International Festival on the theme *"Balancing Heritage Conservation and Community Development".* In the **Philippines**, the Department of Tourism promotes festivals and other cultural events through a monthly calendar, media advertisements, press releases and special event launches. Festival tour packages are developed for international markets. Overseas offices heavily emphasise culture and organise effective familiarisation trips for the media. The product mix ranges from music, art, dance, religious events and cuisine to local traditions and historic villages and towns, for example Intramuros History Town Philippines. The Tourism Master Plan has among its specific objectives for tourism to contribute to social cohesion and cultural preservation. A Cultural Tourism Programme was initiated by the Department of Tourism (DOT) in co-ordination with other official bodies in 2000. The Philippine Tourism Authority became part of the programme in 2001, and a leading cultural tour operator, Viajes Filipinas, was added to this Cultural Tourism Technical Working Group in 2002. A Cultural Tourism Inter-Agency Memorandum of Understanding was signed in June 2002. The DOT is developing a Cultural Tourism Handbook and February has been designated National Arts Month. It is estimated that 30 per cent of tourist arrivals are partly motivated by cultural considerations. Dedicated cultural tourism is largely restricted to students on annual field trips and domestic travellers to festivals. However cultural destinations and activities are part and parcel of the packages sold to overseas visitors and the cultural components appeal particularly to visitors from China, Republic of Korea, Japan, Taiwan (Province of China) and the United States, as well as to second and third generation expatriate Filipinos. **Singapore** has allocated specific resources for culture and heritage as part of its corporate restructure. Its positioning is a progressive, modern city state with a diverse and vibrant cultural background, and it puts major efforts into the development of new cultural products, for example the Malay Heritage Centre, Peranakan Showcase, Little India Interpretative Centre, World War II sites and Heritage Trails. Various festivals supported by the Singapore Tourist Board include Chinese New Year Light Up, the Chinese New Year River Hong Bao, Deepvali, Hari Raya, Heritage, Mid-autumn, Dragon Boat, and the Dumpling Festival. **Malaysia** also focuses above all on its ethnic variety, and its very successful *"Malaysia Truly Asia"* campaign portrays it as a peaceful, colourful and festive nation. Events like the Colours of Malaysia Festival, the Water Festival, and the National

Cultural Celebration are complemented by built heritage gems like Melaka, Malaysia's historic city. An estimated 20 to 30 per cent of visits are culture related. **Myanmar** also offers a varied range of events, including the Taunggyi Tazaungdine Balloon Festival of Lights, the Thingyan Water Festival and Myanmar New Year, and the Phaung Daw Oo Pagoda Festival and One Leg Rowing Competition. These plus historic and religious buildings appeal to visitors from Western Europe and from Japan, Taiwan (Province of China), China and Thailand. An estimated 80 per cent of Myanmar's 217 thousand arrivals are culture related.

The culture and the people are the main attraction in **Bhutan**. The key cultural products are festivals, Dzongs and monasteries. Feasibility studies are to be carried out on cultural, religious and spiritual tourism aimed at overseas generating markets. Of the 6 thousand international arrivals in 2002, 90 per cent came as cultural tourists and 10 per cent for trekking and nature. In **Nepal** pilgrimages to Buddhist site are a key complement to the nature/adventure segment. A special task force has been set up to document and investigate the potentiality of the Buddhist circuit, which appeals to the Indian market as well as to the Buddhist segment from around the world. 5 per cent of incoming tourists have a pilgrimage as their major purpose. However around 60 per cent of tourists take part in some cultural activity. **India** has 22 World Heritage sites, 16 of which are monuments and a multitude of other historic attractions. Conservation, preservation and the integrated development of areas around monuments are providing an opportunity for growth in cultural tourism. Special products have been identified, for example the Bodhgaya-Rajgir-Nalanda-Varansi Buddhist Circuit. According to an International Passenger Survey Report conducted during 1996-1997, 42 per cent of tourists were motivated by cultural activities and resorts. Much of **Pakistan's** cultural promotion centres on its calendar of events. Featured most heavily are the Annual Shandur Polo Festival and Kalash Festivals, the Basant Kite Flying Festival in Lahore, and a Folk Festival in Islamabad, plus of course the annual Silk Road Festival which, together with the Karakoram Car Rally, was introduced in 2001 by the tourism organisation. There are plans to organise Pakistani food/cultural festivals in the Middle East & China. The cultural tourism focus in mountain areas is on young people who will enjoy culture and adventure combined, and in cities on the mature market and seniors. Cultural tourism domestically helps to create harmony and tolerance among different people. To foreign visitors, it presents a positive picture of Pakistani culture, people and society. Approximately 10 per cent of arrivals come for cultural reasons.

In Oceania it is living culture which prevails – for example handicrafts, customs, festivals, song and dance. Culture tends to be more integrated into the overall product, rather than a separate motivation in itself. The **Cook Islands** placed major emphasis on cultural elements during national self-government celebrations. There is also an important role for culture and traditions in schools. Tourists are encouraged to interact freely with locals. Several festivals are held each year, and song and dance groups and traditional motifs are regularly used overseas in promotional campaigns at international fairs and cultural festivals. There is traditional entertainment in most hotels and major efforts are made to assist the development of local artisans' work. Some unusual themes are featured, for example traditional medicine. The mission statement of the **Guam** Visitors Bureau includes the promotion and presentation of the Chamorro culture. Key products included the Chamorro Village night market and a working tour of the famous capital city landmarks. In Guam's big summer festival, the Guam Visitors Bureau promotes street fairs and performing arts fairs. Culinary artefacts are also featured. An estimated 20 per cent of total tour packages include a degree of cultural tourism. Highlights in the **Marshall Islands** are the traditional sailing canoes, handicrafts, cuisine, and, to a lesser extent, pearl farm tours, World War II heritage tours and trips to

Bikini Atoll. Local annual events are also organised. The over-riding aim is to use Marshallese sailing canoes and handicraft originality to cultivate a unique "Marshallese Cultural Experience". Achievements already include a Women's Handicraft Centre and Association and the Waan Aelon in Majol canoe project. An estimated 10 per cent of tourist arrivals and of tours offered are cultural. Main markets are the Japanese and the United States nautical segment for the canoes. In **Papua New Guinea** the National Cultural Commission is responsible for culture. The Tourism Promotion Authority (TPA) works in liaison with them, and promotes the calendar of events which they produce. The TPA has established specific guidelines for the promotion of cultural tourism and for the protection of cultural habits and traditions. It assists regional tourism organisations in promoting cultural events in each province, and offers sponsorship. It also encourages locals to maintain habits and traditions and to look after special sites, for example caves and war memorials. **Samoa** has a special name for its strong living culture: "fa'asamoa". The Tourism Development Plan 2002-2006 strongly supports this concept. All sites are being upgraded and protected. Legends and stories relating to the sites are being documented and researched by a group of cultural experts. Tourists are advised and educated about certain codes of dressing and protocols to be respected in villages. They are also advised to seek permission from village authorities to visit certain areas. Culture ranks fourth as the reason for visiting Samoa, attracting an estimated 20 per cent of Samoa's 89 thousand visitors in 2002. It is a niche market, so Government policy is to encourage operations that offer a combination of opportunities for culture, nature, adventure and coastal tourism, underpinned by the fa'asamoa. Key cultural experiences are the annual Teuila Festival and traditional ceremonies such as the "ava" ceremony, weddings and "matai title bestowals". **Tonga** is aiming to increase visitor interest in festivals. The annual Heilala week festival is now well established and successful. **Tuvalu's** key products include handicrafts, lifestyles, cultural sites and dance performances. They are considering research to identify the benefits and risks of this type of tourism. Miss Tuvalu will be entering the Miss South Pacific Beauty Contest for the first time, a good opportunity to publicise cultural dances, performances and the way of life. Tuvalu is concentrating on ecotourism: if these clients are linked to cultural tourism, then an estimated 50 per cent of arrivals would fall into this joint category. **Yap's** key cultural products are community customs and navigation. The first attempt at reviving traditional navigation took place recently, aiming to restore the link between Yap and Palau. The trial run was successful and future trips are planned. The first of March has been designated Yap Day, when communities throughout the islands assemble to perform cultural activities and display traditional products. A number of film groups visit annually to capture the cultural side of Yap. The islands average 4 thousand foreign visitors annually, but most come for diving.

French Polynesia advocates the type of living, dynamic and communicable culture which stimulates personal development and social cohesion. It stresses the importance of combining the attractive with the authentic. Every year the events calendar is sent to partners in source markets, and distributed widely to trade and customers. Strong cultural components are music, dance, and painting - Paul Gauguin Year is inspiring numerous events and activities. A public organisation - Heiva Nui - has recently been set up to organise and manage attractive cultural events. The main overseas demand comes from Europe, especially France. Cultural themes help particularly to target the seniors market and to support islands like the Marquises and Tahiti. **Vanuatu** aims to concentrate more on the identification of segments which will be attracted by its unique culture and customs, which are different from those of other Melanesian countries. Cultural products will be promoted in collaboration with the Vanuatu Island Bungalows Association. Those travelling to the outer islands (around 30%) are more culturally motivated. **New Caledonia's** slogan is *"Earth, Sea and Culture*". The main market for cultural visits is Europe, especially France. The Tjibaou Cultural Centre is used systematically for cultural events.

Australia set up a National Tourism and Heritage Task Force and an Indigenous Tourism Leadership Group. It is also funding the development of a National Wine Tourism Strategy. The Brand Australia image is based on a combination of the natural environment, the distinctive personality of the people and the free spirited nature of the country's lifestyle and culture. Indigenous tourism appeals to Europeans, especially Britons, while research has indicated a strong growth in food and wine interest and potential across the Japan, New Zealand and Asian markets. An estimated 470 thousand international visitors aged 15 and over (11% of the total) visited wineries during 2001/2002. The International Visitor Survey for the year ending March 2003 identified that 4,1 million international tourists participated in the following cultural activities; performing arts – 545 thousand; museums and art galleries – 1,2 million; art/craft workshops or studios – 280 thousand; festivals, fairs, events – 309 thousand; aboriginal sites/communities – 176 thousand; aboriginal art/craft/cultural displays – 395 thousand; and historic/heritage buildings, sites or monuments – 1,2 million.

Although culture is not normally seen as one of **New Zealand's** iconic strengths, the Ministry of Tourism is well aware of its potential. An informal inter-Governmental Working Group has been meeting regularly to develop proposals. This has resulted in funding to Tourism New Zealand for a three stage research project into international and domestic demand for cultural tourism, and funding to create demand for cultural tourism and to encourage and support the five regions that have established positions as cultural tourism providers to create a cultural tourism development programme focused on capacity and capability building. The first two stages of the research have been completed, with stage three to be delivered in mid 2003. Results already show that the cultural experience, and in particular interaction with the New Zealand people, is a strong driver for international visits. Key products include food, wine, cultural events, films (the Lord of the Rings has been of immense benefit to tourism), and the Maori culture – Tourism New Zealand has appointed a Maori Tourism Development Manager. It is estimated that cultural tourism experiences represent anywhere between 10 and 35 per cent of visitor holidays.

II

Quantitative Analysis of Tourism Results

II Quantitative Analysis of Tourism Results

II.1 Tourism Trends in Asia and the Pacific

In 2002, Asia and the Pacific confirmed the position it reached in 2001, for the first time, as the second region in the world ranking of international tourist arrivals. The last decades the region has made marked progress towards the forefront of the world tourism, showing a significantly rapid growth in terms of both tourist arrivals and tourism receipts. Between 1990 and 2000 international tourist arrivals virtually doubled, from 58 million to 115 million, growing at an annual average rate of 7 per cent, while international tourism receipts (expressed in US dollars) increased on average 8 per cent a year. During this period, the region surpassed successfully the Asian financial crisis of 1997 and 1998, years in which arrivals declined slightly, posting growths of over 10 per cent in the two following years (1999 and 2000). In 2001, again, and in spite of the world economic and political climate, the region showed strong resilience as tourist arrivals grew by 5.1 per cent in a year marked by negative results. Though this growth was behind the performances from previous years, it was still high above the results obtained by other regions and more than 5 per cent above the world's performance for that year (-0.5%). In 2002 the region managed to maintain this positive trend as arrivals grew by 8.4 per cent while arrivals worldwide increased by 2.7 per cent.

Asia and the Pacific: Inbound tourism
International Tourist Arrivals (million)

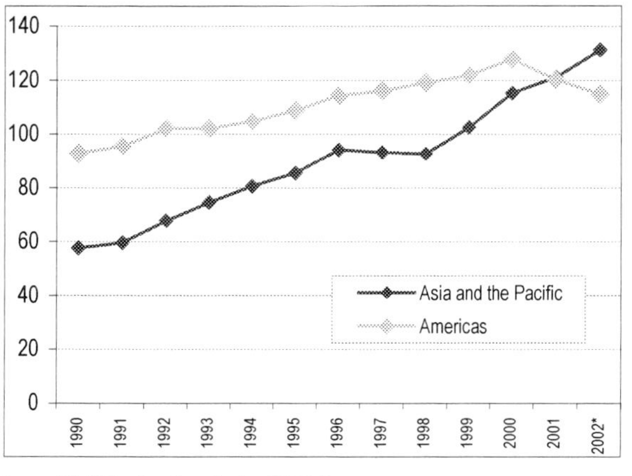

Source: World Tourism Organization (WTO) ©

Asia and the Pacific: Inbound tourism
International Tourist Arrivals (change over previous year, %)

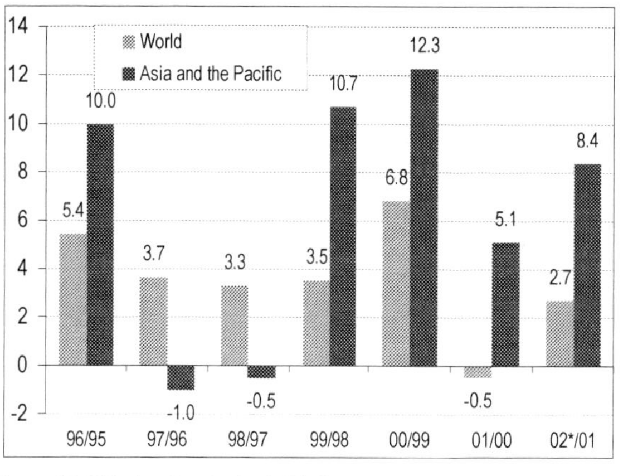

Source: World Tourism Organization (WTO) ©

The rapid and continuous growth in Asia and the Pacific can be attributed to different factors, namely:

- increased government support for tourism;
- strategic development of infrastructures both in terms of access and in terms of the tourism products;
- creation of new destinations and further improvement of the existing ones;
- reduction of legal restrictions on border crossing;
- human resources development;
- increased political and social stability;
- a widespread and active promotional marketing activity.

These factors have determined not only a bigger competitive advantage for the region in the interregional market, but also a significant growth in intraregional traffic. Travel from the same region, driven significantly by the dynamism of the Chinese outbound market, represents already 78 percent of all travel to Asia and the Pacific. In parallel interregional traffic though performing positively has grown at a somewhat slower pace and has consequently lost market share over the years, and in particular in the last two years. Due to its positioning the region has also benefited during 2001 and 2002 from some replacement of long-haul traffic to Americas.

International tourist arrivals

In 2002 Asia and the Pacific attracted more than 131 million tourist arrivals, occupying an 18.7 per cent market share of the world's total international tourist arrivals. This represents significant progress for the region taking into account that in 1990 its market share was of only 13 per cent. Arrivals grew at a significant 8 per cent rate on average a year between 1990 and 1995, and though at a slower pace between 1995 an 2000 due to the dip caused by the Asian financial crisis, still with a 6 per cent average annual growth. In 2002 the region continued to report strong results with an 8.4 per cent increase reinforcing the performance from the previous year (5.1%). Due to these results, and to the fall of arrivals to the Americas, the region confirmed its second position in the world ranking, after Europe (57%), after overtaking the Americas (16%) for the first time in 2001.

World and regions: Inbound tourism
International Tourist Arrivals (change 02*/01, %)

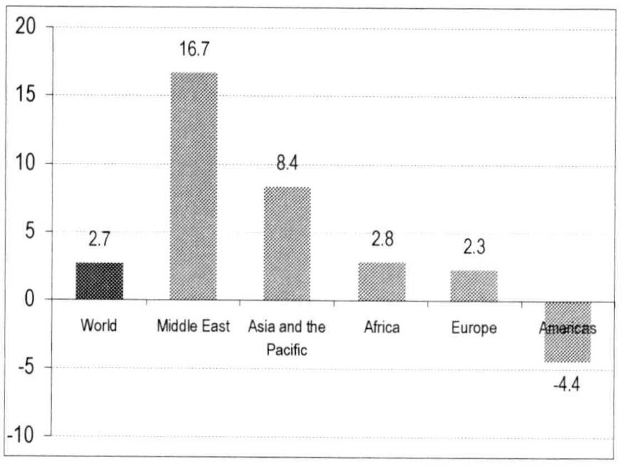

Source: World Tourism Organization (WTO) ©

Asia and the Pacific: Inbound tourism
International Tourist Arrivals (share in world total, %)

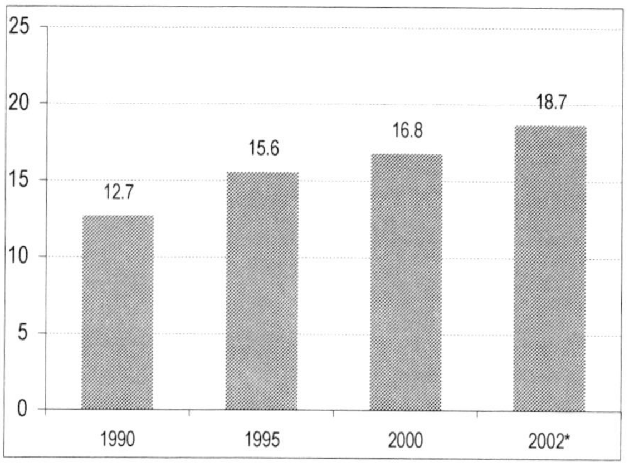

Source: World Tourism Organization (WTO) ©

Asia and the Pacific and subregions: Inbound tourism
International Tourist Arrivals, 2002* (share, %)

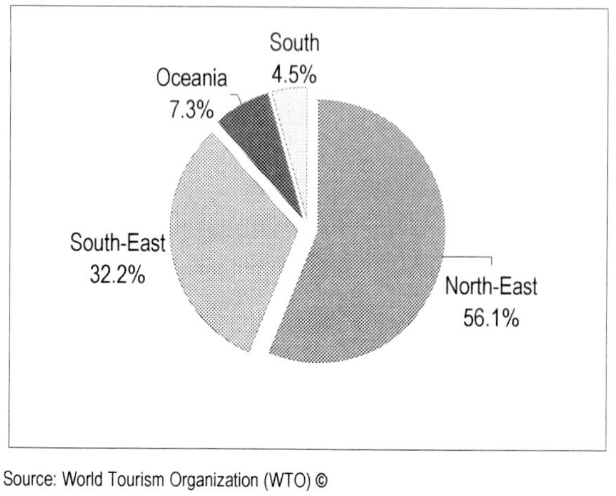

Source: World Tourism Organization (WTO) ©

Asia and the Pacific and subregions: Inbound tourism
International Tourist Arrivals (change 02*/01, %)

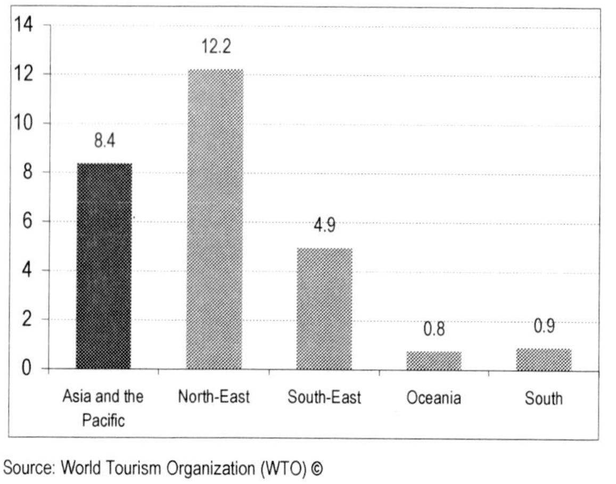

Source: World Tourism Organization (WTO) ©

The growth obtained in 2002 is, for the most part, attributable to the subregions of North-East Asia and South-East Asia, representing shares in the regional total of 56 per cent and 32 respectively. North-East Asia grew at a noteworthy rate of 12.2 per cent driven in particular by the exceptional performances of China and its territories, and gained some 8 million new tourist arrivals. South-East Asia, though hit by the Bali attack in October, still ended the year with a 5 per cent growth, corresponding to 2 million extra arrivals, once tourist arrivals to Malaysia and Thailand continued to grow steadily. In contrast, Oceania affected by constrained air traffic, and in particular by the disappearance of Ansett, grew at a slight 0.8 per cent rate as arrivals to Australia dropped by 0.3 per cent and in spite of New Zealand good results (7.1%). South Asia's growth rate reached 0.9 per cent driven in particular by the decrease for the second consecutive year in tourist arrivals to India (-6.6%).

China, one of the most dynamic countries in the region, continues to lead the way as the main destination with almost 37 million tourist arrivals, corresponding to a significant 28 per cent market share, and a 11 per cent increase over 2001. Hong Kong (China) follows with 16.6 million arrivals, with 12.6 per cent market share and fastest grower among Asia's major destinations with an increase of 21 per cent. Third and fourth positions belong to Malaysia and Thailand with 10.1 and 8.3 per cent market share respectively, both with positive performances in 2002 (+4% and +7.3%). The top ten destination's group in Asia and the Pacific is completed by Singapore (5.3% share), Macao (5.0%), the Republic of Korea (4.1%), Japan (4.0%), Indonesia (3.8%) and Australia (3.7%), all with over 4 million tourist arrivals. In 2002 among these countries only Indonesia and Australia reported negative results, though in the case of Australia the decrease rate was of only 0.3 per cent.

International Tourist Arrivals by (Sub)region

	International Tourist Arrivals (million)					Market share (%)		Growth rate (%)		Average annual growth (%)	
	1990	1995	2000	2001	2002*	1995	2002*	01/00	02*/01	'90-'95	'95-'00
World	**455.9**	**550.4**	**687.3**	**684.1**	**702.6**	**100**	**100**	**-0.5**	**2.7**	**3.8**	**4.5**
Asia and the Pacific	***57.7***	***85.6***	***115.3***	***121.1***	***131.3***	***15.6***	***18.7***	***5.1***	***8.4***	***8.2***	***6.1***
North-East Asia	28.0	44.1	62.5	65.6	73.6	8.0	10.5	5.0	12.2	9.5	7.2
South-East Asia	21.5	29.2	37.0	40.2	42.2	5.3	6.0	8.7	4.9	6.3	4.9
Oceania	5.2	8.1	9.6	9.5	9.6	1.5	1.4	-1.6	0.8	9.4	3.6
South Asia	3.2	4.2	6.1	5.8	5.9	0.8	0.8	-4.5	0.9	6.1	7.5

Source: World Tourism Organization (WTO) © (Data as collected by WTO September 2003)

International tourism receipts

In 2002, Asia and the Pacific earned US$ 94.7 billion from international tourism, representing an increase by US$ 6.7 billion over 2001. It is important to note that for financial data it is always difficult to correctly interpret trends as the figures are expressed in US dollars and are subject to fluctuations in exchange rate versus local currencies. Expressed in (weighted) local currencies in constant prices (i.e. taking account of inflation) international tourism receipts for the region increased by 5.1 per cent, while international tourism receipts for the world as a whole only grew by only 0.3 per cent.

International Tourism Receipts, Asia and the Pacific

	International Tourism Receipts				(billion)	Change current prices (%)			Change constant prices (%)		
	1990	1995	2000	2001	2002*	00/99	01/00	02*/01	00/99	01/00	02*/01
Local currencies						11.5	7.5	6.3	9.9	5.1	5.1
US$	41.3	77.7	86.9	88.0	94.7	8.6	1.2	7.7	5.1	-1.6	6.0
Euro	32.4	59.4	94.1	98.2	100.1	25.4	4.4	2.0	22.5	1.7	-0.3

Source: World Tourism Organization (WTO) © (Data as collected by WTO September 2003)

Asia and the Pacific's world market share of tourism receipts reached 20 per cent in 2002, ranking third after Europe (51%) and the Americas (24%). After a significant increase between 1990 and 1996 the region's market share declined in 1997 and 1998 and has been recovering since 1999, so that in 2002 it reached the same percentage it represented in 1996.

Asia and the Pacific: Inbound tourism
International Tourism Receipts (US$ billion, current prices)

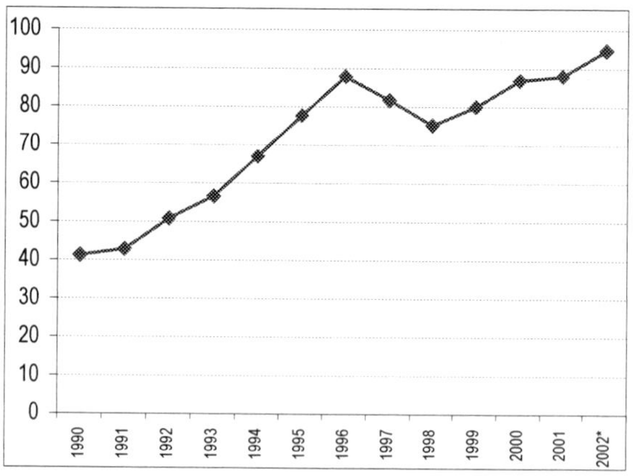

Source: World Tourism Organization (WTO) ©

Asia and the Pacific: Inbound tourism
International Tourism Receipts (share in world total, %)

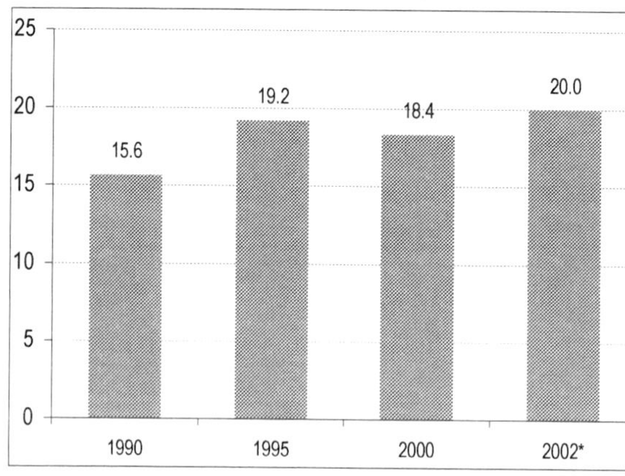

Source: World Tourism Organization (WTO) ©

In 2002, just over half of all international tourism receipts in Asia and the Pacific originated in North-East Asia, while South-East generated 29 per cent, Oceania 15 per cent and South Asia 5 per cent. The share of North-East Asia in the region's tourism receipts grew from 43 per cent in 1990 to almost 51 per cent in 2002, whereas the percentage of tourism receipts generated in South-East Asia lost weight gradually (from 35% in 1990 to 29% in 2002).

Changes expressed in local currencies at constant prices, show that only two subregions posted positive results in 2002: North-East Asia, which peaked with a growth of 11 per cent and Oceania, with a 1.2 per cent rise, but only partly compensating the negative mark of 2001 (-4.2%). On the contrary, after the good results of 2001, both South-East Asia and South Asia recorded decreases of respectively 1.5 and 2.6 per cent in 2002.

The average receipt per arrival in Asia and the Pacific amounted to US$ 721 in 2002. The highest marks of receipt per arrival in the Asian region were recorded by Oceania with US$ 1.498 and by South Asia with US$ 865.

International Tourism Receipts by (Sub)region

	US$ (billion) 2001	US$ (billion) 2002*	US$ Receipts per arrival 2002*	euro (billion) 2001	euro (billion) 2002*	euro Receipts per arrival 2002*	Change[1] (%) 00/99	Change[1] (%) 01/00	Change[1] (%) 02*/01	Market share (%) 2002*
World	**459.5**	**474.2**	**675**	**513.0**	**501.5**	**714**	**9.7**	**-1.0**	**0.3**	**100**
Asia and the Pacific	***88.0***	***94.7***	***721***	***98.2***	***100.1***	***763***	***9.9***	***5.1***	***5.1***	***20.0***
North-East Asia	43.5	47.9	651	48.6	50.7	688	8.0	8.9	11.1	10.1
South-East Asia	26.3	27.4	648	29.3	28.9	685	13.8	4.4	-1.5	5.8
Oceania	13.2	14.3	1,498	14.7	15.2	1,585	9.9	-4.2	1.2	3.0
South Asia	5.0	5.1	865	5.6	5.4	915	4.4	4.5	-2.6	1.1

Source: World Tourism Organization (WTO) © (Data as collected by WTO September 2003)

[1] Local currencies, constant prices

World and regions: Inbound tourism
Receipts per Arrival, 2002* (US$)

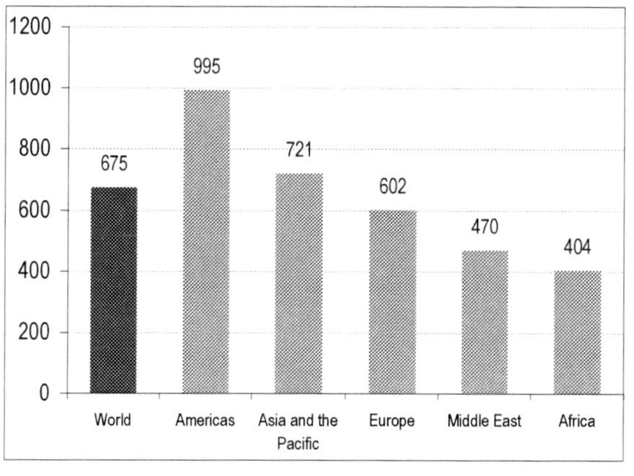

Source: World Tourism Organization (WTO) ©

World and regions: Inbound tourism
International Tourism Receipts (% change 02*/01, local currencies, constant prices)

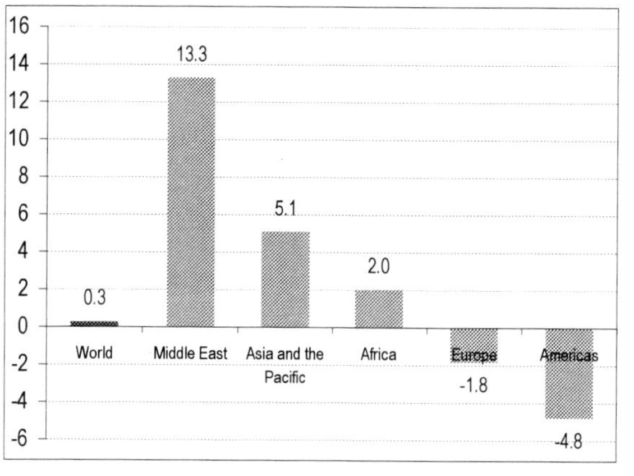

Source: World Tourism Organization (WTO) ©

Asia and the Pacific and subregions: Inbound tourism
International Tourism Receipts, 2002* (share, %)

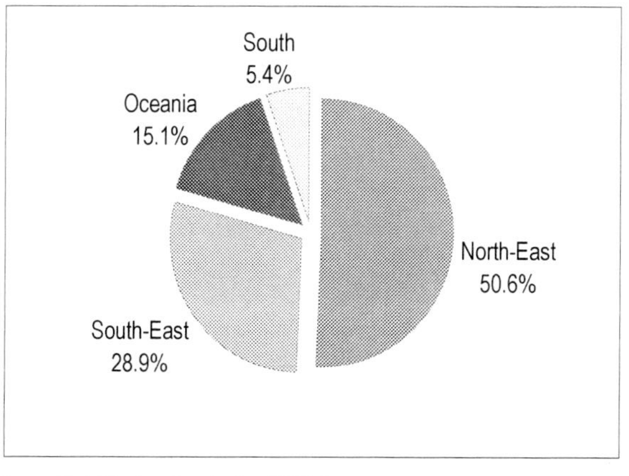

Source: World Tourism Organization (WTO) ©

Asia and the Pacific and subregions: Inbound tourism
Receipts per Arrival, 2002* (US$)

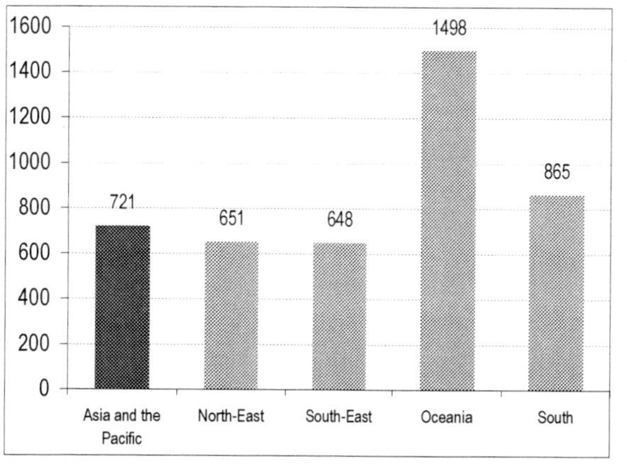

Source: World Tourism Organization (WTO) ©

Inbound tourism by region of origin

In 2002, arrivals to destinations in Asia and the Pacific from both the subregions of East Asia and the Pacific and from South Asia represented 78 per cent of the total arrivals to the region, corresponding to over 102 million tourists. This percentage has been gradually increasing over the years as intraregional arrivals grew at an average annual rate of over 7 per cent between 1990 and 2000. In 2002 intraregional traffic increased by 9 over an already positive previous year (+6%). Likewise arrivals from other regions, which represent a share of nearly 21 per cent, have also shown a positive behaviour, with a 6.7 per cent average annual growth rate in the period 1990-2000 and increases 1.7 and 5.4 per cent respectively in 2001 and 2002.

In 2002, the biggest generating market outside the region was Europe, with 16.4 million arrivals and 12.5 per cent of the total international tourist arrivals to Asia and the Pacific. It was followed at a considerable distance by the Americas with 9 million arrivals and a 7 per cent market share. Africa and the Middle East together contributed 1.2 per cent of the total tourist arrivals to the region. Interregional arrivals to Asia and the Pacific from all world regions showed a positive behaviour in 2002. In particular, the increase in arrivals from the Americas (+5.7%) is remarkable given the overall weak trend in this region.

Asia and the Pacific: Inbound tourism by region of origin
International Tourist Arrivals, 2002* (share, %)

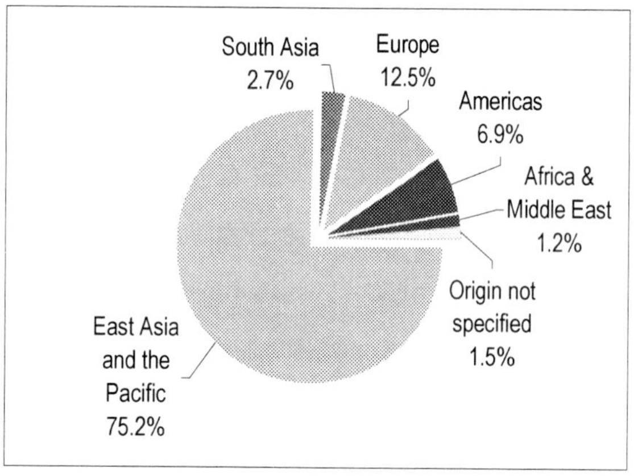

Source: World Tourism Organization (WTO) ©

Asia and the Pacific: Inbound tourism by region of origin
International Tourist Arrivals (share, %)

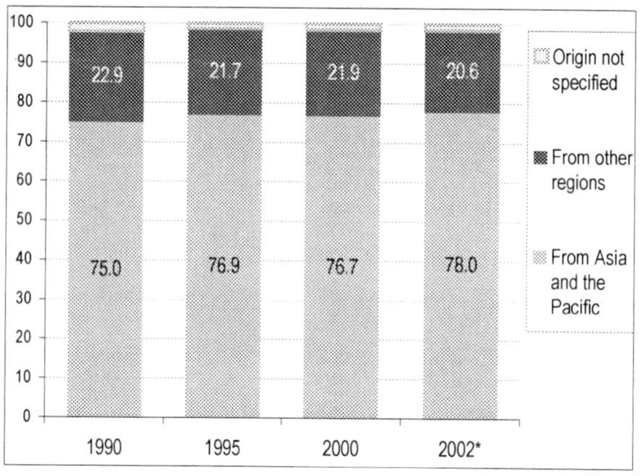

Source: World Tourism Organization (WTO) ©

Asia and the Pacific: Inbound tourism by region of origin
International Tourist Arrivals, 2002* (million)

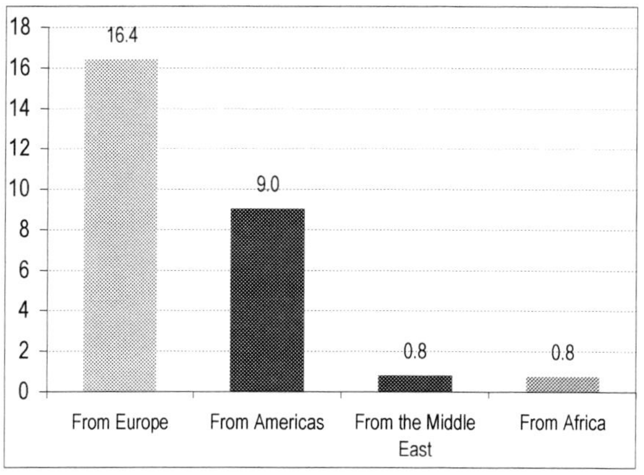

Source: World Tourism Organization (WTO) ©

Asia and the Pacific: Inbound tourism by region of origin
International Tourist Arrivals (change 02*/01, %)

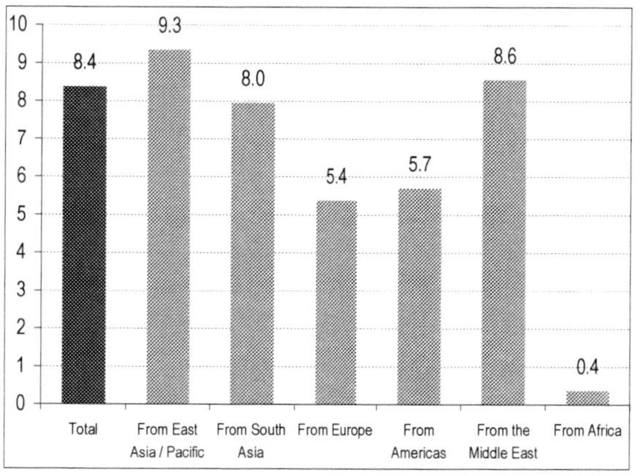

Source: World Tourism Organization (WTO) ©

World and regions: Inbound tourism by region of origin
International Tourist Arrivals, 2002* (share, %)

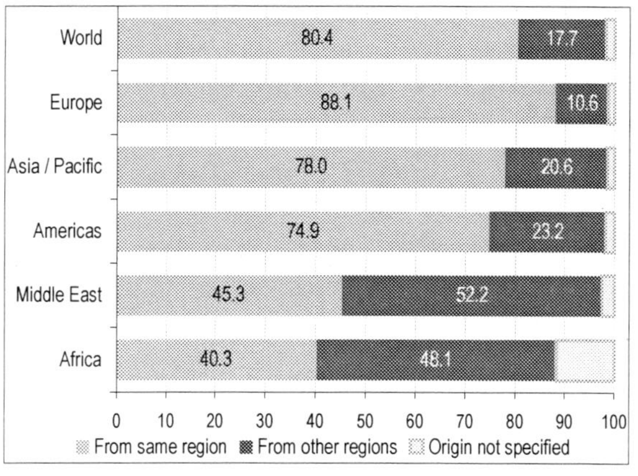

Source: World Tourism Organization (WTO) ©

World regions: Inbound tourism by region of origin
International Tourist Arrivals, 2002* (million)

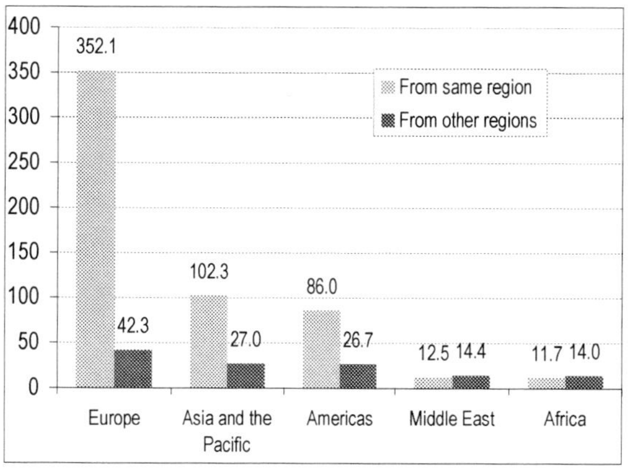

Source: World Tourism Organization (WTO) ©

North-East Asia is characterised by a strong reliance on intraregional tourism, particularly on tourists from East Asia and the Pacific, which is the origin region of over 83 per cent of all international arrivals in the subregion. In 2002, the figure reached a total of almost 61 million arrivals. South Asia is the origin of only 1.2 per cent of arrivals to the North-East Asia (873 thousand). The percentage of interregional arrivals reaches 15 per cent. Europe, which is the main interregional source market, recorded 5.7 million arrivals, corresponding to 7.8 per cent market share, while the Americas holds a 6.6 per cent share with 4.9 million arrivals.

Asia and the Pacific
Inbound Tourism by Region of Origin (including estimations for countries with missing data)

	International Tourist Arrivals (1000)					Market share (%)			Growth rate (%)		Average annual growth (%)	
	1990	1995	2000	2001	2002*	1990	1995	2002*	01/00	02*/01	90-00	95-00
Asia and the Pacific	**57,748**	**85,599**	**115,252**	**121,147**	**131,294**	**100**	**100**	**100**	**5.1**	**8.4**	**7.2**	**6.1**
From:												
East Asia and the Pacific	*41,286*	*63,557*	*85,130*	*90,322*	*98,759*	*71.5*	*74.2*	*75.2*	*6.1*	*9.3*	*7.5*	*6.0*
South Asia	*2,043*	*2,283*	*3,218*	*3,321*	*3,585*	*3.5*	*2.7*	*2.7*	*3.2*	*8.0*	*4.6*	*7.1*
Other regions	*13,217*	*18,568*	*25,198*	*25,624*	*27,014*	*22.9*	*21.7*	*20.6*	*1.7*	*5.4*	*6.7*	*6.3*
Africa	266	496	671	768	771	0.5	0.6	0.6	14.4	0.4	9.7	6.3
Americas	4,846	6,138	8,583	8,542	9,030	8.4	7.2	6.9	-0.5	5.7	5.9	6.9
Europe	7,735	11,467	15,279	15,566	16,402	13.4	13.4	12.5	1.9	5.4	7.0	5.9
Middle East	369	467	665	747	811	0.6	0.5	0.6	12.4	8.6	6.1	7.3
Origin not specified	*1,202*	*1,191*	*1,705*	*1,881*	*1,936*	*2.1*	*1.4*	*1.5*	*10.3*	*3.0*		

Source: World Tourism Organization (WTO) © (Data as collected by WTO September 2003)

As for South-East Asia 76 per cent of its over 42 million international tourists came from the same region (73.6% from East Asia and the Pacific and 2.9% from South Asia). The 22 per cent share of arrivals from other regions is dominated by Europe, with 14 per cent of all arrivals to South-East Asia, followed at a considerable distance by the Americas, with 6 per cent. Africa and the Middle East together accounted for a bit less than 2 per cent of total arrivals.

Asia and the Pacific and subregions: Inbound tourism by region of origin
International Tourist Arrivals, 2002* (share, %)

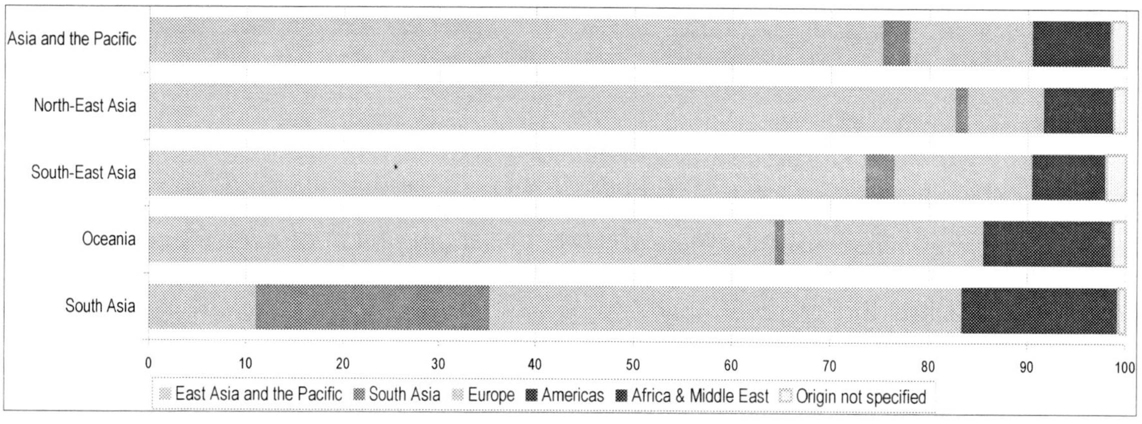

Source: World Tourism Organization (WTO) ©

Nearly two third of total tourist arrivals to Oceania had an Asian country as their origin in 2002. Concretely, most tourists who visited Oceania last year were from East Asia and the Pacific, corresponding to 64 per cent against the 0.9 per cent who came from South Asia. As far as other regions are concerned, the interregional tourists accounted for 33 per cent. European tourists were the ones who visited Oceania the most in 2002 (20%), followed by the Americans, accounting for 12 per cent of total arrivals. Africa and the Middle East together represent 1.4 per cent of total arrivals to this region.

In contrast to other subregions, South Asia is characterized by a strong reliance on interregional tourism and in particular on arrivals from Europe. In 2002, intraregional tourism accounted for only 35 per cent of all tourists in South Asia, being that 24 per cent of total arrivals to South Asia came from South Asia itself, corresponding to 1.4 million tourists and the remaining 11 per cent from East Asia and the Pacific. As for arrivals from other regions Europe was the origin of almost half of all international arrivals in South Asia. Almost 575 thousand tourists from the Americas arrived to South Asia in 2002, accounting for 10 per cent of total arrivals. The neighbouring region of the Middle East was the origin of 255 thousand tourists, corresponding to 4.3 per cent of the total. In addition 108 thousand African tourists visited South Asia in 2002.

As reported, intraregional traffic shows very different weights among the Asian subregions. While it represents nearly 84 per cent in North-East Asia and 76.5 per cent in South-East Asia, in South Asia its share stays below 36 per cent. In fact, arrivals from other regions to South Asia correspond to nearly 65 per cent of all tourist arrivals in the subregion. Interregional traffic to all subregions is dominated by Europe. Traffic from Europe is specially important to South Asia where it reaches 75 per cent of all intraregional arrivals, driven in particular by the British generating market, which ranks first for many countries in the subregion and in particular for its main destination – India. The Americas is second in all subregions and its most significant share occurs in Oceania (12%). Africa and the Middle East show a relatively small weight in arrivals from other regions to all Asian subregions. However, due to its proximity, the Middle East has a significant 4.3 per cent share of tourist arrivals in South Asia, in particular to Iran.

Broken down by region of destination the majority of travel from East Asia and the Pacific is directed to North-East Asia (62%) while South Asia outbound is concentrated within South Asian destinations (40%). As for interregional traffic, the most significant part is aimed to North and South-East Asia (74%). While traffic from Europe is equally distributed over North and South-East Asia (35% and 36% respectively), more than half of the traffic from the Americas goes to North-East Asia (54%). Travellers from Middle East to Asia and the Pacific predominantly end up in South-East Asia (50%).

Asia and the Pacific

Inbound Tourism by Region of Origin (including estimations for countries with missing data), 2002*

		Asia and the Pacific				
		Total	**North-East**	**South-East**	**Oceania**	**South**
		International Tourist Arrivals (000)				
Total		**131,294**	**73,634**	**42,228**	**9,564**	**5,869**
from:	East Asia and the Pacific	98,759	60,875	31,076	6,162	647
	South Asia	3,585	873	1,210	84	1,419
	Other regions	27,014	10,954	9,100	3,194	3,766
	Europe	16,402	5,735	5,908	1,932	2,827
	Americas	9,030	4,884	2,443	1,129	575
	Middle East	811	112	405	39	255
	Africa	771	223	345	95	108
	Origin not specified	1,936	933	842	124	38
		% destination broken down by origin				
Total		**100**	**100**	**100**	**100**	**100**
from:	East Asia and the Pacific	75.2	82.7	73.6	64.4	11.0
	South Asia	2.7	1.2	2.9	0.9	24.2
	Other regions	20.6	14.9	21.6	33.4	64.2
	Europe	12.5	7.8	14.0	20.2	48.2
	Americas	6.9	6.6	5.8	11.8	9.8
	Middle East	0.6	0.2	1.0	0.4	4.3
	Africa	0.6	0.3	0.8	1.0	1.8
	Origin not specified	1.5	1.3	2.0	1.3	0.6
		% origin broken down by destination				
Total		**100**	**56.1**	**32.2**	**7.3**	**4.5**
from:	East Asia and the Pacific	100	61.6	31.5	6.2	0.7
	South Asia	100	24.3	33.7	2.3	39.6
	Other regions	100	40.5	33.7	11.8	13.9
	Europe	100	35.0	36.0	11.8	17.2
	Americas	100	54.1	27.1	12.5	6.4
	Middle East	100	13.8	49.9	4.8	31.5
	Africa	100	28.9	44.7	12.3	14.1
	Origin not specified	100	48.2	43.5	6.4	2.0

Source: World Tourism Organization (WTO) © (Data as collected by WTO September 2003)

Inbound tourism by means of transport

Due to its geographical configuration with many islands and to the long distances between some countries, Asia and the Pacific depends heavily on air transportation. However, though air transport always accounted for at least half of international tourist arrivals to the region during the last decade, its share has been gradually declining, from 58 per cent in 1990 to 50 per cent in 2000. In 2001, it fell further down to 47 per cent, going under the 50 per cent mark for the first time, induced mainly by the exponential growth in arrivals by road. In fact, the major winner during the decade has been road transport, which has increased its market share from 27 per cent in 1990 to 41 per cent in 2001, a year in which road arrivals, unlike arrivals by air, grew substantially. Arrivals by road showed the highest average annual growth rate between 1990 and 2000 (11%). This trend is closely linked to the strong growth of intraregional traffic encouraged by the improved road connections between the countries in the region. It is at the same time the reflection of the increasing weight of North-East Asia in the region, in particular fuelled by traffic to and from mainland China, Hong Kong (China) and Macao (China).

Water transport accounted for a constant share of around 10 per cent of total international tourist arrivals in the region throughout the decade, the highest in all world regions. In 2001, 12 million tourists used this mode of transportation, corresponding to an increase of 4.1 per cent. Unlike arrivals by road, visitors travelling on rail transport, which represented nearly 4 per cent in 1990, suffered a significant fall since and account for no more than 0.5 per cent in 2001.

Asia and the Pacific: Inbound tourism by mode of transport
International Tourist Arrivals (share, %)

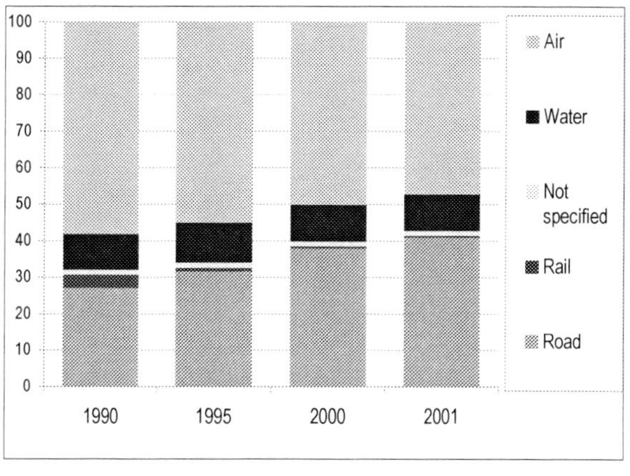

Source: World Tourism Organization (WTO) ©

Asia / Pacific and subregions: Inbound tourism by mode of transport
International Tourist Arrivals, (share, %)

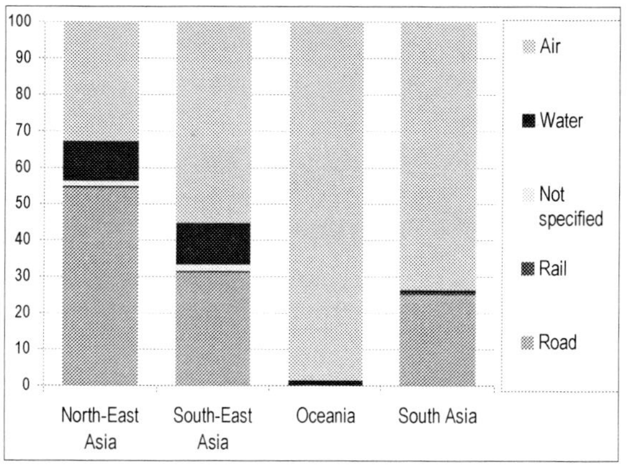

Source: World Tourism Organization (WTO) ©

Asia and the Pacific

Arrivals by mode of transport (including estimations for countries with missing data)

	International Tourist Arrivals (million)				Market share (%)		Growth rate rowth rate (%)		Average annual growth (%)
	1990	1995	2000	2001	1990	2001	00/99	01/00	1990-2000
Total	57.7	85.6	115.3	121.1	100	100	12.3	5.1	7.2
Air	33.6	47.2	57.8	57.3	58.2	47.3	11.4	-0.9	5.6
Road	15.6	27.1	43.6	49.6	27.1	40.9	17.0	13.6	10.8
Rail	2.2	0.8	0.7	0.7	3.8	0.5	15.0	-3.0	-11.0
Water	5.7	9.3	11.6	12.0	9.8	9.9	-0.8	4.1	7.4
Not specified	0.7	1.2	1.6	1.6	1.2	1.3			

Source: World Tourism Organization (WTO) © (Data as collected by WTO September 2003)

Arrivals by air are particularly important in Oceania, with a share of over 98 per cent of all arrivals, but also in South Asia, where tourists travelling by air to the subregion account for almost three quarters of arrivals (4.3 million). In South-East Asia, though air transport also represent the main mode of transport (55%), road transport still accounts for more than 30 per cent of all arrivals to the subregion. By contrast, in North-East Asia road transport leads the ranking with a 54 per cent market share, as the countries in the area share significant borders, while air traffic represents 33 per cent and arrivals by water 11 per cent of all international tourist arrivals.

Arrivals by mode of transport (including estimations for countries with missing data), 2001

	Total	Air	Road	Rail	Water	Not specified
	International Tourist Arrivals (million)					
Asia and the Pacific	121.1	57.3	49.6	0.7	12.0	1.6
North-East Asia	65.6	21.5	35.6	0.4	7.3	0.9
South-East Asia	40.2	22.2	12.5	0.2	4.6	0.7
Oceania	9.5	9.3	0.0	0.0	0.1	0.0
South Asia	5.8	4.3	1.5	0.0	0.0	0.0
	%					
Asia and the Pacific	100	47.3	40.9	0.5	9.9	1.3
North-East Asia	100	32.7	54.2	0.7	11.1	1.3
South-East Asia	100	55.2	31.1	0.4	11.4	1.8
Oceania	100	98.5	0.0	0.0	1.5	0.0
South Asia	100	73.5	25.0	0.8	0.7	0.0

Source: World Tourism Organization (WTO) © (Data as collected by WTO September 2003)

Inbound tourism by purpose of visit

Like in most regions of the world, the majority of arrivals to Asia and the Pacific are for the purpose of leisure, recreation and holidays, accounting for a share of around 60 per cent of all international tourist arrivals to Asia and the Pacific according to figures since 1990. In 2001, 68.8 million tourists visited the region with this purpose (57%). The business and professional market has traditionally represented a share of between 15 and 20 per cent, while the remaining categories, "visiting friends and relatives (VFR), health, religion and other", account for some 20 per cent. Over time, the share of business or professional purposes has increased gradually. This category has shown the fastest growth between 1990 and 2000 (9.3% on average a year) and continued to do so in 2001 (6.7%). In the latter year it was responsible for 19.3 per cent of all arrivals, the world's second highest share by region, after Europe.

Asia and the Pacific: Inbound tourism by purpose of visit
International Tourist Arrivals (share, %)

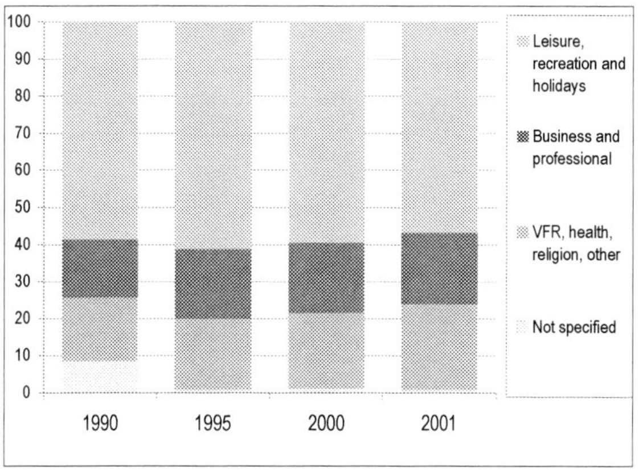

Source: World Tourism Organization (WTO) ©

Asia / Pacific and subregions: Inbound tourism by purpose of visit
International Tourist Arrivals, (share, %)

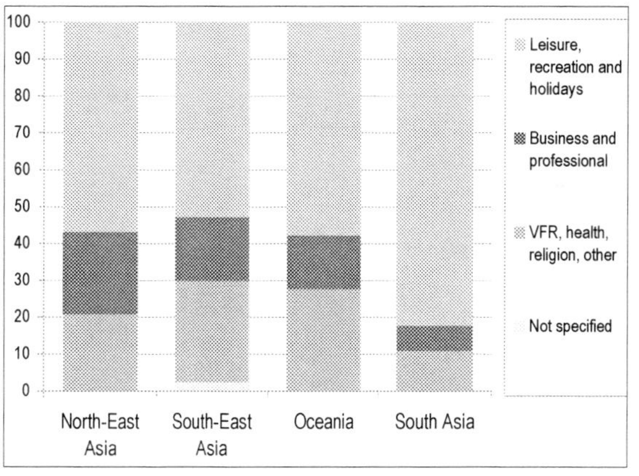

Source: World Tourism Organization (WTO) ©

Asia and the Pacific
Arrivals by purpose of visit (including estimations for countries with missing data)

	International Tourist Arrivals			(million)	Market share	(%)	Growth rate	(%)	Average annual growth (%)
	1990	1995	2000	2001	1990	2001	00/99	01/00	1990-2000
Total	57.7	85.6	115.3	121.1	100	100	12.3	5.1	7.2
Leisure, recreation and holidays	33.9	52.4	68.5	68.8	58.6	56.8	15.9	0.5	7.3
Business and professional	9.0	16.1	21.9	23.4	15.7	19.3	12.1	6.7	9.3
VFR, health, religion, other	9.9	16.3	23.4	28.0	17.2	23.1	2.8	19.5	9.0
Not specified	4.9	0.8	1.5	1.0	8.5	0.8			

Source: World Tourism Organization (WTO) © (Data as collected by WTO September 2003)

Leisure, recreation and holidays ranks first as purpose of visit in all the subregions of Asia and the Pacific, but has a significantly higher weight in South Asia, where it accounts for a share of 82 per cent. The category "visiting friends and relatives (VFR), health, religion and other" is the second most important purpose of visit in all subregions, with the exception of North-East Asia, where the second purpose of visit is "business and professional" (22%).

Besides North-East Asia, business and professional travel has a relative high share in South-East Asia (17%).

Arrivals by purpose of visit (including estimations for countries with missing data), 2001

	Total	Leisure, recreation and holidays	Business and professional	VFR, health, religion, other	Not specified
	International Tourist Arrivals (million)				
Asia and the Pacific	121.1	68.8	23.4	28.0	1.0
North-East Asia	65.6	37.3	14.7	13.6	0.0
South-East Asia	40.2	21.3	6.9	11.1	1.0
Oceania	9.5	5.5	1.4	2.6	0.0
South Asia	5.8	4.8	0.4	0.6	0.0
	%				
Asia and the Pacific	100	56.8	19.3	23.1	0.8
North-East Asia	100	56.8	22.4	20.8	0.0
South-East Asia	100	52.8	17.2	27.5	2.5
Oceania	100	57.8	14.6	27.6	0.0
South Asia	100	82.3	6.8	10.9	0.0

Source: World Tourism Organization (WTO) © (Data as collected by WTO September 2003)

Outbound tourism by (sub)region of destination

Asia and the Pacific generated more than 131 million international arrivals worldwide in 2002. In spite of the Asian financial crisis of 1997 and 1998, outbound tourism originating from this part of the world grew by 7 per cent a year, the fastest pace of all world regions, in the period 1990-2000. Constrained by the world events, outbound tourism from the region went no further than a 2.3 per cent increase in 2001, recovering, nevertheless, subsequently with a 7.9 per cent growth in 2002. The high growth rate of outbound tourism in the region can be interpreted as the result of the improving conditions for international tourism in Asia and the Pacific as travel is becoming more and more accessible to larger parts of the population. In particular, four major countries, China, Japan, Hong Kong (China) and the Republic of Korea, represent prosperous generating markets.

From1990 to 2000 travel to destinations within the region grew at a faster pace (7.4%) than interregional travel (6.1%), a trend that was strongly reinforced in 2001 and 2002. As a result the share of intraregional outbound increased by 6 per cent from 72 per cent in 1990 to 78 per cent in 2002, while outbound tourism to other regions declined from a 28 to a 22 per cent market share. This decline in outbound to destinations outside the region was particularly influenced by the severe two years drop in traffic to the Americas in 2001 and 2002 (-15% and -8% respectively).

In 2002, intraregional traffic in the region exceeded 100 million arrivals for the first time, up from 43 million in 1990. Almost half of all outbound tourism from Asia and the Pacific ended up in North-East Asia, corresponding to 62 million arrivals. Another 32 million arrivals were received in South-East Asia, while Oceania and South Asia received 6 million and 2 million arrivals respectively. Contrary to the overall trend in the world, intraregional traffic to North-East Asia and South-East Asia has grown substantially in both 2001 and 2002, adding almost 10 million and over 4 million arrivals respectively in the two years. Intraregional arrivals to Oceania and South Asia did not increase in this period.

The most visited destination outside the region is Europe, receiving nearly 15 million arrivals in 2002 and accounting for 11 per cent market share. Some 6 per cent of outbound travellers, corresponding to close to 8 million arrivals, headed for the Americas in 2002, almost exclusively to North America. Traffic to both Europe and the Americas grew at a comparatively slower pace between 1990 and 2000, although still above 5 per cent a year. After 2000, traffic to the Americas decreased substantially two years in a row, though in 2002 at a slower pace than in 2001. Traffic to Europe also decreased in 2001, but recovered partly in 2002. Consequently these two regions lost significant market share in recent years, in particular the Americas (from 10% in 1990 to 6% in 2002). In contrast, the Middle East, which saw outbound tourism from Asia and the Pacific growing by 22 per cent in 2002, has been slowly gaining market share (from 3% in 1990 to 4% in 2002).

Asia and the Pacific: Outbound tourism by region of destination
International Tourist Arrivals, 2002* (share, %)

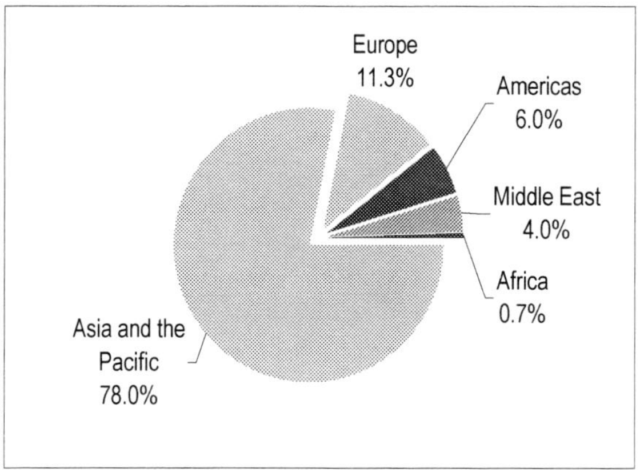

Source: World Tourism Organization (WTO) ©

Asia and the Pacific: Outbound tourism by region of destination
International Tourist Arrivals (share, %)

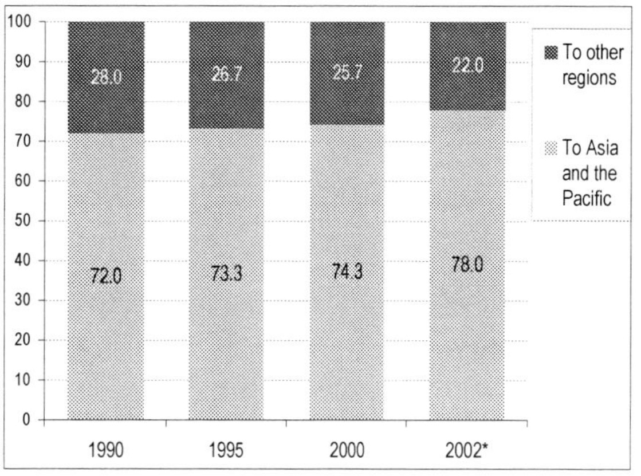

Source: World Tourism Organization (WTO) ©

Asia and the Pacific: Outbound tourism by region of destination
International Tourist Arrivals, 2002* (million)

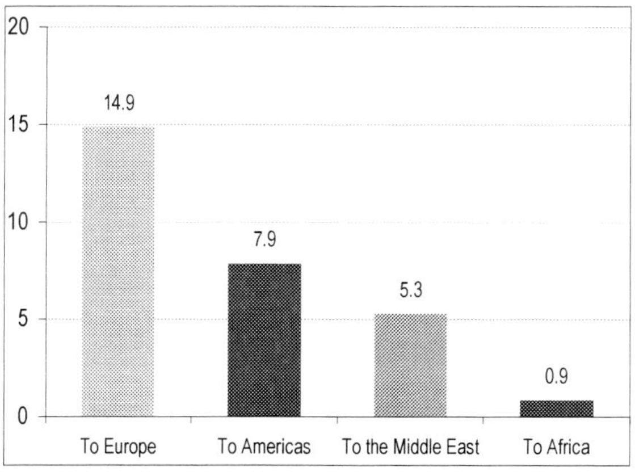

Source: World Tourism Organization (WTO) ©

Asia and the Pacific: Outbound tourism by region of destination
International Tourist Arrivals (change 02*/01, %)

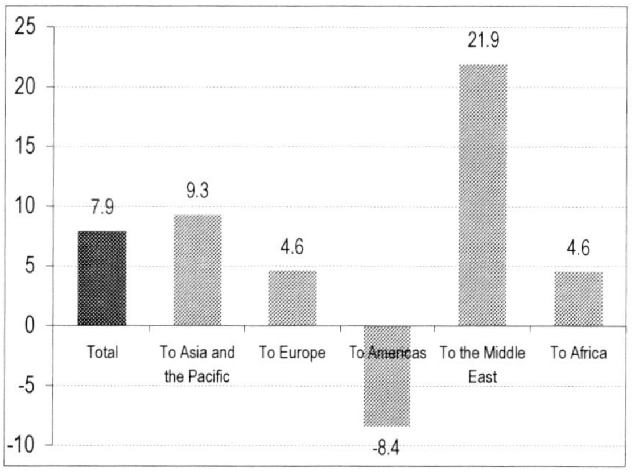

Source: World Tourism Organization (WTO) ©

World and regions: Outbound tourism by region of destination
International Tourist Arrivals, 2002* (share, %)

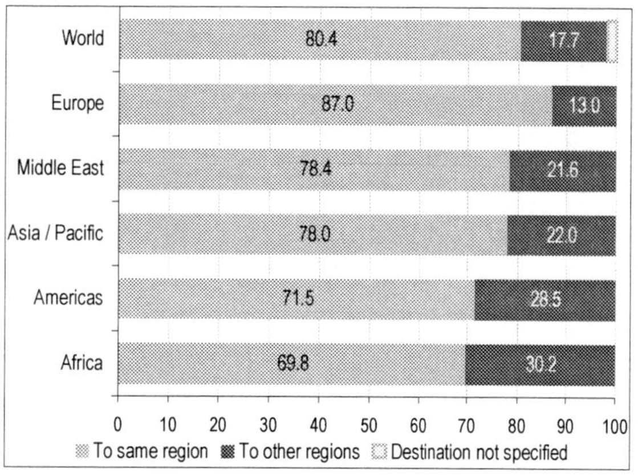

Source: World Tourism Organization (WTO) ©

World regions: Outbound tourism by region of destination
International Tourist Arrivals, 2002* (million)

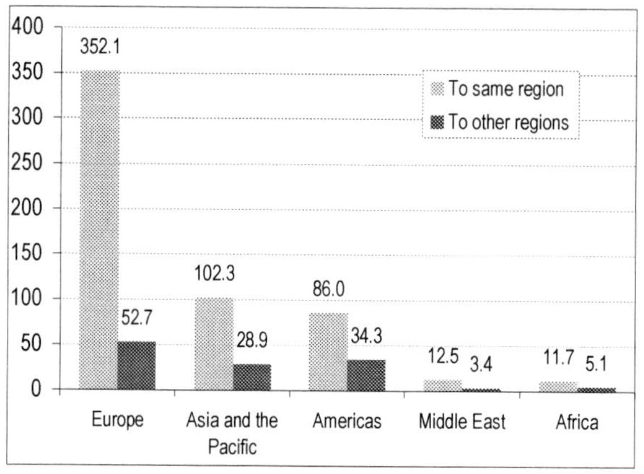

Source: World Tourism Organization (WTO) ©

Asia and the Pacific
Outbound Tourism by (sub)region of destination (including estimations for countries with missing data)

	International Tourist Arrivals (1000)					Market share (%)			Growth rate (%)		Average annual growth (%)	
	1990	1995	2000	2001	2002*	1990	1995	2002*	01/00	02*/01	90-00	95-00
Total	**60,193**	**89,814**	**118,869**	**121,615**	**131,240**	**100**	**100**	**100**	**2.3**	**7.9**	**7.0**	**5.8**
To:												
Asia and the Pacific	***43,329***	***65,840***	***88,348***	***93,642***	***102,344***	***72.0***	***73.3***	***78.0***	***6.0***	***9.3***	***7.4***	***6.1***
North-East Asia	22,357	35,860	51,817	54,824	61,747	37.1	39.9	47.0	5.8	12.6	8.8	7.6
South-East Asia	16,192	22,552	28,000	30,472	32,285	26.9	25.1	24.6	8.8	6.0	5.6	4.4
Oceania	3,398	5,815	6,390	6,288	6,246	5.6	6.5	4.8	-1.6	-0.7	6.5	1.9
South Asia	1,383	1,613	2,142	2,058	2,066	2.3	1.8	1.6	-3.9	0.3	4.5	5.8
Interregional	***16,864***	***23,973***	***30,521***	***27,972***	***28,896***	***28.0***	***26.7***	***22.0***	***-8.3***	***3.3***	***6.1***	***4.9***
Europe	**8,713**	**12,034**	**15,389**	**14,225**	**14,882**	**14.5**	**13.4**	**11.3**	**-7.6**	**4.6**	**5.9**	**5.0**
Northern Europe	1,831	3,140	3,538	3,168	3,177	3.0	3.5	2.4	-10.5	0.3	6.8	2.4
Western Europe	4,201	5,514	7,026	6,375	6,511	7.0	6.1	5.0	-9.3	2.1	5.3	5.0
Central/Eastern Europe	860	1,247	2,044	2,168	2,399	1.4	1.4	1.8	6.1	10.6	9.0	10.4
Southern Europe	1,408	1,481	1,990	1,834	2,016	2.3	1.6	1.5	-7.8	9.9	3.5	6.1
East Mediterranean Eu.	412	652	791	679	780	0.7	0.7	0.6	-14.2	14.9	6.7	3.9
Americas	**6,142**	**8,901**	**10,122**	**8,584**	**7,863**	**10.2**	**9.9**	**6.0**	**-15.2**	**-8.4**	**5.1**	**2.6**
North America	5,946	8,585	9,698	8,171	7,502	9.9	9.6	5.7	-15.7	-8.2	5.0	2.5
Caribbean	26	68	73	70	40	0.0	0.1	0.0	-3.6	-42.7	11.0	1.4
Central America	31	57	67	67	71	0.1	0.1	0.1	-1.2	6.0	8.2	3.3
South America	140	190	283	276	250	0.2	0.2	0.2	-2.7	-9.2	7.3	8.3
Middle East	**1,741**	**2,460**	**4,207**	**4,332**	**5,281**	**2.9**	**2.7**	**4.0**	**3.0**	**21.9**	**9.2**	**11.3**
Africa	**268**	**579**	**803**	**832**	**870**	**0.4**	**0.6**	**0.7**	**3.6**	**4.6**	**11.6**	**6.8**
North Africa	32	46	71	68	72	0.1	0.1	0.1	-4.6	6.9	8.4	9.1
West Africa	30	100	137	144	156	0.0	0.1	0.1	5.4	7.8	16.4	6.6
Central Africa	6	4	15	14	16	0.0	0.0	0.0	-3.1	10.6	9.1	29.9
East Africa	129	217	329	349	330	0.2	0.2	0.3	6.3	-5.5	9.8	8.6
Southern Africa	71	212	252	257	296	0.1	0.2	0.2	1.9	15.5	13.5	3.5

Source: World Tourism Organization (WTO) © (Data as collected by WTO September 2003)

International tourism expenditure & Outbound Trips

Expenditure on international tourism (for both overnight and day trips) by the countries and territories of Asia and the Pacific amounted to an estimated US$ 98 billion in 2002. This represents a 6 per cent increase over 2001, when expenditure in the region dropped by almost 5 per cent.

By subregion, North-East Asia continued by far to spend the most in 2002 (US$ 70 billion), outspending South-East Asia (US$ 16 billion), Oceania (US$ 8 billion) and South Asia (US$ 4 billion) by a considerable margin. In fact, more than 70 per cent of all tourism expenditure generated in the region originates in North-East Asia, and in particular in Japan (US$ 27 billion), China (US$ 15 billion) and Hong Kong (China) (US$ 12 billion). Among these countries, China shows the most dynamic performance, growing by 6 per cent in 2001 and by almost 11 per cent in 2002, while Japan, the top spender in Asia and the Pacific, recovered in 2002 (0.6%) from the major decrease felt the previous year (-17%). In South-East Asia, Singapore and Thailand are the countries that contribute the most to the subregion's expenditure on international tourism, both with significant increases in 2002 (12% and 13% respectively). As for international tourism expenditure registered by Oceania in 2002, the bulk corresponded to Australia (77%) and New Zealand (19%) while more than half of the international tourism expenditure of South Asia in 2002 was accounted for by India. It is important to note that except for the Philippines and Pakistan, all countries in the Asia and the Pacific region increased their tourism expenditure in 2002, many of which with double-digit growth rates.

Data on outbound trips should be taken with care, as figures for many countries are lacking and it is often not clear whether the reported figures refer strictly to tourists (overnight visitors) or to visitors in general (as is obviously the case with Malaysia). Also it is important to note that a single trip can produce arrivals in various destinations. The largest numbers of trips abroad are reported by China and Japan. It is interesting to note that China with an increase of 37 per cent and a total of 16.6 million trips abroad in 2002 surpassed Japan (16.5 million trips) for the first time, although Japanese tourists tend to travel further a field and spend still substantially more. Taiwan and the Republic of Korea followed recording 7.5 million (+4% in 2002) and 7.1 million trips (+17%) respectively. Amongst all Asian countries reporting data on trips abroad in 2002 only Hong Kong (China) showed a slight drop of 1.9 per cent from the previous year. In South-East Asia, major players are Singapore (4.4 million trips) and Malaysia, although the number of overnight trips is unknown in the latter case. Outbound tourism in Oceania is dominated by Australia (3.4 million trips abroad) and New Zealand (1.3 million trips) and in South Asia by India (4.1 million trips) and Iran (2.4 million trips in 2001).

Expenditure per capita reached US$ 47 in Asia and the Pacific while trips per capita went no further that 6 trips per 100 of population. These comparatively modest figures reflect the fact that the ability to engage in international tourism still remains limited to a relatively selective part of the population as well as the fact that many countries in this region have significantly large populations. The highest value in expenditure per capita was reached by Oceania (US$ 253), in contrast to the other subregions with figures ranging between US$ 3 in South Asia to US$ 46 in North-East Asia.

Asia and the Pacific: Outbound tourism
International Tourism Expenditure, 2002* (US$ billion)

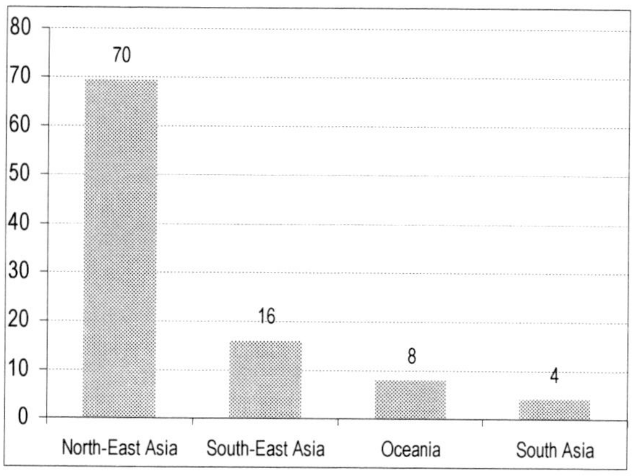

Source: World Tourism Organization (WTO) ©

Asia and the Pacific: Outbound tourism
International Tourism Expenditure, 2002* (US$ per capita)

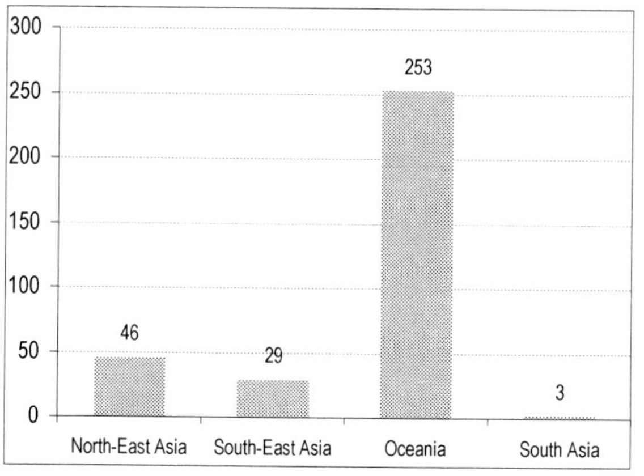

Source: World Tourism Organization (WTO) ©

World and regions: Outbound tourism
International Tourism Expenditure, 2002* (share, %)

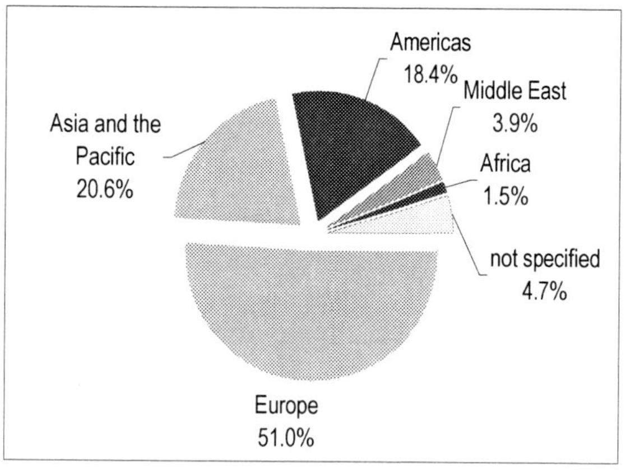

Source: World Tourism Organization (WTO) ©

World and regions: Outbound tourism
International Tourism Expenditure, 2002* (US$ per capita)

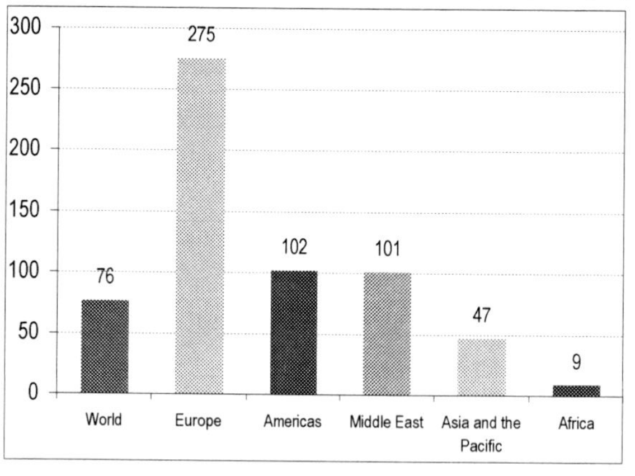

Source: World Tourism Organization (WTO) ©

Outbound Tourism

	International Tourism Expenditure						Trips abroad					
				Growth rate		per				Growth rate		per 100
		(US$ million)			(%)	capita*			(1000)		(%)	popu-
	2000	2001	2002*	01/00	02*/01	US$	2000	2001	2002*	01/00	02*/01	lation*
Asia and the Pacific	***97,139***	***92,583***	***97,737***	***-4.7***	***5.6***	***47***	***102,101***	***109,194***	***114,951***	***6.9***	***5.3***	***6***
North-East Asia	**70,372**	**66,077**	**69,503**	**-6.1**	**5.2**	**46**	**46,096**	**46,848**	**52,937**	**1.6**	**13.0**	**4**
China	13,114	13,909	15,398	6.1	10.7	12	10,473	12,133	16,600	15.9	36.8	1
Hong Kong (China)	12,477	12,316	12,417	-1.3	0.8	1,700	4,611	4,799	4,709	4.1	-1.9	64
Japan	31,886	26,530	26,681	-16.8	0.6	210	17,819	16,216	16,523	-9.0	1.9	13
Korea, Republic of	6,174	6,547	7,642	6.0	16.7	159	5,508	6,084	7,123	10.5	17.1	15
Macao (China)	..	..	..	..	..		144	192	200	33.3	4.2	43
Mongolia	51	55	..	7.8	..	21	..	..	..	..	..	
Taiwan (Pr. of China)	6,376	6,379	6,963	0.0	9.2	310	7,329	7,189	7,507	-1.9	4.4	33
South-East Asia	**14,446**	**15,280**	**16,094**	**5.8**	**5.3**	**29**	**42,239**	**48,433**	**47,672**	**14.7**	**-1.6**	**9**
Cambodia	29	35	..	20.7	..	3	..	..	..	..	..	
Indonesia	3,197	3,406	..	6.5	..	15	..	..	..	..	..	
Lao P.D.R.	8	..	..	..	..	1	..	..	..	..	..	
Malaysia	2,052	2,614	2,618	27.4	0.2	116	30,532	36,248	..	18.7	..	163
Myanmar	25	27	..	8.0	..	1	..	..	..	..	..	
Philippines	1,005	1,229	871	22.3	-29.1	10	1,670	1,787	..	7.0	..	2
Singapore	4,970	4,647	5,213	-6.5	12.2	1,171	4,444	4,363	4,399	-1.8	0.8	99
Thailand	2,775	2,923	3,303	5.3	13.0	52	1,946	2,044	..	5.0	..	3
Oceania	**8,018**	**7,422**	**7,985**	**-7.4**	**7.6**	**253**	**5,194**	**5,130**	**5,232**	**-1.2**	**2.0**	**17**
American Samoa	..	..	..	..	..		41	..	..	..	..	63
Australia	6,131	5,764	6,116	-6.0	6.1	313	3,498	3,443	3,461	-1.6	0.5	18
Cook Is	..	..	..	..	..		9	9	9			43
Fiji	78	..	..	..	..	94	83	85	99	2.4	16.5	12
New Caledonia	..	..	..	..	..		69	68	72	-1.4	5.9	35
New Zealand	1,537	1,334	1,480	-13.2	11.0	379	1,283	1,287	1,293	0.3	0.5	33
Palau	2	2	2	-4.3	3.4	103	..	..	..	..	..	
Papua New Guinea	50	38	..	-24.0	..	8	52	38	92	-26.9	142.1	2
Tonga	..	3	..	..	..	29	..	..	..	..	..	
Vanuatu	9	8	..	-11.1	..	41	12	12	..		..	6
South Asia	**4,303**	**3,804**	**4,155**	**-11.6**	**9.2**	**3**	**8,572**	**8,783**	**9,110**	**2.5**	**3.7**	**1**
Bangladesh	301	166	..	-44.9	..	1	1,128	1,075	..	-4.7	..	1
India	2,567	2,571	2,942	0.2	14.4	3	3,982	4,067	4,205	2.1	3.4	0
Iran	631	238	..	-62.3	..	4	2,286	2,400	..	5.0	..	4
Maldives	46	45	..	-2.2	..	145	42	41	42	-2.4	2.4	13
Nepal	73	80	..	9.6	..	3	155	200	..	29.0	..	1
Pakistan	252	255	179	1.2	-29.8	1	..	..	..	..	..	
Sri Lanka	244	245	253	0.4	3.3	13	524	505	553	-3.6	9.5	3

Source: World Tourism Organization (WTO) © (Data as collected by WTO September 2003)

* values correspond to most recent year with data available

II.2 Tourism Trends by Subregion

II.2.1 North-East Asia

International tourist arrivals

International tourist arrivals to North-East Asia grew again in 2002 at a significant rate (12%), after growths of 5 per cent in 2001 and of 13 per cent in 2000. This represented the best growth rate in the all subregions and exceeded by almost 4 per cent the growth recorded by the region (8.4%). Except for a short stagnation in 1997, growth has been strong during the whole of the last decade. Between 1990 and 2002 international tourist arrivals to the subregion almost tripled, from 28 million in 1990 to the current 74 million. This dynamism is above all the result of the strong expansion of travel to, from and between China and its Special Administrative Regions (SAR) Hong Kong and Macao.

North-East Asia: Inbound tourism
International Tourist Arrivals (million)

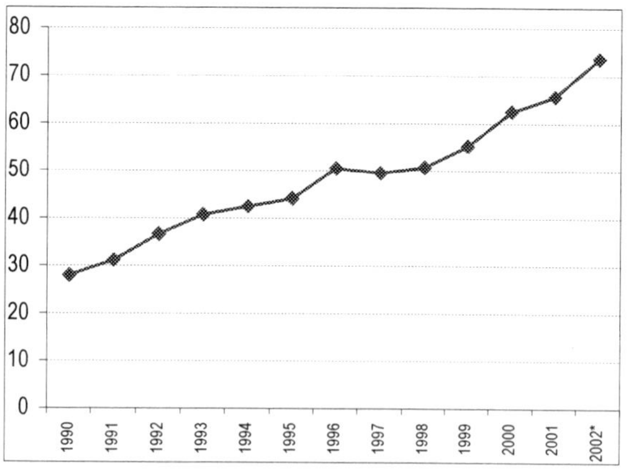

Source: World Tourism Organization (WTO) ©

North-East Asia: Inbound tourism
International Tourist Arrivals (change over previous year, %)

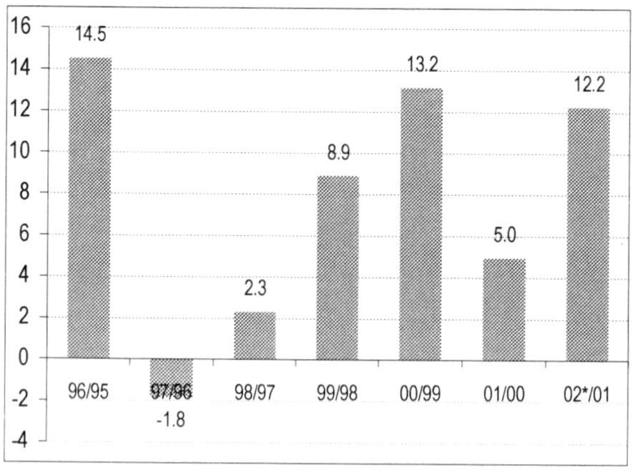

Source: World Tourism Organization (WTO) ©

North-East Asia received more than 73.6 million tourist arrivals in 2002, half of which in China. China alone attracted 36.8 million tourists, marking an 11 per cent growth over 2001. Furthermore, Hong Kong (China) and Macao (China) also performed remarkably, recording 16.6 million (+21%) and 6.6 million tourist arrivals (+12%) respectively. These three Chinese destinations attracted all together 60 million tourists, which represents a share of over four fifth in this subregion and a bit under half of all international tourist arrivals in Asia and the Pacific. The fourth subregional destination was the Republic of Korea, with 5.3 million tourist arrivals, reporting a 4 per cent increase over the previous year. The Republic of Korea and Taiwan (Province of China), both having recorded negative figures in 2001 (-3.3% and –0.3% respectively) bounced back strongly in 2002. Again the dynamism of North-East Asia in recent year was confirmed as all countries registered positive performances, the majority of which above 10 per cent.

International tourism receipts

International tourism receipts in North-East Asia, which correspond to 51 per cent of all receipts generated in the Asia and the Pacific region, grew to an estimated US$ 48 billion in 2002.

As in tourist arrivals, the three Chinese destinations (China, Hong Kong and Macao) are responsible for a very significant share (73%) of international tourism receipts generated in the subregion. China alone accumulated more than US$ 20 billion in tourism receipts (42.5%), followed by Hong Kong (China) with over US$ 10 billion. The third most important earner was the Republic of Korea with an 11 per cent market share and a total of more than US$ 5 billion. It is noteworthy that, except for Mongolia, all countries in North-East Asia recorded tourism receipts over US$ 3 billion.

North-East Asia: Inbound tourism
International Tourism Receipts (US$ billion, current prices)

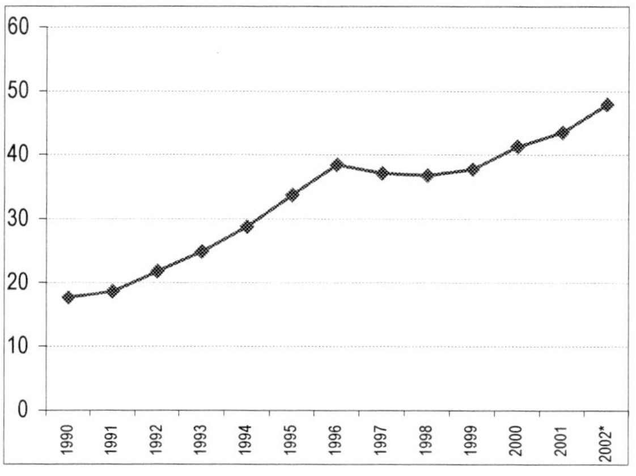

Source: World Tourism Organization (WTO) ©

North-East Asia: Inbound tourism
International arrivals & receipts (share in regional total, %)

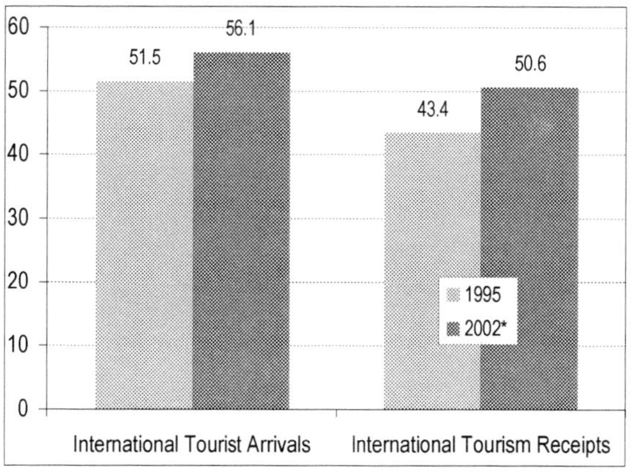

Source: World Tourism Organization (WTO) ©

In terms of receipts per arrival, the subregion reached US$ 653, with the highest values reported by Taiwan (Province of China) with US$ 1.539 and by the Republic of Korea with US$ 987. China and Hong Kong (China) both report receipts per arrival somewhat below the subregional average (US$ 554 and US$ 611 respectively), reflecting the comparatively strong importance of short-stay tourism between both destinations and from other neighbouring countries.

North-East Asia

International Tourist Arrivals and Tourism Receipts by Country of Destination

	Series	1990	1995	2000	2001	2002*	Market share 1995	Market share 2002*	Growth rate 01/00	Growth rate 02*/01	Average annual growth '90-'95	Average annual growth '95-'00
		International Tourist Arrivals (1000)						%		%		%
North-East Asia		**27,969**	**44,102**	**62,507**	**65,604**	**73,634**	**100**	**100**	**5.0**	**12.2**	**9.5**	**7.2**
China	TF	..	20,034	31,229	33,167	36,803	45.4	50.0	6.2	11.0		9.3
Hong Kong (China)	VF	6,581	10,200	13,059	13,725	16,566	23.1	22.5	5.1	20.7	9.2	5.1
Japan	TF	3,236	3,345	4,757	4,772	5,239	7.6	7.1	0.3	9.8	0.7	7.3
Korea, D P Rp	*	115	..	..	..	..						
Korea, Republic of	VF	2,959	3,753	5,322	5,147	5,347	8.5	7.3	-3.3	3.9	4.9	7.2
Macao (China)	TF	2,513	4,202	5,197	5,842	6,565	9.5	8.9	12.4	12.4	10.8	4.3
Mongolia	TF	147	108	158	166	198	0.2	0.3	5.0	19.4	-6.0	7.9
Taiwan (pr. of China)	VF	..	2,332	2,624	2,617	2,726	5.3	3.7	-0.3	4.2		2.4
		International Tourism Receipts (US$ million)						%		%		%
North-East Asia		**17,634**	**33,690**	**41,276**	**43,523**	**47,936**	**100**	**100**	**5.4**	**10.1**	**13.8**	**4.1**
China		2,218	8,733	16,224	17,792	20,385	25.9	42.5	9.7	14.6	31.5	13.2
Hong Kong (China)		5,032	9,604	7,886	8,282	10,117	28.5	21.1	5.0	22.2	13.8	-3.9
Japan		3,578	3,226	3,373	3,301	3,499	9.6	7.3	-2.1	6.0	-2.0	0.9
Korea, Republic of		3,559	5,587	6,811	6,373	5,277	16.6	11.0	-6.4	-17.2	9.4	4.0
Macao (China)		1,473	3,233	3,205	3,745	4,415	9.6	9.2	16.8	17.9	17.0	-0.2
Mongolia		5	21	36	39	..	0.1		8.3		33.2	11.4
Taiwan (pr. of China)		1,740	3,286	3,741	3,991	4,197	9.8	8.8	6.7	5.2	13.6	2.6
		Receipts per Arrival (US$)								%		%
North-East Asia		**1,142**	**766**	**662**	**665**	**653**			**0.5**	**-1.9**	**-7.7**	**-2.9**
China			436	520	536	554			3.3	3.3		3.6
Hong Kong (China)		765	942	604	603	611			-0.1	1.2	4.3	-8.5
Japan		1,106	964	709	692	668			-2.4	-3.5	-2.7	-6.0
Korea, Republic of		1,203	1,489	1,280	1,238	987			-3.3	-20.3	4.4	-3.0
Macao (China)		586	769	617	641	673			3.9	4.9	5.6	-4.3
Mongolia		34	194	228	235				3.2		41.7	3.2
Taiwan (pr. of China)			1,409	1,426	1,525	1,539			7.0	0.9		0.2

Source: World Tourism Organization (WTO) ©

(Data as collected by WTO September 2003)

II.2.2 South-East Asia

International tourist arrivals

In 2002 South-East Asia enjoyed a 5.0 per cent increase in arrivals, attracting over 42 million tourists. This result was due in particular to the growth achieved by its three main destinations - Malaysia, Thailand and Singapore - which together account for nearly 74 per cent of the total international tourist arrivals in the subregion, but also to the general good performances of almost all other countries.

South-East Asia: Inbound tourism
International Tourist Arrivals (million)

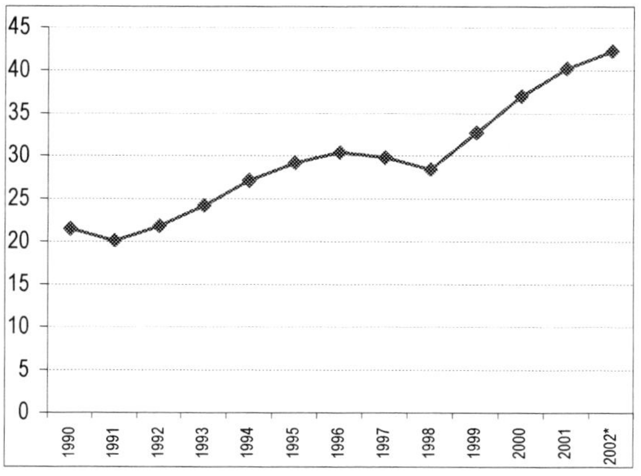

Source: World Tourism Organization (WTO) ©

South-East Asia: Inbound tourism
International Tourist Arrivals (change over previous year, %)

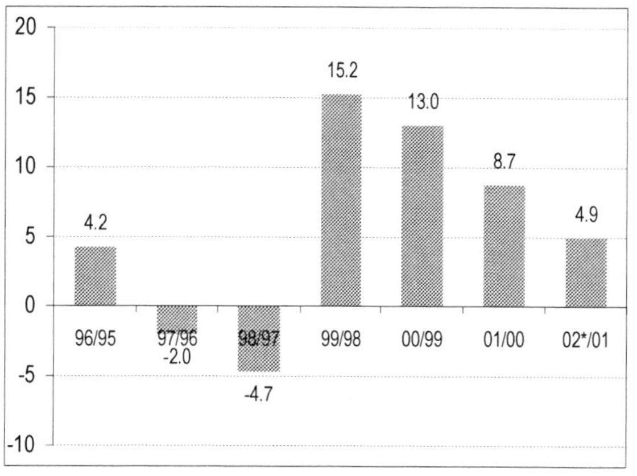

Source: World Tourism Organization (WTO) ©

Malaysia was the top destination in the subregion, accounting for 13.3 million tourist arrivals and a growth of 4 per cent. The country, which has been performing remarkably well recently, with yearly growth rates above 25 per cent between 1999 and 2001, increased its market share from 25.6 per cent in 1995 to 31.5 per cent in 2002. Increases have been driven largely by the growth of inbound arrivals from neighbouring countries: an average annual 7.5 per cent growth in arrivals from Singapore, its main generating market, and an average annual 11.9 per cent growth in arrivals from Thailand between 1995 and 2002. With respect to long-haul markets, it is interesting to note that Malaysia in recent years also has tapped successfully into various Arab markets, such as Saudi Arabia, Syria and United Arab Emirates. Similarly, Thailand and Singapore also recorded significant increases in 2002: 7 and 4 per cent respectively. However, arrivals to Singapore have been growing at a slower pace during recent years when compared to Thailand and Malaysia, and the country has thus lost significant market share since 1995 (22% in 1995 to 17% in 2002). Away from the general trend, the Indonesian tourism industry reflects in 2002 the impact of the October terrorist attack in Bali, with a 2.3 per cent decrease in tourist arrivals, interrupting the growing cycle the country was going through since 1998. The Philippines, which suffered a 9.8 per cent drop in 2001, recovered most of the loss with a 7.6 per cent growth, while Cambodia maintained its excellent 2001 performance growing by another 30 per cent in 2002.

International tourism receipts

International tourism receipts amounted to over US$ 27 billion in South-East Asia, representing almost 30 per cent of all receipts generated by tourism in the Asia and the Pacific region in 2002. As international tourism receipts stagnated between 1995 and 2002 while receipts for North-East Asia on the contrary increased by a notable amount, the regional share of South-East Asia decreased significantly since 1995 when it amounted to over 36 per cent.

South-East Asia: Inbound tourism
International Tourism Receipts (US$ billion, current prices)

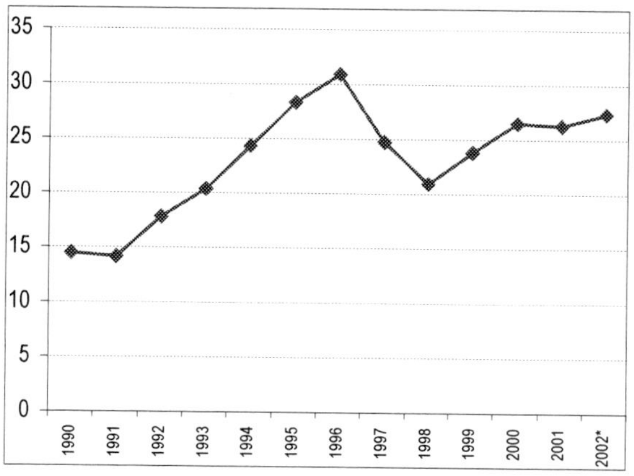

Source: World Tourism Organization (WTO) ©

South-East Asia: Inbound tourism
International arrivals & receipts (share in regional total, %)

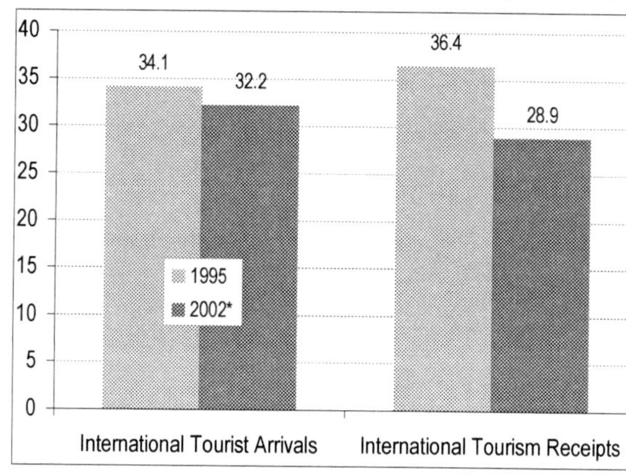

Source: World Tourism Organization (WTO) ©

More than 70 per cent of all tourism receipts in South-East Asia were earned in three countries in 2002: Thailand (29%), Malaysia (25%) and Singapore (18%), with volumes ranging from almost US$ 8 billion in Thailand to nearly US$ 5 billion in Singapore. Though data is not available for Indonesia its 2001 volume of tourism receipts (US$ 5.4 billion) would rank the country third instead of Singapore. It is particularly important to note the evolution of the different market shares among the countries in the subregion. While Malaysia almost doubled its market share between 1995 and 2002, Singapore lost almost 12 per cent in the same period.

In the subregion with the lowest value of receipts per arrivals in Asia and the Pacific (US$ 648), the Philippines enjoyed the highest value of receipts per arrival (US$ 901), whereas Malaysia and Cambodia recorded the lowest figures (US$ 510 and US$ 482 respectively).

South-East Asia

International Tourist Arrivals and Tourism Receipts by Country of Destination

							Market share		Growth rate		Average annual growth	
		1990	1995	2000	2001	2002*	1995	2002*	01/00	02*/01	'90-'95	'95-'00
	Series	International Tourist Arrivals (1000)						%		%		%
South-East Asia		**21,469**	**29,173**	**37,006**	**40,236**	**42,228**	**95**	**100**	**8.7**	**4.9**	**6.3**	**4.9**
Brunei Darussalam	VF	377	498	984	..	..	1.7				5.7	14.6
Cambodia	TF	17	220	466	605	787	0.8	1.9	29.8	30.1	66.9	16.2
Indonesia	TF	2,178	4,324	5,064	5,154	5,033	14.8	11.9	1.8	-2.3	14.7	3.2
Lao P.D.R.	TF	14	60	191	173	215	0.2	0.5	-9.4	24.3	33.8	26.1
Malaysia	TF	7,446	7,469	10,222	12,775	13,292	25.6	31.5	25.0	4.0	0.1	6.5
Myanmar	TF	21	117	208	205	217	0.4	0.5	-1.3	6.0	41.0	12.2
Philippines	TF	1,025	1,760	1,992	1,797	1,933	6.0	4.6	-9.8	7.6	11.4	2.5
Singapore	TF	4,842	6,422	6,917	6,726	6,996	22.0	16.6	-2.8	4.0	5.8	1.5
Thailand	TF	5,299	6,952	9,579	10,133	10,873	23.8	25.7	5.8	7.3	5.6	6.6
Vietnam	TF	250	..	1,383	1,599	..			15.6			
		International Tourism Receipts (US$ million)						%		%		%
South-East Asia		**14,473**	**28,311**	**26,490**	**26,280**	**27,353**	**100**	**100**	**-0.8**	**4.1**	**14.4**	**-1.3**
Brunei Darussalam		..	..	..	..	..						
Cambodia		..	100	228	304	379	0.4	1.4	33.3	24.7		17.9
Indonesia		2,105	5,229	5,749	5,411	..	18.5		-5.9		20.0	1.9
Lao P.D.R.		3	25	114	104	113	0.1	0.4	-8.8	8.7	52.8	35.5
Malaysia		1,667	3,909	4,562	6,374	6,785	13.8	24.8	39.7	6.4	18.6	3.1
Myanmar		9	38	42	45	..	0.1		7.1		33.4	2.0
Philippines		1,306	2,454	2,134	1,723	1,741	8.7	6.4	-19.3	1.0	13.4	-2.8
Singapore		4,937	8,390	6,018	5,081	4,932	29.6	18.0	-15.6	-2.9	11.2	-6.4
Thailand		4,326	8,043	7,489	7,077	7,902	28.4	28.9	-5.5	11.7	13.2	-1.4
Vietnam		85	..	..	..	..						
		Receipts per Arrival (US$)								%		%
South-East Asia		**674**	**970**	**716**	**653**	**648**			**-8.8**	**-0.8**	**7.6**	**-5.9**
Brunei Darussalam												
Cambodia			455	489	502	482			2.7	-4.2		1.5
Indonesia		966	1,209	1,135	1,050				-7.5		4.6	-1.3
Lao P.D.R.		214	417	597	601	526			0.7	-12.6	14.2	7.5
Malaysia		224	523	446	499	510			11.8	2.3	18.5	-3.1
Myanmar		429	325	202	220				8.6		-5.4	-9.0
Philippines		1,274	1,394	1,071	959	901			-10.5	-6.1	1.8	-5.1
Singapore		1,020	1,306	870	755	705			-13.2	-6.7	5.1	-7.8
Thailand		816	1,157	782	698	727			-10.7	4.1	7.2	-7.5
Vietnam		340										

Source: World Tourism Organization (WTO) ©

(Data as collected by WTO September 2003)

[1] Up to 1997 arrivals by air only, from 1998 arrivals by all means of transport.

II.2.3 Oceania

International tourist arrivals

In 2002 Oceania showed a slight 0.8 per cent growth, although not just fully recovering from the previous year decrease. This figure is significantly lower than the growth achieved by Asia and the Pacific as a whole (8.4%) and still much behind the subregion's average annual growth between 1995 and 2000 of 3.6% a year. Arrivals to Oceania peaked in 2000 due in particular to the positive results of Australia and New Zealand, which represent more than 70 per cent of all arrivals, but decreased 1.6 per cent the following year induced by the drop in arrivals to Australia and to Guam. In 2002 the number of tourist arrivals to Oceania grew to 9.6 million, but was still slightly below the 2000 figures.

Oceania: Inbound tourism
International Tourist Arrivals (million)

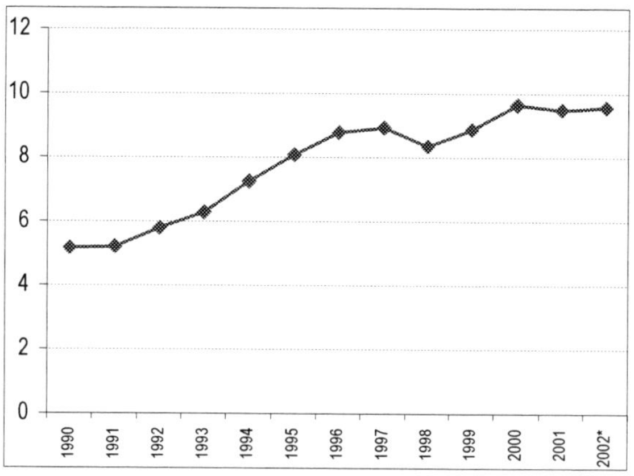

Source: World Tourism Organization (WTO) ©

Oceania: Inbound tourism
International Tourist Arrivals (change over previous year, %)

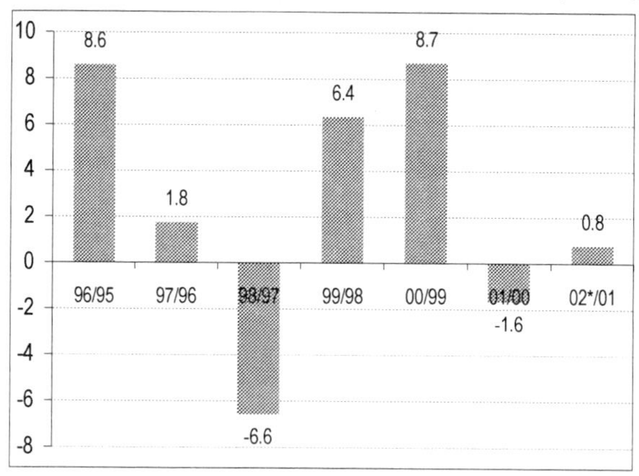

Source: World Tourism Organization (WTO) ©

After the positive impact of the Sydney Olympics in 2000 (+11%), Australia posted two years of negative behaviour in 2001 and 2002 (-1.5% and –0.3%). New Zealand, on the contrary, reported two years of continued strong growth (7% in both 2001 and 2002). The third most important destination in Oceania, Guam, which attracted slightly over one million tourists, continued a decreasing trend initiated in 2001 loosing 18 per cent since. Fiji's strong growth for two consecutive years (18% in 2001 and 14% in 2002) resulted in almost 400 thousand international tourist arrivals to the island in 2002. Among the remaining destinations, all reporting arrivals below 500 thousand tourists, North Mariana Islands, New Caledonia, Palau, Tonga recovered significantly from the decreases of the previous year.

International tourism receipts

Tourism receipts in Oceania amounted to over US$ 14 billion and represent 15 per cent of all receipts earned in Asia and the Pacific in 2002. More than 75 per cent of this volume was generated by Australia and New Zealand, with shares of 56 and 20 per cent respectively.

As the numerous archipelagos distinctly characterize the region's composition, tourism expenditure is understandably very high, causing tourism receipts per person to reach US$ 1,498, the highest among the world's subregions. This figure is twice the average of the Asia and the Pacific region. Australia recorded US$ 1,671 per person and New Zealand's US$ 1,427. In contrast, Tonga earned the least in tourism receipts per arrival in the subregion with US$ 243.

Oceania: Inbound tourism
International Tourism Receipts (US$ billion, current prices)

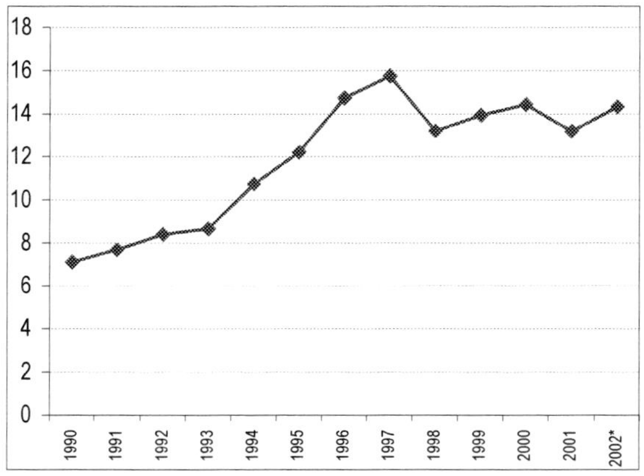

Source: World Tourism Organization (WTO) ©

Oceania: Inbound tourism
International arrivals & receipts (share in regional total, %)

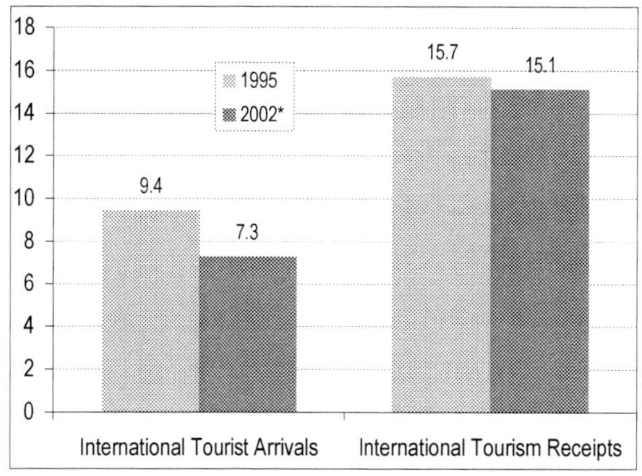

Source: World Tourism Organization (WTO) ©

Oceania
International Tourist Arrivals and Tourism Receipts by Country of Destination

							Market share		Growth rate		Average annual growth	
		1990	1995	2000	2001	2002*	1995	2002*	01/00	02*/01	'90-'95	'95-'00
	Series	International Tourist Arrivals (1000)						%		%		%
Oceania		**5,152**	**8,086**	**9,648**	**9,491**	**9,564**	**100**	**100**	**-1.6**	**0.8**	**9.4**	**3.6**
American Samoa	TF	26	34	44	..	..	0.4				5.5	5.4
Australia	VF	2,215	3,726	4,931	4,856	4,841	46.1	50.6	-1.5	-0.3	11.0	5.8
Cook Is	TF	34	48	73	75	73	0.6	0.8	2.2	-2.1	7.1	8.8
Fiji	TF	279	318	294	348	398	3.9	4.2	18.3	14.4	2.7	-1.6
French Polynesia	TF	132	172	252	228	189	2.1	2.0	-9.8	-16.9	5.5	7.9
Guam	TF	780	1,362	1,287	1,160	1,059	16.8	11.1	-9.9	-8.7	11.8	-1.1
Kiribati	TF	3	4	5	5	5	0.0	0.1	-5.9	18.2	5.6	4.2
Marshall Is	TF	5	6	5	5	6	0.1	0.1	3.8	10.2	1.9	-1.0
Micronesia (Fed.St.of)	TF	..	..	21	15	19		0.2	-25.5	24.8		
N.Mariana Is	TF	426	669	517	438	466	8.3	4.9	-15.3	6.4	9.4	-5.0
New Caledonia	TF	87	86	110	101	104	1.1	1.1	-8.3	3.5	-0.2	4.9
New Zealand	VF	..	1,409	1,787	1,909	2,045	17.4	21.4	6.9	7.1		4.9
Niue	TF	1	2	2	2	2	0.0	0.0	2.9	0.7	16.7	-1.4
Palau	TF	33	53	58	54	59	0.7	0.6	-6.9	9.3	9.9	1.8
Papua New Guinea	TF	41	42	58	54	54	0.5	0.6	-7.2	-0.4	0.6	6.7
Samoa	TF	48	68	88	88	89	0.8	0.9	0.7	0.8	7.3	5.1
Solomon Is	TF	9	12	..	..	..	0.1				5.6	
Tonga	TF	21	30	35	32	37	0.4	0.4	-6.7	14.2	7.0	3.3
Tuvalu	TF	1	1	1	1	1	0.0	0.0	-5.0	8.4	-1.6	5.4
Vanuatu	TF	35	44	58	53	49	0.5	0.5	-7.5	-7.4	4.5	5.7

Continued on the next page.

Oceania

International Tourist Arrivals and Tourism Receipts by Country of Destination

	1990	1995	2000	2001	2002*	Market share 1995	Market share 2002*	Growth rate 01/00	Growth rate 02*/01	Average annual growth '90-'95	Average annual growth '95-'00
	International Tourism Receipts (US$ million)						%		%		%
Oceania	**7,119**	**12,214**	**14,430**	**13,172**	**14,329**	**89**	**100**	**-8.7**	**8.8**	**11.4**	**3.4**
American Samoa	10	..	..	..	..						
Australia	4,088	7,857	8,451	7,624	8,087	64.3	56.4	-9.8	6.1	14.0	1.5
Cook Is	16	28	36	38	46	0.2	0.3	5.6	21.1	11.8	5.2
Fiji	202	283	181	217	267	2.3	1.9	19.9	23.0	7.0	-8.6
French Polynesia	171	326	..	..	..	2.7				13.8	
Guam	936	..	..	..	..						
Kiribati	1	2	3	3	..	0.0		18.5		12.5	8.4
Marshall Is	..	3	4	..	4	0.0	0.0				9.9
N.Mariana Is	455	655	..	..	..	5.4				7.6	
New Caledonia	94	108	110	93	..	0.9		-15.5		2.8	0.4
New Zealand	1,030	1,488	2,240	2,334	2,918	12.2	20.4	4.2	25.0	7.6	8.5
Niue	..	2	..	..	..	0.0					
Papua New Guinea	41	60	92	101	..	0.5		9.8		7.9	8.9
Samoa	20	34	41	40	45	0.3	0.3	-2.4	12.5	11.2	3.8
Solomon Is	7	16	..	..	..	0.1				18.0	
Tonga	9	10	7	7	9	0.1	0.1	0.0	28.6	2.1	-6.9
Vanuatu	39	58	58	46	..	0.5		-20.7		8.3	0.0
	Receipts per Arrival (US$)								%		%
Oceania	**1,382**	**1,511**	**1,496**	**1,388**	**1,498**			**-7.2**	**8.0**	**1.8**	**-0.2**
American Samoa	385										
Australia	1,846	2,109	1,714	1,570	1,671			-8.4	6.4	2.7	-4.1
Cook Is	471	585	493	510	630			3.3	23.7	4.4	-3.3
Fiji	724	889	615	624	671			1.3	7.6	4.2	-7.1
French Polynesia	1,295	1,894								7.9	
Guam	1,200										
Kiribati	333	457	558	703				26.0		6.5	4.1
Marshall Is		454	762		667						10.9
N.Mariana Is	1,068	979								-1.7	
New Caledonia	1,080	1,252	1,004	925				-7.8		3.0	-4.3
New Zealand		1,056	1,254	1,222	1,427			-2.5	16.7		3.5
Niue		740									
Papua New Guinea	1,000	1,418	1,574	1,862				18.3		7.2	2.1
Samoa	417	497	468	453	506			-3.1	11.6	3.6	-1.2
Solomon Is	778	1,357								11.8	
Tonga	429	339	202	216	243			7.1	12.5	-4.6	-9.8
Vanuatu	1,114	1,327	1,007	863				-14.3		3.6	-5.4

Source: World Tourism Organization (WTO) © (Data as collected by WTO September 2003)

II.2.4 South Asia

International tourist arrivals

Under the influence of the attacks of September 11th and particularly of the war in Afghanistan, South Asia's tourist arrivals decreased by 4.5 per cent in 2001, interrupting a growing cycle initiated in 1994. The subregion has nevertheless recovered slightly in 2002 (0.9%) to a total of 5.9 million tourists, a figure that is however still below the peak of 6.1 million recorded in 2000.

South Asia: Inbound tourism
International Tourist Arrivals (million)

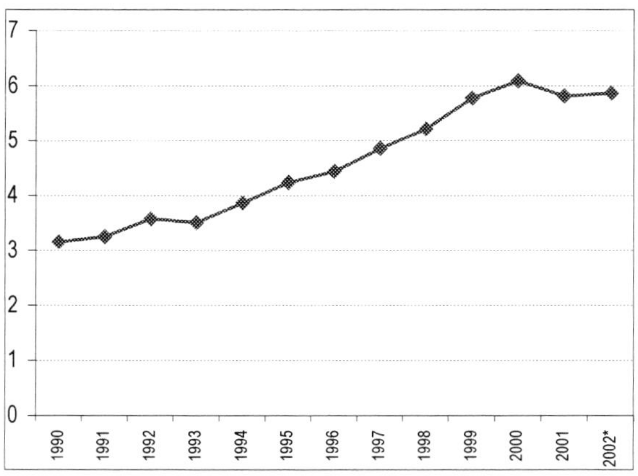

Source: World Tourism Organization (WTO) ©

South Asia: Inbound tourism
International Tourist Arrivals (change over previous year, %)

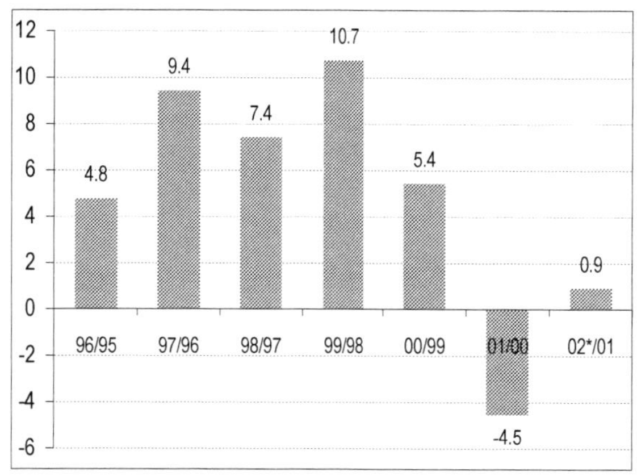

Source: World Tourism Organization (WTO) ©

India, the key destination, responsible for almost 40 per cent of all arrivals in South Asia, has suffered a downtrend in the past two years, with decreases of 4.2 per cent in 2001 and of 6.6 per cent in 2002. Thus the country has seen its market share falling considerably by almost 10 per cent, from half of all international tourist arrivals to the subregion to in 1995 to 40 per cent in 2002. In contrast the Maldives recorded a positive 5.2 per cent growth in midst of difficulties between their neighbouring countries, peaking in terms of tourist arrivals with a new record of 485 thousand. Sri Lanka bounced back successfully from the setbacks of 2001, recording a 17 per cent growth rate over the downfall of the previous year (-16%), but still far from the 436 thousand mark achieved in 1999.

International tourism receipts

South Asia reports a total of US$ 5 billion in international tourism receipts in 2002, which represents 5 per cent of receipts in Asia and the Pacific. Nearly 60 per cent of receipts in the subregion are generated by India, followed at a significant distance by Iran (23% market share in 2001 once data is not available for 2002). Tourism receipts for India have fallen consecutively over the last two years, with decreases of 4 per cent in both 2001 and 2002. Sri Lanka recovered to its 2000 levels, with a 20 per cent growth in 2002, while Pakistan, although showing a negative results in terms of tourist arrivals, achieved a 14 per cent growth in its tourism receipts of US$ 105 million.

South Asia on average collected US$ 865 receipts per arrival in 2002. Only India obtained a higher value than the average receipts per arrival in the subregion (US$ 1,233), reflecting the comparatively large share of longer staying and higher spending long-haul arrivals. In the other destinations receipts per arrival ranged between US$ 211 (Pakistan) and US$ 656 (Maldives) according to data available for 2002.

South Asia: Inbound tourism
International Tourism Receipts (US$ billion, current prices)

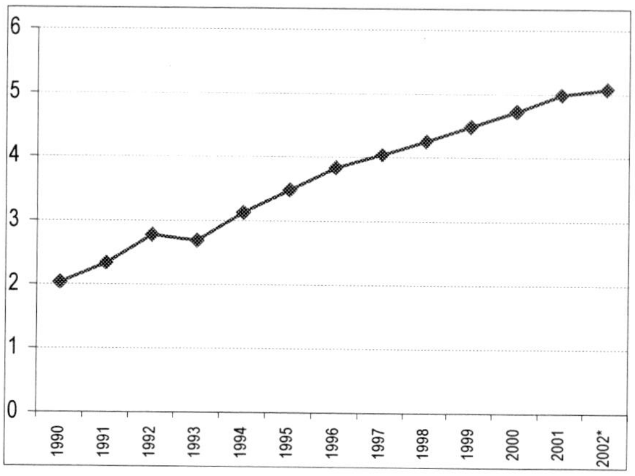

Source: World Tourism Organization (WTO) ©

South Asia: Inbound tourism
International arrivals & receipts (share in regional total, %)

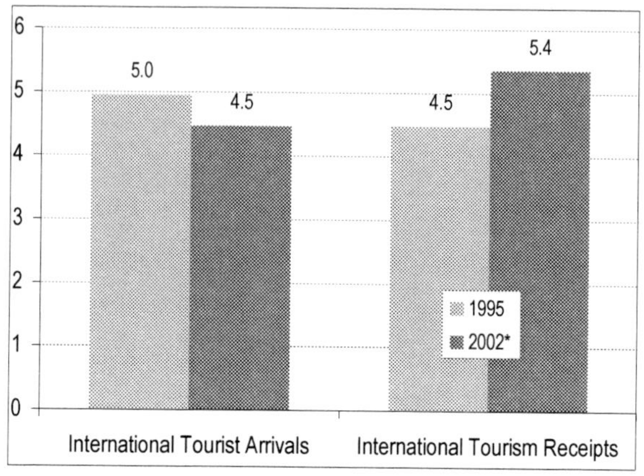

Source: World Tourism Organization (WTO) ©

South Asia

International Tourist Arrivals and Tourism Receipts by Country of Destination

							Market share		Growth rate		Average annual growth	
		1990	1995	2000	2001	2002*	1995	2002*	01/00	02*/01	'90-'95	'95-'00
	Series	International Tourist Arrivals (1000)						%		%		%
South Asia		**3,158**	**4,238**	**6,090**	**5,816**	**5,869**	**100**	**100**	**-4.5**	**0.9**	**6.1**	**7.5**
Afghanistan	*	..	..	..	..	..						
Bangladesh	TF	115	156	199	207	207	3.7	3.5	4.0	0.0	6.3	5.0
Bhutan	TF	2	5	8	6	6	0.1	0.1	-15.7	-5.9	19.0	9.7
India	TF	1,707	2,124	2,649	2,537	2,370	50.1	40.4	-4.2	-6.6	4.5	4.5
Iran	TF	154	489	1,342	1,402	..	11.5		4.5		26.0	22.4
Maldives	TF	195	315	467	461	485	7.4	8.3	-1.3	5.2	10.1	8.2
Nepal	TF	255	363	464	361	..	8.6		-22.1		7.3	5.0
Pakistan	TF	424	378	557	500	498	8.9	8.5	-10.3	-0.3	-2.2	8.0
Sri Lanka	TF	298	403	400	337	393	9.5	6.7	-15.9	16.7	6.2	-0.1
		International Tourism Receipts (US$ million)						%		%		%
South Asia		**2,029**	**3,484**	**4,725**	**4,993**	**5,078**	**100**	**100**	**5.7**	**1.7**	**11.4**	**6.3**
Afghanistan		..	..	..	..	..						
Bangladesh		11	23	50	48	..	0.7		-4.0		15.9	16.8
Bhutan		2	5	10	..	..	0.1				20.1	14.9
India		1,513	2,583	3,168	3,042	2,923	74.1	57.6	-4.0	-3.9	11.3	4.2
Iran		61	205	671	1,122	..	5.9		67.2		27.4	26.8
Maldives		89	211	321	327	318	6.1	6.3	1.9	-2.8	18.8	8.8
Nepal		64	117	167	140	..	3.4		-16.2		12.8	7.4
Pakistan		156	114	84	92	105	3.3	2.1	9.5	14.1	-6.1	-5.9
Sri Lanka		132	225	253	211	253	6.5	5.0	-16.6	19.9	11.3	2.4
		Receipts per Arrival (US$)								%		%
South Asia		**642**	**822**	**776**	**858**	**865**			**10.6**	**0.8**	**5.1**	**-1.2**
Afghanistan												
Bangladesh		96	147	251	232				-7.7		9.0	11.3
Bhutan		1,000	1,049	1,323							1.0	4.7
India		886	1,216	1,196	1,199	1,233			0.3	2.9	6.5	-0.3
Iran		396	419	500	800				60.1		1.2	3.6
Maldives		456	670	687	709	656			3.2	-7.6	8.0	0.5
Nepal		251	322	360	388				7.6		5.1	2.3
Pakistan		368	301	151	184	211			22.0	14.5	-3.9	-12.9
Sri Lanka		443	558	632	626	643			-0.8	2.7	4.7	2.5

Source: World Tourism Organization (WTO) © (Data as collected by WTO September 2003)

III

Tourism Trends by Country

III.1 North-East Asia

III.1.1 China North-East Asia

Profile

China

Capital	Beijing
Year of entry in WTO	1983
Area (1000 km²)	9,598
Population (2002, million)	1,279
Gross Domestic Product (GDP) (2002, US$ million)	1,266,054
GDP per capita (2002, US$)	986
GDP growth (real, %)	
'-> 2001: 7.5; 2002: 8.0; 2003*: 7.5; 2004*: 7.5	

East Asia and the Pacific
North-East Asia

	2000	2001	2002*	2001/2000	2002*/2001
International Arrivals					
Visitors (1000)	83,444	89,013	97,908	6.7	10.0
Tourists (overnight visitors) (1000)	31,229	33,167	36,803	6.2	11.0
- per 100 of inhabitants	2	3	3		
Tourism accommodation[1]					
Number of rooms	948,185	816,260	897,206		9.9
Nights spent in hotels and similar establishments (1000)	432,341	287,810	345,685		20.1
by non-residents (inbound tourism)	78,310	86,765	99,360		14.5
by residents (domestic tourism)	354,031	201,045	246,325		22.5
Outbound Tourism					
Trips abroad (1000)	10,473	12,133	16,600	15.9	36.8
- per 100 of inhabitants	1	1	1		
Receipts and Expenditure for International Tourism					
International Tourism Receipts (US$ million)	16,224	17,792	20,385	9.7	14.6
- per Tourist Arrival (US$)	520	536	554	3.3	3.3
- per Visitor Arrival (US$)	194	200	208	2.8	4.2
- per capita (US$)	13	14	16		
International Fare Receipts (US$ million)	1,087	1,214	..	11.6	
International Tourism Expenditure (US$ million)	13,114	13,909	15,398	6.1	10.7
- per trip (US$)	1,252	1,146	928	-8.4	-19.1
- per capita (US$)	10	11	12		
International Fare Expenditure (US$ million)	1,055	1,083	..	2.7	
△ International Tourism Balance (US$ million)	3,110	3,883	4,987		
△ International Fare Balance (US$ million)	33	131	..		

Source: World Tourism Organization (WTO) (Data as collected by WTO September 2003)

See annex for methodological notes and reference of external sources used.

[1] change of series, from 2001 data only refer to the star-rated hotels

Survey

Contributed by *China National Tourism Administration (CNTA)*
www.cnta.gov.cn (promotional)
www.cnta.gov.cn (institutional/corporate)
www.cnta.gov.cn (research and data)

Tourism development and outlook

Most significant determinant	Beijing will host the 2008 Olympics Shanghai will host the 2010 World Expo China joins the World Trade Organisation Improvements in the infrastructure The destination is safer
Tourism products	Expansion of 145 airports Shanghai, the province of Hainan will apply visa exemption for tourists Twenty two port cities will apply visa on arrival
Generating markets	Notable increase in the fifteen main Markets Growth by more than 20 per cent in near markets: Thailand, Korea, Malaysia, Philippines, Japan, Indonesia
Outlook 2003	Aim: 30 million international Tourists; Income 21.5 million US$
Tourism policy	Strengthen Tourism regulations Promote employment in tourism Invest the state actions fund in infrastructure work in inland areas Improve the information and communication system
Marketing & promotion	Exchange of Tourist Activities with Japan China International Tourism Mart Participation in Tourism Fairs in London, Milan, Zurich, Paris, Madrid

Cultural Tourism (CT)

Specific place for CT in tourism policy: yes.

Main focus of attention supply	Destinations and products like; the Year of Gastronomy, the Year of Traditional Chinese Medicine Tourism, the Year of Martial Arts Tourism, etc.

Specific place for CT in marketing & promotion plan: yes.

Main objectives & programmes	Tourism is promoted by cultural themes, gastronomy, martial arts, traditional Chinese medicine, Beijing opera learning and the Chinese language, etc .
Special activities undertaken	Various Chinese tourism promotion delegations visit other countries to make propaganda about the country.

International Tourism by Origin

China
International Tourist Arrivals at Frontiers

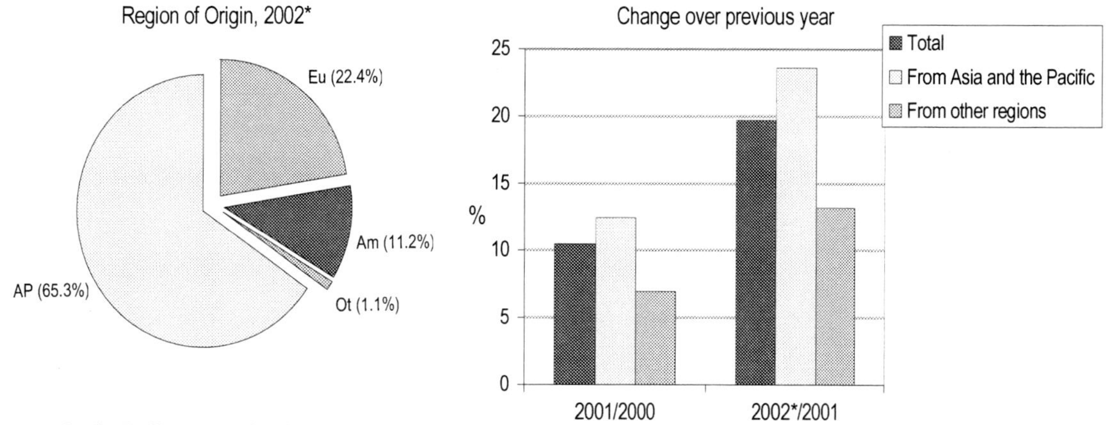

AP: Asia and the Pacific; Eu: Europe; Am: Americas;
Ot: Other;

Source: World Tourism Organization (WTO) ©

China

International Tourist Arrivals at Frontiers (by nationality)

					Market share (%)		Growth rate (%)		Average per year (%)
	1995	2000	2001	2002*	1995	2002*	2001/00	2002*/01	1995-2002*
Total	**5,886,716**	**10,160,432**	**11,226,384**	**13,439,497**	**100**	**100**	**10.5**	**19.7**	**12.5**
From Asia and the Pacific	*3,513,624*	*6,314,210*	*7,100,962*	*8,777,662*	*59.7*	*65.3*	*12.5*	*23.6*	*14.0*
Japan	1,305,190	2,201,528	2,385,700	2,925,553	22.2	21.8	8.4	22.6	12.2
Korea, Republic of	529,467	1,344,721	1,678,836	2,124,310	9.0	15.8	24.8	26.5	22.0
Malaysia	251,758	441,010	468,613	592,447	4.3	4.4	6.3	26.4	13.0
Philippines	219,722	363,852	407,990	508,572	3.7	3.8	12.1	24.7	12.7
Singapore	261,467	399,377	415,047	497,149	4.4	3.7	3.9	19.8	9.6
Mongolia	261,940	399,110	387,057	453,126	4.4	3.4	-3.0	17.1	8.1
Thailand	173,342	241,074	298,417	386,328	2.9	2.9	23.8	29.5	12.1
Australia	129,368	234,102	255,096	291,303	2.2	2.2	9.0	14.2	12.3
Indonesia	132,807	220,554	224,177	274,717	2.3	2.0	1.6	22.5	10.9
India	44,984	120,930	159,361	213,611	0.8	1.6	31.8	34.0	24.9
Vietnam	18,954	82,244	113,823	143,499	0.3	1.1	38.4	26.1	33.5
Pakistan	27,811	40,800	53,061	83,059	0.5	0.6	30.1	56.5	16.9
Korea, D P Rp	66,351	76,385	77,051	79,253	1.1	0.6	0.9	2.9	2.6
New Zealand	22,883	37,595	44,350	50,198	0.4	0.4	18.0	13.2	11.9
Myanmar	19,520	40,806	39,640	44,396	0.3	0.3	-2.9	12.0	12.5
Nepal	8,148	14,255	22,762	25,146	0.1	0.2	59.7	10.5	17.5
Bangladesh	4,728	10,140	17,066	24,709	0.1	0.2	68.3	44.8	26.6
Other intraregional	35,184	45,727	52,915	60,286	0.6	0.4	15.7	13.9	8.0
From other regions	*2,356,219*	*3,842,986*	*4,110,524*	*4,653,720*	*40.0*	*34.6*	*7.0*	*13.2*	*10.2*
Russian Fed	489,329	1,080,209	1,196,175	1,271,635	8.3	9.5	10.7	6.3	14.6
United States	514,850	896,180	949,161	1,121,197	8.7	8.3	5.9	18.1	11.8
United Kingdom	184,912	283,877	302,527	342,967	3.1	2.6	6.6	13.4	9.2
Canada	128,762	236,556	253,876	291,329	2.2	2.2	7.3	14.8	12.4
Germany	166,528	239,062	253,354	281,835	2.8	2.1	6.0	11.2	7.8
France	118,494	184,964	199,523	222,135	2.0	1.7	7.9	11.3	9.4
Former U.S.S.R.	130,877	..	..	..	2.2				
Netherlands	34,948	75,978	92,953	100,405	0.6	0.7	22.3	8.0	16.3
Italy	63,721	77,840	77,684	91,711	1.1	0.7	-0.2	18.1	5.3
Kazakhstan	99,197	67,054	69,273	65,748	1.7	0.5	3.3	-5.1	-5.7
Sweden	35,206	53,570	52,807	62,811	0.6	0.5	-1.4	18.9	8.6
Spain	15,670	34,351	35,914	44,456	0.3	0.3	4.6	23.8	16.1
Denmark	18,066	32,986	34,139	36,812	0.3	0.3	3.5	7.8	10.7
Kyrgyzstan	34,130	28,139	25,769	36,749	0.6	0.3	-8.4	42.6	1.1
Belgium	16,682	30,809	32,469	36,325	0.3	0.3	5.4	11.9	11.8
Portugal	25,649	22,796	26,845	36,092	0.4	0.3	17.8	34.4	5.0
Austria	15,994	31,549	31,401	35,540	0.3	0.3	-0.5	13.2	12.1
Ukraine	7,649	26,028	29,560	34,509	0.1	0.3	13.6	16.7	24.0
Finland	24,341	28,026	27,428	33,621	0.4	0.3	-2.1	22.6	4.7
Switzerland	34,265	30,743	30,816	32,239	0.6	0.2	0.2	4.6	-0.9
Israel	11,306	23,843	25,630	30,141	0.2	0.2	7.5	17.6	15.0
Norway	10,619	24,763	27,138	29,175	0.2	0.2	9.6	7.5	15.5
Turkey	7,067	20,570	16,511	24,787	0.1	0.2	-19.7	50.1	19.6
Poland	10,594	17,120	18,441	23,341	0.2	0.2	7.7	26.6	11.9
Other interregional	157,363	295,973	301,130	368,160	2.7	2.7	1.7	22.3	12.9
Other World/Not specified	*16,873*	*3,236*	*14,898*	*8,115*	*0.3*	*0.1*	*360.4*	*-45.5*	*-9.9*

Source: World Tourism Organization (WTO) © (Data as collected by WTO September 2003)

Note: Excluding ethnic Chinese arriving from Hong Kong (China), Macau (China), Taiwan (Pr. of China) and overseas Chinese.

III.1.2 Democratic People's Republic of Korea — North-East Asia

Profile

Democratic People's Republic of Korea	Capital	Pyongyang
East Asia and the Pacific	Year of entry in WTO	1987
North-East Asia	Area (1000 km²)	121
	Population (2002, million)	22.2

Source: World Tourism Organization (WTO) (Data as collected by WTO September 2003)

See annex for methodological notes and reference of external sources used.

III.1.3 Hong Kong (China) North-East Asia

Profile

Hong Kong (China)

East Asia and the Pacific
North-East Asia

Year of entry in WTO	1999
Population (2002, million)	7.3
Gross Domestic Product (GDP) (2002, US$ million)	161,512
GDP per capita (2002, US$)	23,697
GDP growth (real, %)	
'-> 2001: 0.5; 2002: 2.3; 2003*: 1.5; 2004*: 2.8	

	2000	2001	2002*	2001/2000	2002*/2001
International Arrivals					
Visitors (1000)	13,059	13,725	16,566	5.1	20.7
- per 100 of inhabitants	184	190	227		
Cruise passengers (1000)	9	9	13	6.9	39.9
Tourism accommodation					
Number of rooms	36,438	35,999	..	-1.2	
Outbound Tourism					
Trips abroad (1000)	4,611	4,799	4,709	4.1	-1.9
- per 100 of inhabitants	65	67	64		
Receipts and Expenditure for International Tourism					
International Tourism Receipts (US$ million)	7,886	8,282	10,117	5.0	22.2
- per Visitor Arrival (US$)	604	603	611	-0.1	1.2
- per capita (US$)	1,108	1,149	1,385		
International Tourism Expenditure (US$ million)	12,477	12,316	12,417	-1.3	0.8
- per trip (US$)	2,706	2,566	2,637	-5.2	2.7
- per capita (US$)	1,753	1,708	1,700		
△ International Tourism Balance (US$ million)	-4,591	-4,034	-2,300		

Source: World Tourism Organization (WTO) (Data as collected by WTO September 2003)

See annex for methodological notes and reference of external sources used.

International Tourism by Origin

Hong Kong (China)
International Visitor Arrivals at Frontiers

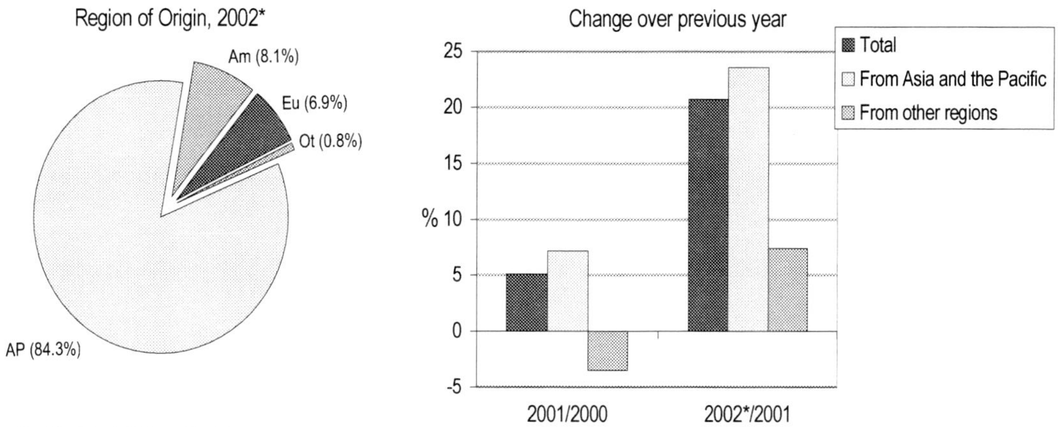

AP: Asia and the Pacific; Am: Americas; Eu: Europe;
Ot: Other;

Source: World Tourism Organization (WTO) ©

Hong Kong (China)
International Visitor Arrivals at Frontiers (by residence)

					Market share (%)		Growth rate (%)		Average per year (%)
	1995	2000	2001	2002*	1995	2002*	2001/00	2002*/01	1995-2002*
Total	**10,199,994**	**13,059,477**	**13,725,332**	**16,566,382**	**100**	**100**	**5.1**	**20.7**	**7.2**
From Asia and the Pacific	*7,960,484*	*10,541,433*	*11,296,095*	*13,957,450*	*78.0*	*84.3*	*7.2*	*23.6*	*8.4*
China	2,243,245	3,785,845	4,448,583	6,825,199	22.0	41.2	17.5	53.4	17.2
Taiwan (Pr. of China)	1,761,111	2,385,739	2,418,827	2,428,776	17.3	14.7	1.4	0.4	4.7
Japan	1,691,283	1,382,417	1,336,538	1,395,020	16.6	8.4	-3.3	4.4	-2.7
Macao (China)	155,915	449,947	532,391	534,590	1.5	3.2	18.3	0.4	19.2
Korea, Republic of	352,981	372,639	425,732	457,438	3.5	2.8	14.2	7.4	3.8
Singapore	279,514	450,569	421,513	426,166	2.7	2.6	-6.4	1.1	6.2
Australia	280,080	352,409	324,156	343,294	2.7	2.1	-8.0	5.9	2.9
Philippines	295,018	278,460	293,105	329,604	2.9	2.0	5.3	12.5	1.6
Malaysia	222,319	314,857	286,338	318,854	2.2	1.9	-9.1	11.4	5.3
Thailand	265,844	228,774	241,480	259,336	2.6	1.6	5.6	7.4	-0.4
Indonesia	184,417	236,275	212,260	223,590	1.8	1.3	-10.2	5.3	2.8
India	86,151	131,368	161,752	193,705	0.8	1.2	23.1	19.8	12.3
New Zealand	50,130	58,185	57,501	61,887	0.5	0.4	-1.2	7.6	3.1
Pakistan	23,550	32,241	39,138	55,415	0.2	0.3	21.4	41.6	13.0
Bangladesh	16,073	25,243	30,540	33,032	0.2	0.2	21.0	8.2	10.8
Vietnam	9,821	20,269	28,157	23,838	0.1	0.1	38.9	-15.3	13.5
Sri Lanka	9,851	11,492	10,834	12,691	0.1	0.1	-5.7	17.1	3.7
Other intraregional	33,181	24,704	27,250	35,015	0.3	0.2	10.3	28.5	0.8
From other regions	*2,235,874*	*2,518,044*	*2,429,237*	*2,608,932*	*21.9*	*15.7*	*-3.5*	*7.4*	*2.2*
United States	748,911	966,008	935,717	1,000,844	7.3	6.0	-3.1	7.0	4.2
United Kingdom	360,545	367,938	360,581	379,965	3.5	2.3	-2.0	5.4	0.8
Canada	174,656	253,095	249,707	264,967	1.7	1.6	-1.3	6.1	6.1
Germany	249,266	193,837	173,359	172,654	2.4	1.0	-10.6	-0.4	-5.1
France	129,676	142,487	136,876	146,714	1.3	0.9	-3.9	7.2	1.8
Italy	75,766	70,743	65,753	71,969	0.7	0.4	-7.1	9.5	-0.7
Netherlands	53,972	61,479	65,574	67,073	0.5	0.4	6.7	2.3	3.2
Israel	17,366	32,825	33,001	33,661	0.2	0.2	0.5	2.0	9.9
Switzerland	60,729	38,169	35,131	33,303	0.6	0.2	-8.0	-5.2	-8.2
South Africa	32,983	30,908	32,504	30,793	0.3	0.2	5.2	-5.3	-1.0
Spain	18,604	25,946	25,311	29,974	0.2	0.2	-2.4	18.4	7.1
Sweden	33,171	30,103	26,111	29,412	0.3	0.2	-13.3	12.6	-1.7
Belgium	20,390	20,069	18,813	20,062	0.2	0.1	-6.3	6.6	-0.2
Mexico	4,150	14,369	13,661	19,031	0.0	0.1	-4.9	39.3	24.3
Turkey	7,079	15,773	10,872	17,495	0.1	0.1	-31.1	60.9	13.8
Denmark	16,868	16,225	15,155	17,155	0.2	0.1	-6.6	13.2	0.2
Austria	30,229	16,379	15,088	16,303	0.3	0.1	-7.9	8.1	-8.4
Brazil	15,527	13,467	13,684	15,654	0.2	0.1	1.6	14.4	0.1
Ireland	9,001	15,765	13,163	14,996	0.1	0.1	-16.5	13.9	7.6
Mauritius	5,865	9,221	11,546	14,287	0.1	0.1	25.2	23.7	13.6
Norway	11,650	11,597	12,146	13,576	0.1	0.1	4.7	11.8	2.2
Finland	8,541	9,127	8,640	13,033	0.1	0.1	-5.3	50.8	6.2
Russian Fed	3,537	9,767	9,777	12,852	0.0	0.1	0.1	31.5	20.2
Portugal	33,053	10,915	9,248	10,793	0.3	0.1	-15.3	16.7	-14.8
Other interregional	114,339	141,832	137,819	162,366	1.1	1.0	-2.8	17.8	5.1
Other World/Not specified	*3,636*	..	..	..	*0.0*				

Source: World Tourism Organization (WTO) © (Data as collected by WTO September 2003)

III.1.4 Japan North-East Asia

Profile

Japan

Capital	Tokyo
Year of entry in WTO	1978
Area (1000 km²)	378
Population (2002, million)	127
Gross Domestic Product (GDP) (2002, US$ million)	3,986,347
GDP per capita (2002, US$)	31,300
GDP growth (real, %)	
'-> 2001: 0.4; 2002: 0.2; 2003*: 2.0; 2004*: 1.4	

East Asia and the Pacific
North-East Asia

	2000	2001	2002*	2001/2000	2002*/2001
International Arrivals					
Tourists (overnight visitors) (1000)	4,757	4,772	5,239	0.3	9.8
- per 100 of inhabitants	4	4	4		
Tourism accommodation					
Number of rooms	1,574,132	1,572,131	..	-0.1	
Nights spent in hotels and similar establishments (1000)					
by residents (domestic tourism)	313,000	284,000	286,000	-9.3	0.7
Outbound Tourism					
Trips abroad (1000)	17,819	16,216	16,523	-9.0	1.9
- per 100 of inhabitants	14	13	13		
Receipts and Expenditure for International Tourism					
International Tourism Receipts (US$ million)	3,373	3,301	3,499	-2.1	6.0
- per Tourist Arrival (US$)	709	692	668	-2.4	-3.5
- per capita (US$)	27	26	28		
International Fare Receipts (US$ million)	2,600	2,440	..	-6.2	
International Tourism Expenditure (US$ million)	31,886	26,530	26,681	-16.8	0.6
- per trip (US$)	1,789	1,636	1,615	-8.6	-1.3
- per capita (US$)	252	209	210		
International Fare Expenditure (US$ million)	10,760	9,000	..	-16.4	
△ International Tourism Balance (US$ million)	-28,513	-23,229	-23,182		
△ International Fare Balance (US$ million)	-8,160	-6,560	..		

Source: World Tourism Organization (WTO) (Data as collected by WTO September 2003)

See annex for methodological notes and reference of external sources used.

Survey

Contributed by *Japan National Tourist Organization (JNTO)*
www.jnto.go.jp (promotional)
www.jnto.go.jp (research and data)

Tourism development and outlook

Most significant determinant

Visitor arrivals to Japan were 5,238,963 (a 9.8% increase), mainly due to increasing visitor arrivals from the East Asian countries, especially from China and South Korea. Also the Hong Kong and Taiwan markets were better than expected. The total arrivals from the four markets constitute 55.2 per cent of total visitor arrivals to Japan.

In the East Asian countries, the consumer made short-haul travel within the area, avoiding long-haul travel, after 11 September 2001.

With the inauguration of the second runway of Narita Airport (Tokyo), short-haul flights to Asian capitals, such as Taipei, Hong Kong, Seoul and major cities in China, were almost doubled.

Re-evaluation of good security and hygiene in Japan. Japan's mild weather and beautiful natural scenery attracted the family consumer from Asian countries. Natural hot springs have been more appreciated than ever by the Asian tourist.

Exchange rate of the Japanese Yen against the United States Dollar was stable in 2002. The consumer prices in Japan showed a –9 per cent decrease in comparison to 2001, with four years consecutive decrease. Domestic travel was depressed by economic recession.

These economic and social factors favourable to consumers makes it easier for foreign tourists to come to Japan.

Tourism products

Positive factor:
The World Cup Football Championship was held in Korea and Japan in June 2002. These matches brought almost 50,000 football supporters from overseas countries, of which 60 per cent were from European countries.

Access

The second provisional runaway (2,180 meters) of the Narita Airport, Tokyo began operating in April 2002.

Outlook 2003

The original forecast for 2003 was almost the same percentage increase as in 2002 (9.8%). SARS spread in the most important generating market for Japan from March to June 2003. It is difficult to estimate an expected number of tourists this year. We estimate that there will be a relatively fast recovery in the Chinese and Korean markets and slow growth in the Hong Kong and Taiwan markets.

Tourism policy

In Japan, the importance of international tourism has been recently recognized by central and local governments and economic federations. For the fiscal year 2003 a new budget was approved (almost 9 million US dollars) for the implementation of the "Visit Japan Campaign", which was put into operation in five major markets (Korea, The United States of America, China, Taiwan and Hong Kong) as from April 2003.

Marketing & promotion

With all the different methods of promotion, it is felt that invitations to travel agents and other media (newspaper, magazine and television crews) is much more effective.

Cultural Tourism (CT)

Main objectives & instruments

In Japan it is abundant the material of Cultural Tourism, however it is not yet established as one of important field of Tourism. It is becoming more indispensable nowadays in the package tour included some factors of "Do", "Study with pleasure" and experience local delicious dishes of the region. In the domestic tourism, there are Special Interested Tours (SIT), specialized in Cultural Tourism. But the market in this field is not so big.

Main focus of attention supply

In domestic travel, the following experiences are popular: the experience of agriculture (the transplantation of rice and the harvesting of rice), a snow storm experience, participation at local festival dances, fire-fly watching, the experience of fishing (watching fish catching from another boat), whale watching, etc.

Main focus of attention demand

The main segment of cultural tourism is school student excursions. Almost 3.8 million students participated in school excursions in 2002 domestically, and 210 thousand students went overseas to neighbour countries, mainly to Korea and China. Families with small children are expected to be a good target, but the segment size is not. Also the seniors will be a future market, because of the abundant number of baby-boomers who are already in their middle of fifties.

Main objectives & programmes

As cultural tourism is not clearly classified as one of the segments in inbound tourism, it still occupies a minor position in Japan. But considering the repeat tourists to Japan, cultural tourism can be seen to be an increasing factor. They enjoy the natural wonders and mild climate of Japan e.g. the special flowers of the north: lavender and the potato flower, salmon returning to their native rivers from the sea and monkeys enjoying hot spring baths on winter snow fall days.

Special activities undertaken

For attracting school excursions from Korea and China, we are promoting the cultural tourism factor or attraction, in addition to the historical factor.

International Tourism by Origin

Japan
International Tourist Arrivals at Frontiers

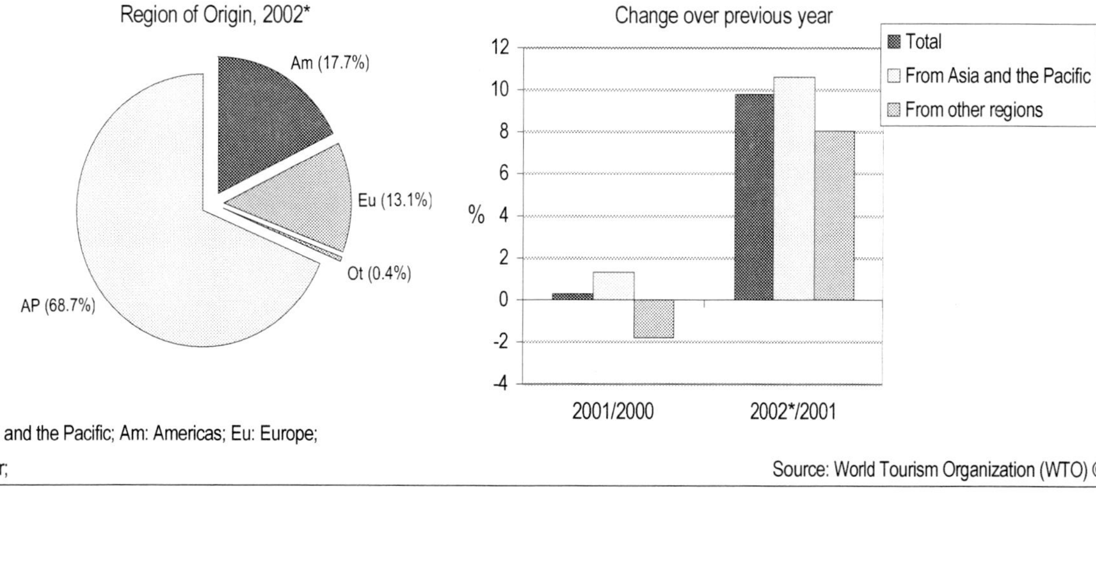

AP: Asia and the Pacific; Am: Americas; Eu: Europe;
Ot: Other;

Source: World Tourism Organization (WTO) ©

Japan

International Tourist Arrivals at Frontiers (by nationality)

					Market share (%)		Growth rate (%)		Average per year (%)
	1995	2000	2001	2002*	1995	2002*	2001/00	2002*/01	1995-2002*
Total	**3,345,274**	**4,757,146**	**4,771,555**	**5,238,963**	**100**	**100**	**0.3**	**9.8**	**6.6**
From Asia and the Pacific	*2,191,277*	*3,212,643*	*3,255,379*	*3,601,069*	*65.5*	*68.7*	*1.3*	*10.6*	*7.4*
Korea, Republic of	873,635	1,064,390	1,133,971	1,271,835	26.1	24.3	6.5	12.2	5.5
Taiwan (Pr. of China)	578,651	912,814	807,202	877,709	17.3	16.8	-11.6	8.7	6.1
China	220,715	351,788	391,384	452,420	6.6	8.6	11.3	15.6	10.8
Hong Kong (China)	97,865	243,149	262,229	290,624	2.9	5.5	7.8	10.8	16.8
Australia	77,102	147,393	149,621	164,896	2.3	3.1	1.5	10.2	11.5
Philippines	76,605	112,182	124,072	129,914	2.3	2.5	10.6	4.7	7.8
Singapore	40,729	73,745	69,517	76,688	1.2	1.5	-5.7	10.3	9.5
Thailand	53,941	64,778	66,174	72,696	1.6	1.4	2.2	9.9	4.4
Malaysia	47,744	62,163	59,122	64,346	1.4	1.2	-4.9	8.8	4.4
Indonesia	36,035	53,838	56,557	55,668	1.1	1.1	5.1	-1.6	6.4
India	24,452	38,767	40,345	45,394	0.7	0.9	4.1	12.5	9.2
New Zealand	27,428	31,252	33,196	32,762	0.8	0.6	6.2	-1.3	2.6
Vietnam	4,863	9,964	11,722	14,158	0.1	0.3	17.6	20.8	16.5
Sri Lanka	4,837	6,494	7,257	8,684	0.1	0.2	11.7	19.7	8.7
Pakistan	4,680	6,451	6,112	5,599	0.1	0.1	-5.3	-8.4	2.6
Bangladesh	3,316	4,645	4,853	5,072	0.1	0.1	4.5	4.5	6.3
Iran	2,611	3,950	3,734	4,142	0.1	0.1	-5.5	10.9	6.8
Other Asia	6,928	13,258	16,413	16,251	0.2	0.3	23.8	-1.0	13.0
Other Oceania	2,561	2,925	2,867	3,131	0.1	0.1	-2.0	9.2	2.9
Other intraregional	6,579	8,697	9,031	9,080	0.2	0.2	3.8	0.5	4.7
From other regions	*1,152,120*	*1,541,793*	*1,513,967*	*1,635,940*	*34.4*	*31.2*	*-1.8*	*8.1*	*5.1*
United States	539,899	725,954	692,192	731,900	16.1	14.0	-4.7	5.7	4.4
United Kingdom	126,967	192,930	197,965	219,271	3.8	4.2	2.6	10.8	8.1
Canada	75,303	119,168	125,570	131,542	2.3	2.5	5.4	4.8	8.3
Germany	68,317	88,309	87,740	93,936	2.0	1.8	-0.6	7.1	4.7
France	54,069	79,079	82,710	87,034	1.6	1.7	4.6	5.2	7.0
Russian Fed	25,979	32,000	34,771	37,963	0.8	0.7	8.7	9.2	5.6
Italy	24,896	33,506	35,254	36,396	0.7	0.7	5.2	3.2	5.6
Netherlands	19,663	27,506	24,039	24,050	0.6	0.5	-12.6	0.0	2.9
Mexico	7,512	12,433	11,987	23,699	0.2	0.5	-3.6	97.7	17.8
Sweden	15,667	20,916	19,525	20,973	0.5	0.4	-6.7	7.4	4.3
Ireland	6,890	10,627	10,654	17,771	0.2	0.3	0.3	66.8	14.5
Switzerland	17,086	17,152	17,068	17,509	0.5	0.3	-0.5	2.6	0.3
Spain	11,378	14,161	13,097	15,344	0.3	0.3	-7.5	17.2	4.4
Brazil	49,320	16,953	13,934	14,513	1.5	0.3	-17.8	4.2	-16.0
Belgium	8,031	11,062	10,989	11,596	0.2	0.2	-0.7	5.5	5.4
Denmark	8,757	10,139	9,794	10,924	0.3	0.2	-3.4	11.5	3.2
Israel	6,032	11,660	10,313	10,620	0.2	0.2	-11.6	3.0	8.4
Austria	8,344	9,976	9,661	10,150	0.2	0.2	-3.2	5.1	2.8
Finland	7,664	11,107	9,791	9,391	0.2	0.2	-11.8	-4.1	2.9
Portugal	4,246	7,785	6,917	9,246	0.1	0.2	-11.1	33.7	11.8
Romania	1,617	4,826	6,123	7,166	0.0	0.1	26.9	17.0	23.7
Norway	6,038	7,164	6,733	6,906	0.2	0.1	-6.0	2.6	1.9
Other interregional	58,445	77,380	77,140	88,040	1.7	1.7	-0.3	14.1	6.0
Other World/Not specified	*1,877*	*2,710*	*2,209*	*1,954*	*0.1*	*0.0*	*-18.5*	*-11.5*	*0.6*

Source: World Tourism Organization (WTO) © (Data as collected by WTO September 2003)

III.1.5 Macao (China) North-East Asia

Profile

Macao (China)

Year of entry in WTO	1981
Population (2002, 1000)	462

East Asia and the Pacific
North-East Asia

	2000	2001	2002*	2001/2000	2002*/2001
International Arrivals					
Visitors (1000)	9,162	10,279	11,531	12.2	12.2
Tourists (overnight visitors) (1000)	5,197	5,842	6,565	12.4	12.4
- per 100 of inhabitants	1,166	1,288	1,422		
Same-day visitors (1000)	3,965	4,437	4,966	11.9	11.9
Tourism accommodation					
Number of rooms	9,201	9,030	..	-1.9	
Nights spent in hotels and similar establishments (1000)	3,446	3,572	3,874	3.7	8.5
by non-residents (inbound tourism)	3,219	3,344	3,656	3.9	9.3
by residents (domestic tourism)	227	228	218	0.4	-4.4
Outbound Tourism					
Trips abroad (1000)	144	192	200	33.3	4.2
- per 100 of inhabitants	32	42	43		
Receipts and Expenditure for International Tourism					
International Tourism Receipts (US$ million)	3,205	3,745	4,415	16.8	17.9
- per Tourist Arrival (US$)	617	641	673	3.9	4.9
- per Visitor Arrival (US$)	350	364	383	4.2	5.1
- per capita (US$)	7,193	8,254	9,560		

Source: World Tourism Organization (WTO) (Data as collected by WTO September 2003)

See annex for methodological notes and reference of external sources used.

Survey

Contributed by *Macau Government Tourist Office*
www.macau.tourism.gov.mo (promotional)
www.macau.tourism.gov.mo (institutional/corporate)
www.dsec.gov.mo ; www.dse.gov.mo (research and data)

Tourism development and outlook

Tourism products

New Projects for Gaming Concessions,

Sociedade de Jogos de Macau (SJM)

Investment MOP 4.75 billion (US$ 594 million). Extension of Hotel Lisboa gambling palace, construction of Fisherman's Wharf and Inner Harbour Reform as set out below.

Fisherman's Wharf:
It is one of the most ambitious tourist attractions ever to be undertaken in the Pearl River Delta region. The MOP$ 950 million (US$ 119 million) complex is to be constructed in the Outer Harbour and will be completed in 2004. The complex will occupy an estimated one million square feet site and revolve around three major themes:

- Dynasty Wharf which encapsulates Chinese history and culture;
- East Meets West will include a 30 meter tall man-made volcano complete with waterfalls, volcanic eruptions and night time laser shows plus ceramic crucibles and mine carts to ride inside for the Indiana Jones experience. An African Fort and Greek Square will serve as a leisure park;
- Legend Wharf will feature a Portuguese restaurant, French inns and galleon museum, a disco, games center and a pool area complete with dolphins.

Theme Park at Ponte 16 (Inner Harbour):
SJM announced plans for a theme park to be constructed in Macau's Inner Harbour as part of a 4.75 billion pataca (US$ 594 million) development scheme. The 23,000 square meter area under development will comprise a public park, entertainment areas, retail space, a hotel and a cultural activity center. The new project kicks off the redevelopment of the Inner Harbour which is rich in historic interest. The project will be completed in two to three years time.

Wynn Resorts Macau Ltd.:
Investment MOP 4 billion (US$ 500 million). Gaming and entertainment resorts.
Wynn Resorts (Macau) is developing Wynn Macau, a luxury hotel and destination casino resort and retail/entertainment complex located on the Macau Peninsula adjacent to the Hotel Lisboa on a 16 acre site. Wynn Resorts' first Macau casino is scheduled to open in 2004 and the second phase is currently scheduled to open 7-9 months later.

Galaxy Casino Company Ltd.:
Investment MOP 8.8 billion (US$ 1.1 billion). Luxury resort with casino, multi-purpose trade show and conference facilities.
A Venetian style hotel-casino joint venture. The Sands Casino - the first phase of the project scheduled for completion this year. In the second phase, the Venetian complex, to be located in the Cotai reclamation area between Taipa and Coloane Islands, when completed will comprise a casino covering 100,000 square metres, three exhibition and convention centers which will be able to accommodate 25,000 people, a hotel boasting more than 3,000 rooms, an art museum, a hall for variety shows and more than 10 restaurants.

– *Other Attractions:*

A-Ma Cultural Village:
To promote the A-Ma culture (A-Ma, the Taoist goddess also known as Tin Hau is particularly revered in Macau and is the deity of fisher folk and other seafarers and the name Macau is derived from this goddess) and enrich the tourism resources of Macau, the A-Ma Cultural Village will be established on Alto de Coloane where the highest white *marble* statue of A-Ma stands.
The Cultural Village is a religious and cultural tourist complex with the A-Ma Statue as the core architecture. Apart from the religious structure, the tourist district also includes a cable car, A-Ma cultural museum, a large-scale stone carving structure, a nunnery, vegetarian restaurant, Macanese and Taiwanese snack stalls, folk handicrafts and souvenirs stores and other tourist facilities.

East Asia Satellite Television (EAST) TV City:
eSun Holdings Limited announced the construction of MOP 300 million (US$ 38 million) television production center and tourist facility in Macau on reclaimed land between Taipa and Coloane Island in an area known as Cotai. EAST-TV City will be one of the largest production facilities in Asia and the state-of-the-art facility will occupy 150,000 square meters. When fully operational, EAST-TV City will initially be capable of producing 5,000 hours of programming each year and will include in its production complex nine production studios, location and post-production facilities plus tourist attractions consisting of studio tours, restaurants and shops and is to be completed in 2004.

Cultural Centre Plaza:
Total investment MOP 18.67 million (US$ 2.3 million) with an area of 25,000 square meters. The plaza will hold 4,000 to 5,000 people.

Macau Stadium for the 2005 East Asian Games total area 35,500 square meters.

Nam Van Lake Square: Total investment MOP 34.8 million (US$ 43.8 thousand) with an area of 30,600 square meters.

Macau East Asian Games Dome:
The dome occupies 45,000 square meters, major venues will be at the west and north areas. The central area will be used as complementary venue and the south area is a multi-functional venue. Approximately 640 million patacas (US$ 80 million) will be spent for the construction and is to be completed in 2005.

Macau Science Center:
Mr. Ieoh Ming Pei will design the Macau Science Center with a total area of 2 million square meters. The construction fee and purchase of exhibits will be around MOP 700 million (US$ 88 million).

New developments planned to enhance picturesque and historic Taipa Village:
Taipa Village which is comprised of 20 hectares has historic buildings preserved with both Chinese and Western architecture, some with 100 or more years of history which give the area a unique combination of European touches within a typical Chinese village. To expand the area of the tourist district and boost the business for the village shops, the Macau SAR Government is planning to spend 15 million patacas (US$ 1.9 million) to renovate village facilities. New pedestrian passageways will be introduced to link the attractions that form the leisure and cultural zone.

New museum preserves part of Macau's valuable heritage - Heritage Exhibition of a Traditional Pawnshop Business:
A museum dedicated to the tradition of Chinese pawnshops, which before the establishment of a modern banking system were an important part of everyday life for people in Macau and elsewhere in China. Tak Seng Pawnshop was established in 1917 and belonged initially to Mr. Kou Ho Ning a wealthy Macau merchant. The architectural design and layout, interior décor and equipment of this establishment is very similar *to* pawnshops in mainland China at the time.
Today, this kind of pawnshop has been relegated to the annals of history, but as part of its mission to preserve the cultural heritage of Macau, the Cultural Institute of the Macau SAR Government has restored "Tak Seng On" to its original condition. By visiting this historic establishment, locals and tourists can glimpse the heyday of the pawn business in Macau.

Sound of the Century Museum:
Macau now has yet another new and interesting museum. The Sound of the Century museum is a private collection which opened in December. The museum displays more than 200 antique gramophones, many old wooden telephones, early model radios and sound equipment that bear witness to the history of electronic appliances.

Access

Border Gate Checkpoint:

The border between Macau and mainland China situated at the northern most point of Macau was officially opened to foreigners in 1979, and since then an increasing number of locals and tourists cross through the Macau Border Gate to visit China. This is an important mode of entry into Macau and in 2002, 4.8 million visitors used the Border Gate with an increase of 18.8 per cent compared to 2001. The total area is 28,000 square meters and the construction cost over MOP 134 million (US$ 167 thousand) and is to be completed in 2003.

The Third Macau - Taipa Bridge:

The building cost for the six-lane bridge is around 560 million patacas (US$ 70 million) and will be completed within 28 months and open to traffic in early 2005. The new bridge is 1,720 meters and connects the western parts of the Macau peninsula and Taipa Island. It comprises a fully-closed second floor for operation during the typhoon and monsoon seasons.

In 2002, Air Macau inaugurated regular flights to Singapore and Malaysia, our regional destinations.

As a means of encouraging tourism development and to lift the restrictions on mainland visitors coming to Macau, the central government has approved 528 mainland tour operators under the Macau Tour Scheme. Moreover, 76 travel agencies in Macau were admitted as ground-receiving agents and both tour operators on the mainland and ground-receiving agents in Macau are ready to initiate the "Macau Tour" business.

In this connection, MGTO will organize more tourism promotions in all major cities on mainland China to provide a platform for mainland agents and the Macau trade to conduct business.

Further visa exemption was added for holders of the Republic of Croatia Passports entering Macau with a valid passport for a stay of up to 90 days.

Generating markets

Major generating markets:

In 2002 the total visitor arrivals in Macau exceeded 11.5 million with a year-on-year surge of 12 per cent compared with 2001. At present, Macau's major source markets are Hong Kong, Mainland China, Taiwan, Japan and the United States of America, representing percentage shares of 44 per cent, 37 per cent, 13 per cent, 1 per cent and 1 per cent respectively.

Compared with previous years, there is a change in the tourism source markets of Macau. The proportion of visitors from mainland China is becoming bigger and visitor rates continue to grow rapidly by 41 per cent with 4.24 million visitors. Mainland China has become a huge and a very important tourism source market for Macau. Followed by Taiwan, Japan and the United States of America with an increase of 6 per cent, 1 per cent and 4 per cent respectively. However the Hong Kong market registered a decrease of 1.8 per cent.

Following the relaxation iin the Hong Kong/Macau Tour policy, the Guangdong province announced various measures, which allow more citizens of Guangdong and citizens of other provinces residing in Guangdong to visit Hong Kong and Macau, implying that Macau will receive more mainland visitors in the future.

Meanwhile, MGTO will continue to consolidate and organize promotional activities in important source markets such as Hong Kong, Taiwan, Japan, Korea, Singapore, Malaysia, India and Thailand.

MGTO and SilkAir signed a memorandum of understanding in May 2002 to jointly develop the Singapore-Macau route and to encourage visitors from Singapore and other East Asian countries to travel to Macau and vice versa. The existence of this connection will also help to facilitate the market development in Southeast Asian countries.

Also in 2002, Air Macau inaugurated regular flights to Singapore and Malaysia, our regional destinations.

The Macau tourism sector will assume an even greater role in stimulating the growth of the economy in the years to come with the liberalization of the gaming industry.

Outlook 2003

The Macau SAR has defined tourism and the gaming industry as the leading industry for its economy. The tourism authorities will follow this direction to eventually make Macau an international MICE (Meeting, Incentive, Convention, Exhibition) and leisure destination by striving to develop cultural and leisure tourism resources as well as convention and incentive tourism. Macau will also further enrich its tourism products and enhance co-operation with nearby regions such as Guangdong and Hong Kong, to establish regional tourism.

Macau is working closely with regional destinations to capitalize on its competitive edge and characteristics through resource sharing, pooling its strengths with other cities in the region and synergy in marketing power.

MGTO will set up a MICE Research and Information Center to study and plan for future development and invite scholars to provide training to nurture professionals for the MICE industry.

For the tourism industry to achieve sustainable development, Macau will attach great importance to service quality. In view of this, MGTO will continue activities such as the "Macau Tourism Awareness Campaign", to arouse the awareness of tourism employees and local residents on the significance of tourism and hospitality and to support various training programs.

With the liberalization of gaming concessions, international investors are attracted to invest in Macau. In addition, the meeting facilities to be established will raise the profile of Macau internationally.

Cultural Tourism (CT)

Specific place for CT in tourism policy: yes.

Main objectives & instruments

Cultural tourism has a specific place within the tourism policy of our administration and tourism board.

Macau has its cultural and architectonic heritage, the fundamental element of its tourism product. For the last two decades, Macau cultural heritage preservation has been marked by an appreciation of the delicate balance between the need to preserve important aspects of Macau's uniqueness and the need to pursue economic development. There has also been a balance between old and new, preservation and progress and the government views education along these lines as an essential element of its work.

Recognizing the contribution of tourism to the city's economy in recent years, the Macau SAR Government and private investors have worked together to improve the quality of cultural tourism in Macau.

History and culture are Macau's biggest attraction. The cultural interpenetration of centuries has created a proper identity evident in the vast and diversified architectonic and cultural heritage, and confers to Macau a unique atmosphere resulting from the harmonious blend of Chinese and Portuguese elements.

Macau is one of the oldest meeting places of the East and the West, a tradition that not only continues but also has become an important part of our tourism activity. The unique cultural identity of Macau has remained after China resumed sovereignty of Macau.

Specific place for CT in marketing & promotion plan: yes.

Main objectives & programmes

Cultural tourism has a specific place in our marketing and promotion plan.

Macau SAR has been striving hard to promote itself as a cultural tourism destination. Aside from package tours, tourists nowadays prefer to visit Macau as FITs so as to take a closer look at the mix and match of the eastern and western cultures over 400 years of history. To promote cultural tourism, advertisements, road shows, product presentations, travel fairs, promotional activities and conferences are held in different countries and regions throughout the year to introduce Macau to the outside world. In addition, MGTO has especially designed and published brochures to introduce cultural sites and tourist attractions to visitors.

Through cultural tourism, Macau strengthens its own identity and can assert itself on the regional and international stage.

Most tourists come to Macau for its unique culture and heritage. The Macau Government Tourist Office has been putting great effort into promoting Macau and its cultural heritage assets to the world, while the Macau SAR government has invested heavily in preserving historical sites.

Decree Law No.56/84/M of 1984 - Defense of the architectural, environmental and cultural heritage. The Government is concerned to preserve and revive the historic, cultural and architectural heritage of Macau. An important step towards this end was the creation of the Cultural Institute that combines cultural heritage, activities, training and research. Its aim was to assist in drafting and implementing the Territory's policies on culture and academic research by organizing activities relating to Sino-Portuguese cultural interchange and by disseminating and stimulating an interest in Portuguese language and culture in this part of the world.

The cultural heritage department of Cultural Institute focuses on classifying, restoring, renovating and up-grading Macau's cultural heritage, including both buildings and artifacts. Of particular importance are the monuments, classified urban areas and sites whose environment must be protected.

On the other hand, within a global strategy for the preservation of the cultural heritage tourism, the fiscal treatment of the material assumes particular importance as a means to prevent the demolition of classified buildings or those forming part of a complex on classified sites or in protected areas and promote their recuperation.

The government has selected 128 attractions from Macau manmade and natural heritage assets including temples, churches, fortresses, historic buildings and parks which have been listed in Decree Law No. 83/92/M of 31 December 1992. The listed assets benefit from legal protection and are subject to conservation measures to ensure their preservation.

Moreover, the Cultural Institute is responsible for the heritage conservation with its aims to strengthen the cultural identity of Macau and to provide greater protection for Macau's unique cultural heritage. At the end of 2001, Macau SAR has formally submitted a proposal include Macau's truly unique heritage sites and buildings on the UNESCO's World Heritage sites list and will be decided by UNESCO by 2004/2005.

Last year, the Cultural Institute trained 58 Young Heritage Ambassadors to take groups of their peers around heritage sites. They will also promote cultural heritage tourism of Macau in other countries.

Under the activities of the Macau Tourism Awareness Campaign organized by the Macau Government Tourist Office, the Tourism Ambassadors have visited different schools in Macau aiming to disseminate the idea of "Be my guest, feel at home" as a crucial factor in the success of Macau Tourism and its development as a tourist destination, as well as to convey to the community that Macau is a unique place where cultures blend in various components, architecture, social life and leisure.

During the overseas promotional activities, road shows and travel fairs, the theme of "City of Culture" has been used to promote the cultural heritage of Macau.

Special activities undertaken

The three Cultural Heritage Tours of Macau designed by the Cultural Institute are being promoted to tourists and travellers to explore the cultural treasures of Macau on foot so that they can experience the essence of the development of the history of Macau.

International Tourism by Origin

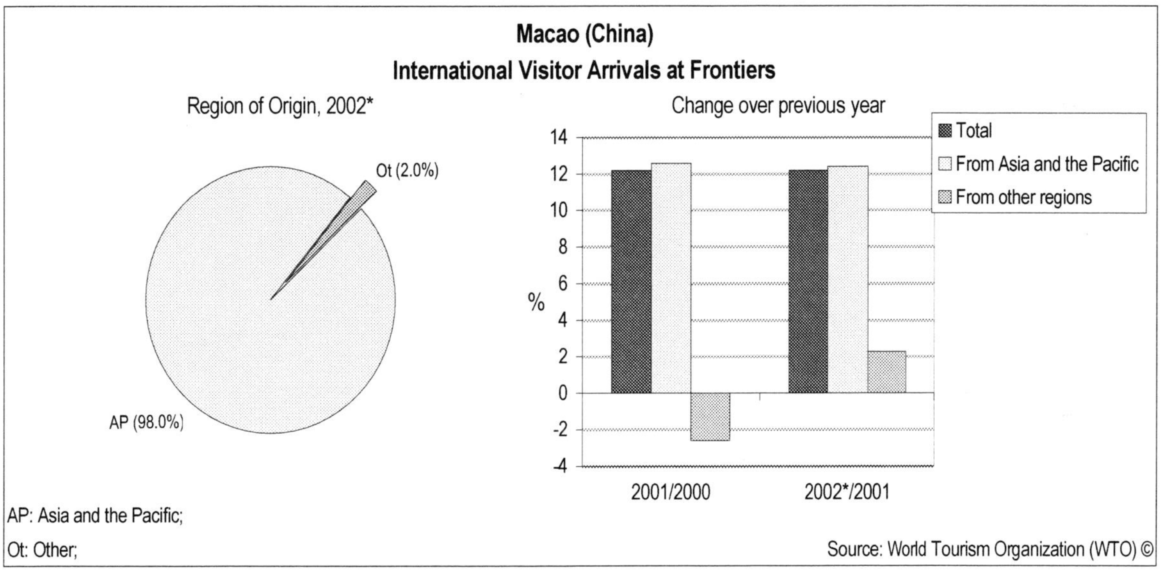

Macao (China)
International Visitor Arrivals at Frontiers (by residence)

					Market share (%)		Growth rate (%)		Average per year (%)
	1995	2000	2001	2002*	1995	2002*	2001/00	2002*/01	1995-2002*
Total	**7,752,495**	**9,162,212**	**10,278,973**	**11,530,841**	**100**	**100**	**12.2**	**12.2**	**5.8**
From Asia and the Pacific	*7,434,402*	*8,927,441*	*10,050,226*	*11,296,966*	*95.9*	*98.0*	*12.6*	*12.4*	*6.2*
Hong Kong (China)	5,952,523	4,954,619	5,196,136	5,101,437	76.8	44.2	4.9	-1.8	-2.2
China	550,294	2,274,713	3,005,722	4,240,446	7.1	36.8	32.1	41.1	33.9
Taiwan (Pr. of China)	250,690	1,311,035	1,451,826	1,532,929	3.2	13.3	10.7	5.6	29.5
Japan	379,861	144,888	140,937	142,588	4.9	1.2	-2.7	1.2	-13.1
Philippines	35,521	42,111	50,705	54,739	0.5	0.5	20.4	8.0	6.4
Korea, Republic of	78,272	45,365	48,274	50,447	1.0	0.4	6.4	4.5	-6.1
Malaysia	30,160	25,753	27,254	31,323	0.4	0.3	5.8	14.9	0.5
Australia	31,466	28,809	29,334	31,028	0.4	0.3	1.8	5.8	-0.2
Singapore	29,935	26,026	25,702	30,940	0.4	0.3	-1.2	20.4	0.5
Thailand	65,437	24,396	21,572	24,625	0.8	0.2	-11.6	14.2	-13.0
Indonesia	10,626	16,920	16,771	19,423	0.1	0.2	-0.9	15.8	9.0
India	6,321	7,530	8,659	10,574	0.1	0.1	15.0	22.1	7.6
New Zealand	5,987	5,122	6,061	5,489	0.1	0.0	18.3	-9.4	-1.2
Pakistan	..	..	..	2,446		0.0			
Nepal	..	..	..	2,248		0.0			
Bangladesh	..	..	..	1,564		0.0			
Korea, D P Rp	..	..	..	1,528		0.0			
Other North-East Asia	945	1,992	1,891	1,183	0.0	0.0	-5.1	-37.4	3.3
Other South-East Asia	2,810	6,640	8,021	10,126	0.0	0.1	20.8	26.2	20.1
Other South Asia	2,969	9,106	9,179	..	0.0		0.8		
Other Oceania	585	2,416	2,182	1,883	0.0	0.0	-9.7	-13.7	18.2
From other regions	*270,177*	*234,586*	*228,521*	*233,674*	*3.5*	*2.0*	*-2.6*	*2.3*	*-2.1*
United States	76,232	74,353	73,607	76,904	1.0	0.7	-1.0	4.5	0.1
United Kingdom	51,476	45,558	44,666	40,517	0.7	0.4	-2.0	-9.3	-3.4
Canada	21,703	25,482	26,448	28,552	0.3	0.2	3.8	8.0	4.0
France	14,369	16,186	15,986	16,304	0.2	0.1	-1.2	2.0	1.8
Germany	38,728	14,396	12,176	10,721	0.5	0.1	-15.4	-11.9	-16.8
Portugal	15,059	12,364	9,824	10,057	0.2	0.1	-20.5	2.4	-5.6
Netherlands	..	..	..	4,781		0.0			
Italy	5,077	4,513	4,315	4,327	0.1	0.0	-4.4	0.3	-2.3
All Africa	5,064	4,182	3,823	..	0.1		-8.6		
Switzerland	..	..	..	2,771		0.0			
Sweden	..	..	..	2,524		0.0			
Brazil	..	..	..	2,485		0.0			
Spain	..	..	..	2,110		0.0			
South Africa	..	..	..	1,658		0.0			
Ireland	..	..	..	1,651		0.0			
Mexico	..	..	..	1,623		0.0			
Austria	..	..	..	1,452		0.0			
All Middle East	1,964	871	1,059	..	0.0		21.6		
Other Africa	..	..	..	5,107		0.0			
Other Americas	9,029	8,791	8,989	5,819	0.1	0.1	2.3	-35.3	-6.1
Other Europe	31,476	27,890	27,628	14,311	0.4	0.1	-0.9	-48.2	-10.6
Other World/Not specified	*47,916*	*185*	*226*	*201*	*0.6*	*0.0*	*22.2*	*-11.1*	*-54.3*

Source: World Tourism Organization (WTO) ©

(Data as collected by WTO September 2003)

Macao (China)
Nights of International Tourists in Hotels and Similar Establishments (by residence)

	1995	2000	2001	2002*	Market share (%) 1995	Market share (%) 2002*	Growth rate (%) 2001/00	Growth rate (%) 2002*/01	Average per year (%) 1995-2002*
Total	**2,929,611**	**3,219,037**	**3,344,070**	**3,656,239**	**100**	**100**	**3.9**	**9.3**	**3.2**
From Asia and the Pacific	*2,777,005*	*3,100,580*	*3,251,702*	*3,566,311*	*94.8*	*97.5*	*4.9*	*9.7*	*3.6*
China	696,995	1,199,402	1,308,556	1,726,084	23.8	47.2	9.1	31.9	13.8
Hong Kong (China)	1,743,842	1,458,748	1,533,688	1,513,772	59.5	41.4	5.1	-1.3	-2.0
Taiwan (Pr. of China)	128,503	311,105	269,037	201,253	4.4	5.5	-13.5	-25.2	6.6
Japan	105,899	62,288	72,301	54,443	3.6	1.5	16.1	-24.7	-9.1
Korea, Republic of	26,391	17,314	20,695	20,156	0.9	0.6	19.5	-2.6	-3.8
Singapore	10,532	8,930	8,333	13,206	0.4	0.4	-6.7	58.5	3.3
Australia	10,700	7,327	7,392	8,903	0.4	0.2	0.9	20.4	-2.6
Thailand	32,154	15,231	9,002	7,924	1.1	0.2	-40.9	-12.0	-18.1
Malaysia	9,416	5,511	6,489	7,585	0.3	0.2	17.7	16.9	-3.0
Philippines	2,748	6,035	7,352	4,654	0.1	0.1	21.8	-36.7	7.8
Indonesia	4,646	5,424	4,590	3,915	0.2	0.1	-15.4	-14.7	-2.4
India	3,361	1,868	2,614	2,528	0.1	0.1	39.9	-3.3	-4.0
New Zealand	1,818	1,397	1,653	1,888	0.1	0.1	18.3	14.2	0.5
From other regions	*120,789*	*93,446*	*71,543*	*75,037*	*4.1*	*2.1*	*-23.4*	*4.9*	*-6.6*
United States	18,087	30,708	21,752	22,560	0.6	0.6	-29.2	3.7	3.2
United Kingdom	17,859	15,573	11,674	11,312	0.6	0.3	-25.0	-3.1	-6.3
Canada	9,754	12,163	7,930	10,976	0.3	0.3	-34.8	38.4	1.7
Portugal	48,315	8,975	6,029	8,508	1.6	0.2	-32.8	41.1	-22.0
France	10,350	8,106	7,298	7,422	0.4	0.2	-10.0	1.7	-4.6
Germany	5,753	3,930	5,461	4,073	0.2	0.1	39.0	-25.4	-4.8
Italy	1,578	1,055	1,827	2,346	0.1	0.1	73.2	28.4	5.8
Other Europe	9,093	12,936	9,572	7,840	0.3	0.2	-26.0	-18.1	-2.1
Other World/Not specified	*31,817*	*25,011*	*20,825*	*14,891*	*1.1*	*0.4*	*-16.7*	*-28.5*	*-10.3*

Source: World Tourism Organization (WTO) © (Data as collected by WTO September 2003)

III.1.6 Mongolia North-East Asia

Profile

Mongolia		
	Capital	Ulan Bator
	Year of entry in WTO	1990
	Area (1000 km²)	1,567
	Population (2002, million)	2.7
	Gross Domestic Product (GDP) (2002, US$ million)	1,092
	GDP per capita (2002, US$)	447
East Asia and the Pacific	GDP growth (real, %)	
North-East Asia	'-> 2001: 1.0; 2002: 3.9; 2003*: 5.0; 2004*: 5.3	

	2000	2001	2002*	2001/2000	2002*/2001
International Arrivals					
Visitors (1000)	158	192	230	21.4	19.9
Tourists (overnight visitors) (1000)	158	166	198	5.0	19.4
- per 100 of inhabitants	6	6	7		
Receipts and Expenditure for International Tourism					
International Tourism Receipts (US$ million)	36	39	..	8.3	
- per Tourist Arrival (US$)	228	235	..	3.2	
- per Visitor Arrival (US$)	228	203	..	-10.8	
- per capita (US$)	14	15	..		
International Fare Receipts (US$ million)	7	10	..	42.9	
International Tourism Expenditure (US$ million)	51	55	..	7.8	
- per capita (US$)	20	21	..		
International Fare Expenditure (US$ million)	3	5	..	66.7	
△ International Tourism Balance (US$ million)	-15	-16	..		
△ International Fare Balance (US$ million)	4	5	..		

Source: World Tourism Organization (WTO) (Data as collected by WTO September 2003)

See annex for methodological notes and reference of external sources used.

International Tourism by Origin

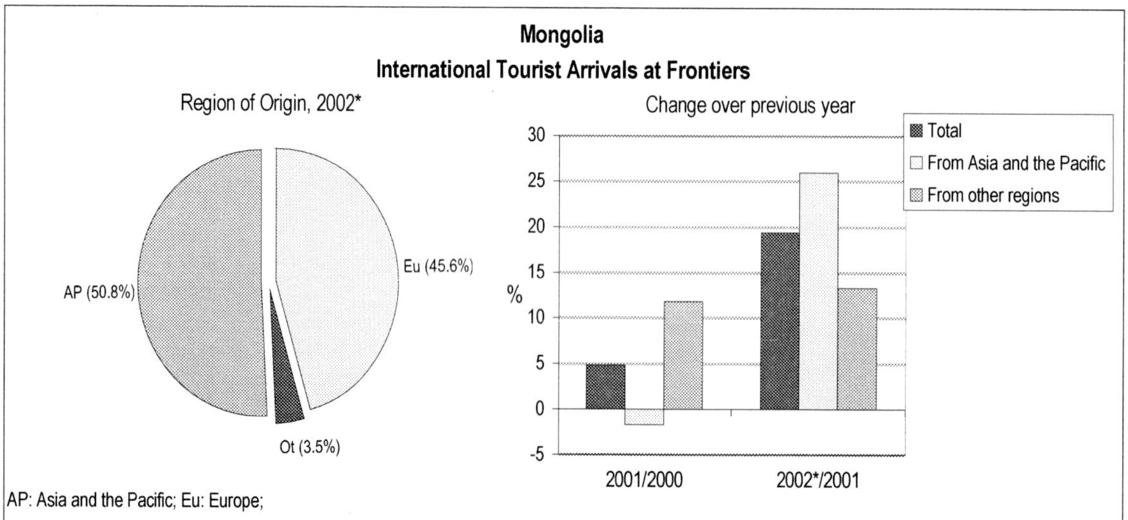

AP: Asia and the Pacific; Eu: Europe;

Ot: Other;

Source: World Tourism Organization (WTO) ©

Mongolia
International Tourist Arrivals at Frontiers (by nationality)

					Market share (%)		Growth rate (%)		Average per year (%)
	1995	2000	2001	2002*	1995	2002*	2001/00	2002*/01	1995-2002*
Total	**108,434**	**158,205**	**165,890**	**198,057**	**100**	**100**	**4.9**	**19.4**	**9.0**
From Asia and the Pacific	*61,796*	*81,345*	*79,953*	*100,700*	*57.0*	*50.8*	*-1.7*	*25.9*	*7.2*
China	47,721	57,546	57,440	70,860	44.0	35.8	-0.2	23.4	5.8
Korea, Republic of	2,561	8,039	8,372	12,331	2.4	6.2	4.1	47.3	25.2
Japan	8,976	11,392	10,247	12,312	8.3	6.2	-10.1	20.2	4.6
Australia	892	1,008	1,139	1,513	0.8	0.8	13.0	32.8	7.8
Singapore	256	383	433	969	0.2	0.5	13.1	123.8	20.9
New Zealand	230	438	423	572	0.2	0.3	-3.4	35.2	13.9
Taiwan (Pr. of China)	..	578	488	484		0.2	-15.6	-0.8	
Malaysia	147	203	217	291	0.1	0.1	6.9	34.1	10.2
Hong Kong (China)	..	184	187	248		0.1	1.6	32.6	
India	305	337	270	197	0.3	0.1	-19.9	-27.0	-6.1
Korea, D P Rp	..	295	179	195		0.1	-39.3	8.9	
Philippines	103	249	149	195	0.1	0.1	-40.2	30.9	9.5
Vietnam	69	114	118	102	0.1	0.1	3.5	-13.6	5.7
Pakistan	204	172	62	86	0.2	0.0	-64.0	38.7	-11.6
Thailand	97	141	52	78	0.1	0.0	-63.1	50.0	-3.1
Indonesia	49	73	35	72	0.0	0.0	-52.1	105.7	5.7
Other intraregional	186	193	142	195	0.2	0.1	-26.4	37.3	0.7
From other regions	*46,638*	*76,860*	*85,937*	*97,344*	*43.0*	*49.1*	*11.8*	*13.3*	*11.1*
Russian Fed	28,390	49,456	58,534	65,537	26.2	33.1	18.4	12.0	12.7
Germany	3,502	4,206	4,661	6,110	3.2	3.1	10.8	31.1	8.3
United States	3,987	6,451	5,446	5,747	3.7	2.9	-15.6	5.5	5.4
France	1,523	1,841	2,600	3,084	1.4	1.6	41.2	18.6	10.6
United Kingdom	1,752	2,800	2,549	2,976	1.6	1.5	-9.0	16.8	7.9
Netherlands	820	1,391	1,273	1,607	0.8	0.8	-8.5	26.2	10.1
Kazakhstan	173	1,677	1,291	1,369	0.2	0.7	-23.0	6.0	34.4
Sweden	850	904	1,274	1,187	0.8	0.6	40.9	-6.8	4.9
Italy	648	743	921	954	0.6	0.5	24.0	3.6	5.7
Canada	318	611	691	895	0.3	0.5	13.1	29.5	15.9
Switzerland	302	637	612	816	0.3	0.4	-3.9	33.3	15.3
Ukraine	280	781	643	773	0.3	0.4	-17.7	20.2	15.6
Denmark	1,497	602	558	706	1.4	0.4	-7.3	26.5	-10.2
Poland	233	325	460	703	0.2	0.4	41.5	52.8	17.1
Norway	288	373	505	648	0.3	0.3	35.4	28.3	12.3
Austria	277	502	573	599	0.3	0.3	14.1	4.5	11.6
Finland	102	283	304	453	0.1	0.2	7.4	49.0	23.7
Czech Rep	200	415	416	449	0.2	0.2	0.2	7.9	12.2
Israel	43	208	299	431	0.0	0.2	43.8	44.1	39.0
Spain	99	245	226	270	0.1	0.1	-7.8	19.5	15.4
Turkey	300	371	234	236	0.3	0.1	-36.9	0.9	-3.4
Ireland	86	76	84	198	0.1	0.1	10.5	135.7	12.7
Kyrgyzstan	62	74	103	188	0.1	0.1	39.2	82.5	17.2
Belgium	100	383	456	142	0.1	0.1	19.1	-68.9	5.1
Belarus	34	152	125	142	0.0	0.1	-17.8	13.6	22.7
Other interregional	772	1,353	1,099	1,124	0.7	0.6	-18.8	2.3	5.5
Other World/Not specified	..	..	..	*13*		*0.0*			

Source: World Tourism Organization (WTO) © (Data as collected by WTO September 2003)

III.1.7 Republic of Korea North-East Asia

Profile

Republic of Korea

East Asia and the Pacific
North-East Asia

Capital	Seoul
Year of entry in WTO	1975
Area (1000 km²)	99
Population (2002, million)	48.0
Gross Domestic Product (GDP) (2002, US$ million)	476,690
GDP per capita (2002, US$)	9,918
GDP growth (real, %)	
'-> 2001: 3.1; 2002: 6.3; 2003*: 2.5; 2004*: 4.7	

	2000	2001	2002*	2001/2000	2002*/2001
International Arrivals					
Visitors (1000)	5,322	5,147	5,347	-3.3	3.9
- per 100 of inhabitants	11	11	11		
Tourism accommodation					
Number of rooms	51,189	53,478	..	4.5	
Outbound Tourism					
Trips abroad (1000)	5,508	6,084	7,123	10.5	17.1
- per 100 of inhabitants	12	13	15		
Receipts and Expenditure for International Tourism					
International Tourism Receipts (US$ million)	6,811	6,373	5,277	-6.4	-17.2
- per Visitor Arrival (US$)	1,280	1,238	987	-3.3	-20.3
- per capita (US$)	144	134	110		
International Fare Receipts (US$ million)	1,693	..	..		
International Tourism Expenditure (US$ million)	6,174	6,547	7,642	6.0	16.7
- per trip (US$)	1,121	1,076	1,073	-4.0	-0.3
- per capita (US$)	131	137	159		
International Fare Expenditure (US$ million)	813	..	..		
△ International Tourism Balance (US$ million)	637	-174	-2,365		
△ International Fare Balance (US$ million)	880	..	..		

Source: World Tourism Organization (WTO) (Data as collected by WTO September 2003)

See annex for methodological notes and reference of external sources used.

Survey

Contributed by *Ministry of Culture and Tourism*
www.tour2korea.com ; www.korea.net ; www.goodwillguide.com (promotional)
www.mct.go.kr ; www.knto.or.kr ; www.ktri.re.kr (institutional/corporate)
www.knto.or.kr (research and data)

Tourism development and outlook

Most significant determinant

Establishment of the tourism sector support system to successfully host large-scale international events including the 2002 FIFA World Cup Korea/Japan, the 2002 Busan Asian Games, etc. and maximizing tourism benefits from the 2002 FIFA World Cup Korea/Japan.

Weathering the drop in tourist arrivals and the downturn in the tourism industry, brought about by the impact of 11 September 2001 event.

The surge in national tourism demand, including a sharp increase in international travel and the consequent aggravation of the tourism balance.

Tourism products

The holding of large-scale international events like the 2002 FIFA World Cup Korea/Japan and the 2002 Busan Asian Games providing an opportunity to develop and operate various cultural tourism products and experiences:

- Tourism products that enable tourists to experience Korea such as experiencing herbal medicine, kimchi making, etc.
- The development and operation of traditional cultural and tourism programmes such as the Royal Guards Changing Ceremony, the Coronation Ceremony of King Sejong, etc.
- At 33 temples nationwide, the Temple Stay Program was offered during 2002 FIFA World Cup. Visitors could participate in everyday Buddhist activities and experience the unique traditional culture of Korea.

The Government secured a total of 178,000 rooms, including the designation of 135,000 rooms in ten World Cup venues as recommended lodging facilities, to prepare for a transient surge in demand during the World Cup. In addition, among the designated inns the Government named outstanding facilities as " World Inns", equipping them with Internet reservation systems.

To resolve inconvenience stemming from language barriers, interpretation phones that enabled three people to talk together have been installed in accommodation facilities and taxis. The "Before Babel Brigade" (BBB) translation service offers interpretation assistance by volunteers through mobile phones.

Access

In April 2002, Yangyang International Airport opened. It is forecasted that the increase of accessibility to the Gangwon province region with abundant tourism resources will contribute to the increase in inbound tourists (for skiing, enjoying the autumn foliage etc.).

As of April 2002, there are 259 routes (including freight) and 1,073 passenger flights a week for international flights. This is an increase of 20 routes and 142 flights in the number of passenger flights compared to April 2001.

Generating markets

In the first half of 2002, the number of inbound travelers decreased compared to the number of travelers during the same period the previous year due to the impact of the 11 September 2001attacks. However, in the second half of the year, thanks to the improvement of international awareness and the national image of Korea from hosting the 2002 FIFA World Cup, there has been a gradual recovery.

By region, owing to the effects from hosting the 2002 FIFA World Cup, the share of arrivals from Europe and the Americas, which has been on the decline, increased to 19.8 per cent in 2002 from 18.1 per cent in 2001. In the case of Japan, the largest market in Korea, visitors accounted for 43.4 per cent of the total inbound travelers, which is a drop from 46.2 per cent in 2001. This is attributable to the decline in the number of arrivals from Japan (-2.4%) for two consecutive years from 2001 due to the aftermath of the 11 September 2001 incident and the co-hosting of the 2002 FIFA World Cup. Arrivals from China, which positioned itself as the second largest market in Korea in 2001 by outpacing the United States of America, grew by 11.9 per cent in 2002. The share of visitors in the winter (December) from major Southeast Asian countries (Hong Kong, Singapore, Malaysia, etc.) increased with the favorable conditions of winter tourism products.

Other Issues

A trial overland tour to Mt. Kumgang was carried out.

Outlook 2003

Due to the impact of SARS, the number of inbound and outbound travellers started to decline from March 2003 compared to the number of travellers during the same period the previous year and in April, the number plummeted. In the case of Korea, the proportion of inbound travelers from Asia and outbound travellers to Asia is relatively high, accounting for 60 to 70 per cent of the total. Thus, it is expected that Korea will be greatly influenced by the implications from the SARS epidemic. It is forecasted that the number of inbound travellers in 2003 will decrease nearly 17 per cent compared to the number of travelers during same period the previous year - about 4.4 million.

Tourism policy

With the end of the 1st National Tourism Resources Development Plan in 2001, the 2nd National Tourism Resources Development Plan was implemented in 2002. The new plan includes a new vision, strategy and basic direction for nationwide tourism development to respond to changes in the tourism environment.

ISP (Information Strategic Plan) in the tourism sector was set up to respond to advancements in digitalization. The primary establishment of the Comprehensive Tourism Information System, which provides and collects tourism-related information systematically and comprehensively has been undertaken.

Related laws and regulations such as the Foreign Investment Promotion Act and the Restriction of Preferential Taxation Act have been amended to positively induce foreign investment in the tourism industry and increase tax exemption and reduction for businesses.

Marketing & promotion

In 2002, the 2002 FIFA World Cup Korea/Japan and the 2002 Busan Asian Games were held in Korea. Taking full advantage of the two large-scale international events, priority was put on introducing Korean tourism products and promoting unique features of Korean tourism. Joint marketing efforts were made by World Cup venues, the World Cup Organizing Committee and the tourism sector, etc., to improve Korea's national image as an advanced nation in culture and tourism and achieve globalization of regional cities. In addition, because 2002 was the second year of the "Visit Korea Year" campaign, we focused on overseas promotion along with efforts to improve tourism infrastructure to heighten the satisfaction level of foreign travelers.

As part of the efforts, from January to March 2002, "2002 World Cup Special Tourism Promotion Teams" were dispatched to 21 cities in 12 countries in Europe, North America, South America and Asia for publicity and promotion activities under the slogan of "Dynamic Korea, The Hub of Asia". The dispatch reaped great results in promotion. For instance, 19 explanatory meetings were held with local journalists participating from 503 media and 20 Korea tourism trade fairs were held with 4,170 participants.

On the occasion of the 2002 FIFA World Cup, four tourism promotional commercials were made, tailored to each market. They were aired on 42 major broadcasting systems including CNN, Eurosport, STAR Sports, etc. in three phases (before, during and after the World Cup).

It has been recognized recently that not only off-line but also on-line promotion has tremendous efficacy. Consequently, active efforts have been made in online promotion. The Korean tourism portal site www.tour2korea.com, which is provided in seven languages, was advertised through banners on the FIFA World Cup website and various other events were held. Promotion activities have been made on renowned search engines like Yahoo, AOL, MSN, etc.

Cultural Tourism (CT)

Specific place for CT in tourism policy: yes.

Main objectives & instruments

Main Goals:
- To make Korea an attractive tourist destination by transforming historical and cultural resources dispersed in various regions into tourism resources through efficient preservation and management.
- To achieve regional economic development and balanced nationwide development by developing unique cultural tourism resources by region.
- To preserve and improve historical and cultural resources by establishing culture-oriented mindset and cultural identity.

One of the strategies included in the 2nd National Tourism Resource Development Plan is "promote systematic transformation of cultural resources into tourism products". The main points of the strategy are stated below:
- To pursue development of cultural tourism resources: the development project for Seven Major Cultural Tourism Regions, the development of the North Gyeongbuk Confucian Cultural Zone, etc.
- To facilitate development of cultural tourism products (cultural tourism festivals and tourist souvenirs).
- To establish the basic infrastructure for cultural tourism: build a Cultural Tourism Information System and foster cultural tourism guides.

Main focus of attention supply

Korea gives priority to developing and commercializing Korea's traditional culture.

With respect to developing tourist attractions, since 2000, the Korean government has been endeavoring vigorously with a ten-year plan to make the North Gyeongbuk region, which has well-preserved traditional Confucian culture, into an international tourist attraction by developing its Confucian cultural resource.

The government is aiming to commercialize traditional culture such as festivals, permanent cultural tourism programs, tourist souvenirs, etc. Festivals that are based on traditional culture are being fostered into cultural tourism festivals. In 2002, 29 festivals including the Bullfighting Festival in Cheongdo, the World Taekwondo Festival, the International Mask Dance Festival in Andong, etc. were selected. Moreover, with the development of unique traditional art performances of each region into standing cultural tourism products like the Royal Guard Changing Ceremony and the traditional Korean Music Performances, visitors will be able to see and enjoy various events.

To fulfill the cultural needs of visitors, guides that can provide professional explanations on historical background, behind-the-scenes stories and an unofficial history of cultural tourism resources will be fostered.

Main focus of attention demand

In the markets of Europe and the Americas, focus will be made on segments that are interested in Asian culture. We are publicizing and commercializing Korea's traditional culture such as cultural heritage, programs for experiencing Korean culture (Taekwondo, Temple Stay), etc. We are also making efforts to differentiate Korea's culture from that of neighboring countries.

In Japan, China and Southeast Asia, Korean television dramas and movies have been gaining great popularity. Consequently, we are deriving visits from these countries by developing tourism products that are related to the starring actors and/or actresses and filming sites. In general, travellers tend to prefer tours that enable them to experience the culture and history. Therefore, efforts are being made to develop culture and tourism products that provide a chance for tourists to have first-hand experience and participation.

Specific place for CT in marketing & promotion plan: yes.

Main objectives & programmes

Support for promotions of local festivals based on traditional regional culture has been reinforced. Moreover, we are striving to attract more tourists by utilizing the promotion of Korean dramas and films.

Special activities undertaken

Since 1998, the National Tourist Souvenir Contest has been held to facilitate development of various tourist souvenirs and artistic cultural products. Every year, cultural tourism festivals are selected and not only funding but also overall know-how for operating the festival such as marketing techniques are provided. Also, journalists and travel agencies are invited for familiarization tours to visit festival venues. The Seoul World Food Expo has been held since 2002 to publicize and commercialize Korean food.

Importance of cultural tourism:

- in total tourism offer

According to a survey conducted by the Korean National Tourism Organization (KNTO) in 2002 on foreign tourists, travelers who participated in cultural events, traditional cultural events and festivals during their visit to Korea was 8.8 per cent, which is a 1.1 per cent increase from 2000. In addition, when asked what was the most memorable while traveling in Korea, 34.7 per cent replied "the unique culture".

In developing tourism resources, our main focus is on cultural tourism resource development. Of the government budget provided for tourism resource and product development in 2002, 45 per cent was allocated to the cultural tourism sector including development of Confucian cultural tourism, festivals, souvenirs, etc.

International Tourism by Origin

Republic of Korea
International Visitor Arrivals at Frontiers

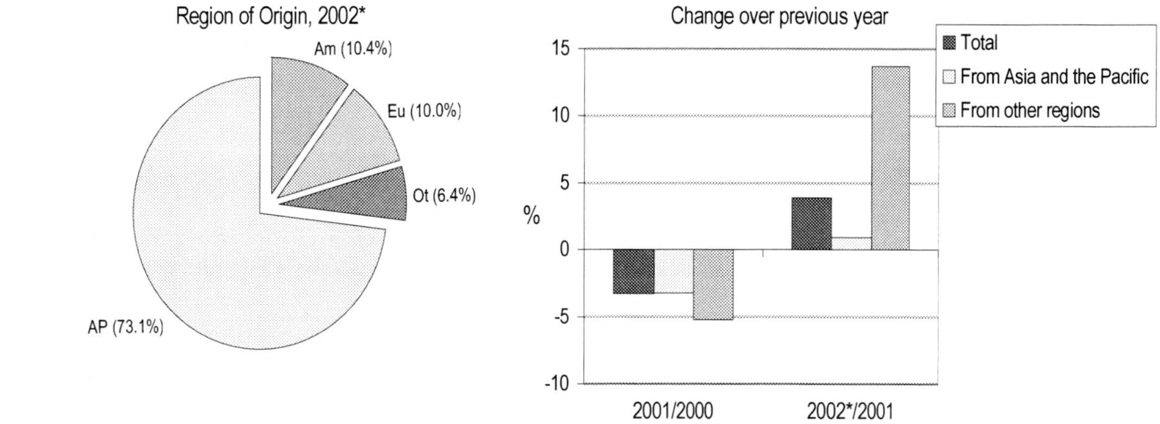

AP: Asia and the Pacific; Am: Americas; Eu: Europe;
Ot: Other;

Source: World Tourism Organization (WTO) ©

Republic of Korea
International Visitor Arrivals at Frontiers (by nationality)

					Market share (%)		Growth rate (%)		Average per year (%)
	1995	2000	2001	2002*	1995	2002*	2001/00	2002*/01	1995-2002*
Total	**3,753,197**	**5,321,792**	**5,147,204**	**5,347,469**	**100**	**100**	**-3.3**	**3.9**	**5.2**
From Asia and the Pacific	*2,557,258*	*4,005,104*	*3,875,694*	*3,911,196*	*68.1*	*73.1*	*-3.2*	*0.9*	*6.3*
Japan	1,667,203	2,472,054	2,377,321	2,320,837	44.4	43.4	-3.8	-2.4	4.8
China	178,359	442,794	482,227	539,466	4.8	10.1	8.9	11.9	17.1
Philippines	163,228	248,737	210,975	215,848	4.3	4.0	-15.2	2.3	4.1
Hong Kong (China)	100,407	200,874	204,959	179,299	2.7	3.4	2.0	-12.5	8.6
Taiwan (Pr. of China)	130,147	127,120	129,410	136,921	3.5	2.6	1.8	5.8	0.7
Malaysia	31,145	59,933	55,848	82,720	0.8	1.5	-6.8	48.1	15.0
Singapore	38,577	82,871	71,240	79,403	1.0	1.5	-14.0	11.5	10.9
Thailand	73,770	87,885	73,163	74,000	2.0	1.4	-16.8	1.1	0.0
Indonesia	37,723	59,085	57,288	65,093	1.0	1.2	-3.0	13.6	8.1
India	35,668	51,369	47,657	52,725	1.0	1.0	-7.2	10.6	5.7
Australia	27,251	39,614	44,295	49,759	0.7	0.9	11.8	12.3	9.0
Myanmar	18,520	37,794	30,955	33,559	0.5	0.6	-18.1	8.4	8.9
Vietnam	16,720	21,483	20,399	23,574	0.4	0.4	-5.0	15.6	5.0
New Zealand	6,499	9,890	12,086	13,355	0.2	0.2	22.2	10.5	10.8
Mongolia	3,792	12,156	11,614	8,567	0.1	0.2	-4.5	-26.2	12.3
Pakistan	9,295	15,775	10,082	8,087	0.2	0.2	-36.1	-19.8	-2.0
Iran	2,655	8,967	7,116	7,743	0.1	0.1	-20.6	8.8	16.5
Bangladesh	9,662	10,529	9,502	6,479	0.3	0.1	-9.8	-31.8	-5.5
Sri Lanka	3,135	5,905	3,630	3,624	0.1	0.1	-38.5	-0.2	2.1
Other intraregional	3,502	10,269	15,927	10,137	0.1	0.2	55.1	-36.4	16.4
From other regions	*860,281*	*1,039,165*	*984,925*	*1,119,738*	*22.9*	*20.9*	*-5.2*	*13.7*	*3.8*
United States	358,872	458,617	426,817	459,362	9.6	8.6	-6.9	7.6	3.6
Russian Fed	155,098	155,392	134,727	165,341	4.1	3.1	-13.3	22.7	0.9
Canada	34,475	56,304	59,720	67,041	0.9	1.3	6.1	12.3	10.0
United Kingdom	46,923	57,895	60,080	66,696	1.3	1.2	3.8	11.0	5.2
Germany	46,634	51,093	52,916	59,698	1.2	1.1	3.6	12.8	3.6
France	22,295	33,991	35,598	41,207	0.6	0.8	4.7	15.8	9.2
Ukraine	8,308	14,914	14,496	17,743	0.2	0.3	-2.8	22.4	11.4
Netherlands	13,182	15,611	14,952	16,288	0.4	0.3	-4.2	8.9	3.1
Italy	13,312	13,578	12,832	14,981	0.4	0.3	-5.5	16.7	1.7
Poland	22,175	18,292	9,454	11,082	0.6	0.2	-48.3	17.2	-9.4
Turkey	5,280	5,891	6,227	10,325	0.1	0.2	5.7	65.8	10.1
Uzbekistan	4,747	10,971	9,785	10,288	0.1	0.2	-10.8	5.1	11.7
Greece	14,591	9,899	9,038	9,068	0.4	0.2	-8.7	0.3	-6.6
Bulgaria	3,374	6,105	7,569	8,794	0.1	0.2	24.0	16.2	14.7
Mexico	2,626	4,453	4,908	8,335	0.1	0.2	10.2	69.8	17.9
Denmark	5,409	6,140	6,063	8,024	0.1	0.2	-1.3	32.3	5.8
Sweden	6,900	8,336	7,589	7,769	0.2	0.1	-9.0	2.4	1.7
Brazil	9,362	4,492	4,734	7,278	0.2	0.1	5.4	53.7	-3.5
Portugal	3,876	7,170	6,905	7,114	0.1	0.1	-3.7	3.0	9.1
Croatia	3,198	4,955	5,732	7,105	0.1	0.1	15.7	24.0	12.1
Norway	6,421	7,500	7,069	7,050	0.2	0.1	-5.7	-0.3	1.3
Switzerland	8,157	6,013	6,419	6,694	0.2	0.1	6.8	4.3	-2.8
Other interregional	65,066	81,553	81,295	102,455	1.7	1.9	-0.3	26.0	6.7
Nationals residing abroad	*335,658*	*277,523*	*286,585*	*316,535*	*8.9*	*5.9*	*3.3*	*10.5*	*-0.8*

Source: World Tourism Organization (WTO) © (Data as collected by WTO September 2003)

III.1.8 Taiwan (Pr. of China) North-East Asia

Profile

Taiwan (Pr. of China)

East Asia and the Pacific
North-East Asia

Population (2002, million)	22.5
Gross Domestic Product (GDP) (2002, US$ million)	281,572
GDP per capita (2002, US$)	12,455
GDP growth (real, %)	
-> 2001: -2.2; 2002: 3.5; 2003*: 2.7; 2004*: 3.8	

	2000	2001	2002*	2001/2000	2002*/2001
International Arrivals					
Visitors (1000)	2,624	2,617	2,726	-0.3	4.2
- per 100 of inhabitants	12	12	12		
Tourism accommodation					
Number of rooms	19,928	20,789	..	4.3	
Nights spent in collective establishments (1000)					
by non-residents (inbound tourism)	16,487	16,987	18,188	3.0	7.1
Outbound Tourism					
Trips abroad (1000)	7,329	7,189	7,507	-1.9	4.4
- per 100 of inhabitants	33	32	33		
Receipts and Expenditure for International Tourism					
International Tourism Receipts (US$ million)	3,741	3,991	4,197	6.7	5.2
- per Visitor Arrival (US$)	1,426	1,525	1,539	7.0	0.9
- per capita (US$)	169	179	187		
International Fare Receipts (US$ million)	3,202	2,607	2,621	-18.6	0.5
International Tourism Expenditure (US$ million)	6,376	6,379	6,963	0.0	9.2
- per trip (US$)	870	887	928	2.0	4.5
- per capita (US$)	288	286	310		
International Fare Expenditure (US$ million)	5,806	5,341	5,113	-8.0	-4.3
△ International Tourism Balance (US$ million)	-2,635	-2,388	-2,766		
△ International Fare Balance (US$ million)	-2,604	-2,734	-2,492		

Source: World Tourism Organization (WTO) (Data as collected by WTO September 2003)

See annex for methodological notes and reference of external sources used.

Survey

Contributed by *Ministry of Transportation and Communications - Tourism Bureau*
http://taiwan.net.tw (promotional)
www.tbroc.gov.tw (institutional/corporate)
www.tbroc.gov.tw (research and data)

Tourism development and outlook

Most significant determinant

Completed "Doubling of Tourist Arrivals Plan" to boost yearly visitor arrivals to five million in 2008.

Promotional marketing campaigns overseas in 2002 include:
- Japan market promotion campaign;
- Hong Kong market promotion campaign;
- Malaysia market promotion campaign.

Tourism products

Positive factor:
Events (12 Major Festivals in 2002).

Negative factor:
Price competition.

Access

Entry formalities for visitors from Hong Kong, Singapore and Malaysia were eased by offering landing visas and visa-free entry.
Increase in international flights:
- Taiwan-Japan: 168 flights weekly to 176 flights weekly;
- Taiwan-Hong Kong: 121 flights weekly to 153 flights weekly.

Generating markets

Existing markets: Japan, overseas Chinese, Hong Kong, South East Asia, and MICE.
Emerging market: Cruise tours and China.

Other Issues

Strengthening of hardware and software facilities for package tour routes.
Designation of 2004 as the "Taiwan Tourism Year".

Outlook 2003

Target of the achievement of 3.0 million arrivals in 2003. Foreign visitors who come for tourism purposes are targeted to double from the current one million to two million in 2008.

Tourism policy

Five key tasks of the “Doubling of Tourist Arrivals” Plan are:
- Preparation of package tour itineraries;
- Development of new itineraries and tourist attractions;
- Establishment of a visitor-service network;
- Launching of international advertising and promotion campaigns;
- Promotion of the MICE (meetings, incentives, conference and exhibitions) industry.

Marketing & promotion

Attending travel trade shows, publishing of publicity materials and commercial advertisements.
Special overseas promotion campaigns.
Enhanced web site: <http://taiwan.net.tw>.
Provide half-day tours to transit passengers.

Cultural Tourism (CT)

Specific place for CT in tourism policy: yes.

Main objectives & instruments	"12 Major Festivals in Taiwan 2003" encompasses folk art, fine cuisine and scenic attractions. Each month, there is an event held in a different city/county of Taiwan. The events are expressions of the passion of the people of Taiwan.
Main focus of attention supply	Tourism products.
Main focus of attention demand	Discovery of the lifestyle, history, art, etc., of the local Taiwanese people.

Specific place for CT in marketing & promotion plan: yes.

Main objectives & programmes	Most of our overseas promotional campaigns have cultural performances (tea ceremony performance) and gastronomic performances (pearl milk tea and Chinese Dim Sum).
Special activities undertaken	A special Taiwan festival is promoted each month. These 12 events are great expressions of the passion of the people of Taiwan. The Tourism Bureau promotes these festivals by attending overseas trade shows and organizing overseas promotional campaigns.

Importance of cultural tourism:

- in total tourism offer	Forty per cent of international arrivals visit historic sites and attend festival events.

International Tourism by Origin

Taiwan (Pr. of China)
International Visitor Arrivals at Frontiers

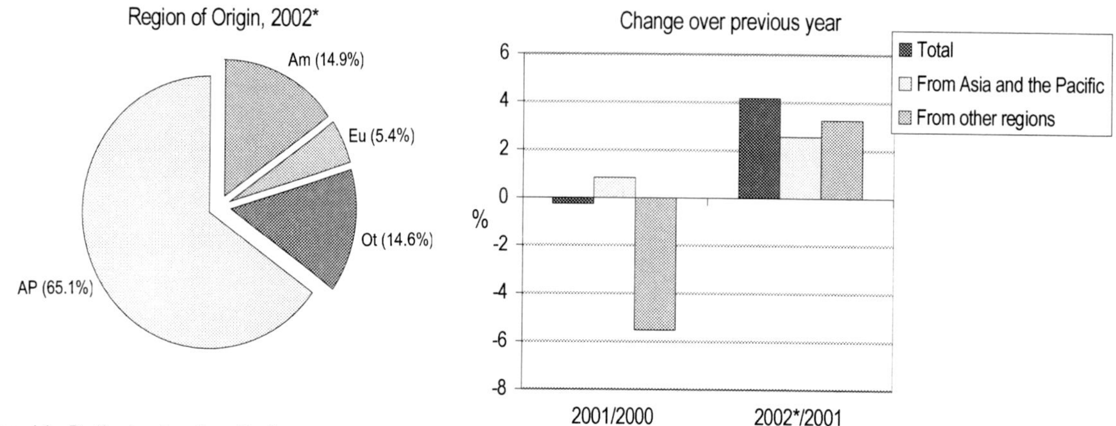

AP: Asia and the Pacific; Am: Americas; Eu: Europe;
Ot: Other;

Source: World Tourism Organization (WTO) ©

Taiwan (Pr. of China)
Nights of International Tourists in All Accommodation Establishments

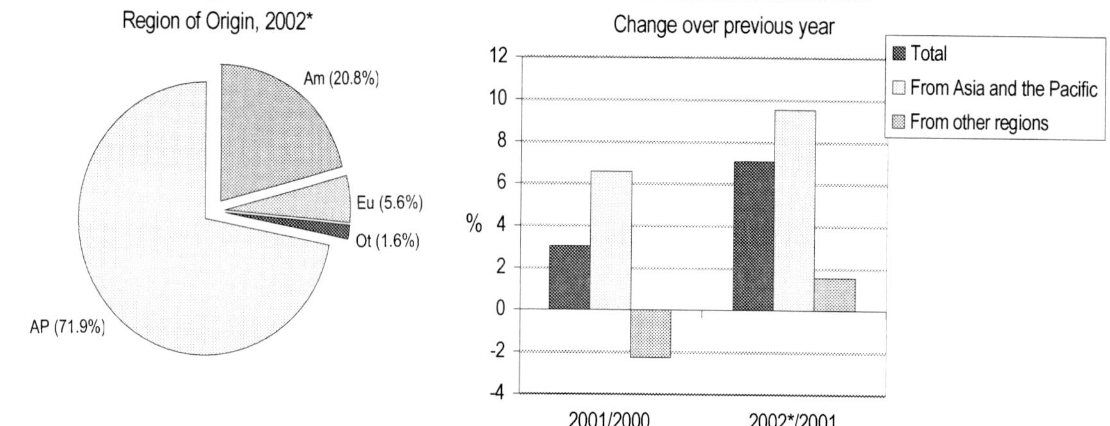

AP: Asia and the Pacific; Am: Americas; Eu: Europe;
Ot: Other;

Source: World Tourism Organization (WTO) ©

Taiwan (Pr. of China)
International Visitor Arrivals at Frontiers (by residence)

					Market share (%)		Growth rate (%)		Average per year (%)
	1995	2000	2001	2002*	1995	2002*	2001/00	2002*/01	1995-2002*
Total	**2,331,934**	**2,624,037**	**2,617,137**	**2,726,411**	**100**	**100**	**-0.3**	**4.2**	**2.3**
From Asia and the Pacific	*1,587,331*	*1,717,079*	*1,731,396*	*1,775,605*	*68.1*	*65.1*	*0.8*	*2.6*	*1.6*
Japan	907,338	914,884	970,741	985,564	38.9	36.1	6.1	1.5	1.2
Singapore	69,665	94,691	96,645	107,069	3.0	3.9	2.1	10.8	6.3
Thailand	146,632	132,998	116,296	105,688	6.3	3.9	-12.6	-9.1	-4.6
Indonesia	45,857	106,787	89,027	86,098	2.0	3.2	-16.6	-3.3	9.4
Korea, Republic of	140,469	82,480	82,081	79,874	6.0	2.9	-0.5	-2.7	-7.7
Hong Kong (China)	39,269	73,708	80,752	76,690	1.7	2.8	9.6	-5.0	10.0
Philippines	89,490	83,137	68,955	74,022	3.8	2.7	-17.1	7.3	-2.7
Malaysia	53,620	57,728	56,615	64,483	2.3	2.4	-1.9	13.9	2.7
Australia	26,112	31,711	29,978	31,477	1.1	1.2	-5.5	5.0	2.7
India	9,553	13,195	13,062	13,945	0.4	0.5	-1.0	6.8	5.6
New Zealand	4,875	5,973	5,768	6,124	0.2	0.2	-3.4	6.2	3.3
Other South-East Asia	..	47,880	47,427	71,382		2.6	-0.9	50.5	
Other Asia	..	71,542	73,654	72,941		2.7	3.0	-1.0	
Other East Asia/Pacific	54,451	..	..	..	2.3				
Other Oceania	..	365	395	248		0.0	8.2	-37.2	
From other regions	*474,785*	*586,346*	*553,974*	*572,006*	*20.4*	*21.0*	*-5.5*	*3.3*	*2.7*
United States	273,606	356,535	338,548	353,411	11.7	13.0	-5.0	4.4	3.7
Canada	25,944	38,016	40,176	42,815	1.1	1.6	5.7	6.6	7.4
United Kingdom	28,796	35,471	33,569	34,082	1.2	1.3	-5.4	1.5	2.4
Germany	32,667	34,769	33,687	33,470	1.4	1.2	-3.1	-0.6	0.3
France	21,587	23,675	20,988	20,179	0.9	0.7	-11.3	-3.9	-1.0
Italy	12,239	12,055	10,639	10,664	0.5	0.4	-11.7	0.2	-1.9
Netherlands	9,935	12,592	11,032	10,237	0.4	0.4	-12.4	-7.2	0.4
All Middle East	10,066	11,202	9,194	9,929	0.4	0.4	-17.9	8.0	-0.2
South Africa	5,671	4,849	5,151	5,724	0.2	0.2	6.2	11.1	0.1
Switzerland	6,238	6,325	5,909	5,639	0.3	0.2	-6.6	-4.6	-1.4
Sweden	4,751	5,585	4,845	4,927	0.2	0.2	-13.2	1.7	0.5
Austria	4,227	4,238	4,313	4,098	0.2	0.2	1.8	-5.0	-0.4
Belgium	3,745	4,147	3,506	3,833	0.2	0.1	-15.5	9.3	0.3
Spain	3,685	4,063	3,736	3,826	0.2	0.1	-8.0	2.4	0.5
Brazil	4,095	2,767	2,155	2,206	0.2	0.1	-22.1	2.4	-8.5
Mexico	1,034	1,876	1,605	2,195	0.0	0.1	-14.4	36.8	11.4
Greece	1,797	1,193	1,094	1,174	0.1	0.0	-8.3	7.3	-5.9
Nigeria	856	930	1,020	835	0.0	0.0	9.7	-18.1	-0.4
Argentina	813	1,052	888	552	0.0	0.0	-15.6	-37.8	-5.4
Mauritius	624	348	281	336	0.0	0.0	-19.3	19.6	-8.5
Madagascar	64	28	14	17	0.0	0.0	-50.0	21.4	-17.3
Other Africa	2,624	2,512	2,197	2,208	0.1	0.1	-12.5	0.5	-2.4
Other Americas	5,688	5,503	5,135	5,048	0.2	0.2	-6.7	-1.7	-1.7
Other Europe	14,033	16,615	14,292	14,601	0.6	0.5	-14.0	2.2	0.6
Nationals residing abroad	*265,601*	*313,367*	*325,266*	*372,394*	*11.4*	*13.7*	*3.8*	*14.5*	*4.9*
Other World/Not specified	*4,217*	*7,245*	*6,501*	*6,406*	*0.2*	*0.2*	*-10.3*	*-1.5*	*6.2*

Source: World Tourism Organization (WTO) © (Data as collected by WTO September 2003)

Taiwan (Pr. of China)
Nights of International Tourists in All Accommodation Establishments (by residence)

	1995	2000	2001	2002*	Market share (%) 1995	Market share (%) 2002*	Growth rate (%) 2001/00	Growth rate (%) 2002*/01	Average per year (%) 1995-2002*
Total	**14,833,868**	**16,487,081**	**16,986,990**	**18,187,898**	**100**	**100**	**3.0**	**7.1**	**3.0**
From Asia and the Pacific	*9,854,986*	*11,207,821*	*11,943,594*	*13,082,906*	*66.4*	*71.9*	*6.6*	*9.5*	*4.1*
Japan	4,185,449	4,294,752	4,489,876	4,506,849	28.2	24.8	4.5	0.4	1.1
Hong Kong (China)	1,769,740	1,774,908	1,818,696	2,653,257	11.9	14.6	2.5	45.9	6.0
Singapore	586,201	683,370	719,359	762,479	4.0	4.2	5.3	6.0	3.8
Indonesia	284,168	540,439	503,754	499,814	1.9	2.7	-6.8	-0.8	8.4
Malaysia	440,984	475,689	445,369	499,243	3.0	2.7	-6.4	12.1	1.8
Korea, Republic of	526,474	406,927	433,070	408,011	3.5	2.2	6.4	-5.8	-3.6
Thailand	289,984	340,192	338,499	346,215	2.0	1.9	-0.5	2.3	2.6
Philippines	395,594	332,749	319,005	285,725	2.7	1.6	-4.1	-10.4	-4.5
Australia	215,003	223,116	217,945	219,083	1.4	1.2	-2.3	0.5	0.3
India	77,729	99,328	105,650	111,513	0.5	0.6	6.4	5.5	5.3
New Zealand	48,265	49,521	46,797	48,515	0.3	0.3	-5.5	3.7	0.1
Other South-East Asia	68,079	225,848	272,570	341,337	0.5	1.9	20.7	25.2	25.9
Other Asia	963,583	1,757,224	2,229,906	2,398,400	6.5	13.2	26.9	7.6	13.9
Other Oceania	3,733	3,758	3,098	2,465	0.0	0.0	-17.6	-20.4	-5.8
From other regions	*4,635,933*	*4,998,562*	*4,885,807*	*4,962,286*	*31.3*	*27.3*	*-2.3*	*1.6*	*1.0*
United States	2,973,822	3,238,125	3,205,110	3,322,580	20.0	18.3	-1.0	3.7	1.6
Canada	282,995	361,683	365,659	377,030	1.9	2.1	1.1	3.1	4.2
Germany	265,810	276,393	268,977	254,570	1.8	1.4	-2.7	-5.4	-0.6
United Kingdom	201,632	238,442	233,443	235,864	1.4	1.3	-2.1	1.0	2.3
France	179,915	175,901	161,003	154,739	1.2	0.9	-8.5	-3.9	-2.1
All Middle East	65,249	71,262	59,583	63,202	0.4	0.3	-16.4	6.1	-0.5
Italy	106,719	73,010	67,054	61,625	0.7	0.3	-8.2	-8.1	-7.5
Netherlands	69,286	74,881	64,017	61,209	0.5	0.3	-14.5	-4.4	-1.8
South Africa	46,551	44,628	46,439	49,841	0.3	0.3	4.1	7.3	1.0
Switzerland	45,396	50,247	47,430	39,901	0.3	0.2	-5.6	-15.9	-1.8
Austria	42,816	38,198	42,114	37,844	0.3	0.2	10.3	-10.1	-1.7
Sweden	30,943	34,354	30,706	32,621	0.2	0.2	-10.6	6.2	0.8
Spain	24,695	25,444	22,684	22,654	0.2	0.1	-10.8	-0.1	-1.2
Brazil	57,083	30,786	23,457	21,712	0.4	0.1	-23.8	-7.4	-12.9
Belgium	25,470	24,361	21,769	19,617	0.2	0.1	-10.6	-9.9	-3.7
Mexico	6,607	12,566	13,187	14,477	0.0	0.1	4.9	9.8	11.9
Nigeria	6,972	14,109	15,405	12,333	0.0	0.1	9.2	-19.9	8.5
Argentina	18,352	12,438	10,808	7,873	0.1	0.0	-13.1	-27.2	-11.4
Greece	5,168	5,825	6,601	6,060	0.0	0.0	13.3	-8.2	2.3
Mauritius	5,327	2,920	1,866	3,050	0.0	0.0	-36.1	63.5	-7.7
Madagascar	1,245	397	83	258	0.0	0.0	-79.1	210.8	-20.1
Other Africa	16,365	17,732	17,844	15,653	0.1	0.1	0.6	-12.3	-0.6
Other Americas	67,785	54,660	50,184	46,777	0.5	0.3	-8.2	-6.8	-5.2
Other Europe	89,730	120,200	110,384	100,796	0.6	0.6	-8.2	-8.7	1.7
Other World/Not specified	*342,949*	*280,698*	*157,589*	*142,706*	*2.3*	*0.8*	*-43.9*	*-9.4*	*-11.8*

Source: World Tourism Organization (WTO) © (Data as collected by WTO September 2003)

III.2 South-East Asia

III.2.1 Brunei Darussalam South-East Asia

Profile

Brunei Darussalam

Capital	Bandar Seri Begawan
Area (100 km²)	58
Population (2002, 1000)	351
Gross Domestic Product (GDP) (2002, US$ million)	4,044
GDP per capita (2002, US$)	11,509
GDP growth (real, %)	
'-> 2001: 0.8; 2002: 3.0; 2003*: 5.1; 2004*: 0.1	

East Asia and the Pacific
South-East Asia

	2000	2001	2002*	2001/2000	2002*/2001
International Arrivals					
Visitors (1000)	984	..	..		
- per 100 of inhabitants	293	..	..		
Tourism accommodation					
Number of rooms	2,412	..	..		

Source: World Tourism Organization (WTO) (Data as collected by WTO September 2003)
See annex for methodological notes and reference of external sources used.

International Tourism by Origin

Brunei Darussalam
International Visitor Arrivals at Frontiers

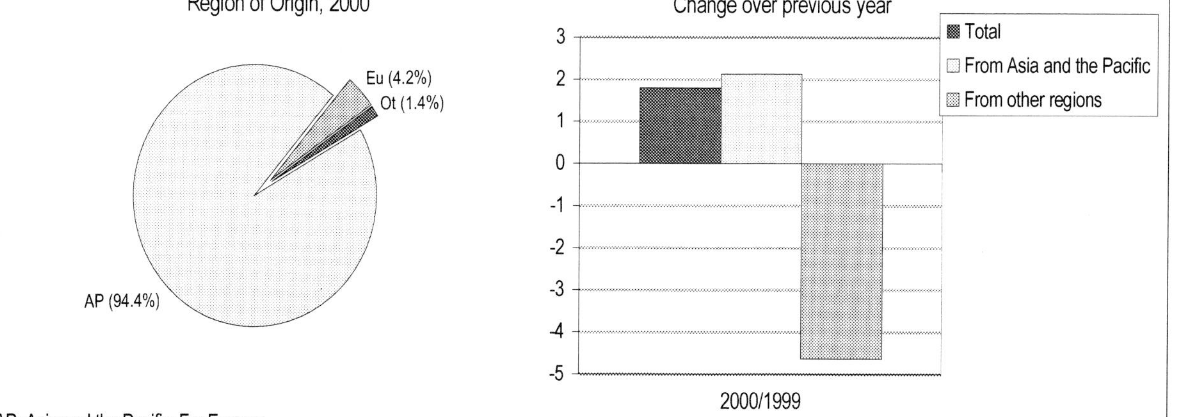

AP: Asia and the Pacific; Eu: Europe;
Ot: Other;
Source: World Tourism Organization (WTO) ©

Brunei Darussalam

International Visitor Arrivals at Frontiers (by nationality)

	1995	1999	2000	2001	Market share (%) 1995	Market share (%) 2001	Growth rate (%) 2000/99	Growth rate (%) 2001/00	Average per year (%) 1995-2001
Total	..	**966,684**	**984,093**	..			**1.8**		
From Asia and the Pacific	..	*909,426*	*928,835*	..			*2.1*		
Malaysia	..	757,588	756,026	..			-0.2		
Philippines	..	37,559	48,878	..			30.1		
Indonesia	..	37,732	38,325	..			1.6		
Singapore	..	23,226	21,966	..			-5.4		
Australia	..	13,178	11,962	..			-9.2		
Thailand	..	8,898	9,857	..			10.8		
Taiwan (Pr. of China)	..	6,608	9,449	..			43.0		
Nepal	..	4,316	7,120	..			65.0		
India	..	5,724	6,237	..			9.0		
Japan	..	3,172	3,967	..			25.1		
New Zealand	..	3,736	2,801	..			-25.0		
Korea, Republic of	..	1,544	1,741	..			12.8		
Pakistan	..	1,228	1,053	..			-14.3		
Hong Kong (China)	..	557	618	..			11.0		
Sri Lanka	..	616	528	..			-14.3		
Myanmar	..	621	381	..			-38.6		
Vietnam	..	923	381	..			-58.7		
Cambodia	..	145	105	..			-27.6		
Other South Asia	..	617	1,230	..			99.4		
Other Asia	..	1,438	6,210	..			331.8		
From other regions	..	*54,502*	*51,978*	..			*-4.6*		
United Kingdom	..	33,793	30,533	..			-9.6		
United States	..	4,643	5,164	..			11.2		
Canada	..	4,108	4,305	..			4.8		
Germany	..	3,031	4,175	..			37.7		
Netherlands	..	3,547	3,250	..			-8.4		
France	..	1,768	1,394	..			-21.2		
All Middle East	..	886	781	..			-11.9		
Switzerland	..	420	383	..			-8.8		
Norway	..	354	349	..			-1.4		
Sweden	..	384	349	..			-9.1		
Ireland	..	454	299	..			-34.1		
Italy	..	203	232	..			14.3		
Belgium	..	238	197	..			-17.2		
Denmark	..	348	191	..			-45.1		
Austria	..	192	187	..			-2.6		
Spain	..	63	136	..			115.9		
Finland	..	70	53	..			-24.3		
Other World/Not specified	..	*2,756*	*3,280*	..			*19.0*		

Source: World Tourism Organization (WTO) ©

(Data as collected by WTO September 2003)

III.2.2 Cambodia South-East Asia

Profile

Cambodia

Capital	Phnom-Penh
Year of entry in WTO	1975
Area (1000 km²)	181
Population (2002, million)	12.9
Gross Domestic Product (GDP) (2002, US$ million)	3,663
GDP per capita (2002, US$)	272
GDP growth (real, %)	
'-> 2001: 6.3; 2002: 5.5; 2003*: 4.7; 2004*: 5.8	

East Asia and the Pacific
South-East Asia

	2000	2001	2002*	2001/2000	2002*/2001
International Arrivals					
Tourists (overnight visitors) (1000)	466	605	787	29.8	30.1
- per 100 of inhabitants	4	5	6		
Tourism accommodation					
Number of rooms	9,673	10,804	11,426	11.7	5.8
Receipts and Expenditure for International Tourism					
International Tourism Receipts (US$ million)	228	304	379	33.3	24.7
- per Tourist Arrival (US$)	489	502	482	2.7	-4.2
- per capita (US$)	18	24	29		
International Fare Receipts (US$ million)	41	49	..	18.0	
International Tourism Expenditure (US$ million)	29	35	..	20.7	
- per capita (US$)	2	3	..		
International Fare Expenditure (US$ million)	19	22	..	17.9	
△ International Tourism Balance (US$ million)	199	269	..		
△ International Fare Balance (US$ million)	22	26	..		

Source: World Tourism Organization (WTO) (Data as collected by WTO September 2003)

See annex for methodological notes and reference of external sources used.

International Tourism by Origin

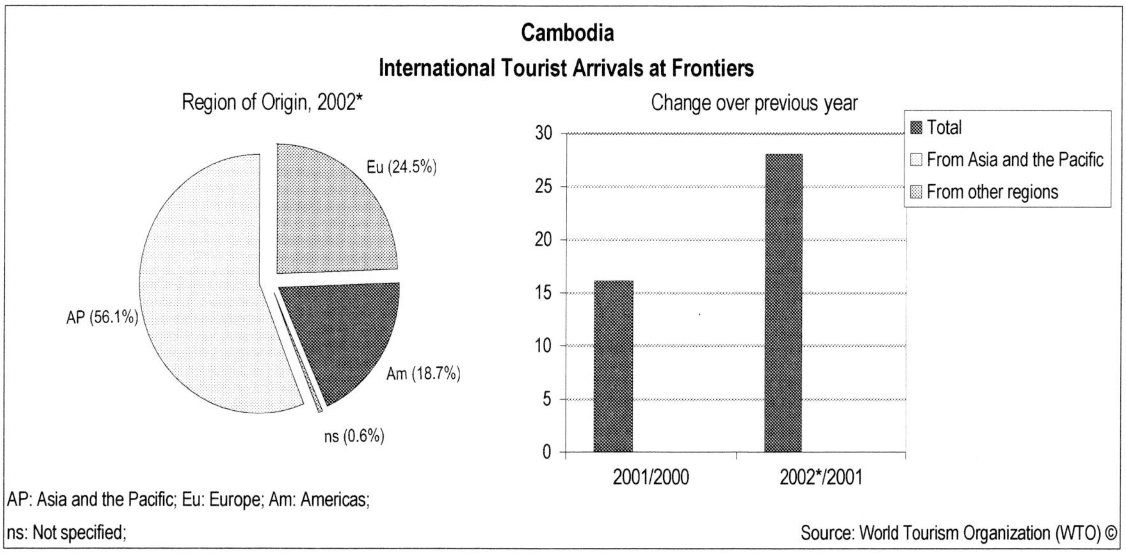

Cambodia

International Tourist Arrivals at Frontiers (by residence)

	1995	2000	2001	2002*	Market share (%) 1995	Market share (%) 2002*	Growth rate (%) 2001/00	Growth rate (%) 2002*/01	Average per year (%) 1995-2002*
Total	**219,680**	**351,661**	**408,377**	**522,980**	**100**	**100**	**16.1**	**28.1**	**13.2**
From Asia and the Pacific	*156,978*	*155,350*	*163,098*	*293,648*	*71.5*	*56.1*	*5.0*	*80.0*	*9.4*
Japan	21,629	19,906	17,952	96,796	9.8	18.5	-9.8	439.2	23.9
China	22,886	30,586	32,002	32,958	10.4	6.3	4.6	3.0	5.3
Taiwan (Pr. of China)	22,422	21,626	23,098	32,149	10.2	6.1	6.8	39.2	5.3
Thailand	13,595	16,550	17,496	26,099	6.2	5.0	5.7	49.2	9.8
Korea, Republic of	4,141	7,536	9,579	25,861	1.9	4.9	27.1	170.0	29.9
Australia	6,634	11,350	13,078	22,240	3.0	4.3	15.2	70.1	18.9
Malaysia	11,553	14,701	15,994	15,341	5.3	2.9	8.8	-4.1	4.1
Singapore	9,155	10,734	10,982	11,166	4.2	2.1	2.3	1.7	2.9
Vietnam	1,834	8,333	7,828	8,507	0.8	1.6	-6.1	8.7	24.5
Philippines	..	2,112	2,622	3,474		0.7	24.1	32.5	
India	1,158	1,767	2,271	3,373	0.5	0.6	28.5	48.5	16.5
New Zealand	1,334	1,887	2,188	3,294	0.6	0.6	16.0	50.5	13.8
Indonesia	1,488	1,704	1,734	2,953	0.7	0.6	1.8	70.3	10.3
Hong Kong (China)	1,656	3,646	1,769	2,526	0.8	0.5	-51.5	42.8	6.2
Bangladesh	..	381	1,433	..			276.1		
Other East Asia/Pacific	37,493	162	378	4,264	17.1	0.8	133.3	1028.0	-26.7
Other intraregional	..	2,369	2,694	2,647		0.5	13.7	-1.7	
From other regions	*59,445*	*107,813*	*109,993*	*226,251*	*27.1*	*43.3*	*2.0*	*105.7*	*21.0*
United States	17,846	35,814	37,033	79,363	8.1	15.2	3.4	114.3	23.8
France	19,437	24,883	23,328	49,165	8.8	9.4	-6.2	110.8	14.2
United Kingdom	5,809	15,912	17,686	24,565	2.6	4.7	11.1	38.9	22.9
Germany	3,499	7,298	6,861	15,137	1.6	2.9	-6.0	120.6	23.3
Canada	3,692	5,646	6,191	11,330	1.7	2.2	9.7	83.0	17.4
Italy	1,810	3,060	3,170	6,048	0.8	1.2	3.6	90.8	18.8
Switzerland	1,832	2,604	2,548	5,484	0.8	1.0	-2.2	115.2	17.0
Belgium	..	2,510	2,180	4,363		0.8	-13.1	100.1	
Netherlands	..	1,905	2,423	3,085		0.6	27.2	27.3	
Austria	..	628	655	2,358		0.5	4.3	260.0	
Denmark	..	879	982	1,639		0.3	11.7	66.9	
Norway	..	652	821	1,379		0.3	25.9	68.0	
Sweden	..	1,283	..	..					
Spain	..	1,014	1,044	..			3.0		
Finland	..	443	563	818		0.2	27.1	45.3	
Ireland	..	535	706	..			32.0		
Portugal	..	621	..	..					
Russian Fed	..	483	513	..			6.2		
Poland	..	183	235	..			28.4		
Mexico	..	200	225	..			12.5		
Turkey	..	141	..	..					
Iceland	..	104	..	..					
Brazil	..	104	90	..			-13.5		
Argentina	..	..	85	..					
Other Americas	..	392	281	7,240		1.4	-28.3	2476.5	
Other interregional	5,520	519	2,373	14,277	2.5	2.7	357.2	501.6	14.5
Other World/Not specified	*3,257*	*88,498*	*135,286*	*3,081*	*1.5*	*0.6*	*52.9*	*-97.7*	*-0.8*

Source: World Tourism Organization (WTO) © (Data as collected by WTO September 2003)

III.2.3 Indonesia South-East Asia

Profile

Indonesia

East Asia and the Pacific
South-East Asia

Capital	Jakarta
Year of entry in WTO	1975
Area (1000 km²)	1,905
Population (2002, million)	231
Gross Domestic Product (GDP) (2002, US$ million)	173,290
GDP per capita (2002, US$)	804
GDP growth (real, %)	
'-> 2001: 3.4; 2002: 3.7; 2003*: 3.5; 2004*: 4.0	

	2000	2001	2002*	2001/2000	2002*/2001
International Arrivals					
Tourists (overnight visitors) (1000)	5,064	5,154	5,033	1.8	-2.3
- per 100 of inhabitants	2	2	2		
Tourism accommodation					
Number of rooms	252,984	259,450	..	2.6	
Nights spent in collective establishments (1000)					
by non-residents (inbound tourism)	62,087	54,062	..	-12.9	
Nights spent in hotels and similar establishments (1000)					
by non-residents (inbound tourism)	49,397	43,023	..	-12.9	
Receipts and Expenditure for International Tourism					
International Tourism Receipts (US$ million)	5,749	5,411	..	-5.9	
- per Tourist Arrival (US$)	1,135	1,050	..	-7.5	
- per capita (US$)	26	24	..		
International Tourism Expenditure (US$ million)	3,197	3,406	..	6.5	
- per capita (US$)	14	15	..		
△ International Tourism Balance (US$ million)	2,552	2,005	..		

Source: World Tourism Organization (WTO) (Data as collected by WTO September 2003)

See annex for methodological notes and reference of external sources used.

Survey

Contributed by *Ministry for Culture and Tourism*
www.budpar.go.id ; www.my-indonesia.info (promotional)
www.budpar.go.id (institutional/corporate)
www.budpar.go.id (research and data)

Tourism development and outlook

Most significant determinant

The bomb blast that shook Bali has impacted the Indonesian tourism sector significantly. There was a huge downturn in visitors at the end of last year.

Tourism products

Product diversification has been directed towards the development of the MICE industry, ecotourism, marine tourism and cruises to attract niche markets with higher spending patterns. Furthermore, with the objective of maximizing the equitable distribution of the benefits of tourism in the country, the tourism policy has shifted to a focus on the development of community-based tourism.

Access

Many regions do not have a good local transport infrastructure to link intra and inter island, inter cities, from cities to the countryside and rural areas.

Other Issues

The other important factor is development of competency-based training programs aim at strengthening the human resources of tourism administrations and of tourism enterprises to meet certain standards of competency in various tourism-related occupations.

Outlook 2003

We have a pessimistic forecast for international visitor arrivals and only estimate approximately 3.6 to 3.8 million in 2003.

Tourism policy

Several breakthrough strategies were implemented to maintain the positive growth of tourism in Indonesia e.g. specific public relations, market redistribution, image positioning and enhancement of domestic tourism.

Marketing & promotion

In the effort to recover from the present crisis in Bali, the government of Indonesia launched a national tourism recovery programme with the main thrust being to regain confidence in the international market. The recovery programme consists of four phases:

- Rescue Phase (October- December 2002);
- Rehabilitation Phase (January-June 2003);
- Normalization Phase (July- December 2003);
- Expansion Phase (2004 onward).

The activities include : intensive public relations, promotion (peace mission and anti-terrorism campaign), communication networking (establishing a media center), image campaign (road-shows to Europe, Asia, ASEAN and Australia), and redistribution of overall demand focusing on regional and domestic tourism.

Cultural Tourism (CT)

Specific place for CT in tourism policy: yes.

Main objectives & instruments	One of the objectives is to empower the local community at places where cultural tourism has flourished. In this matter, more opportunities are given to local government to expose their attraction and develop tourism in their respective region, underlining its local uniqueness in line with the national guidelines.
Main focus of attention supply	Due to its ethnic diversity, Indonesia is richly endowed with cultural attractions including the world heritage site of Borobudur Temple. There are more than 500 ethnic groups maintaining their distinctiveness in terms of cultures, traditions, crafts and folklore that have a competitive edge in cultural tourism

Specific place for CT in marketing & promotion plan: yes.

Main objectives & programmes	To increase its competitive edge over other Asia/Pacific nations, Indonesia has to promote its mega-diversity in culture and maintain the distinct features and strengths of destinations. On 11-17 June 2003 Borobudur International Festival with the theme "Balancing Heritage Conservation and Community Development " will be held in Central Java, Indonesia.

International Tourism by Origin

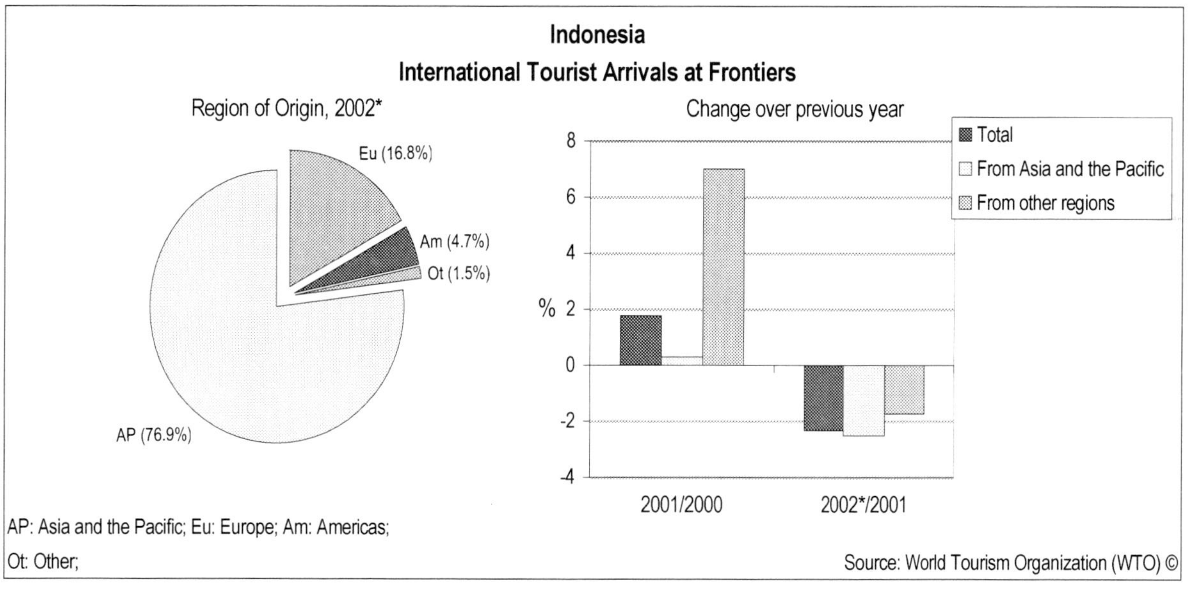

Indonesia

International Tourist Arrivals at Frontiers (by residence)

					Market share (%)		Growth rate (%)		Average per year (%)
	1995	2000	2001	2002*	1995	2002*	2001/00	2002*/01	1995-2002*
Total	**4,324,229**	**5,064,217**	**5,153,620**	**5,033,297**	**100**	**100**	**1.8**	**-2.3**	**2.2**
From Asia and the Pacific	*3,263,898*	*3,959,354*	*3,971,406*	*3,871,592*	*75.5*	*76.9*	*0.3*	*-2.5*	*2.5*
Singapore	1,046,533	1,427,886	1,477,132	1,436,906	24.2	28.5	3.4	-2.7	4.6
Japan	486,278	643,794	611,314	599,922	11.2	11.9	-5.0	-1.9	3.0
Malaysia	511,903	475,845	484,692	469,582	11.8	9.3	1.9	-3.1	-1.2
Australia	320,494	459,994	397,982	389,262	7.4	7.7	-13.5	-2.2	2.8
Taiwan (Pr. of China)	352,797	356,436	391,696	383,634	8.2	7.6	9.9	-2.1	1.2
Korea, Republic of	115,091	213,762	212,233	205,031	2.7	4.1	-0.7	-3.4	8.6
Philippines	96,242	79,682	82,828	80,157	2.2	1.6	3.9	-3.2	-2.6
Hong Kong (China)	93,163	72,461	70,112	68,911	2.2	1.4	-3.2	-1.7	-4.2
Thailand	38,908	48,477	50,489	49,162	0.9	1.0	4.2	-2.6	3.4
India	31,968	34,221	34,962	34,023	0.7	0.7	2.2	-2.7	0.9
New Zealand	28,339	32,659	32,898	32,413	0.7	0.6	0.7	-1.5	1.9
China	38,895	29,352	32,197	31,428	0.9	0.6	9.7	-2.4	-3.0
Brunei Darussalam	11,641	12,787	14,526	14,228	0.3	0.3	13.6	-2.1	2.9
Pakistan	7,352	6,254	6,439	6,296	0.2	0.1	3.0	-2.2	-2.2
Sri Lanka	5,068	5,618	5,495	5,362	0.1	0.1	-2.2	-2.4	0.8
Bangladesh	6,513	4,167	4,327	4,225	0.2	0.1	3.8	-2.4	-6.0
Other South-East Asia	..	5,324	4,890	4,674		0.1	-8.2	-4.4	
Other Asia	70,330	48,666	55,199	54,434	1.6	1.1	13.4	-1.4	-3.6
Other Oceania	2,383	1,969	1,995	1,942	0.1	0.0	1.3	-2.7	-2.9
From other regions	*1,060,331*	*1,104,863*	*1,182,214*	*1,161,705*	*24.5*	*23.1*	*7.0*	*-1.7*	*1.3*
United Kingdom	165,788	161,662	189,027	186,010	3.8	3.7	16.9	-1.6	1.7
United States	155,111	176,379	177,869	174,646	3.6	3.5	0.8	-1.8	1.7
Germany	167,653	151,897	159,881	156,121	3.9	3.1	5.3	-2.4	-1.0
Netherlands	136,858	105,109	114,656	112,440	3.2	2.2	9.1	-1.9	-2.8
France	80,422	93,477	98,807	97,422	1.9	1.9	5.7	-1.4	2.8
Italy	55,725	63,208	59,519	59,510	1.3	1.2	-5.8	0.0	0.9
All Africa	38,128	37,573	40,282	39,498	0.9	0.8	7.2	-1.9	0.5
Saudi Arabia	24,571	33,027	34,381	34,291	0.6	0.7	4.1	-0.3	4.9
Canada	30,700	29,952	34,941	34,142	0.7	0.7	16.7	-2.3	1.5
Spain, Portugal	14,780	34,572	33,725	33,227	0.3	0.7	-2.4	-1.5	12.3
Switzerland	44,016	33,740	32,852	32,114	1.0	0.6	-2.6	-2.2	-4.4
Sweden	21,177	26,592	32,646	31,793	0.5	0.6	22.8	-2.6	6.0
Belgium	17,436	23,495	26,832	26,447	0.4	0.5	14.2	-1.4	6.1
Austria	18,275	18,791	21,784	21,476	0.4	0.4	15.9	-1.4	2.3
Norway	10,702	18,158	19,826	19,365	0.2	0.4	9.2	-2.3	8.8
Denmark	17,888	16,375	19,663	19,231	0.4	0.4	20.1	-2.2	1.0
All South America	11,903	16,562	19,223	18,885	0.3	0.4	16.1	-1.8	6.8
All Central America	3,435	9,224	11,064	11,079	0.1	0.2	19.9	0.1	18.2
Former U.S.S.R.	7,232	10,954	10,873	10,579	0.2	0.2	-0.7	-2.7	5.6
Finland	7,601	8,900	8,756	8,464	0.2	0.2	-1.6	-3.3	1.5
Egypt	1,118	1,714	1,765	1,721	0.0	0.0	3.0	-2.5	6.4
Bahrain	1,523	663	719	711	0.0	0.0	8.4	-1.1	-10.3
Other Central/Eastern Europe	12,155	13,205	14,415	14,149	0.3	0.3	9.2	-1.8	2.2
Other Europe	16,134	19,634	18,708	18,384	0.4	0.4	-4.7	-1.7	1.9

Source: World Tourism Organization (WTO) ©

(Data as collected by WTO September 2003)

III.2.4 Lao People's Democratic Republic — South-East Asia

Profile

Lao People's Democratic Republic

East Asia and the Pacific
South-East Asia

Capital	Vientiane
Year of entry in WTO	1975
Area (1000 km²)	237
Population (2002, million)	5.8
Gross Domestic Product (GDP) (2002, US$ million)	1,858
GDP per capita (2002, US$)	333
GDP growth (real, %)	
'-> 2001: 5.8; 2002: 5.9; 2003*: 5.5; 2004*: 6.0	

	2000	2001	2002*	2001/2000	2002*/2001
International Arrivals					
Visitors (1000)	737	674	736	-8.5	9.2
Tourists (overnight visitors) (1000)	191	173	215	-9.4	24.3
- per 100 of inhabitants	3	3	4		
Same-day visitors (1000)	546	501	521	-8.2	4.0
Tourism accommodation					
Number of rooms	7,333	8,797	..	20.0	
Receipts and Expenditure for International Tourism					
International Tourism Receipts (US$ million)	114	104	113	-8.8	8.7
- per Tourist Arrival (US$)	597	601	526	0.7	-12.6
- per Visitor Arrival (US$)	155	154	154	-0.2	-0.5
- per capita (US$)	21	18	20		
International Tourism Expenditure (US$ million)	8	..	..		
- per capita (US$)	1	..	..		
△ International Tourism Balance (US$ million)	106	..	..		

Source: World Tourism Organization (WTO) (Data as collected by WTO September 2003)

See annex for methodological notes and reference of external sources used.

International Tourism by Origin

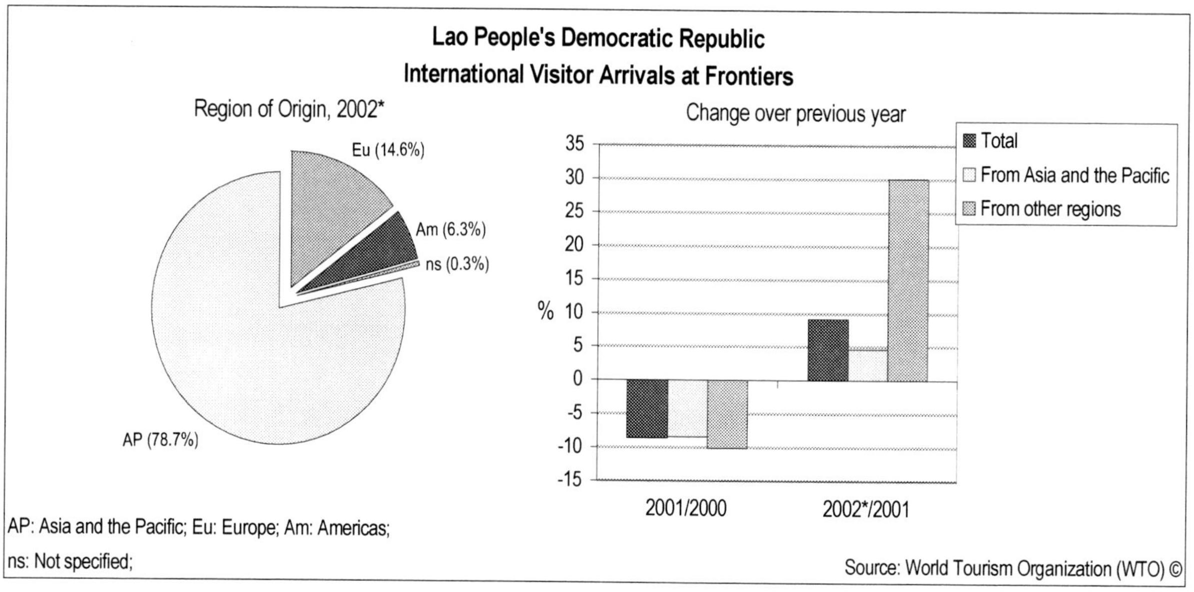

Lao People's Democratic Republic
International Visitor Arrivals at Frontiers (by nationality)

					Market share (%)		Growth rate (%)		Average per year (%)
	1995	2000	2001	2002*	1995	2002*	2001/00	2002*/01	1995-2002*
Total	**346,460**	**737,208**	**673,823**	**735,662**	**100**	**100**	**-8.6**	**9.2**	**11.4**
From Asia and the Pacific	*314,470*	*604,254*	*553,249*	*579,031*	*90.8*	*78.7*	*-8.4*	*4.7*	*9.1*
Thailand	233,779	442,564	376,685	422,766	67.5	57.5	-14.9	12.2	8.8
Vietnam	48,860	68,751	82,411	71,001	14.1	9.7	19.9	-13.8	5.5
China	4,076	28,215	40,644	21,724	1.2	3.0	44.1	-46.6	27.0
Japan	4,318	20,687	15,547	19,801	1.2	2.7	-24.8	27.4	24.3
Australia	3,833	10,168	9,547	12,611	1.1	1.7	-6.1	32.1	18.5
Korea, Republic of	356	4,944	4,051	4,891	0.1	0.7	-18.1	20.7	45.4
Taiwan (Pr. of China)	2,099	2,940	2,461	3,918	0.6	0.5	-16.3	59.2	9.3
Malaysia	1,061	4,211	2,544	3,543	0.3	0.5	-39.6	39.3	18.8
Cambodia	..	1,841	1,806	2,620		0.4	-1.9	45.1	
Philippines	436	3,452	2,240	2,549	0.1	0.3	-35.1	13.8	28.7
Singapore	722	2,514	2,055	2,454	0.2	0.3	-18.3	19.4	19.1
India	11,396	3,309	2,693	2,319	3.3	0.3	-18.6	-13.9	-20.3
New Zealand	703	3,385	2,521	2,271	0.2	0.3	-25.5	-9.9	18.2
Indonesia	372	2,403	2,082	1,903	0.1	0.3	-13.4	-8.6	26.3
Myanmar	72	2,086	1,459	1,365	0.0	0.2	-30.1	-6.4	52.2
Bangladesh	463	472	738	669	0.1	0.1	56.4	-9.3	5.4
Brunei Darussalam	..	531	855	582		0.1	61.0	-31.9	
Sri Lanka	580	288	132	278	0.2	0.0	-54.2	110.6	-10.0
Pakistan	652	116	225	251	0.2	0.0	94.0	11.6	-12.7
Nepal	424	96	124	171	0.1	0.0	29.2	37.9	-12.2
Other South Asia	..	65	225	75		0.0	246.2	-66.7	
Other East Asia/Pacific	268	1,216	2,204	1,269	0.1	0.2	81.3	-42.4	24.9
From other regions	*31,654*	*131,814*	*118,523*	*154,143*	*9.1*	*21.0*	*-10.1*	*30.1*	*25.4*
United States	9,001	32,869	25,779	35,734	2.6	4.9	-21.6	38.6	21.8
France	9,210	24,534	21,662	26,748	2.7	3.6	-11.7	23.5	16.5
United Kingdom	3,090	15,204	15,722	21,749	0.9	3.0	3.4	38.3	32.2
Germany	2,498	11,580	10,322	12,777	0.7	1.7	-10.9	23.8	26.3
Canada	1,868	8,330	7,174	9,060	0.5	1.2	-13.9	26.3	25.3
Netherlands	432	5,035	4,498	6,656	0.1	0.9	-10.7	48.0	47.8
Israel	..	3,241	3,417	5,515		0.7	5.4	61.4	
Sweden	1,002	3,986	3,710	4,507	0.3	0.6	-6.9	21.5	24.0
Switzerland	754	3,305	3,597	4,480	0.2	0.6	8.8	24.5	29.0
Belgium	408	3,363	3,301	4,111	0.1	0.6	-1.8	24.5	39.1
Italy	1,047	4,061	3,128	3,517	0.3	0.5	-23.0	12.4	18.9
Denmark	272	2,855	2,874	3,345	0.1	0.5	0.7	16.4	43.1
Norway	207	1,506	1,380	2,110	0.1	0.3	-8.4	52.9	39.3
Spain	139	753	908	1,450	0.0	0.2	20.6	59.7	39.8
Russian Fed	..	2,415	1,533	1,371		0.2	-36.5	-10.6	
Finland	..	1,772	704	1,072		0.1	-60.3	52.3	
Austria	195	1,375	1,405	890	0.1	0.1	2.2	-36.7	24.2
Greece	83	139	216	489	0.0	0.1	55.4	126.4	28.8
Other Americas	150	912	1,417	1,910	0.0	0.3	55.4	34.8	43.8
Other Europe	1,298	4,579	5,776	6,652	0.4	0.9	26.1	15.2	26.3
Other World/Not specified	*336*	*1,140*	*2,051*	*2,488*	*0.1*	*0.3*	*79.9*	*21.3*	*33.1*

Source: World Tourism Organization (WTO) © (Data as collected by WTO September 2003)

III.2.5 Malaysia — South-East Asia

Profile

Malaysia

East Asia and the Pacific
South-East Asia

Capital	Kuala Lumpur
Year of entry in WTO	1991
Area (1000 km²)	330
Population (2002, million)	22.7
Gross Domestic Product (GDP) (2002, US$ million)	94,875
GDP per capita (2002, US$)	3,868
GDP growth (real, %)	

'-> 2001: 0.3; 2002: 4.1; 2003*: 4.2; 2004*: 5.3

	2000	2001	2002*	2001/2000	2002*/2001
International Arrivals					
Visitors (1000)	17,213	22,995	..	33.6	
Tourists (overnight visitors) (1000)	10,222	12,775	13,292	25.0	4.0
- per 100 of inhabitants	47	57	59		
Same-day visitors (1000)	6,991	10,219	..	46.2	
Tourism accommodation					
Number of rooms	134,503	130,757	..	-2.8	
Nights spent in hotels and similar establishments (1000)	40,984	42,193		2.9	
by non-residents (inbound tourism)	21,296	20,450	..	-4.0	
by residents (domestic tourism)	19,688	21,743	..	10.4	
Outbound Tourism					
Trips abroad (1000)	30,532	36,248	..	18.7	
- per 100 of inhabitants	140	163	..		
Receipts and Expenditure for International Tourism					
International Tourism Receipts (US$ million)	4,562	6,374	6,785	39.7	6.4
- per Tourist Arrival (US$)	446	499	510	11.8	2.3
- per Visitor Arrival (US$)	265	277	..	4.6	
- per capita (US$)	209	287	299		
International Fare Receipts (US$ million)	991	..	..		
International Tourism Expenditure (US$ million)	2,052	2,614	2,618	27.4	0.2
- per trip (US$)	67	72	..	7.3	
- per capita (US$)	94	118	116		
International Fare Expenditure (US$ million)	468	..	..		
△ International Tourism Balance (US$ million)	2,510	3,760	4,167		
△ International Fare Balance (US$ million)	523	..	..		

Source: World Tourism Organization (WTO) (Data as collected by WTO September 2003)

See annex for methodological notes and reference of external sources used.

Survey

Contributed by *Ministry of Culture, Arts and Tourism*
www.tourism.gov.my (promotional)
www.mocat.gov.my (institutional/corporate)
www.tourism.gov.my/statistic/statistic.asp (research and data)

Tourism development and outlook

Most significant determinant	The main determinant was the stable political and economic situation.
Tourism products	The promotion of "Malaysia truly Asia" as a brand.
Access	Facilitation of entry formalities such as the granting of visas upon arrival.
Generating markets	Tourist arrivals from China and India increased by 23 per cent and 27.8 per cent respectively.
Other Issues	Close partnership with public and private sectors.
Outlook 2003	Tourist arrivals are expected to decrease by 20-30 per cent this year (2003). Tourist arrivals for 2004 are expected to increase through aggressive promotion and marketing.
Tourism policy	The encouragement of domestic tourism. Promotion will be based on "unique selling point" in target markets. To encourage quality tourism. The encouragement of local community participation in tourism activities. To encourage local private investors in the tourism sector.
Marketing & promotion	More focussed promotion and marketing in traditional and new markets. Promotion via electronic media, print and sales missions.

Cultural Tourism (CT)

Specific place for CT in tourism policy: yes.

Main objectives & instruments	The setting up of cultural books overseas to portray Malaysia's multiracial culture through the "Malaysia truly Asia" campaign.
Main focus of attention supply	Both destination and products e.g. Melaka, historic city of Malaysia and the "Colours of Malaysia" festivals.
Main focus of attention demand	Generating markets and segments.

Specific place for CT in marketing & promotion plan: yes.

Main objectives & programmes	The "Malaysia truly Asia" portrays Malaysia as a peaceful, colourful and festive nation.
Special activities undertaken	The following special programmes have been undertaken: - Colours of Malaysia; - The Water Festival; - The National Cultural Celebration.

Importance of cultural tourism:

- in total tourism offer	Twenty to thirty per cent.
- in intern. arrivals	Twenty to thirty per cent.

International Tourism by Origin

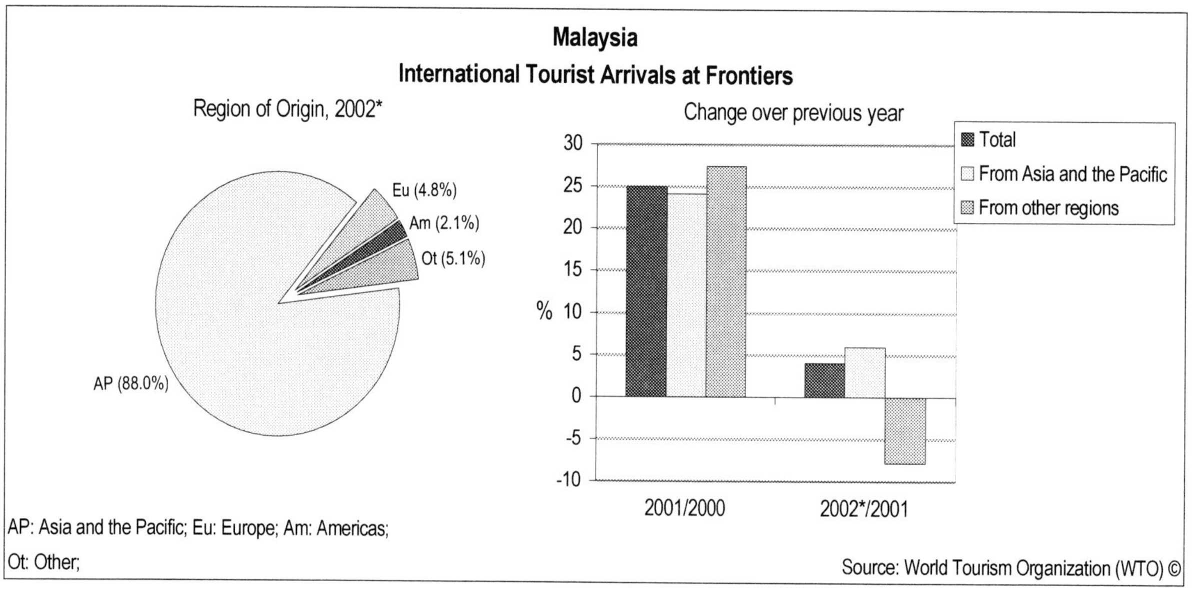

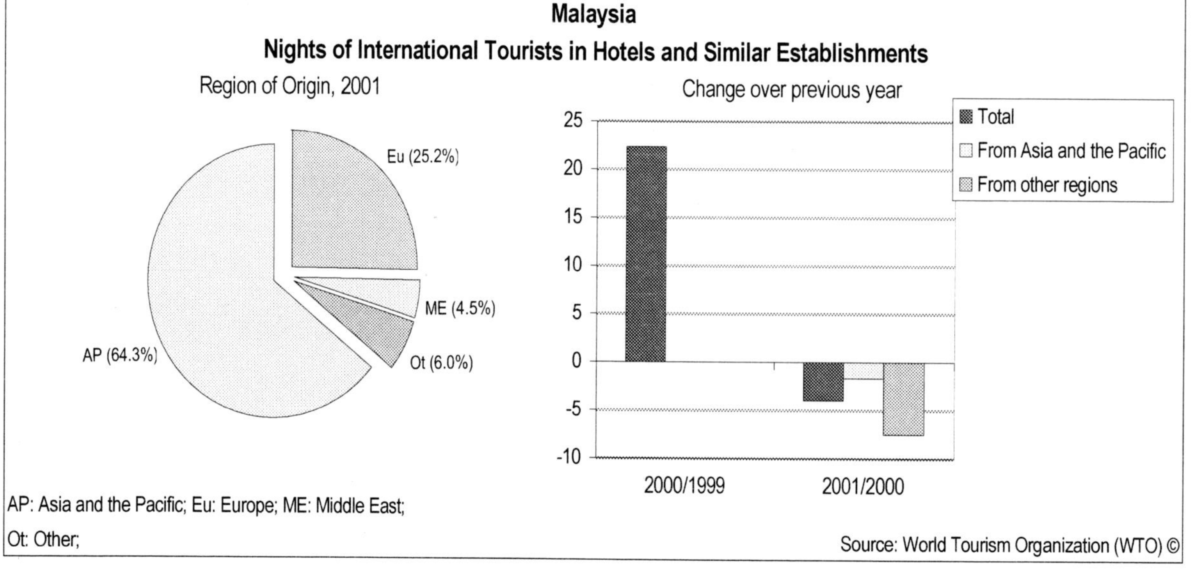

Malaysia
International Tourist Arrivals at Frontiers (by residence)

	1995	2000	2001	2002*	Market share (%) 1995	Market share (%) 2002*	Growth rate (%) 2001/00	Growth rate (%) 2002*/01	Average per year (%) 1995-2002*
Total	**7,468,749**	**10,221,582**	**12,775,073**	**13,292,010**	**100**	**100**	**25.0**	**4.0**	**8.6**
From Asia and the Pacific	*6,723,990*	*8,896,445*	*11,044,618*	*11,700,354*	*90.0*	*88.0*	*24.1*	*5.9*	*8.2*
Singapore	4,537,347	5,420,200	6,951,594	7,547,761	60.8	56.8	28.3	8.6	7.5
Thailand	530,254	940,215	1,018,797	1,166,937	7.1	8.8	8.4	14.5	11.9
Indonesia	233,996	545,051	777,449	769,128	3.1	5.8	42.6	-1.1	18.5
China	103,130	425,246	453,246	557,647	1.4	4.2	6.6	23.0	27.3
Japan	330,725	455,981	397,639	354,563	4.4	2.7	-12.8	-10.8	1.0
Brunei Darussalam	189,657	195,059	309,529	256,952	2.5	1.9	58.7	-17.0	4.4
Taiwan (Pr. of China)	293,896	213,016	249,811	209,706	3.9	1.6	17.3	-16.1	-4.7
Australia	136,300	236,775	222,340	193,794	1.8	1.5	-6.1	-12.8	5.2
India	27,701	132,127	143,513	183,360	0.4	1.4	8.6	27.8	31.0
Hong Kong (China)	146,603	76,344	144,611	116,409	2.0	0.9	89.4	-19.5	-3.2
Philippines	46,058	81,927	122,428	107,527	0.6	0.8	49.4	-12.2	12.9
Korea, Republic of	71,622	72,443	66,343	64,301	1.0	0.5	-8.4	-3.1	-1.5
New Zealand	19,374	19,351	29,893	25,157	0.3	0.2	54.5	-15.8	3.8
Vietnam	4,775	7,969	18,729	21,158	0.1	0.2	135.0	13.0	23.7
Bangladesh	..	6,241	13,552	17,450		0.1	117.1	28.8	
Sri Lanka	..	16,500	13,171	12,882		0.1	-20.2	-2.2	
Other North-East Asia	1,812	5,831	13,771	12,081	0.0	0.1	136.2	-12.3	31.1
Other South-East Asia	..	4,977	9,360	8,889		0.1	88.1	-5.0	
Other South Asia	35,972	6,232	10,674	9,522	0.5	0.1	71.3	-10.8	-17.3
Other Asia	6,443	..	..	..	0.1				
Other Oceania	8,325	11,500	37,385	35,223	0.1	0.3	225.1	-5.8	22.9
Other intraregional	..	23,460	40,783	29,907		0.2	73.8	-26.7	
From other regions	*598,784*	*1,016,975*	*1,295,875*	*1,194,327*	*8.0*	*9.0*	*27.4*	*-7.8*	*10.4*
United Kingdom	164,489	237,757	262,423	239,294	2.2	1.8	10.4	-8.8	5.5
United States	97,547	184,100	145,827	127,920	1.3	1.0	-20.8	-12.3	3.9
Germany	63,915	74,556	70,401	54,645	0.9	0.4	-5.6	-22.4	-2.2
All the Caribbean	2,279	33,994	57,492	52,193	0.0	0.4	69.1	-9.2	56.4
Saudi Arabia	..	27,808	39,957	45,007		0.3	43.7	12.6	
Netherlands	18,097	35,400	52,034	39,303	0.2	0.3	47.0	-24.5	11.7
Canada	29,223	55,799	38,935	34,996	0.4	0.3	-30.2	-10.1	2.6
Spain	..	5,706	31,733	34,477		0.3	456.1	8.6	
Sweden	17,920	48,739	35,053	29,044	0.2	0.2	-28.1	-17.1	7.1
All Middle East	28,923	..	..	..	0.4				
France	28,741	31,785	32,922	27,434	0.4	0.2	3.6	-16.7	-0.7
Syrian Arab Republic	..	2,784	18,205	21,109		0.2	553.9	16.0	
All Central America	2,078	7,761	19,005	17,771	0.0	0.1	144.9	-6.5	35.9
All North Africa	2,946	8,151	18,418	17,332	0.0	0.1	126.0	-5.9	28.8
Denmark	11,008	10,599	19,770	17,297	0.1	0.1	86.5	-12.5	6.7
Italy	17,444	34,548	20,636	16,805	0.2	0.1	-40.3	-18.6	-0.5
Switzerland	24,217	10,213	20,429	15,614	0.3	0.1	100.0	-23.6	-6.1
Untd Arab Emirates	..	2,391	13,762	14,124		0.1	475.6	2.6	
South Africa	17,058	11,540	20,766	13,720	0.2	0.1	79.9	-33.9	-3.1
Finland	4,568	22,667	15,284	12,908	0.1	0.1	-32.6	-15.5	16.0
Other interregional	68,331	170,677	362,823	363,334	0.9	2.7	112.6	0.1	27.0
Other World/Not specified	*145,975*	*308,162*	*434,580*	*397,329*	*2.0*	*3.0*	*41.0*	*-8.6*	*15.4*

Source: World Tourism Organization (WTO) © (Data as collected by WTO September 2003)

Malaysia

Nights of International Tourists in Hotels and Similar Establishments (by residence)

					Market share (%)		Growth rate (%)		Average per year (%)
	1995	**1999**	**2000**	**2001**	**1995**	**2001**	**2000/99**	**2001/00**	**1995-2001**
Total	**13,376,029**	**17,410,073**	**21,295,679**	**20,450,452**	**100**	**100**	**22.3**	**-4.0**	**7.3**
From Asia and the Pacific	*8,017,521*	*9,688,152*	*13,365,929*	*13,145,680*	*59.9*	*64.3*	*38.0*	*-1.6*	*8.6*
Singapore	2,102,578	3,149,319	3,602,965	3,710,450	15.7	18.1	14.4	3.0	9.9
Japan	2,558,143	1,673,424	1,976,115	1,675,966	19.1	8.2	18.1	-15.2	-6.8
China	296,088	1,070,741	1,252,308	1,250,812	2.2	6.1	17.0	-0.1	27.1
Australia	651,597	1,167,941	1,541,954	1,234,651	4.9	6.0	32.0	-19.9	11.2
Hong Kong (China)	561,993	826,321	1,068,251	1,008,066	4.2	4.9	29.3	-5.6	10.2
Taiwan (Pr. of China)	1,216,814	835,971	1,084,451	850,215	9.1	4.2	29.7	-21.6	-5.8
Indonesia	..	580,253	794,950	847,587		4.1	37.0	6.6	
Thailand	259,927	301,450	388,315	448,247	1.9	2.2	28.8	15.4	9.5
Brunei Darussalam	77,951	..	358,430	382,183	0.6	1.9		6.6	30.3
India	57,697	..	265,943	339,001	0.4	1.7		27.5	34.3
Korea, Republic of	95,914	..	178,258	311,194	0.7	1.5		74.6	21.7
Philippines	90,496	..	312,426	273,277	0.7	1.3		-12.5	20.2
Vietnam	..	..	37,838	168,052		0.8		344.1	
Bangladesh	..	..	39,777	161,486		0.8		306.0	
New Zealand	48,323	82,732	158,887	148,042	0.4	0.7	92.1	-6.8	20.5
Sri Lanka	..	..	33,476	66,045		0.3		97.3	
Pakistan	..	..	34,460	43,166		0.2		25.3	
Other Asia	..	..	237,125	227,240		1.1		-4.2	
From other regions	*2,440,189*	*3,521,288*	*7,543,141*	*6,977,471*	*18.2*	*34.1*	*114.2*	*-7.5*	*19.1*
United Kingdom	983,719	2,378,094	2,911,502	1,844,437	7.4	9.0	22.4	-36.6	11.0
All Middle East	89,732	..	643,833	921,602	0.7	4.5		43.1	47.4
Netherlands	62,357	..	739,921	532,125	0.5	2.6		-28.1	43.0
United States	474,462	560,782	629,814	527,019	3.5	2.6	12.3	-16.3	1.8
Germany	530,736	582,412	582,683	501,160	4.0	2.5	0.0	-14.0	-1.0
Luxembourg	2,902	..	15,911	240,405	0.0	1.2		1410.9	108.8
France	98,130	..	221,130	175,553	0.7	0.9		-20.6	10.2
Switzerland	..	..	213,225	175,509		0.9		-17.7	
Italy	..	..	181,565	158,403		0.8		-12.8	
Canada	59,024	..	134,952	145,620	0.4	0.7		7.9	16.2
Austria	..	..	131,434	131,294		0.6		-0.1	
Sweden	55,453	..	159,755	130,177	0.4	0.6		-18.5	15.3
South Africa	..	..	129,813	112,958		0.6		-13.0	
Denmark	25,593	..	78,166	74,621	0.2	0.4		-4.5	19.5
Norway	16,039	..	56,429	73,910	0.1	0.4		31.0	29.0
Belgium	24,930	..	78,902	66,945	0.2	0.3		-15.2	17.9
Finland	9,144	..	81,656	61,424	0.1	0.3		-24.8	37.4
Commonwealth Indep. States	..	..	48,034	60,041		0.3		25.0	
Spain	..	..	39,502	44,971		0.2		13.8	
Ireland	7,968	..	27,351	41,153	0.1	0.2		50.5	31.5
Other Africa	..	..	33,721	38,538		0.2		14.3	
Other Americas	..	..	71,530	70,667		0.3		-1.2	
Other Western Europe	..	..	5,085	581,357		2.8		11332.8	
Other Europe	..	..	327,227	267,582		1.3		-18.2	
Other World/Not specified	*2,918,319*	*4,200,633*	*386,609*	*327,301*	*21.8*	*1.6*	*-90.8*	*-15.3*	*-30.6*

Source: World Tourism Organization (WTO) ©

(Data as collected by WTO September 2003)

III.2.6 Myanmar South-East Asia

Profile

Myanmar		
	Capital	Yangon
	Area (1000 km²)	677
	Population (2002, million)	42.3
	Gross Domestic Product (GDP) (2002, US$ million)	9,135
	GDP per capita (2002, US$)	175
East Asia and the Pacific	GDP growth (real, %)	
South-East Asia	-> 2001: 10.5; 2002: 5.5; 2003*: 5.1; 2004*: 4.3	

	2000	**2001**	**2002***	**2001/2000**	**2002*/2001**
International Arrivals					
Visitors (1000)	418	478	489	14.4	2.3
Tourists (overnight visitors) (1000)	208	205	217	-1.3	6.0
- per 100 of inhabitants	0	0	1		
Same-day visitors (1000)	209	270	270	29.2	
Cruise passengers (1000)	1	3	2	200.0	-33.3
Tourism accommodation					
Number of rooms	16,157	15,752	..	-2.5	
Nights spent in hotels and similar establishments (1000)					
by non-residents (inbound tourism)	1,444	1,434	1,521	-0.7	6.0
Receipts and Expenditure for International Tourism					
International Tourism Receipts (US$ million)	42	45	..	7.1	
- per Tourist Arrival (US$)	202	220	..	8.6	
- per Visitor Arrival (US$)	100	94	..	-6.3	
- per capita (US$)	1	1	..		
International Fare Receipts (US$ million)	32	25	..	-21.9	
International Tourism Expenditure (US$ million)	25	27	..	8.0	
- per capita (US$)	1	1	..		
International Fare Expenditure (US$ million)	5	5	..		
△ International Tourism Balance (US$ million)	17	18	..		
△ International Fare Balance (US$ million)	27	20	..		

Source: World Tourism Organization (WTO) (Data as collected by WTO September 2003)

See annex for methodological notes and reference of external sources used.

Survey

Contributed by *Ministry of Hotels and Tourism*
www.hotel-tourism.gov.mm ; www.myanmar.com/Ministry/Hotel-Tour ;
www.myanmars.net.mtt (promotional)
www.myanmar.com/Ministry/Hotel_Tour (institutional/corporate)
www.myanmar.com/Ministry/Hotel_Tour (research and data)

Tourism development and outlook

Most significant determinant	Safe and secure access to main tourist sites of Mandalay and Bagan throughout the year, even during the rainy season.
Tourism products	Naga New Year Festival, Kachin Manaw Festival, Saloe Festival. Balloons over Bagan/ Inlay lake and Kachin Manaw Festival. 15 Ecotourism sites. Pilgrimage Tourism. Forum/ National Seminars. Caravan Tours. Mandalay Thingyan.
Access	Yangon International Airport, Mandalay International Airport. MAI, TG (daily) flight to Singapore and Bangkok. Domestic Airlines (daily) Myanmar Airways, Air Mandalay,Yangon Airways. Direct connections to Kumming, Calcutta, Dhaka Kuala Lumpur, Bhutan and Taipei. Phuket - Mandalay (two flights a week). Kumming - Mandalay (four flights a week). Business + Tourist Visa of 28 days (may be extended for another 14 days). Visa granted on arrival for Charter Flights, Cruise Liners and Package Groups.
Generating markets	Arrivals from Asia 57 per cent (Taiwan 10%, Japan 9.5%, China 8%, Thailand 9.8%, etc.). Arrivals from Europe 30 per cent (French 6.5%, Germans 6%, British 4%, Italian 3.6%, etc.).
Other Issues	Potential sites developed are Myitkyina, Putao, Kawthaung, Myeik Archipelago, Ngwe Saung Beach, Mrauk-U.
Outlook 2003	Participation in International Tourism Fairs. Updates on the ASEAN Website, BIMST- EC Website and the Myanmar Website. Kachin Manaw Festival in January 2004. Naga New Year Festival in January 2004. Salone Festival in February 2004. Forecast: 1 million arrivals.
Tourism policy	Only FITs are to exchange US$ 200 for Foreign Exchange Certificates on arrival at Yangon. Tourism Development and Management Committee. Myanmar Tourism Promotion Board. Union of Myanmar Travel Association. Union of Myanmar Hotel Association.

	3rd Phase of Tourism Manpower Training Programme with STB and SHATEC (Singapore). Under the Initiative for ASEAN Integration, Hospitality and Tourism Executive Programme for Myanmar with STB and RITC (Singapore).
Marketing & promotion	Distribution of Visitors' Guide Books, Pamphlets, Brochure, Maps, CD ROMs, Betacams to Myanmar Embassies Abroad, Fairs, Seminars, and Workshops. Regional cooperation within ASEAN, GMS, BIMST-EC and AMTA. AMTA Newsletter. International Fairs (ITB, WTM, PATA, ATF). ASEAN/ Mekong PATA Website. Roadshows. Collaboration with PATA and WTO.

Cultural Tourism (CT)

Specific place for CT in tourism policy: yes.

Main objectives & instruments	Myanmar Hotels and Tourism Law (1993): - To encourage a systematic development of the hotel and tourism industry; - To enable tourists to observe Myanmar's cultural heritage and natural scenic beauty; - To prevent destruction and damage of Myanmar's cultural heritage and natural scenic beauty, due to the hotel and tourism industry; - To contribute to international friendship and tourism industry; - To develop technical knowledge relating to the hotel tourism industry and to open up more employment opportunities; - To provide security for and the satisfaction of tourists.
Main focus of attention supply	Yangon (Shwedagon Pagoda), Bagan, Mandalay, Inlay Lake, Pindaya, Mrauk-U and Kakku.
Main focus of attention demand	France, Germany, Spain and Italy in Europe. Japan, Taiwan, China and Thailand in Asia.

Specific place for CT in marketing & promotion plan: yes.

Main objectives & programmes	Implementation of Sisters Cities (Bagan + Angkor Wat) between Myanmar and Cambodia. Two Countries - One Destination between Myanmar and Thailand. Four Countries - One Destination (Myanmar, Cambodia, Laos and Thailand). Agreement of the Approved Destination Status for Chinese citizens to visit Myanmar.
Special activities undertaken	Taunggyi Tazaungdine Balloon Festival of Lights (November). Thingyan Water Festival and Myanmar New Year (April). Phaung Daw Oo Pagoda Festival and One Leg Rowing Competition (November).

Importance of cultural tourism:

- in total tourism offer	Eighty (80) per cent of the total arrivals (209,315) 2002- 2003.

International Tourism by Origin

Myanmar

International Tourist Arrivals at Frontiers

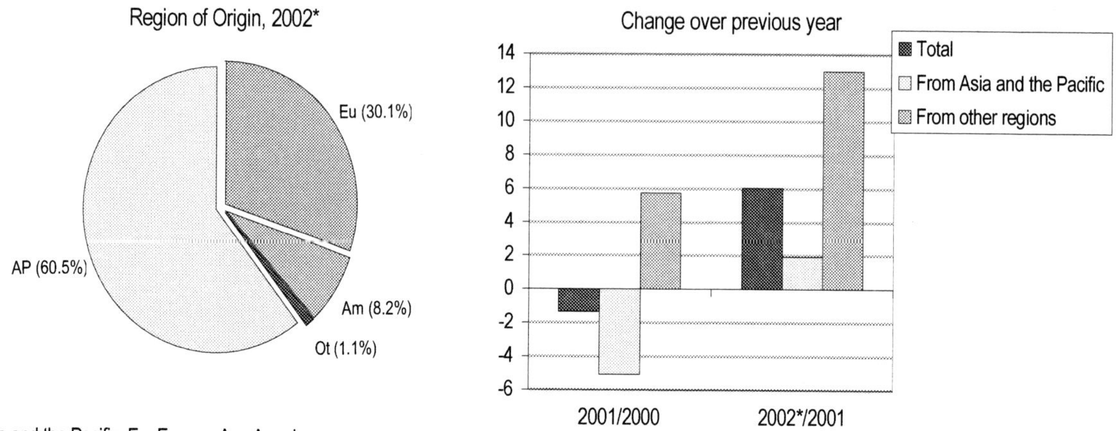

AP: Asia and the Pacific; Eu: Europe; Am: Americas;
Ot: Other;

Source: World Tourism Organization (WTO) ©

Myanmar

Nights of International Tourists in Hotels and Similar Establishments

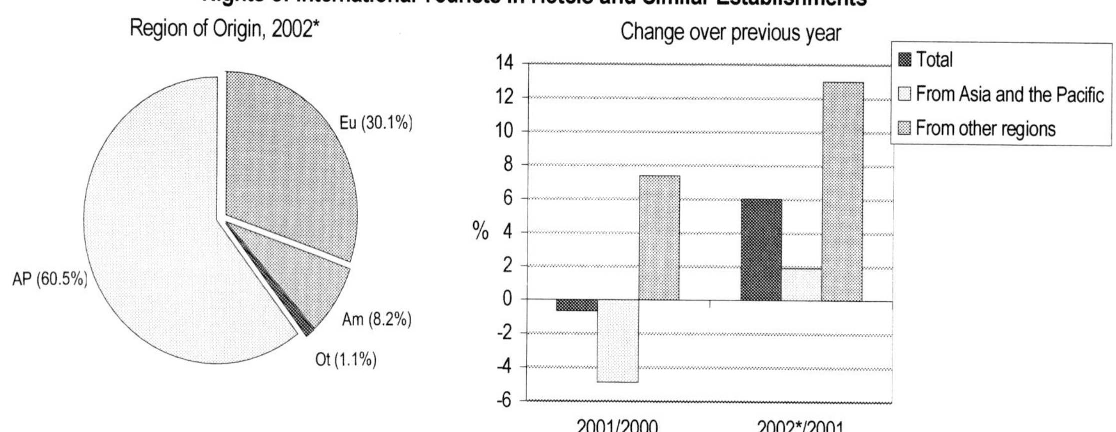

AP: Asia and the Pacific; Eu: Europe; Am: Americas;
Ot: Other;

Source: World Tourism Organization (WTO) ©

Myanmar

International Tourist Arrivals at Frontiers (by nationality)

	1995	2000	2001	2002*	Market share (%) 1995	Market share (%) 2002*	Growth rate (%) 2001/00	Growth rate (%) 2002*/01	Average per year (%) 1995-2002*
Total	**117,000**	**207,665**	**204,862**	**217,212**	**100**	**100**	**-1.3**	**6.0**	**9.2**
From Asia and the Pacific	*66,790*	*135,881*	*128,973*	*131,459*	*57.1*	*60.5*	*-5.1*	*1.9*	*10.2*
Taiwan (Pr. of China)	..	32,098	26,020	22,849		10.5	-18.9	-12.2	
Japan	16,095	21,930	20,118	20,744	13.8	9.6	-8.3	3.1	3.7
China	..	14,336	16,788	17,732		8.2	17.1	5.6	
Thailand	11,659	19,070	17,123	16,936	10.0	7.8	-10.2	-1.1	5.5
Malaysia	..	9,938	11,296	12,532		5.8	13.7	10.9	
Singapore	..	11,645	9,939	11,310		5.2	-14.7	13.8	
Korea, Republic of	..	7,423	7,581	7,890		3.6	2.1	4.1	
India	603	5,605	5,572	5,691	0.5	2.6	-0.6	2.1	37.8
Australia	1,863	4,120	4,442	5,194	1.6	2.4	7.8	16.9	15.8
Bangladesh	..	929	1,074	1,488		0.7	15.6	38.5	
Hong Kong (China)	..	1,742	1,408	1,277		0.6	-19.2	-9.3	
New Zealand	636	596	627	718	0.5	0.3	5.2	14.5	1.7
Pakistan	402	..	..	..	0.3				
Other South Asia	199	..	..	..	0.2				
Other Asia	35,333	6,449	6,985	7,098	30.2	3.3	8.3	1.6	-20.5
From other regions	*42,983*	*71,784*	*75,889*	*85,753*	*36.7*	*39.5*	*5.7*	*13.0*	*10.4*
United States	7,914	12,669	13,524	14,477	6.8	6.7	6.7	7.0	9.0
France	8,218	13,313	12,461	14,108	7.0	6.5	-6.4	13.2	8.0
Germany	4,639	9,920	11,450	12,952	4.0	6.0	15.4	13.1	15.8
United Kingdom	6,727	9,020	8,424	8,620	5.7	4.0	-6.6	2.3	3.6
Italy	4,533	6,852	6,618	7,908	3.9	3.6	-3.4	19.5	8.3
Switzerland	2,609	3,128	3,602	4,695	2.2	2.2	15.2	30.3	8.8
Spain	..	2,478	3,277	3,856		1.8	32.2	17.7	
Austria	..	1,727	2,126	3,616		1.7	23.1	70.1	
Canada	1,189	2,022	2,340	2,476	1.0	1.1	15.7	5.8	11.0
Belgium	..	2,334	2,408	2,364		1.1	3.2	-1.8	
All Middle East	..	1,263	1,416	2,022		0.9	12.1	42.8	
Russian Fed	..	308	434	556		0.3	40.9	28.1	
All Africa	..	304	312	430		0.2	2.6	37.8	
Other Americas	..	621	807	871		0.4	30.0	7.9	
Other Central/Eastern Europe	..	..	1,108	1,521		0.7		37.3	
Other Europe	7,154	5,825	5,582	5,281	6.1	2.4	-4.2	-5.4	-4.2
Other World/Not specified	*7,227*	..	..	..	*6.2*				

Source: World Tourism Organization (WTO) © (Data as collected by WTO September 2003)

Myanmar

Nights of International Tourists in Hotels and Similar Establishments (by nationality)

	1995	2000	2001	2002*	Market share (%) 1995	2002*	Growth rate (%) 2001/00	2002*/01	Average per year (%) 1995-2002*
Total	**813,213**	**1,443,671**	**1,434,034**	**1,520,505**	**100**	**100**	**-0.7**	**6.0**	**9.4**
From Asia and the Pacific	*483,955*	*948,988*	*902,811*	*920,213*	*59.5*	*60.5*	*-4.9*	*1.9*	*9.6*
Taiwan (Pr. of China)	..	224,686	182,140	159,943		10.5	-18.9	-12.2	
Japan	104,617	151,361	140,826	145,208	12.9	9.5	-7.0	3.1	4.8
China	..	100,352	117,516	124,124		8.2	17.1	5.6	
Thailand	75,783	133,490	119,861	118,552	9.3	7.8	-10.2	-1.1	6.6
Malaysia	16,126	69,566	79,072	87,724	2.0	5.8	13.7	10.9	27.4
Singapore	33,150	81,515	69,573	79,170	4.1	5.2	-14.7	13.8	13.2
Korea, Republic of	..	51,961	53,067	55,230		3.6	2.1	4.1	
India	..	39,235	39,004	39,837		2.6	-0.6	2.1	
Australia	12,109	28,840	31,094	36,358	1.5	2.4	7.8	16.9	17.0
Bangladesh	..	6,503	7,518	10,416		0.7	15.6	38.5	
Hong Kong (China)	8,372	12,194	9,856	8,939	1.0	0.6	-19.2	-9.3	0.9
New Zealand	4,134	4,142	4,389	5,026	0.5	0.3	6.0	14.5	2.8
Other Asia	229,664	45,143	48,895	49,686	28.2	3.3	8.3	1.6	-19.6
From other regions	*329,258*	*494,683*	*531,223*	*600,292*	*40.5*	*39.5*	*7.4*	*13.0*	*9.0*
United States	54,441	80,878	94,668	101,339	6.7	6.7	17.1	7.0	9.3
France	53,417	93,191	87,227	98,756	6.6	6.5	-6.4	13.2	9.2
Germany	30,153	69,440	80,150	90,664	3.7	6.0	15.4	13.1	17.0
United Kingdom	43,725	63,140	58,968	60,340	5.4	4.0	-6.6	2.3	4.7
Italy	29,464	47,964	46,326	55,356	3.6	3.6	-3.4	19.5	9.4
Switzerland	16,958	21,896	25,214	32,865	2.1	2.2	15.2	30.3	9.9
Spain	..	17,346	22,939	26,992		1.8	32.2	17.7	
Austria	7,403	12,089	14,882	25,312	0.9	1.7	23.1	70.1	19.2
Canada	7,728	14,154	16,380	17,332	1.0	1.1	15.7	5.8	12.2
Belgium	10,530	16,338	16,856	16,548	1.3	1.1	3.2	-1.8	6.7
All Middle East	18,276	8,841	9,912	14,154	2.2	0.9	12.1	42.8	-3.6
Denmark	5,447	..	..	..	0.7				
Russian Fed	..	2,156	3,038	3,892		0.3	40.9	28.1	
All Africa	..	2,128	2,184	3,010		0.2	2.6	37.8	
Former U.S.S.R.	2,008	..	..	..	0.2				
Sweden	1,007	..	..	..	0.1				
Other Americas	2,200	4,347	5,649	6,097	0.3	0.4	30.0	7.9	15.7
Other Central/Eastern Europe	..	..	7,756	10,668		0.7		37.5	
Other Europe	46,501	40,775	39,074	36,967	5.7	2.4	-4.2	-5.4	-3.2

Source: World Tourism Organization (WTO) ©

(Data as collected by WTO September 2003)

III.2.7 Philippines South-East Asia

Profile

Philippines

East Asia and the Pacific
South-East Asia

Capital	Manila
Year of entry in WTO	1991
Area (1000 km²)	300
Population (2002, million)	83.0
Gross Domestic Product (GDP) (2002, US$ million)	77,932
GDP per capita (2002, US$)	980
GDP growth (real, %)	
'-> 2001: 4.5; 2002: 4.4; 2003*: 4.0; 2004*: 4.0	

	2000	2001	2002*	2001/2000	2002*/2001
International Arrivals					
Tourists (overnight visitors) (1000)	1,992	1,797	1,933	-9.8	7.6
- per 100 of inhabitants	2	2	2		
Cruise passengers (1000)	7	4	..	-42.9	
Tourism accommodation					
Number of rooms	26,876	28,971	..	7.8	
Nights spent in hotels and similar establishments (1000)					
by non-residents (inbound tourism)	13,063	..	..		
Outbound Tourism					
Trips abroad (1000)	1,670	1,787	..	7.0	
- per 100 of inhabitants	2	2	..		
Receipts and Expenditure for International Tourism					
International Tourism Receipts (US$ million)	2,134	1,723	1,741	-19.3	1.0
- per Tourist Arrival (US$)	1,071	959	901	-10.5	-6.1
- per capita (US$)	27	21	21		
International Fare Receipts (US$ million)	243	99	..	-59.3	
International Tourism Expenditure (US$ million)	1,005	1,229	871	22.3	-29.1
- per trip (US$)	602	688	..	14.3	
- per capita (US$)	13	15	10		
International Fare Expenditure (US$ million)	316	335	..	6.0	
△ International Tourism Balance (US$ million)	1,129	494	870		
△ International Fare Balance (US$ million)	-73	-236	..		

Source: World Tourism Organization (WTO) (Data as collected by WTO September 2003)

See annex for methodological notes and reference of external sources used.

Survey

Contributed by *Department of Tourism*
www.tourism.gov.ph ; ww.wowphilippines.com (promotional)
www.tourism.gov.ph ; www.wowphilippines.com (institutional/corporate)
www.tourism.gov.ph ; www.wowphilippines.com (research and data)

Tourism development and outlook

Most significant determinant

The development of a focused and aggressive international marketing campaign for "Visit Philippines Year 2003" resulted in a significant increase in arrivals for the first time in several years. On the whole, the most significant determinants of a state Philippine tourism include: a) the political and economic situation, which resulted in better and more stable peace and order in the country; b) better security measures not only in the domestic and international airports but also in tourist establishments and destinations; and c) travel preference of tourists for the Asia/Pacific region. Visitor arrivals in 2002 grew by 7.6 per cent which can be attributed to the following factors:

- Aggressive marketing and promotions in domestic and international markets;
- Attendance/participation in regional and international tourist-related events; and
- Strong government support for tourism programs.

Tourism products

To come up with a more diverse tourism product mix, the Department of Tourism (DOT) launched culture and nature-based tourism products as well as other special products such as ecotourism, adventure tourism (e.g. surfing, caving, trekking, and adventure races), cultural tourism and health/spa tourism.

Use of positive and unique branding - WOW Philippines, More Than The Usual - significantly increased awareness and product recall in the international market.

New adventure experiences and special sports events introduced the Philippines as a viable destination for the younger and more adventurous traveller, i.e., white-water rafting, surfing, triathlons, spelunking.

Development of new and affordable international tour packages such as the "WOW Packages", and VIPS Travel Package (in collaboration with Singapore) provided a competitive marketing platform for the Philippines.

New promotional materials such as posters, monthly calendar of events, flyers, brochures and maps were effective means of disseminating important information to the markets.

Closer collaboration with provincial, municipal and city governments through regional educational programmess and the production of special collateral materials (posters, brochures, tour packages) resulted in an increase in visitor arrivals in the different regions and provinces.

Access

Positive factors:

- Closer co-ordination with counter-part government agencies in countries such as the United States of America, China, and Japan for more carefully worded advisories;
- There were several air and water transport developments and enhancement of projects initiated by the Department of Transportation and Communications in 2002 which are hoped to complement tourism development initiatives. Among these projects are the following:

- Construction of new airports:
- Sta. Barbara Airport in Iloilo Province (International Standard);
- Laginlingan Airport in Misamis Orientalo;
- Improvement and rehabilitation of selected airports:
- New Bacolod Airport;
- Tacloban Airport;
- Davao Airport;
- Butuan Airport;
- Pagadian Airport;
- Puerto Princesa Airport;
- Cotabato Airport; and
- Dipolog Airport.
- Completion of the following airports, also turned over to local government units:
- Atimonan Feeder Port, Quezon Province;
- Caramoan Feeder Port, Camarines Sur;
- Pasacao Feeder Port, Camarines Sur;
- San Jose Feeder Port, Camarines Sur;
- Tamban Feeder Port, Camarines Sur.

Negative factors:
- Low frequencies or no flights to key cities in Europe and China which limits access to important markets;
- Long process of visa facilitation in new markets such as China and India due to lack of tourism offices and strict visa policies in these areas.

Generating markets

Positive factors:
- Extensive promotions in growth markets such as Korea, Hong Kong SAR, and Singapore compensated the decline in arrivals from top source markets such as the United States of America and Japan.
- The utilization of Filipino Communities in key cities through the Tourism Volunteer 12 Program was a major factor in inviting large numbers of tourists at very minimal costs.
- Growth in special interests markets such as Golf, Student/Education/, Eco-adventure, Shopping, as well as Gender and Age submarkets, i.e., Young Office Ladies, Youth Market, Senior Citizens and Retirees, guided the direction of the development of marketing campaigns (TVCs, tour packages, special attractions/events promotional collaterals).
- The emerging significance of the Chinese market resulted in specialized tourism products for Chinese tourists and closer co-ordination with the Chinese government on issues such as "zero tour fares and shopping scams".
- The sales missions to China significantly increased the appeal of the Philippines as a tourist destination and opened up a major growth market.
- The Philippines was able to win bids to host prestigious international Meetings, Incentives, Conventions and Exhibitions (M.I.C.E.) such as the International Society of Tropical Pediatrics in 2008, the Asian Conference of Pediatric Infectious Diseases in 2006, and the Asia Pacific Hospice Palliative Care Network in 2007.
- As far as an increase in visitor arrivals to the Philippines is concerned, travel decisions of tourists to stick to nearer destinations became a positive factor due to drastic changes in their travelling activities and preferences.

Negative factor:
Sudden and misinformed negative travel advisories periodically affected travel to the Philippines.

Outlook 2003

Philippine tourism is expected to grow significantly this year as a result of its international and domestic campaign. Visitor arrivals in 2002 increased by 7.7 percent after several years of negative growth. For the first time, the country also recorded successive monthly growth over the same period the previous year.

For January 2003, the arrival figure was already up by 13.2 percent from the previous period. A complete calendar of local and international events will occur nationwide during Visit Philippines Year 2003. The program is designed to become a template for tourism campaigns in succeeding years. Furthermore, the media mileage and networking opportunities gained from the 2002 campaign is expected to contribute positively to continuing promotional efforts.

The occurrence of the United States of America/Iraq war somehow predicted the fate of tourism and all other industries in the world this early part of the year. It is expected to have a remarkably negative effect on tourism, the impact of which will be on the security and safety of the travel market. The Middle East countries serve as stopover routes for most of the European market and outbound Asian travellers, thus affecting people moving in and out of South-East Asian destinations. Countries in the East Asia and the Pacific Region including the Philippines will have to double their efforts in rebuilding their individual images as the safest and the most risk-free destination. As the war progresses, other obvious effects such as the currency crisis, travel advisories, low morale of the people, possible shortage of oil supply, price increases, etc. will refrain people from going to places, thus, cancellations or scarcity of bookings and reservations can cause a lull in business. This could almost dim hopes for better days to come, but this will not occur in the near future.

The impending effect of external conflict on the country's tourism development is as much a concern of the government as that of the internal conflict in Southern Philippines. Movements of people and products from major gateways of the country to Mindanao are restrained due to safety hazards posed by terrorist activities. Delivery of services, infrastructure projects and implementation of national programmes geared towards recovery of the local economy are hampered and suspended. It is within these realities that the DOT should strategize its response to position itself as one of the government's major driving forces in getting the country back on the road to economic recovery and development.

Activities in major generating markets, promotional campaigns, upcoming special events, etc., are the following:

- In celebration of the "Visit Philippines Year 2003" and in line with the continuing promotional and marketing efforts of the DOT WOW Philippines Campaign, various activities have been prepared for the major and second priority international markets.
- The 365-day Celebration at the Intramuros for 2003 showcases the various indigenous presentations, specialties and products of each province and/or region at the Intramuros Clamshell. A specific month has been scheduled for every market, such as February for the Japanese market, May for the Korean market, June for the Spanish market, etc. Also various activities are simultaneously being performed on the streets of Intramuros for the public to see and enjoy, e.g., painting and tattoo designs to choose, musicians performing, and clowns with comedy acts, etc.
- Aside from vigorous media and travel trade invitations, the DOT is undertaking multimedia promotions, will conduct sales missions and road show presentations and participate in major travel trade and consumer fairs, such as:
- Sales missions/Road shows to Korea in April, Australia in May, North America (including Guam and Hawaii) and Japan (date to be announced later);
- Promotion of the Volunteer 12 Program, wherein the Filipino overseas workers and Filipino communities abroad take major part in promoting the Philippines;

- The Visit Philippines 2003 Project and the Visit ASEAN 2003 Program;
- Attendance and participation in major travel fairs and exhibitions such as the ASEAN Tourism Forum (ATF), China 1st Solo Exhibition, Marine Diving Fair, the Asia Dive Expo (ADEX), the National Association of Travel Agents Singapore (NATAS), MATTA International Travel Fair (MATTA) and the World Travel Mart (WTM), etc.

Tourism policy

The Philippine government has highlighted tourism as a major engine for growth. Budget allocation was increased for 2003 and all government agencies have been encouraged to support tourism promotions efforts.

A domestic tourism advocacy program was also introduced from the grass-roots to the corporate level to inculcate a "Culture of Tourism". The program was designed to emphasize the importance of tourism in generating jobs and revenues. Local government units put in place systems for tourist assistance and encouraged the community to provide a favourable atmosphere for tourists.

The preparation of Area-Specific Master Plans for various destinations in the country such as Bohol, Pinatubo, Guimaras, Marinduque and Camiguin was one of the major tasks undertaken to improve the tourism sector. Completion of the said plans will set the design for tourism development in the above areas for the improvement of life of the local communities without compromising the environment.

The DOT and the Department of Environment and Natural Resources (DENR) also pursued the finalization of the National Ecotourism Strategy (NES) which provides an integrated management plan to warrant a comprehensive direction for the future of ecotourism in the country. The NES served as a guideline in the identification of banner sites from the key ecotourism sites in order to set an image and to position the Philippines in the international and domestic markets.

Marketing & promotion

The launching of DOT's promotional campaign tagged as "WOW Philippines" set out the theme and direction for the country's tourism marketing programs and promotional strategies. It emphasizes the country's diverse color and riches from natural assets, to people and wares, to festivals and celebrations, daring the rest of the world to experience the Philippines' Wealth of Wonders.

A majority of the tourism budget was earmarked for international tourism promotions. A major campaign to develop and release media advertisements and marketing collaterals was undertaken in important marketing channels such as print and television.

New designs for posters, flyers, and brochures were made to replace the old promotional collaterals.

The conduct of major international Sales Missions composed of government and private sector (airlines, travel agents, tour operators, hotels, resorts) executives provide the means to touch base with foreign government officials, travel trade executives, international media, consumers and Filipino communities.

Although the Philippines is not able to compete with its neighboring ASEAN countries, especially with Thailand, Malaysia and Singapore in terms of the tourism promotional budget, the DOT is able to advertise on CNN/BBC, featuring the WOW Philippines/More Than The Usual campaign.

The currently operating websites, <www.wowphilippines.gov.ph> and <www.thephilippinesnow.gov.ph> are available for those who would like to inquire about the Philippines as a tourism destination, or for research purposes.

The DOT's International Marketing Plan, which has identified Japan, Korea, Taiwan, and China as major sources of tourist arrivals, will focus its marketing and promotional efforts in said markets. Other nearer (short-haul) markets will be considered such as Australia, notwithstanding the importance of the USA market, which has been the overall number one source of visitor arrivals to the Philippines.

Cultural Tourism (CT)

Specific place for CT in tourism policy: yes.

Main objectives & instruments

The Visit Philippines Year 2003 (VPY 2003) celebrations are centered on the "Best of the Regions" program in Intramuros, a historic Spanish enclave transformed into a showcase of the country's best music, dances, arts and crafts, culture and festivals. Already the "Best of the Regions" is emerging as a popular destination for domestic and international tourists.

The Philippines is also the site for numerous festivals and events which depict the different indigenous cultures. The Department of Tourism (DOT) has intensified promotions of festivals and encouraged the development of new regional or provincial events. Among these are religious and cultural parades, exhibits and displays, film showings, culinary offerings, and musical/dance performances.

The month of February is also designated as National Arts Month, which features the works of renowned and emerging local artists. The DOT also includes the importance of cultural endowments such as ancient art and artifacts, native jewelry and clothing, and customs and traditions as part of educational programs for the local tourism industry.

The Philippine Tourism Master Plan (TMP) completed in 1991 serves as a blueprint for tourism development in the Philippines until 2010. Among its specific objectives is for tourism to contribute to social cohesion and cultural preservation.Though numerous cultural tourism projects have been implemented in the past, the DOT saw a need to come up with an organized programme for cultural tourism development identifying interventions at various levels. The Cultural Tourism Programme was considered to lay down the foundation for a sustainable and concerted development of culture and heritage-related projects and programmes in the Philippines.The cultural Tourism Programme in the Philippines was initiated by the DOT in coordination with the National Commission for Culture and the Arts (NCCA), the National Museum (NM), the National Historical Institute (NHI), and the Philippine Convention and Visitors Corporation (PCVC) in 2000. The Philippine Tourism Authority (PTA) became part of the program in 2001. In efforts to involve the private sector in this undertaking, Viajes Filipinas, a leading cultural tour operator was invited to be part of the team in 2002. The said agencies comprise the Cultural Tourism Technical Working Group. A Cultural Tourism Inter-agency Memorandum of Understanding was signed by the heads of the agencies last June 2002.

Main focus of attention supply

The focus is more on destinations. The DOT has sought to promote existing events and develop new destinations.

The following areas are being promoted by the DOT:
- UNESCO World Heritage Sites;
- Cultural/historical towns and villages such Intramuros History Town Philippines;
- Festivals and local traditions;
- Selected Cultural Communities and Traditional Arts;
- Cultural shows.

Main focus of attention demand	Our focus is on major markets such as China, Korea, Japan, Taiwan and the United States of America. Important market segments are second- and third-generation Filipino expatriates, family groups, business travellers, and FITs.

Specific place for CT in marketing & promotion plan: yes.

Main objectives & programmes

The objective of cultural tourism is to promote the Philippine's rich cultural heritage through a variety of events such as festivals and special events. The DOT has been extensively promoting world-renowned local festivals as well as a variety of minor festivals through promotional collaterals and tour packages.

Cultural tourism has always been part and parcel of tourism promotion of the DOT.

Activities related to cultural tourism such as festivals, travel marts and other events are being marketed and promoted by the DOT throughout the country in coordination with the local government units, various cultural agencies, and the private sector.

The DOT is also developing a cultural tourism handbook to feature information on the country's cultural and historical assets and destinations. This will assist in further promoting cultural tourism.

Cultural tourism has a specific place in the DOT's international marketing and promotion plan. The Visit Philippines 2003's main feature includes monthly regional and provincial activities that highlight the captivating and unique cultural values and traditions of each province.As earlier mentioned, Intramuros, the focal point of the 365-day Visit Philippines Year in Manila, likiewise serves as a venue in emphasizing the value of the Philippine culture, both to domestic and international tourists.

Special activities undertaken

The DOT extensively promotes festivals and other cultural events through the Monthly Calendar of Events, media advertisements and press releases, and special event launches. In particular, the "Best of the Regions" is a venue to promote scheduled major festivals and special events. Festival tour packages have also been developed for the international market in cooperation with local tour operators.

The Monthly Calendar of Events, inclusive of the specific Destination's Theme in cognizance of a particular destination's activity is incorporated in the WOW Philippines Tour Packages. The tourist is not only given the opportunity to travel and see the Philippines, but also to participate in the Events, Festivals, and Fiestas in specific destinations. Likewise, under the WOW Philippines campaign, the DOT-Regional Offices are actively making campaigns and promotional efforts in close coordination with the DOT-Main Office, other concerned government agencies and the private sector in their respective areas of jurisdiction. The DOT-Overseas Offices on the other hand, are carrying out aggressive marketing of the Philippine Culture. One of the most effective marketing efforts is its endorsement to the Head Office, of the thoroughly screened groups of foreign media who would want to conduct familiarization tours to the Philippines and cover the events, festivals and fiestas.

Importance of cultural tourism:

- in total tourism offer

Thirty percent of tourist arrivals.

At the moment, cultural tourism is largely engaged in by students through their annual field trips and domestic tourists who flock to the various festivals in the different regions of the country.

Cultural destinations and activities are part and parcel of the packages being sold to the foreign markets. While cultural tourism is most important in our country, the DOT is not in a position to estimate its current size.

International Tourism by Origin

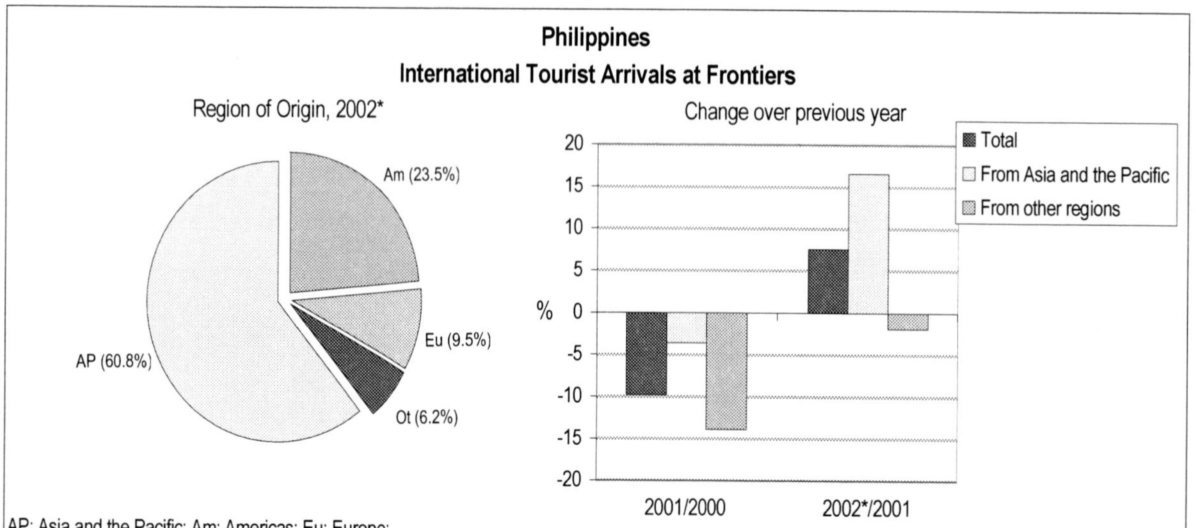

AP: Asia and the Pacific; Am: Americas; Eu: Europe;
Ot: Other;

Source: World Tourism Organization (WTO) ©

Philippines

International Tourist Arrivals at Frontiers (by residence)

	1995	2000	2001	2002*	Market share (%) 1995	Market share (%) 2002*	Growth rate (%) 2001/00	Growth rate (%) 2002*/01	Average per year (%) 1995-2002*
Total	**1,760,063**	**1,992,169**	**1,796,893**	**1,932,677**	**100**	**100**	**-9.8**	**7.6**	**1.3**
From Asia and the Pacific	*951,115*	*1,046,059*	*1,008,134*	*1,175,261*	*54.0*	*60.8*	*-3.6*	*16.6*	*3.1*
Japan	323,199	390,517	343,840	341,867	18.4	17.7	-12.0	-0.6	0.8
Korea, Republic of	121,559	174,966	207,957	288,468	6.9	14.9	18.9	38.7	13.1
Hong Kong (China)	107,151	146,858	134,408	155,964	6.1	8.1	-8.5	16.0	5.5
Taiwan (Pr. of China)	190,423	75,722	85,231	103,024	10.8	5.3	12.6	20.9	-8.4
Australia	75,898	75,706	68,541	70,735	4.3	3.7	-9.5	3.2	-1.0
Singapore	27,327	50,276	44,155	57,662	1.6	3.0	-12.2	30.6	11.3
Malaysia	34,863	42,067	30,498	31,735	2.0	1.6	-27.5	4.1	-1.3
China	8,606	14,724	18,937	27,803	0.5	1.4	28.6	46.8	18.2
Guam	457	741	2,746	25,013	0.0	1.3	270.6	810.9	77.1
Thailand	14,185	15,652	15,063	18,817	0.8	1.0	-3.8	24.9	4.1
Indonesia	12,723	16,272	16,307	15,352	0.7	0.8	0.2	-5.9	2.7
India	12,440	18,570	15,391	14,826	0.7	0.8	-17.1	-3.7	2.5
New Zealand	7,822	9,078	7,832	6,569	0.4	0.3	-13.7	-16.1	-2.5
Vietnam	1,160	3,814	4,198	4,577	0.1	0.2	10.1	9.0	21.7
Brunei Darussalam	2,607	1,827	1,786	2,136	0.1	0.1	-2.2	19.6	-2.8
Myanmar	..	2,314	2,394	1,982		0.1	3.5	-17.2	
Pakistan	3,918	1,167	1,998	1,591	0.2	0.1	71.2	-20.4	-12.1
Bangladesh	1,715	1,037	1,537	1,457	0.1	0.1	48.2	-5.2	-2.3
Other intraregional	5,062	4,751	5,315	5,683	0.3	0.3	11.9	6.9	1.7
From other regions	*642,317*	*778,960*	*670,581*	*657,542*	*36.5*	*34.0*	*-13.9*	*-1.9*	*0.3*
United States	342,189	445,043	392,099	395,323	19.4	20.5	-11.9	0.8	2.1
Canada	45,725	61,004	54,942	54,563	2.6	2.8	-9.9	-0.7	2.6
United Kingdom	70,591	74,507	60,147	48,478	4.0	2.5	-19.3	-19.4	-5.2
Germany	50,766	51,131	40,605	39,103	2.9	2.0	-20.6	-3.7	-3.7
France	18,044	19,179	13,918	12,498	1.0	0.6	-27.4	-10.2	-5.1
Switzerland	14,727	14,710	12,268	12,145	0.8	0.6	-16.6	-1.0	-2.7
Netherlands	12,209	16,150	13,540	12,015	0.7	0.6	-16.2	-11.3	-0.2
Saudi Arabia	12,116	10,444	10,409	11,341	0.7	0.6	-0.3	9.0	-0.9
Italy	12,745	12,454	8,994	8,483	0.7	0.4	-27.8	-5.7	-5.6
Denmark	5,445	10,239	7,902	7,164	0.3	0.4	-22.8	-9.3	4.0
Norway	5,459	7,726	6,650	7,025	0.3	0.4	-13.9	5.6	3.7
Sweden	8,178	9,197	7,330	6,612	0.5	0.3	-20.3	-9.8	-3.0
Spain	5,307	7,486	5,624	6,349	0.3	0.3	-24.9	12.9	2.6
Austria	7,253	7,761	6,548	6,281	0.4	0.3	-15.6	-4.1	-2.0
Belgium	5,289	6,536	5,450	5,512	0.3	0.3	-16.6	1.1	0.6
Commonwealth Indep. States	..	2,487	2,773	3,562		0.2	11.5	28.5	
Untd Arab Emirates	1,066	1,568	2,160	3,460	0.1	0.2	37.8	60.2	18.3
Former U.S.S.R.	3,175	..	..	..	0.2				
Israel	2,558	2,808	2,470	2,062	0.1	0.1	-12.0	-16.5	-3.0
Ireland	2,342	2,678	2,323	1,864	0.1	0.1	-13.3	-19.8	-3.2
Finland	2,345	2,955	2,016	1,597	0.1	0.1	-31.8	-20.8	-5.3
Kuwait	1,567	1,007	1,164	1,469	0.1	0.1	15.6	26.2	-0.9
Other interregional	13,221	11,890	11,249	10,636	0.8	0.6	-5.4	-5.4	-3.1
Nationals residing abroad	*149,903*	*150,386*	*98,831*	*83,754*	*8.5*	*4.3*	*-34.3*	*-15.3*	*-8.0*
Other World/Not specified	*16,728*	*16,764*	*19,347*	*16,120*	*1.0*	*0.8*	*15.4*	*-16.7*	*-0.5*

Source: World Tourism Organization (WTO) © (Data as collected by WTO September 2003)

III.2.8 Singapore South-East Asia

Profile

Singapore

East Asia and the Pacific
South-East Asia

Capital	Singapore
Area (10 km²)	62
Population (2002, million)	4.5
Gross Domestic Product (GDP) (2002, US$ million)	86,969
GDP per capita (2002, US$)	20,887
GDP growth (real, %)	

-> 2001: -2.4; 2002: 2.2; 2003*: 0.5; 2004*: 4.2

	2000	2001	2002*	2001/2000	2002*/2001
International Arrivals					
Visitors (1000)	7,691	7,522	7,567	-2.2	0.6
Tourists (overnight visitors) (1000)	6,917	6,726	6,996	-2.8	4.0
- per 100 of inhabitants	167	156	157		
Same-day visitors (1000)	774	796	571	2.8	-28.3
Tourism accommodation					
Number of rooms	35,625	35,674	35,800	0.1	0.4
Outbound Tourism					
Trips abroad (1000)	4,444	4,363	4,399	-1.8	0.8
- per 100 of inhabitants	107	101	99		
Receipts and Expenditure for International Tourism					
International Tourism Receipts (US$ million)	6,018	5,081	4,932	-15.6	-2.9
- per Tourist Arrival (US$)	870	755	705	-13.2	-6.7
- per Visitor Arrival (US$)	782	675	652	-13.7	-3.5
- per capita (US$)	1,450	1,182	1,108		
International Tourism Expenditure (US$ million)	4,970	4,647	5,213	-6.5	12.2
- per trip (US$)	1,118	1,065	1,185	-4.8	11.3
- per capita (US$)	1,197	1,081	1,171		
△ International Tourism Balance (US$ million)	1,048	434	-281		

Source: World Tourism Organization (WTO) (Data as collected by WTO September 2003)

See annex for methodological notes and reference of external sources used.

Survey

Contributed by *Singapore Tourism Board*
www.visitsingapore.com
http://www.meet-in-singapore.com.sg/secb/homepage/cgi-bin/main.pl (promotional)
www.stb.com.sg (institutional/corporate)
www.cybrary.com.sg (research and data)

Tourism development and outlook

Most significant determinant

Despite the Bali bombings in October 2002, visitor arrivals for the month registered a double-digit growth of 12 per cent with all major markets, apart from Australia, recording a positive growth in visitor arrivals.

Tourism products

Cultural events (e.g. Hari Raya Lightup, Chingay etc.), the Arts (e.g. Singapore Arts Festival), Sports (e.g. Caltex Masters) and Fashion and Food events.

Generating markets

For 2002, visitor arrivals grew 0.6 per cent to reach 7,566,237. China rose from the 5th to 3rd position, overtaking Malaysia and Australia while India rose from the 9th to 7th position, overtaking the United States of America and South Korea.

Outlook 2003

The current forecast for Visitor Arrivals this year has to be revised due to the unexpected SARs situation in the region of the ASEAN countries.

Tourism policy

One of the major developments to stimulate tourism development recently is a realignment of the Singapore Tourism Board (STB) and management directions to reflect its full functional footprint as a national development agency. Management policy and resources are now geared towards an emphasis on increasing tourism's contribution to the economy. In the past, tourism performance was measured by the number of visitor arrivals. To better reflect the new emphasis, the key tourism performance indicator will now be the total tourism receipts generated, and Singapore's market share of total Asia-Pacific tourism receipts.

To help us market better to our visitors, the organisation has been realigned into strategic tourism business units to reflect the main purposes of visit. The intention is to fully develop these different purpose of visits to enhance visitor experience in Singapore. With tourism being a multi-dimensional industry, there will be units looking into shared tourism clusters and inter-agency collaboration to facilitate overall tourism sector development and to focus on improving service quality.

Marketing & promotion

In the area of marketing and promotions, the new strategic thrust is to focus on Asian markets.Traditional markets such as Indonesia and Malaysia will be given a renewed focus, while emerging markets like China and India will be aggressively tapped on. More resources will be redeployed to these markets, and plans are underway to establish more presence in these markets through the setting up of more regional offices. In addition to the shift in geographic focus, STB will also be creating new market segments such as health and education services, through brand-building initiatives and aggressive information-channel development.

Cultural Tourism (CT)

Specific place for CT in tourism policy: yes.

Main objectives & instruments	As part of our STB's corporate restructure exercise, specific resources are now been allocated and teams formed to oversee the development and marketing of the different cultural and heritage experiences that Singapore has to offer. These experiences reflect the diversity of Singapore's unique and multi-faceted social fabric: Chinese, Indian, Malay/Arab, Colonial and Peranakan.
Main focus of attention supply	Product development: to facilitate the development of new projects e.g., the Malay Heritage Centre, the Peranakan showcase, the Little India Interpretative Centre, World War II sites and heritage trails.
Main focus of attention demand	Positioning Singapore as the epicentre of discovery and lifestyle escapism where one of the key themes is Cultural and Heritage pursuits (Chinese, Malay, Indian, Arab, Peranakan and Colonial). The unique blend of a progressive cosmopolitan/modern city state with its diverse and vibrant cultural background makes Singapore a unique destination.

Specific place for CT in marketing & promotion plan: yes.

Main objectives & programmes	It is articulated in the brochures that are produced as well as an essential component in the itinerary of any media and agents familiarisation trips to Singapore. The marketing of key cultural events also forms an integral role in our advertising and promotion plans.
Special activities undertaken	Various festivals that the STB supports include: - Chinese New Year Light Up; - Chinese New Year River Hong Bao (Festival Village by the River); - Deepavali Light Up; - Hari Raya Light Up; - Heritage Festival; - Mid-Autumn Festival; - Dragon Boat Festival; - Dumpling Festival.

International Tourism by Origin

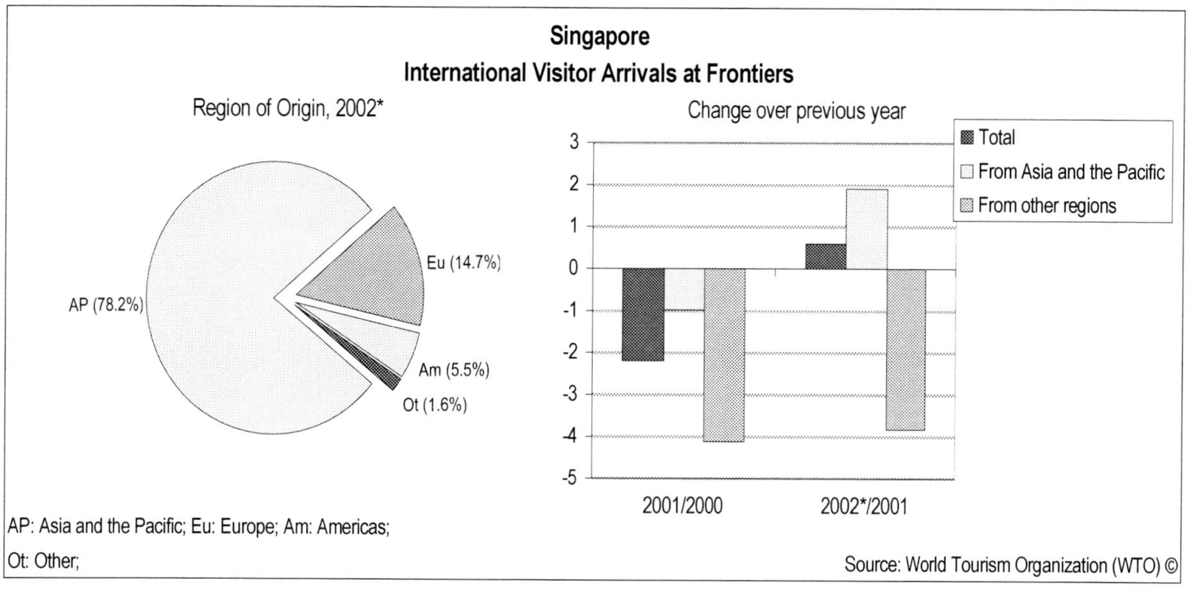

Singapore

International Visitor Arrivals at Frontiers (by residence)

	1995	2000	2001	2002*	Market share (%) 1995	2002*	Growth rate (%) 2001/00	2002*/01	Average per year (%) 1995-2002*
Total	**7,136,538**	**7,691,399**	**7,522,163**	**7,567,039**	**100**	**100**	**-2.2**	**0.6**	**0.8**
From Asia and the Pacific	*5,601,760*	*5,863,611*	*5,806,123*	*5,916,417*	*78.5*	*78.2*	*-1.0*	*1.9*	*0.8*
Indonesia	1,050,064	1,313,316	1,364,380	1,392,999	14.7	18.4	3.9	2.1	4.1
Japan	1,178,906	929,895	755,766	723,422	16.5	9.6	-18.7	-4.3	-6.7
China	201,953	434,335	497,398	670,093	2.8	8.9	14.5	34.7	18.7
Malaysia	681,138	564,750	578,719	548,653	9.5	7.3	2.5	-5.2	-3.0
Australia	346,763	510,347	550,681	538,402	4.9	7.1	7.9	-2.2	6.5
India	188,494	346,356	339,813	375,658	2.6	5.0	-1.9	10.5	10.4
Korea, Republic of	350,975	354,353	359,083	371,050	4.9	4.9	1.3	3.3	0.8
Hong Kong (China)	279,791	285,975	276,157	265,970	3.9	3.5	-3.4	-3.7	-0.7
Thailand	257,110	246,750	260,958	263,864	3.6	3.5	5.8	1.1	0.4
Taiwan (Pr. of China)	563,287	290,904	222,087	209,317	7.9	2.8	-23.7	-5.7	-13.2
Philippines	124,160	181,032	190,630	195,561	1.7	2.6	5.3	2.6	6.7
New Zealand	66,197	94,274	94,283	94,115	0.9	1.2	0.0	-0.2	5.2
Brunei Darussalam	59,279	57,913	62,264	60,052	0.8	0.8	7.5	-3.6	0.2
Sri Lanka	48,787	63,170	56,248	54,690	0.7	0.7	-11.0	-2.8	1.6
Vietnam	17,991	31,837	34,633	40,651	0.3	0.5	8.8	17.4	12.4
Bangladesh	45,092	38,646	42,415	27,551	0.6	0.4	9.8	-35.0	-6.8
Myanmar	32,864	22,091	21,675	22,339	0.5	0.3	-1.9	3.1	-5.4
Nepal	16,923	12,674	14,780	13,202	0.2	0.2	16.6	-10.7	-3.5
Pakistan	51,059	42,495	40,842	10,569	0.7	0.1	-3.9	-74.1	-20.1
Other intraregional	40,927	42,498	43,311	38,259	0.6	0.5	1.9	-11.7	-1.0
From other regions	*1,534,438*	*1,784,133*	*1,710,653*	*1,645,219*	*21.5*	*21.7*	*-4.1*	*-3.8*	*1.0*
United Kingdom	288,670	444,976	460,018	458,522	4.0	6.1	3.4	-0.3	6.8
United States	345,512	385,585	343,805	327,646	4.8	4.3	-10.8	-4.7	-0.8
Germany	190,230	169,408	166,981	157,507	2.7	2.1	-1.4	-5.7	-2.7
France	74,631	74,773	71,456	72,152	1.0	1.0	-4.4	1.0	-0.5
Netherlands	70,588	77,326	74,989	71,651	1.0	0.9	-3.0	-4.5	0.2
Canada	61,869	71,393	69,273	67,969	0.9	0.9	-3.0	-1.9	1.4
Switzerland	54,290	48,323	46,519	45,233	0.8	0.6	-3.7	-2.8	-2.6
Italy	46,945	42,230	35,739	36,737	0.7	0.5	-15.4	2.8	-3.4
Sweden	34,554	42,415	38,439	36,411	0.5	0.5	-9.4	-5.3	0.8
South Africa	51,404	43,119	35,558	30,524	0.7	0.4	-17.5	-14.2	-7.2
Denmark	25,187	25,243	25,431	25,706	0.4	0.3	0.7	1.1	0.3
Ireland	8,242	20,330	21,763	23,202	0.1	0.3	7.0	6.6	15.9
Commonwealth Indep. States	24,125	21,383	22,227	23,169	0.3	0.3	3.9	4.2	-0.6
Norway	20,537	23,914	23,138	22,820	0.3	0.3	-3.2	-1.4	1.5
Untd Arab Emirates	16,508	21,017	21,619	20,784	0.2	0.3	2.9	-3.9	3.3
Belgium	17,556	22,436	21,895	20,357	0.2	0.3	-2.4	-7.0	2.1
Spain	15,618	15,117	15,268	17,324	0.2	0.2	1.0	13.5	1.5
Austria	21,613	15,979	14,051	14,645	0.3	0.2	-12.1	4.2	-5.4
Mauritius	12,325	21,141	17,292	13,927	0.2	0.2	-18.2	-19.5	1.8
Greece	14,462	13,170	11,319	12,801	0.2	0.2	-14.1	13.1	-1.7
Turkey	11,876	14,422	10,418	12,183	0.2	0.2	-27.8	16.9	0.4
Finland	13,182	18,171	14,123	11,317	0.2	0.1	-22.3	-19.9	-2.2
Other interregional	114,514	152,262	149,332	122,632	1.6	1.6	-1.9	-17.9	1.0
Other World/Not specified	*340*	*43,655*	*5,387*	*5,403*	*0.0*	*0.1*	*-87.7*	*0.3*	*48.5*

Source: World Tourism Organization (WTO) © (Data as collected by WTO September 2003)

III.2.9 Thailand — South-East Asia

Profile

Thailand

Capital	Bangkok
Year of entry in WTO	1996
Area (1000 km²)	513
Population (2002, million)	63.6
Gross Domestic Product (GDP) (2002, US$ million)	126,473
GDP per capita (2002, US$)	1,990
GDP growth (real, %)	
'-> 2001: 1.9; 2002: 5.3; 2003*: 5.0; 2004*: 5.1	

East Asia and the Pacific
South-East Asia

	2000	2001	2002*	2001/2000	2002*/2001
International Arrivals					
Visitors (1000)	10,096	10,751	..	6.5	
Tourists (overnight visitors) (1000)	9,579	10,133	10,873	5.8	7.3
- per 100 of inhabitants	15	16	17		
Same-day visitors (1000)	517	618	..	19.5	
Tourism accommodation					
Number of rooms	318,812	320,565	..	0.5	
Nights spent in hotels and similar establishments (1000)	171,196	183,389		7.1	
by non-residents (inbound tourism)	73,855	79,796	..	8.0	
by residents (domestic tourism)	97,341	103,593	..	6.4	
Outbound Tourism					
Trips abroad (1000)	1,946	2,044	..	5.0	
- per 100 of inhabitants	3	3	..		
Receipts and Expenditure for International Tourism					
International Tourism Receipts (US$ million)	7,489	7,077	7,902	-5.5	11.7
- per Tourist Arrival (US$)	782	698	727	-10.7	4.1
- per Visitor Arrival (US$)	742	658	..	-11.3	
- per capita (US$)	120	112	124		
International Fare Receipts (US$ million)	2,447	2,306	2,491	-5.8	8.0
International Tourism Expenditure (US$ million)	2,775	2,923	3,303	5.3	13.0
- per trip (US$)	1,426	1,430	..	0.3	
- per capita (US$)	45	46	52		
International Fare Expenditure (US$ million)	446	412	583	-7.6	41.5
△ International Tourism Balance (US$ million)	4,714	4,154	4,599		
△ International Fare Balance (US$ million)	2,001	1,894	1,908		

Source: World Tourism Organization (WTO) (Data as collected by WTO September 2003)

See annex for methodological notes and reference of external sources used.

Survey

Contributed by *Tourism Authority of Thailand*
www.tourismthailand.org / www.tat.or.th (promotional)
www.tourismthailand.org / www.tat.or.th (institutional/corporate)
www.tourismthailand.org / www.tat.or.th (research and data)

Tourism development and outlook

Most significant determinant	Safety, economy and promotion.
Tourism products	Positive factors: - Price level; - Varieties of tourism products.
Access	Positive factors: - International Airport, - Ports (Land, Sea). Negative factor: Lack of marine transport, sea ports, marina.
Generating markets	All markets.
Other Issues	Standard services and compatible manposers in the industry.
Outlook 2003	Long stay / Health and Spa. MICE
Tourism policy	Tourism Master Plans. Human Resource. Development Public – private partnership. SMEs.
Marketing & promotion	All as indicated in the left box as our office has been substantively focusing on marketing.

Cultural Tourism (CT)

Specific place for CT in tourism policy: no.

Specific place for CT in marketing & promotion plan: no.

International Tourism by Origin

Thailand

International Tourist Arrivals at Frontiers

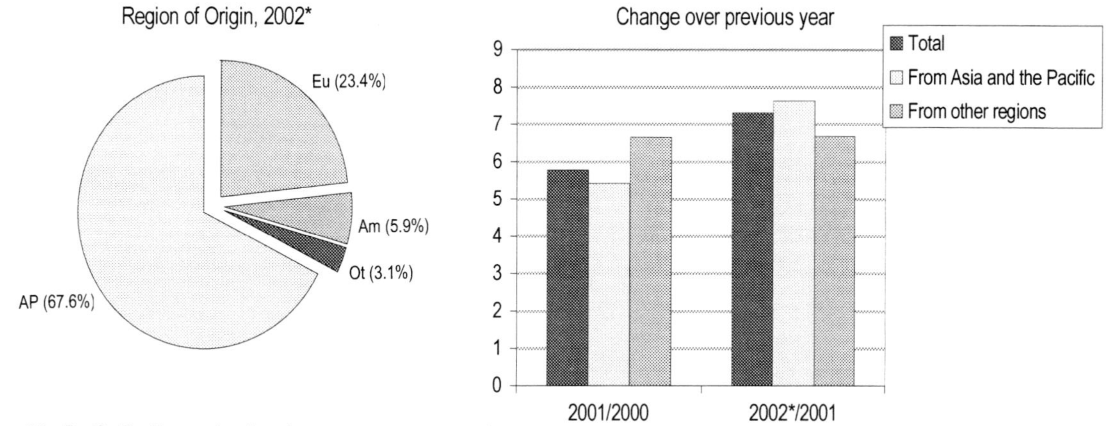

AP: Asia and the Pacific; Eu: Europe; Am: Americas;
Ot: Other;

Source: World Tourism Organization (WTO) ©

Thailand

Nights of International Tourists in Hotels and Similar Establishments

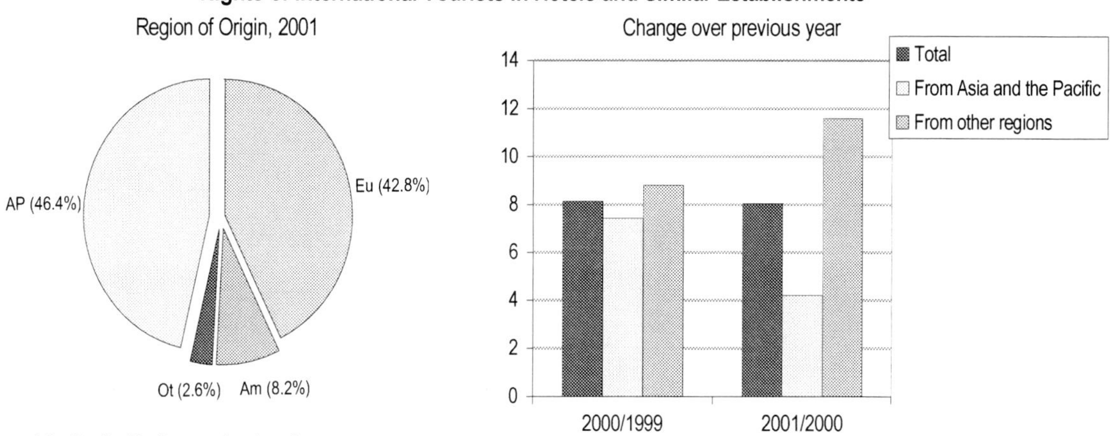

AP: Asia and the Pacific; Eu: Europe; Am: Americas;
Ot: Other;

Source: World Tourism Organization (WTO) ©

Thailand

International Tourist Arrivals at Frontiers (by residence)

	1995	2000	2001	2002*	Market share (%) 1995	Market share (%) 2002*	Growth rate (%) 2001/00	Growth rate (%) 2002*/01	Average per year (%) 1995-2002*
Total	**6,951,566**	**9,578,826**	**10,132,509**	**10,872,976**	**100**	**100**	**5.8**	**7.3**	**6.6**
From Asia and the Pacific	*4,857,239*	*6,473,748*	*6,825,038*	*7,345,792*	*69.9*	*67.6*	*5.4*	*7.6*	*6.1*
Malaysia	1,077,005	1,054,469	1,159,630	1,296,109	15.5	11.9	10.0	11.8	2.7
Japan	814,706	1,197,931	1,168,548	1,222,270	11.7	11.2	-2.5	4.6	6.0
China	375,564	704,080	694,886	763,139	5.4	7.0	-1.3	9.8	10.7
Korea, Republic of	456,228	447,798	552,977	716,778	6.6	6.6	23.5	29.6	6.7
Singapore	430,824	655,767	664,980	683,296	6.2	6.3	1.4	2.8	6.8
Taiwan (Pr. of China)	492,189	707,305	724,769	673,652	7.1	6.2	2.5	-7.1	4.6
Hong Kong (China)	346,254	487,151	523,465	526,138	5.0	4.8	7.5	0.5	6.2
Australia	192,573	323,275	363,696	355,529	2.8	3.3	12.5	-2.2	9.2
India	123,650	202,868	206,132	253,110	1.8	2.3	1.6	22.8	10.8
Indonesia	93,274	145,066	153,458	164,994	1.3	1.5	5.8	7.5	8.5
Philippines	69,046	106,724	129,818	142,940	1.0	1.3	21.6	10.1	11.0
Vietnam	23,327	56,959	80,071	97,996	0.3	0.9	40.6	22.4	22.8
Lao P.D.R.	94,056	74,832	86,357	94,052	1.4	0.9	15.4	8.9	0.0
Cambodia	17,810	43,104	54,399	79,219	0.3	0.7	26.2	45.6	23.8
New Zealand	28,173	55,775	61,190	64,771	0.4	0.6	9.7	5.9	12.6
Myanmar	56,938	47,164	42,903	42,266	0.8	0.4	-9.0	-1.5	-4.2
Bangladesh	53,222	29,708	32,941	41,145	0.8	0.4	10.9	24.9	-3.6
Sri Lanka	20,533	29,586	29,147	32,441	0.3	0.3	-1.5	11.3	6.8
Pakistan	53,420	49,148	35,737	29,902	0.8	0.3	-27.3	-16.3	-8.0
Nepal	15,487	19,603	19,009	23,001	0.2	0.2	-3.0	21.0	5.8
Brunei Darussalam	5,842	12,762	13,912	13,755	0.1	0.1	9.0	-1.1	13.0
Other intraregional	17,118	22,673	27,013	29,289	0.2	0.3	19.1	8.4	8.0
From other regions	*2,094,327*	*3,034,875*	*3,236,912*	*3,453,275*	*30.1*	*31.8*	*6.7*	*6.7*	*7.4*
United Kingdom	274,366	476,387	517,974	569,812	3.9	5.2	8.7	10.0	11.0
United States	285,486	473,285	485,276	509,841	4.1	4.7	2.5	5.1	8.6
Germany	365,812	378,562	398,034	403,240	5.3	3.7	5.1	1.3	1.4
France	197,713	239,532	237,511	253,463	2.8	2.3	-0.8	6.7	3.6
Sweden	77,549	209,092	223,040	220,866	1.1	2.0	6.7	-1.0	16.1
Netherlands	81,519	119,533	136,929	140,966	1.2	1.3	14.6	2.9	8.1
Italy	127,765	119,677	119,953	126,222	1.8	1.2	0.2	5.2	-0.2
Switzerland	103,276	112,035	120,507	126,217	1.5	1.2	7.6	4.7	2.9
Canada	53,495	86,279	92,803	101,369	0.8	0.9	7.6	9.2	9.6
Israel	43,888	73,470	91,166	98,629	0.6	0.9	24.1	8.2	12.3
Denmark	45,786	79,915	78,728	84,617	0.7	0.8	-1.5	7.5	9.2
Norway	25,249	64,550	72,785	74,947	0.4	0.7	12.8	3.0	16.8
Russian Fed	43,692	49,586	58,927	68,978	0.6	0.6	18.8	17.1	6.7
Finland	22,417	55,144	58,530	64,115	0.3	0.6	6.1	9.5	16.2
Belgium	40,661	50,374	54,350	56,179	0.6	0.5	7.9	3.4	4.7
Spain	41,109	33,954	38,812	48,491	0.6	0.4	14.3	24.9	2.4
Austria	42,200	44,793	46,461	48,067	0.6	0.4	3.7	3.5	1.9
Untd Arab Emirates	22,910	34,124	36,692	43,549	0.3	0.4	7.5	18.7	9.6
South Africa	26,610	37,521	42,026	37,721	0.4	0.3	12.0	-10.2	5.1
Kuwait	8,726	19,699	22,167	28,448	0.1	0.3	12.5	28.3	18.4
Other interregional	164,098	277,363	304,241	347,538	2.4	3.2	9.7	14.2	11.3
Nationals residing abroad	..	*70,203*	*70,559*	*73,909*		*0.7*	*0.5*	*4.7*	

Source: World Tourism Organization (WTO) ©

(Data as collected by WTO September 2003)

Thailand

Nights of International Tourists in Hotels and Similar Establishments (by nationality)

	1995	1999	2000	2001	Market share (%) 1995	Market share (%) 2001	Growth rate (%) 2000/99	Growth rate (%) 2001/00	Average per year (%) 1995-2001
Total	**52,375,093**	**68,293,242**	**73,855,073**	**79,795,758**	**100**	**100**	**8.1**	**8.0**	**7.3**
From Asia and the Pacific	*26,416,197*	*33,088,720*	*35,549,829*	*37,049,268*	*50.4*	*46.4*	*7.4*	*4.2*	*5.8*
Japan	4,710,970	6,533,321	7,107,340	7,353,189	9.0	9.2	8.8	3.5	7.7
China	2,763,534	5,194,214	4,801,086	4,694,111	5.3	5.9	-7.6	-2.2	9.2
Taiwan (Pr. of China)	3,138,417	3,424,797	4,140,658	4,340,866	6.0	5.4	20.9	4.8	5.6
Malaysia	3,523,208	3,497,136	3,835,991	4,071,954	6.7	5.1	9.7	6.2	2.4
Australia	1,774,384	2,647,164	2,858,305	3,245,643	3.4	4.1	8.0	13.6	10.6
Korea, Republic of	1,849,861	1,767,050	2,174,454	2,628,060	3.5	3.3	23.1	20.9	6.0
Singapore	1,598,329	2,294,331	2,355,680	2,328,384	3.1	2.9	2.7	-1.2	6.5
India	1,788,463	1,687,813	1,867,591	1,817,514	3.4	2.3	10.7	-2.7	0.3
Hong Kong (China)	1,228,125	1,134,924	1,097,338	1,081,634	2.3	1.4	-3.3	-1.4	-2.1
Lao P.D.R.	..	935,443	1,000,092	1,033,101		1.3	6.9	3.3	
Philippines	529,772	625,492	744,925	882,680	1.0	1.1	19.1	18.5	8.9
Indonesia	357,991	534,715	610,134	648,086	0.7	0.8	14.1	6.2	10.4
New Zealand	371,332	599,453	576,832	607,679	0.7	0.8	-3.8	5.3	8.6
Vietnam	..	230,376	291,368	419,102		0.5	26.5	43.8	
Myanmar	..	..	404,997	334,011		0.4		-17.5	
Pakistan	433,145	350,769	479,135	330,860	0.8	0.4	36.6	-30.9	-4.4
Cambodia	..	..	242,566	313,177		0.4		29.1	
Bangladesh	392,478	127,066	151,064	171,767	0.7	0.2	18.9	13.7	-12.9
Sri Lanka	133,619	156,641	154,770	168,279	0.3	0.2	-1.2	8.7	3.9
Other South Asia	33,331	57,364	53,772	66,070	0.1	0.1	-6.3	22.9	12.1
Other Asia	1,623,088	1,116,803	424,365	307,953	3.1	0.4	-62.0	-27.4	-24.2
Other Oceania	15,781	17,678	13,157	12,426	0.0	0.0	-25.6	-5.6	-3.9
Other intraregional	150,369	156,170	164,209	192,722	0.3	0.2	5.1	17.4	4.2
From other regions	*25,958,896*	*35,204,522*	*38,305,244*	*42,746,490*	*49.6*	*53.6*	*8.8*	*11.6*	*8.7*
United Kingdom	4,258,513	6,075,985	7,116,127	7,793,463	8.1	9.8	17.1	9.5	10.6
Germany	5,045,056	6,168,600	6,107,472	6,274,350	9.6	7.9	-1.0	2.7	3.7
United States	2,794,796	3,989,289	4,562,050	5,003,958	5.3	6.3	14.4	9.7	10.2
Sweden	981,124	1,725,257	2,144,666	3,457,701	1.9	4.3	24.3	61.2	23.4
France	2,254,430	2,884,819	2,921,237	2,886,627	4.3	3.6	1.3	-1.2	4.2
Netherlands	1,190,311	1,746,053	1,886,107	2,182,765	2.3	2.7	8.0	15.7	10.6
Switzerland	1,516,759	1,627,578	1,581,087	1,673,278	2.9	2.1	-2.9	5.8	1.7
Italy	1,439,887	1,461,392	1,539,099	1,444,855	2.7	1.8	5.3	-6.1	0.1
Canada	707,551	1,019,421	1,088,178	1,257,896	1.4	1.6	6.7	15.6	10.1
Denmark	632,793	1,112,267	1,097,920	1,165,930	1.2	1.5	-1.3	6.2	10.7
Israel	510,081	737,479	902,637	1,156,087	1.0	1.4	22.4	28.1	14.6
Norway	322,379	677,819	762,326	1,068,461	0.6	1.3	12.5	40.2	22.1
Finland	293,178	601,096	686,268	881,514	0.6	1.1	14.2	28.5	20.1
Belgium	557,953	701,379	705,391	731,590	1.1	0.9	0.6	3.7	4.6
Austria	563,775	890,392	768,684	730,556	1.1	0.9	-13.7	-5.0	4.4
Russian Fed	442,908	408,035	530,382	634,610	0.8	0.8	30.0	19.7	6.2
Spain	392,051	255,896	290,501	332,761	0.7	0.4	13.5	14.5	-2.7
South Africa	178,837	212,906	257,845	295,686	0.3	0.4	21.1	14.7	8.7
Untd Arab Emirates	127,749	193,729	226,778	231,849	0.2	0.3	17.1	2.2	10.4
Kuwait	90,287	162,601	196,402	217,866	0.2	0.3	20.8	10.9	15.8
Other interregional	1,658,478	2,552,529	2,934,087	3,324,687	3.2	4.2	14.9	13.3	12.3

Source: World Tourism Organization (WTO) ©

(Data as collected by WTO September 2003)

III.2.10 Timor-Leste South-East Asia

Profile

Timor-Leste

East Asia and the Pacific
South-East Asia

Capital	Dili
Area (100 km²)	149
Population (2002, 1000)	953

Source: World Tourism Organization (WTO) (Data as collected by WTO September 2003)

See annex for methodological notes and reference of external sources used.

III.2.11 Vietnam — South-East Asia

Profile

Vietnam

East Asia and the Pacific
South-East Asia

Capital	Hanoi
Year of entry in WTO	1981
Area (1000 km²)	332
Population (2002, million)	80.6
Gross Domestic Product (GDP) (2002, US$ million)	34,138
GDP per capita (2002, US$)	428
GDP growth (real, %)	

'-> 2001: 5.0; 2002: 5.8; 2003*: 6.0; 2004*: 7.0

	2000	2001	2002*	2001/2000	2002*/2001
International Arrivals					
Visitors (1000)	2,140	2,330	2,628	8.9	12.8
Tourists (overnight visitors) (1000)	1,383	1,599	..	15.6	
- per 100 of inhabitants	2	2	..		
Same-day visitors (1000)	501	446	..	-11.0	
Cruise passengers (1000)	256	285	309	11.3	8.4
Tourism accommodation					
Number of rooms	66,700	74,000	..	10.9	
Nights spent in hotels and similar establishments (1000)	24,227	25,513		5.3	
by non-residents (inbound tourism)	6,307	6,873	..	9.0	
by residents (domestic tourism)	17,920	18,640	..	4.0	

Source: World Tourism Organization (WTO) (Data as collected by WTO September 2003)

See annex for methodological notes and reference of external sources used.

International Tourism by Origin

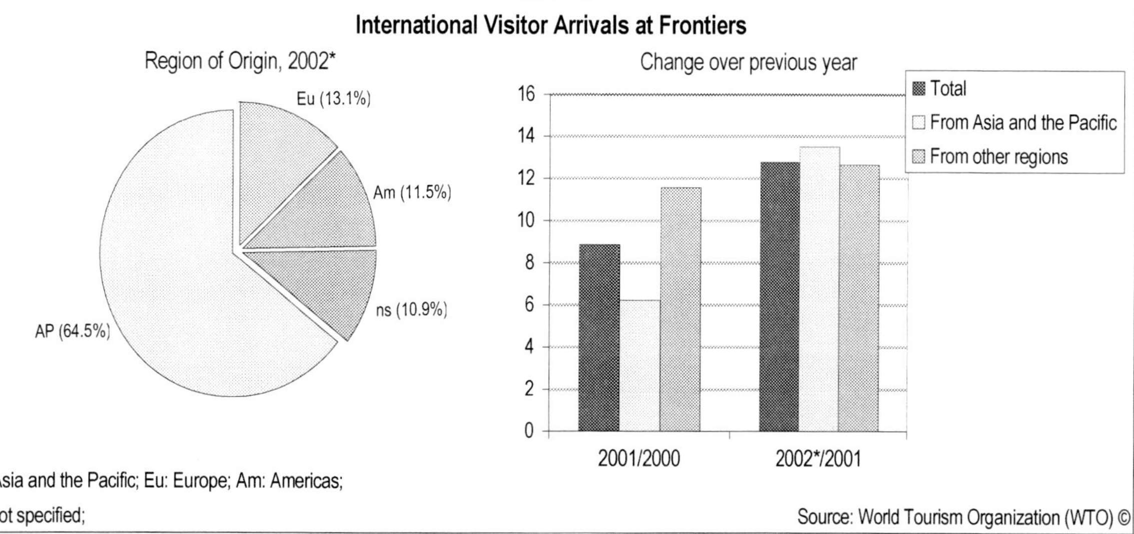

AP: Asia and the Pacific; Eu: Europe; Am: Americas;
ns: Not specified;

Source: World Tourism Organization (WTO) ©

Vietnam

International Visitor Arrivals at Frontiers (by residence)

	1995	2000	2001	2002*	Market share (%) 1995	Market share (%) 2002*	Growth rate (%) 2001/00	Growth rate (%) 2002*/01	Average per year (%) 1995-2002*
Total	**1,351,296**	**2,140,000**	**2,330,050**	**2,627,988**	**100**	**100**	**8.9**	**12.8**	**10.0**
From Asia and the Pacific	*450,557*	*1,405,524*	*1,492,885*	*1,694,624*	*33.3*	*64.5*	*6.2*	*13.5*	*20.8*
China	62,640	626,476	672,846	724,385	4.6	27.6	7.4	7.7	41.9
Japan	119,540	152,755	204,860	279,769	8.8	10.6	34.1	36.6	12.9
Taiwan (Pr. of China)	224,127	212,370	200,061	211,072	16.6	8.0	-5.8	5.5	-0.9
Korea, Republic of	..	53,452	75,167	105,060		4.0	40.6	39.8	
Australia	..	68,162	84,085	96,624		3.7	23.4	14.9	
Cambodia	..	124,557	76,620	69,538		2.6	-38.5	-9.2	
Malaysia	..	20,378	26,265	46,086		1.8	28.9	75.5	
Thailand	23,117	26,366	31,789	40,999	1.7	1.6	20.6	29.0	8.5
Lao P.D.R.	..	27,918	40,696	37,237		1.4	45.8	-8.5	
Singapore	..	29,100	32,110	35,261		1.3	10.3	9.8	
Philippines	..	18,760	20,035	25,306		1.0	6.8	26.3	
Hong Kong (China)	21,133	22,170	..	..	1.6				
Indonesia	..	7,061	11,116	13,456		0.5	57.4	21.1	
New Zealand	..	5,285	6,897	8,266		0.3	30.5	19.8	
India	..	4,812	5,844	..			21.4		
Myanmar	..	839	1,837	1,131		0.0	119.0	-38.4	
Sri Lanka	..	665	658	..			-1.1		
Pakistan	..	552	637	..			15.4		
Brunei Darussalam	..	359	415	434		0.0	15.6	4.6	
Other North-East Asia	..	153	..	..					
Other South Asia	..	610	947	..			55.2		
Other Asia	..	2,724	..	..					
From other regions	*379,800*	*514,598*	*574,155*	*646,879*	*28.1*	*24.6*	*11.6*	*12.7*	*7.9*
United States	189,090	208,642	230,470	259,967	14.0	9.9	10.5	12.8	4.7
France	137,890	86,492	99,700	111,546	10.2	4.2	15.3	11.9	-3.0
United Kingdom	52,820	56,355	64,673	69,682	3.9	2.7	14.8	7.7	4.0
Germany	..	32,058	39,096	46,327		1.8	22.0	18.5	
Canada	..	30,845	35,963	43,552		1.7	16.6	21.1	
Netherlands	..	12,347	15,592	18,125		0.7	26.3	16.2	
Sweden	..	9,347	10,877	14,444		0.5	16.4	32.8	
Switzerland	..	12,337	13,797	13,394		0.5	11.8	-2.9	
Italy	..	10,138	11,608	12,221		0.5	14.5	5.3	
Denmark	..	9,785	10,780	11,815		0.4	10.2	9.6	
Belgium	..	8,556	8,944	10,325		0.4	4.5	15.4	
Portugal	..	5,577	7,406	10,306		0.4	32.8	39.2	
Norway	..	6,425	7,920	8,586		0.3	23.3	8.4	
Russian Fed	..	6,017	8,092	7,964		0.3	34.5	-1.6	
Austria	..	4,011	4,570	4,476		0.2	13.9	-2.1	
Finland	..	2,771	3,565	4,149		0.2	28.7	16.4	
South Africa	..	646	..	..					
Other interregional	..	12,249	1,102	..			-91.0		
Other World/Not specified	*520,939*	*219,878*	*263,010*	*286,485*	*38.6*	*10.9*	*19.6*	*8.9*	*-8.2*

Source: World Tourism Organization (WTO) ©

(Data as collected by WTO September 2003)

III.3 Oceania

III.3.1 American Samoa — Oceania

Profile

American Samoa

Capital	Pago Pago
Area (10 km²)	20
Population (2002, 1000)	69

East Asia and the Pacific
Oceania

	2000	2001	2002*	2001/2000	2002*/2001
International Arrivals					
Tourists (overnight visitors) (1000)	44	..	..		
- per 100 of inhabitants	67	..	..		
Outbound Tourism					
Trips abroad (1000)	41	..	..		
- per 100 of inhabitants	63	..	..		

Source: World Tourism Organization (WTO) (Data as collected by WTO September 2003)

See annex for methodological notes and reference of external sources used.

International Tourism by Origin

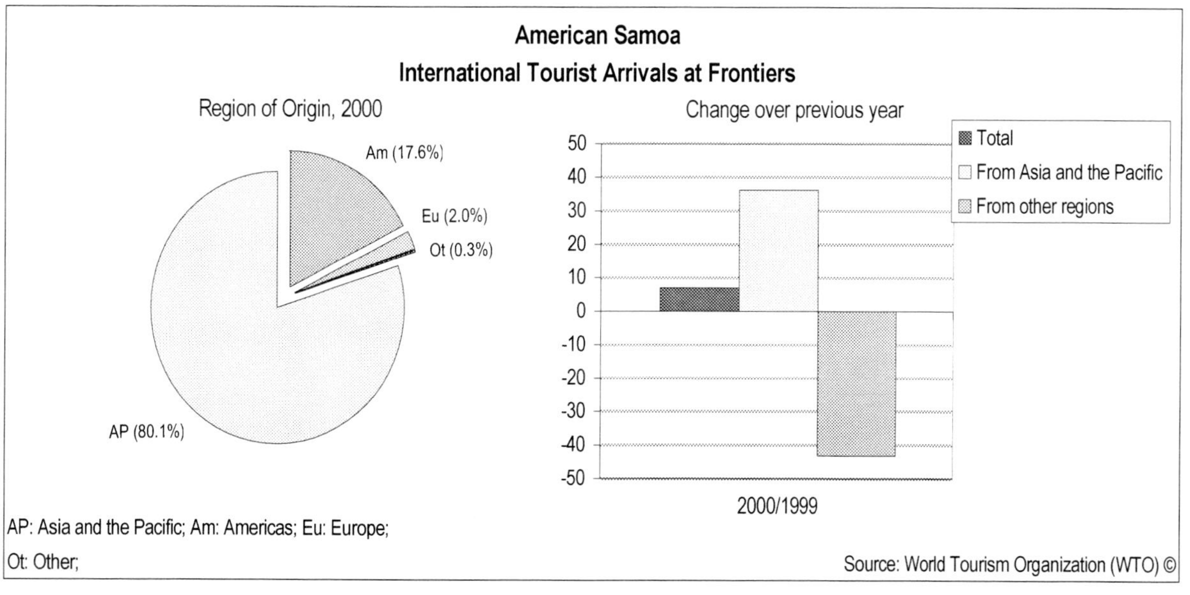

American Samoa

International Tourist Arrivals at Frontiers (by nationality)

	1995	1999	2000	2001	Market share (%) 1995	Market share (%) 2001	Growth rate (%) 2000/99	Growth rate (%) 2001/00	Average per year (%) 1995-2001
Total	**17,522**	**41,287**	**44,158**	..	**100**		**7.0**		
From Asia and the Pacific	*7,910*	*25,980*	*35,379*	..	*45.1*		*36.2*		
Samoa	..	20,738	28,004	..			35.0		
New Zealand	4,231	3,711	3,916	..	24.1		5.5		
Australia	736	732	717	..	4.2		-2.0		
Fiji	279	123	685	..	1.6		456.9		
Tonga	838	253	519	..	4.8		105.1		
China	258	37	351	..	1.5		848.6		
Taiwan (Pr. of China)	324	..	..	..	1.8				
Philippines	400	60	304	..	2.3		406.7		
Solomon Is	17	6	194	..	0.1		3133.3		
Korea, Republic of	338	69	147	..	1.9		113.0		
Papua New Guinea	29	7	121	..	0.2		1628.6		
Japan	130	72	93	..	0.7		29.2		
India	46	40	46	..	0.3		15.0		
Malaysia	3	8	27	..	0.0		237.5		
Singapore	7	20	27	..	0.0		35.0		
Thailand	3	5	18	..	0.0		260.0		
Micronesia (Fed.St.of)	68	35	15	..	0.4		-57.1		
Palau	10	..	..	..	0.1				
Indonesia	20	3	9	..	0.1		200.0		
Sri Lanka	5	..	6	..	0.0				
Kiribati	21	6	6	..	0.1		0.0		
Vietnam	6	..	..	..	0.0				
Other intraregional	141	55	174	..	0.8		216.4		
From other regions	*9,603*	*15,302*	*8,688*	..	*54.8*		*-43.2*		
United States	8,383	14,671	7,521	..	47.8		-48.7		
France	77	32	498	..	0.4		1456.3		
All South America	58	14	103	..	0.3		635.7		
Canada	182	102	95	..	1.0		-6.9		
United Kingdom	228	156	84	..	1.3		-46.2		
Germany	220	121	68	..	1.3		-43.8		
Sweden	88	33	64	..	0.5		93.9		
Italy	33	38	45	..	0.2		18.4		
All Central America	43	8	30	..	0.2		275.0		
All Middle East	18	8	24	..	0.1		200.0		
Portugal	71	12	20	..	0.4		66.7		
Netherlands	35	15	18	..	0.2		20.0		
Mexico	29	4	14	..	0.2		250.0		
All Africa	2	9	14	..	0.0		55.6		
Denmark	29	25	11	..	0.2		-56.0		
All Central/Eastern Europe	29	2	11	..	0.2		450.0		
Finland	3	9	9	..	0.0		0.0		
Spain	6	3	9	..	0.0		200.0		
Other Europe	15	9	40	..	0.1		344.4		
Other interregional	54	31	10	..	0.3		-67.7		
Other World/Not specified	*9*	*5*	*91*	..	*0.1*		*1720.0*		

Source: World Tourism Organization (WTO) © (Data as collected by WTO September 2003)

III.3.2 Australia Oceania

Profile

Australia

East Asia and the Pacific
Oceania

Capital	Canberra
Area (1000 km²)	7,741
Population (2002, million)	19.5
Gross Domestic Product (GDP) (2002, US$ million)	398,157
GDP per capita (2002, US$)	20,220
GDP growth (real, %)	
'-> 2001: 2.7; 2002: 3.6; 2003*: 3.0; 2004*: 3.5	

	2000	2001	2002*	2001/2000	2002*/2001
International Arrivals					
Visitors (1000)	4,931	4,856	4,841	-1.5	-0.3
- per 100 of inhabitants	26	25	25		
Tourism accommodation					
Number of rooms	194,926	198,133	..	1.6	
Nights spent in collective establishments (1000)	175,911				
by non-residents (inbound tourism)	41,080	41,176	42,148	0.2	2.4
by residents (domestic tourism)	134,831	..	..		
Nights spent in hotels and similar establishments (1000)	84,753				
by non-residents (inbound tourism)	17,469	17,542	17,768	0.4	1.3
by residents (domestic tourism)	67,284	..	..		
Outbound Tourism					
Trips abroad (1000)	3,498	3,443	3,461	-1.6	0.5
- per 100 of inhabitants	18	18	18		
Receipts and Expenditure for International Tourism					
International Tourism Receipts (US$ million)	8,451	7,624	8,087	-9.8	6.1
- per Visitor Arrival (US$)	1,714	1,570	1,671	-8.4	6.4
- per capita (US$)	441	394	414		
International Fare Receipts (US$ million)	3,727	3,580	..	-3.9	
International Tourism Expenditure (US$ million)	6,131	5,764	6,116	-6.0	6.1
- per trip (US$)	1,753	1,674	1,767	-4.5	5.6
- per capita (US$)	320	298	313		
International Fare Expenditure (US$ million)	2,393	2,193	..	-8.4	
△ International Tourism Balance (US$ million)	2,320	1,860	1,971		
△ International Fare Balance (US$ million)	1,333	1,387	..		

Source: World Tourism Organization (WTO) (Data as collected by WTO September 2003)

See annex for methodological notes and reference of external sources used.

Survey

Contributed by *Department of Industry, Tourism & Resources*
www.australia.com ; www.seeaustralia.com.au ; www.dimia.gov.au (for visa requirements) (promotional)
www.industry.gov.au ; www.atc.australia.com/ ; www.joehockey.com (institutional/corporate)
www.btr.gov.au (tourism research & tourism-specific surveys) ; www.abs.gov.au (tourism & general stats, including TSA) (research and data)

Tourism development and outlook

Most significant determinant

Ongoing impacts from September 11 – Australia experienced a decline in overall inbound tourist numbers in 2002, of -0.3 per cent, following a decline of -1.5 in 2001. Increased global uncertainty, including uncertain global economic environments and security have contributed to this decline. Bali Bombing - October 2002, heightened security concerns in the region. Public Liability Insurance – Rapid increases in the price of public liability insurance and difficulty in obtaining the insurance was a top concern for many small businesses involved in tourism. Sectors particularly affected included adventure and tour operators and the horse riding industry. Bushfires - 3 states were affected by bushfires during the holiday period in December 2002 / January 2003. This was coupled with drought conditions in some states.

Tourism products

Accommodation Capacity - The number of rooms available in hotels, motels, guesthouses and serviced apartments with 15 or more rooms decreased marginally by 0.9 per cent in 2002, compared with 2001, as operators shed excess capacity. Room demand showed only a marginal increase of 2.4 per cent, reflecting the downturn in international visitor arrivals in 2002, and the marginal growth of 1 per cent in domestic visitor nights. Overall, capital cities, particularly those depending significantly on international tourism were worst affected, while destinations within drive distance from major population centres were least adversely affected.

Quality - The Australian Government continues to work cooperatively with industry to help develop and encourage participation in voluntary tourism accreditation schemes. These are designed to help industry continue to improve on its already high standards and to benchmark best practice for industry. Key schemes in which the Government has an involvement include an overarching scheme for tourism businesses, and improving the standard of service provided by tour guides. Additional $ 8 million in funding for the Regional Tourism Program over 2002-2003 to 2005-2006 period. The program boosts the capacity of tourism businesses to deliver higher quality tourism products and services in regional Australia. Events - The Gay Games held in Sydney in November 2002. The Games attracted approximately 30,000 competitors to Sydney.

Access

Aviation Positive - Virgin Blue continued to expand its domestic network including to a range of domestic tourism destinations. Qantas' new low cost international carrier, Australian Airlines commenced operations to a range of Asian destinations from its base in Cairns. The sale of Ansett's Sydney terminal and its development as a common user facility helped to facilitate expansion by other airlines. Negative - Consumer confidence in air travel domestically was damaged by the continuing uncertainty and the eventual grounding of Ansett and liquidation after a deal to sell the airline as a going concern fell-through. The Bali bombing in October and subsequent terrorist threats further undermined traveller confidence. Visas The Electronic Travel Authority (ETA) continued to expand in 2002, with residents from 34 countries able to apply for visas via the Internet and check the validity of an existing ETA issued via the Internet. Working Holiday Maker arrangements have now been extended to 14 countries, and the Department of Immigration and Multicultural and Indigenous Affairs (DIMIA) are currently negotiating to develop working holiday arrangements with a number of countries including Belgium, Italy, France, Taiwan and Greece.

Generating markets

In 2002 there were 4.8 million international visitors to Australia, a decline of 0.3 per cent on 2001. Visitor nights declined by 3 per cent compared to year ended December 2001, however, expenditure rose by 5 per cent. While overall activity was flat between 2001 and 2002, there was significant falls in the number of visitor nights spent in Australia by international visitors travelling mainly for holiday (down 10%) and visiting friends and relatives (down 7%) purposes. These falls were offset mainly by continued strong growth in travel by overseas students studying in Australia (visitor nights up 21%). International visitor nights spent in Australia by people travelling for the purposes of employment (up 10%) and business (up 9%) also contributed to offsetting the fall in holiday and visiting friends and relatives nights.

China - During 2001 and 2002, tourist arrivals from China grew by 31.7 per cent 22.6 per cent respectively. The onset of SARS saw a decrease of almost 60 per cent in the June 2003 quarter, due to Chinese travel authorities placing a ban on outbound travel in China's 3 strongest travel provinces. The Government is finalising arrangements with the Chinese Government to expand the Approved Destination Status (ADS) group leisure travel arrangement. The expansion will allow residents of six new regions to travel to Australia.

Japan - After the events of September 11, the Japanese outbound market shrunk by 33 per cent. Coupled with the demise of Ansett (a major Australian Airline), this saw Australia's short term position weaken with an estimated decline of 24 per cent in Japanese arrivals in the four months to December 2001 (a total decline of 6.6 per cent for 2001). An aggressive marketing campaign by the Australian Tourism Commission (ATC), coupled with slowly improving air capacity, steered the market back into growth of 6.2 per cent, a total of 715,500 arrivals by 2002.

Backpackers – Backpackers constitute 10 per cent of visitors to Australia and contribute 22 per cent of expenditure by international tourists. Backpackers and visitors coming to Australia for the purposes of education and employment are important segments of the market because of their long stays compared to other visitor types. Together they account for only 16 per cent of visitors but over half (52%) the nights and 45 per cent of total expenditure.

In 2001 the ATC launched a global strategy to build the awareness of Australia as an incentive and business tourism destination which included advertising in key business publications and television networks. The next stage of the strategy is now being introduced across key markets in Europe, North America and Asia. The campaigns address several of the barriers or challenges which face Australia as an incentive destination by moving key decision makers towards conversion.

Other Issues

In 2001-2002: Tourism consumption was 70.8 billion dollar, a drop of 0.7 per cent on 2000-2001. Both domestic and international tourism consumption dropped. Tourism GDP fell slightly in absolute numbers, but its contribution to total GDP dropped significantly to 4.5 per cent, from 4.8 per cent in 2000-2001. This reflects the strong growth (6.5%) of the total economy. Tourism employed 549,000 persons, a marginal decrease on 2000-2001. Its share of total employment dropped to 5.9 per cent from 6.0 per cent in 2000-2001. Tourism exports were 17.1 billion dollar. While this was a very marginal decline, total exports also dropped very slightly and tourism maintained its share of total exports at 11.2 per cent.

Outlook 2003

International visitor arrivals are forecast to grow at an average annual rate of 4.6 per cent, from 4.8 million in 2002 to 7.6 million in 2012. The Iraqi conflict and onset of Severe Acute Respiratory Syndrome (SARS) has revised forecasts for 2003 with a fall of 5.3 per cent in total visitor arrivals in 2003 to 4.6 million visitors. Asia totals approximately 43 per cent of Australia's total inbound market and was forecast to grow by 5.4 per cent in 2003. Since the Iraqi conflict and the onset of SARS, revised figures from the Tourism Forecasting Council (TPC) forecast that arrivals from Asia will fall by 10 per cent in 2003.

Strong growth of 15.4 per cent is forecast for 2004, bringing the total number of visitor arrivals to almost 2.2 million, marginally higher than 2002. Average annual growth of 5.5 per cent is forecast for Asia for the period 2003 to 2012. Japan - SARS and the Iraqi conflict are expected to drive a decline of 6.9 per cent in 2003, with strong growth of 12.5 per cent forecast for 2004. In the period to 2012, average annual growth for the Japan market is forecast to increase by 2.7 per cent per annum to 930,000 visitor arrivals in 2012.China - Total arrivals from China are forecast to decline by 17.7 per cent for 2003. Strong growth of 29.7 per cent is forecast for 2004, with an average annual growth rate of 12.6 percent per annum forecast until 2012, bringing the total number of visitor arrivals from China to 623,000 in 2012. The TPC expects domestic visitor nights to increase by 1.9 per cent in 2003, with growth being driven by people's reluctance to travel overseas.

The Council expects an improvement over the next ten years with an expected average annual growth in domestic visitor nights of 1.9 per cent. Having grown by just 0.1 per cent in 2002, outbound tourism is expected to remain static with just 0.3 per cent growth in 2003. The TFC has revised it average annual growth rate for the next ten years to 2.7 percent. The Rugby World Cup (RWC) will be held in Australia from October through to November 2003. RWC matches will be played at 10 locations in seven states. Australia is anticipating around 40,000 international visitors to attend matches. The RWC will be viewed by 1.3 billion people in 130 countries.

Tourism policy

Tourism Master Plans: The Minister for Small Business and Tourism recently released a tourism Green Paper "A Medium to Long Term Strategy for Tourism". The Paper will be developed into a White Paper, which will form the basis of the strategic development for the Australian tourism industry for the next 10 years. The Green Paper canvasses the key issues for developing a medium to long term strategy and has 5 key themes:

- Diversification of Australia from a travel destination to a lifetime experience.
- Diversification of Australian tourism product.
- Focus on business yield and niche markets.
- Enhancing business profitability to better position the industry against volatility and global uncertainly.
- Improving asset utilisation and coordination across public and private sectors.
- National Tourism Issues Response Plan:

The National Tourism Issues Response Plan was developed after the events of September 11 and the collapse of Ansett and involves Tourism Ministers, State and Territory Tourism Organisations, the Australian Tourist Commission and the Commonwealth Department of Industry, Tourism and Resources (ITR). The Plan sets out a process for delivering a coherent national response aimed at minimising the impact of crisis events. The Plan was initiated for the Iraq War and extended to cover SARS.

'Building Momentum: Japanese Tourism to Australia' is an action plan that identifies fundamentals issues that need to be addressed to continue to maintain and grow inbound tourists from Japan. The Report identifies a series of actions against four key areas to remove impediments to growth. A similar report focusing on the South Korean market will be produced in 2003-2004.

Marketing & promotion

The ATC received 24 million dollar boost over 5 years to implement a business and leisure tourism market re-development package. A new AU$ 6 million TV campaign was launched in the United States promoting Australia as a realistic and affordable 2 week holiday destination. The ATC global consumer site, Australia.com, was redeveloped and relaunched in May 2002. Celebrate Australia 2002 launched in Singapore, a joint marketing initiative by the ATC, the Australia Trade Commission and the Australia Trade Commission in Singapore. The Australian Tourism Data Warehouse (ATDW), a new online database coordinated by the State and Territory tourism organisations and the ATC, aims to catalogue all tourism products Australia wide. By June 2002, 10,500 operators were featured. The Government provided an additional 8 million dollar over 4 years to extend the existing See Australia marketing initiative, focusing on domestic tourism in regional and rural Australia.

Cultural Tourism (CT)

Specific place for CT in tourism policy: yes.

Main objectives & instruments

Several Commonwealth agencies are responsible for the development and management of cultural tourism in Australia. Cultural Heritage Tourism "Going Places – Developing natural and cultural heritage tourism in Australia" is a plan developed under the National Tourism and Heritage Taskforce.

- The Plan identified several key opportunities for natural and cultural tourism:
- Developing the product.
- Managing tourism at natural and cultural heritage places
- Planning and coordination and
- Supporting people and products.

Indigenous Tourism:
The Indigenous Tourism Leadership Group (ITLG) is an industry group set up in 2001 to provide advice and to pursue strategies to develop indigenous tourism in Australia. Building partnerships between the mainstream tourism industry and indigenous business enterprises or communities is a potential means for growing product. The ITLG is an industry based group consisting of Indigenous tourism operators, government representatives, tourism industry representatives and mainstream business organisations.

Food and Wine:
Funding the development and implementation of The National Wine Tourism Strategy and Implementation Plan.

Main focus of attention supply

Indigenous tourism - As this segments grows, the ATC - in partnership with the State and Territory Tourist Organisations (STOs) - is providing assistance to ensure that Aboriginal tourism products fully understand the tourism industry, both domestically and internationally. The ATC is continually consulting with key industry and community members to maintain relevance and effectiveness of marketing activities. The ATC aims to foster the integration of marketing and industry development activities across all States and Territories, ensuring the sustainable growth of Aboriginal tourism at an international level.

Main focus of attention demand

ATC is currently developing the cultural tourism segments of food and wine tourism and Indigenous tourism. Indigenous tourism - Western markets (the United Kingdom and Europe in particular) hold most potential overall for Indigenous tourism, with higher levels of awareness, interest and participation. Food and Wine tourism - The Bureau of Tourism Research (BTR) estimates that around 470,700 international visitors aged 15 and over visited wineries within Australia during 2001-2002. This represented 11 per cent of total visitors to Australia. Research commissioned by the

ATC indicated a strong growth in food and wine interest and potential across the Japan, New Zealand and Asian markets.

Specific place for CT in marketing & promotion plan: yes.

Main objectives & programmes

The Brand Australia image is based on a combination of, Australia's natural environment, the distinctive personality of the Australian people and the free spirited nature of the country's lifestyle and culture.

Special activities undertaken

Food and wine - A full-colour motivational brochure featuring information on food and wine, eating out, bush tucker and fast facts on the industry in each Australian State and Territory. A range of wine tourism itinerary options for travellers, across each Australian state and territory. Tourism information for the wine industry. A map highlighting the main international wine regions across Australia. Indigenous - The ATC has also developed a motivational brochure on Indigenous tourism in Australia in conjunction with the STOs and the Commonwealth Department of Industry, Tourism and Resources.

Importance of cultural tourism:

- in total tourism offer

Attend theatre, concerts or other performing arts: 545,777
Visit museums or art galleries: 1,173,853
Visit art / craft workshops / studios: 280,389
Attend festivals / fairs or cultural events: 308,820
Visit an aboriginal site / community: 175,546
Experience aboriginal art/craft, cultural displays: 394,770
Visit history / heritage buildings, sites or monuments: 1,231,448
Total: 4,110,603
The International Visitor Survey, year ending March 2003 identified that international tourists to Australia participated in the following cultural activities;

International Tourism by Origin

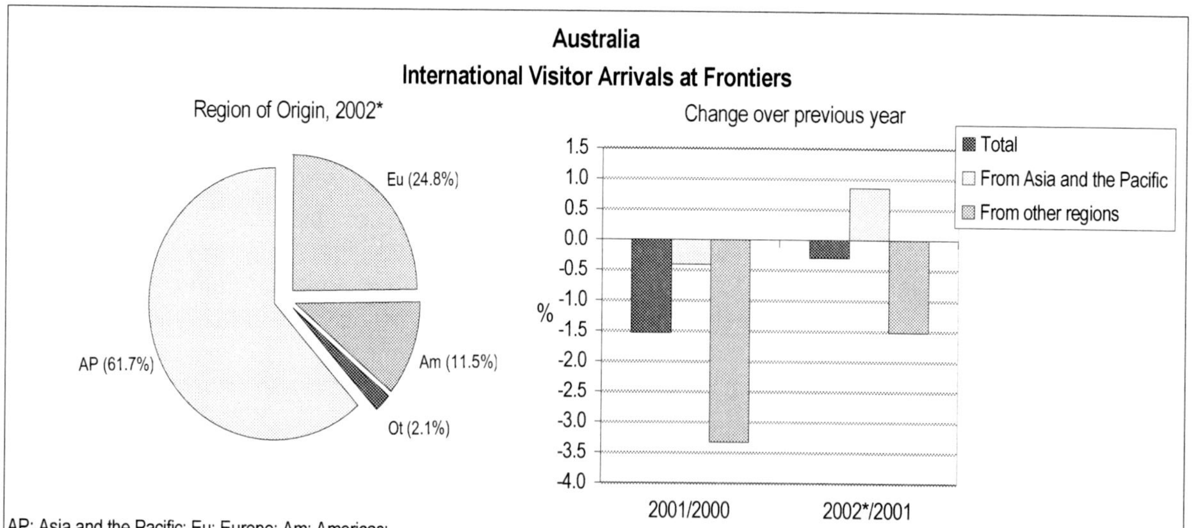

AP: Asia and the Pacific; Eu: Europe; Am: Americas;
Ot: Other;

Source: World Tourism Organization (WTO) ©

Australia

International Visitor Arrivals at Frontiers (by residence)

	1995	2000	2001	2002*	Market share (%) 1995	2002*	Growth rate (%) 2001/00	2002*/01	Average per year (%) 1995-2002*
Total	**3,725,800**	**4,931,336**	**4,855,669**	**4,841,152**	**100**	**100**	**-1.5**	**-0.3**	**3.8**
From Asia and the Pacific	*2,518,200*	*2,971,580*	*2,959,430*	*2,984,845*	*67.6*	*61.7*	*-0.4*	*0.9*	*2.5*
New Zealand	538,400	817,024	814,874	790,068	14.5	16.3	-0.3	-3.0	5.6
Japan	782,700	720,973	673,577	715,458	21.0	14.8	-6.6	6.2	-1.3
Singapore	202,400	285,729	296,007	286,852	5.4	5.9	3.6	-3.1	5.1
China	42,600	120,259	157,955	190,016	1.1	3.9	31.3	20.3	23.8
Korea, Republic of	168,000	157,375	175,587	189,729	4.5	3.9	11.6	8.1	1.8
Malaysia	108,200	152,074	149,415	158,990	2.9	3.3	-1.7	6.4	5.7
Hong Kong (China)	131,700	154,079	154,149	150,943	3.5	3.1	0.0	-2.1	2.0
Taiwan (pr. of China)	152,000	134,349	110,070	97,429	4.1	2.0	-18.1	-11.5	-6.2
Indonesia	135,000	98,106	97,877	89,432	3.6	1.8	-0.2	-8.6	-5.7
Thailand	81,300	72,750	79,940	82,671	2.2	1.7	9.9	3.4	0.2
India	17,100	41,452	48,227	45,022	0.5	0.9	16.3	-6.6	14.8
Papua New Guinea	42,300	44,461	38,960	31,247	1.1	0.6	-12.4	-19.8	-4.2
New Caledonia	21,400	25,281	28,720	30,514	0.6	0.6	13.6	6.2	5.2
Philippines	27,000	39,185	30,412	28,453	0.7	0.6	-22.4	-6.4	0.8
Fiji	19,000	23,169	24,516	23,168	0.5	0.5	5.8	-5.5	2.9
Other intraregional	49,100	85,314	79,144	74,853	1.3	1.5	-7.2	-5.4	6.2
From other regions	*1,204,200*	*1,947,144*	*1,882,288*	*1,853,753*	*32.3*	*38.3*	*-3.3*	*-1.5*	*6.4*
United Kingdom	347,900	579,751	615,634	640,782	9.3	13.2	6.2	4.1	9.1
United States	304,900	488,105	446,443	434,470	8.2	9.0	-8.5	-2.7	5.2
Germany	124,200	143,273	147,613	134,806	3.3	2.8	3.0	-8.7	1.2
Canada	58,400	88,292	93,134	90,874	1.6	1.9	5.5	-2.4	6.5
Netherlands	34,500	61,251	56,508	52,992	0.9	1.1	-7.7	-6.2	6.3
South Africa	32,700	59,513	54,943	50,971	0.9	1.1	-7.7	-7.2	6.5
France	35,200	57,312	50,022	49,557	0.9	1.0	-12.7	-0.9	5.0
Ireland	17,400	46,449	51,564	48,048	0.5	1.0	11.0	-6.8	15.6
Italy	36,800	57,933	43,297	43,300	1.0	0.9	-25.3	0.0	2.4
Switzerland	35,300	47,844	46,217	41,509	0.9	0.9	-3.4	-10.2	2.3
Sweden	22,400	36,785	31,651	30,905	0.6	0.6	-14.0	-2.4	4.7
Austria	17,000	18,559	17,945	19,008	0.5	0.4	-3.3	5.9	1.6
Denmark	15,800	20,693	18,348	18,870	0.4	0.4	-11.3	2.8	2.6
Norway	6,600	16,575	16,574	16,876	0.2	0.3	0.0	1.8	14.4
Israel	8,100	13,121	14,574	15,072	0.2	0.3	11.1	3.4	9.3
Untd Arab Emirates	..	13,449	13,970	13,286		0.3	3.9	-4.9	
Spain	7,300	16,360	12,415	12,451	0.2	0.3	-24.1	0.3	7.9
Belgium	7,000	11,811	10,483	10,803	0.2	0.2	-11.2	3.1	6.4
Brazil	4,700	13,391	11,609	10,247	0.1	0.2	-13.3	-11.7	11.8
Poland	3,400	6,789	6,463	8,775	0.1	0.2	-4.8	35.8	14.5
Greece	7,600	9,639	7,063	7,027	0.2	0.1	-26.7	-0.5	-1.1
Finland	5,800	9,445	7,245	6,529	0.2	0.1	-23.3	-9.9	1.7
Mexico	1,900	6,228	4,689	5,404	0.1	0.1	-24.7	15.2	16.1
Russian Fed	..	6,167	4,405	4,373		0.1	-28.6	-0.7	
Argentina	4,600	9,582	7,868	4,358	0.1	0.1	-17.9	-44.6	-0.8
Other interregional	64,700	108,827	91,611	82,460	1.7	1.7	-15.8	-10.0	3.5
Other World/Not specified	*3,400*	*12,612*	*13,951*	*2,554*	*0.1*	*0.1*	*10.6*	*-81.7*	*-4.0*

Source: World Tourism Organization (WTO) ©

(Data as collected by WTO September 2003)

III.3.3 Cook Islands Oceania

Profile

Cook Islands

East Asia and the Pacific
Oceania

Capital	Avarua
Area (10 km²)	23
Population (2002, 1000)	21

	2000	2001	2002*	2001/2000	2002*/2001
International Arrivals					
Tourists (overnight visitors) (1000)	73	75	73	2.2	-2.1
- per 100 of inhabitants	358	362	351		
Tourism accommodation					
Number of rooms	783	..	..		
Nights spent in hotels and similar establishments (1000)					
by non-residents (inbound tourism)	219	225	165	2.7	-26.7
Outbound Tourism					
Trips abroad (1000)	9	9	9		
- per 100 of inhabitants	44	44	43		
Receipts and Expenditure for International Tourism					
International Tourism Receipts (US$ million)	36	38	46	5.6	21.1
- per Tourist Arrival (US$)	493	510	630	3.3	23.7
- per capita (US$)	1,764	1,844	2,210		

Source: World Tourism Organization (WTO) (Data as collected by WTO September 2003)

See annex for methodological notes and reference of external sources used.

Survey

Contributed by *Cook Islands Tourism Corporation*
www.cook-islands.com (promotional)
www.cook-islands.com (institutional/corporate)
www.cook-islands.com (research and data)

Tourism development and outlook

Most significant determinant

The effect of international crises: 11 September 2001 and the Bali bombings, etc.

The collapse of major carriers effecting distribution and visitor flows. The collapse of Canada 300 removed an important link to the Canadian market. The collapse of Ansett Australia and the near collapse of Air New Zealand impacted heavily on visitor flows from the Australian market.

Low level of the European markets in the first three quarters of the year.

Directional traffic flows through Asia and into the Pacific region in general was greatly affected. Key markets for the Cook Islands (Europe, the United States of America, Canada and Australia) all suffered.

Fortunately, New Zealand compensated for the declines in all markets with an overall increase of 23 per cent for the year. Accessibility from this market with daily non-stop services greatly assisted in holding up visitor numbers.

Tourism products

Several new upmarket boutique properties opened in 2002 and one luxury resort on the island of Aitutaki. Several private home rentals also commenced operations. Existing operations focussed on upgrading during the year.

New activities commenced operations: an ecotour operation and a lagoon cruise.

Access

The Cook Islands maintains its visa-free policy for bonafide visitors staying up to 31 days.

Accessibility improved from New Zealand, a key gateway offering daily services with Air New Zealand using B767 aircraft.

Services also provided by this carrier with three Los Angeles/Raratonga services per week and one service via Tahiti.

One service per week from Fiji connecting with Auckland services.

Commencement of Aloha Airlines services linking Vancouver and the United States West coast cities to the Cook Islands via Honolulu.

Generating markets

Overall slowdown in long-haul traffic due to international crisis.

Strong growth in the weddings and honeymoon market and special interest markets, particularly bone fishing and deep-sea fishing.

Cultural and educational tours also increased.

Other Issues

Tourism in the Cook Islands has been concentrated on only two of the 15 islands in the group. The government has embraced a policy to develop tourism in the other islands to stimulate economic development in these islands. The focus of such development will be on the basis of small-scale, low-key development in keeping with the life style of the islands.

Outlook 2003

Visitor arrivals marginally declined by 2 per cent in 2002 against the previous year of 74,575 arrivals. The industry bounced back in the last quarter of 2002 with growth from all key markets aided by strong marketing campaigns.

Projected annual growth of 6 per cent set for the next five years.

Tourism policy

A major Tourism Forum was held in December 2002 calling for the updating of the Tourism Master Plan of 1992 and Island-Specific Strategic Development Plans of 1994 and 1995.

Major emphasis was placed on human resource development and training.

Co-operative marketing initiatives between the Tourism Corporation and the private sector partners were strengthened.

Marketing & promotion

The main marketing thrust was made in Europe, North America, Australia and New Zealand.

Emphasis was put on trade seminars, co-operative advertising with tour operators, trade and media visitation programmes and the establishment was made of a Cook Islands Specialist Programme.

Cultural Tourism (CT)

Specific place for CT in tourism policy: yes.

Main objectives & instruments	Culture is a key component of Cook Islands tourism. This is reflected in the customs and traditions and in the daily lives of its people. Major emphasis has been placed on cultural celebrations during national self-government celebrations. Cultural development within primary and secondary schools has progressed very well. Strong emphasis is being placed on language and culture in all schools. Restoration of historical sites is gaining strong interest as is the development of local artisans work. Traditional ceremonies remain a living component of Cook Islands culture.
Main focus of attention supply	The destination depends on the culture of the people and visitors interact freely with the host population.Traditional entertainment features prominently in most hotels. Arts and crafts, traditional medicines and cultural and historical tours are key components of the cultural product.
Main focus of attention demand	Being a small destination, the cultural component of the tourism product is integrated into the overall visitor experience.

Specific place for CT in marketing & promotion plan: yes.

Main objectives & programmes	Because culture is very much a part of the tourism product, it is effectively promoted in song and dance form in promotional campaigns through the use of cultural groups and traditional motifs and art.
Special activities undertaken	Cultural groups regularly travel internationally to promote culture and tourism in key markets. They also participate in international cultural festivals. Several cultural festivals are programmed throughout the calendar year and these are promoted through our website and through tourism literature and the annual calendar of events.

Importance of cultural tourism:

- in total tourism offer	As culture is engrained in our mainstream tourism product it is difficult to estimate the actual component of total tourism revenue. It suffices to say that tourism contributes 54 per cent of GDP.

International Tourism by Origin

Cook Islands
International Tourist Arrivals at Frontiers

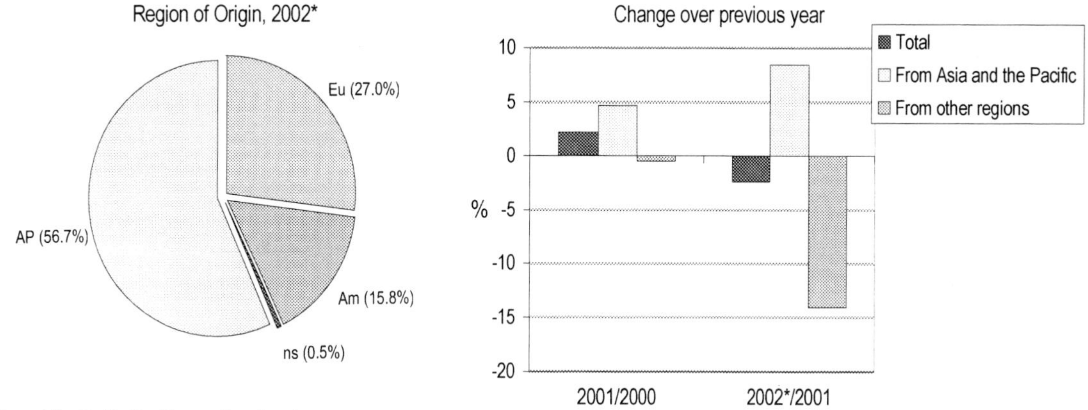

AP: Asia and the Pacific; Eu: Europe; Am: Americas;
ns: Not specified;

Source: World Tourism Organization (WTO) ©

Cook Islands
International Tourist Arrivals at Frontiers (by residence)

					Market share (%)		Growth rate (%)		Average per year (%)
	1995	2000	2001	2002*	1995	2002*	2001/00	2002*/01	1995-2002*
Total	**47,899**	**72,994**	**74,575**	**72,781**	**100**	**100**	**2.2**	**-2.4**	**6.2**
From Asia and the Pacific	*20,788*	*36,359*	*38,061*	*41,277*	*43.4*	*56.7*	*4.7*	*8.4*	*10.3*
New Zealand	14,161	22,020	24,328	28,841	29.6	39.6	10.5	18.6	10.7
Australia	4,361	12,128	11,826	9,952	9.1	13.7	-2.5	-15.8	12.5
French Polynesia	1,620	756	538	936	3.4	1.3	-28.8	74.0	-7.5
All Asia	646	654	459	503	1.3	0.7	-29.8	9.6	-3.5
Other Oceania	..	801	910	1,045		1.4	13.6	14.8	
From other regions	*26,537*	*36,409*	*36,229*	*31,135*	*55.4*	*42.8*	*-0.5*	*-14.1*	*2.3*
All Europe	18,600	..	..	..	38.8				
United Kingdom	..	12,392	12,694	10,612		14.6	2.4	-16.4	
United States	5,270	6,734	7,143	6,716	11.0	9.2	6.1	-6.0	3.5
Canada	2,667	5,992	6,270	4,789	5.6	6.6	4.6	-23.6	8.7
Germany	..	5,232	3,945	3,298		4.5	-24.6	-16.4	
Sweden	..	835	1,011	1,183		1.6	21.1	17.0	
Italy	..	857	746	895		1.2	-13.0	20.0	
Switzerland	..	1,121	821	771		1.1	-26.8	-6.1	
Norway	..	649	655	643		0.9	0.9	-1.8	
Austria	..	500	397	344		0.5	-20.6	-13.4	
France	..	267	273	312		0.4	2.2	14.3	
Belgium	..	108	254	196		0.3	135.2	-22.8	
Denmark	..	345	258	191		0.3	-25.2	-26.0	
Spain	..	270	188	177		0.2	-30.4	-5.9	
Finland	..	81	94	118		0.2	16.0	25.5	
Netherlands	..	199	173	113		0.2	-13.1	-34.7	
Other Europe	..	827	1,307	777		1.1	58.0	-40.6	
Other World/Not specified	*574*	*226*	*285*	*369*	*1.2*	*0.5*	*26.1*	*29.5*	*-6.1*

Source: World Tourism Organization (WTO) © (Data as collected by WTO September 2003)

III.3.4 Fiji Oceania

Profile

Fiji

East Asia and the Pacific
Oceania

Capital	Suva
Year of entry in WTO	1997
Area (100 km²)	183
Population (2002, 1000)	856
Gross Domestic Product (GDP) (2002, US$ million)	1,828
GDP per capita (2002, US$)	2,169
GDP growth (real, %)	
'-> 2001: 4.3; 2002: 4.4; 2003*: 5.2; 2004*: 3.2	

	2000	2001	2002*	2001/2000	2002*/2001
International Arrivals					
Visitors (1000)	435	447	462	2.7	3.4
Tourists (overnight visitors) (1000)	294	348	398	18.3	14.4
- per 100 of inhabitants	35	41	46		
Same-day visitors (1000)	131	92	58	-29.8	-37.0
Cruise passengers (1000)	10	7	6	-30.0	-14.3
Tourism accommodation					
Number of rooms	5,602	5,520	..	-1.5	
Nights spent in hotels and similar establishments (1000)	1,849	1,784	2,259	-3.5	26.6
by non-residents (inbound tourism)	1,519	1,463	1,871	-3.7	27.9
by residents (domestic tourism)	330	321	388	-2.7	20.9
Outbound Tourism					
Trips abroad (1000)	83	85	99	2.4	16.5
- per 100 of inhabitants	10	10	12		
Receipts and Expenditure for International Tourism					
International Tourism Receipts (US$ million)	181	217	267	19.9	23.0
- per Tourist Arrival (US$)	615	624	671	1.3	7.6
- per Visitor Arrival (US$)	416	485	578	16.7	19.1
- per capita (US$)	217	257	312		
International Tourism Expenditure (US$ million)	78	..	..		
- per trip (US$)	940	..	..		
- per capita (US$)	94	..	..		
△ International Tourism Balance (US$ million)	103	..	..		

Source: World Tourism Organization (WTO) (Data as collected by WTO September 2003)

See annex for methodological notes and reference of external sources used.

International Tourism by Origin

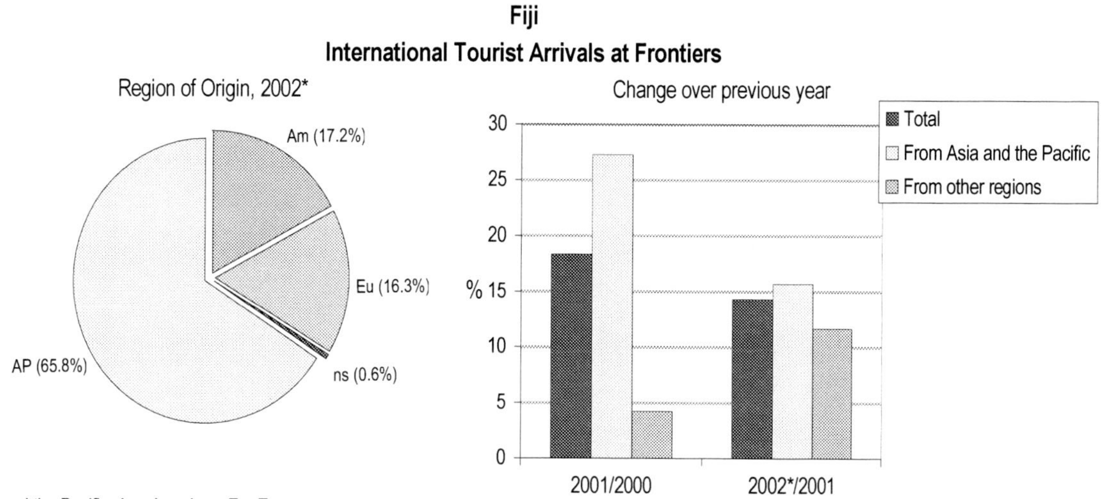

AP: Asia and the Pacific; Am: Americas; Eu: Europe;
ns: Not specified;

Source: World Tourism Organization (WTO) ©

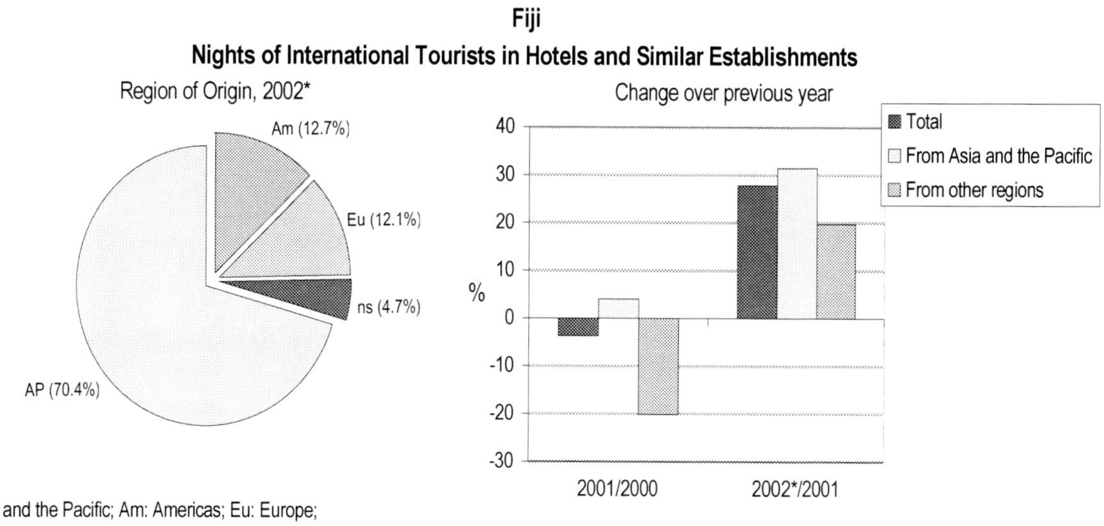

AP: Asia and the Pacific; Am: Americas; Eu: Europe;
ns: Not specified;

Source: World Tourism Organization (WTO) ©

Fiji

International Tourist Arrivals at Frontiers (by residence)

	1995	2000	2001	2002*	Market share (%) 1995	Market share (%) 2002*	Growth rate (%) 2001/00	Growth rate (%) 2002*/01	Average per year (%) 1995-2002*
Total	**318,495**	**294,070**	**348,014**	**397,859**	**100**	**100**	**18.3**	**14.3**	**3.2**
From Asia and the Pacific	*211,618*	*177,697*	*226,190*	*261,690*	*66.4*	*65.8*	*27.3*	*15.7*	*3.1*
Australia	78,503	76,883	98,213	123,606	24.6	31.1	27.7	25.9	6.7
New Zealand	59,019	49,470	66,472	68,293	18.5	17.2	34.4	2.7	2.1
Japan	45,300	19,674	20,411	26,382	14.2	6.6	3.7	29.3	-7.4
Korea, Republic of	5,475	3,386	8,143	6,992	1.7	1.8	140.5	-14.1	3.6
Taiwan (Pr. of China)	789	610	776	922	0.2	0.2	27.2	18.8	2.3
Malaysia	334	277	304	316	0.1	0.1	9.7	3.9	-0.8
Other Asia	4,737	5,863	8,263	11,128	1.5	2.8	40.9	34.7	13.0
Other East Asia/Pacific	17,461	21,534	23,608	24,051	5.5	6.0	9.6	1.9	4.7
From other regions	*105,525*	*114,787*	*119,688*	*133,664*	*33.1*	*33.6*	*4.3*	*11.7*	*3.4*
United States	39,736	52,534	57,511	58,815	12.5	14.8	9.5	2.3	5.8
United Kingdom	24,409	29,215	30,508	43,393	7.7	10.9	4.4	42.2	8.6
Canada	10,412	10,532	10,752	9,802	3.3	2.5	2.1	-8.8	-0.9
Germany	13,472	7,467	6,062	6,104	4.2	1.5	-18.8	0.7	-10.7
Italy	2,793	2,411	2,136	2,457	0.9	0.6	-11.4	15.0	-1.8
Sweden	1,822	2,098	1,931	2,139	0.6	0.5	-8.0	10.8	2.3
Switzerland	3,635	1,873	2,110	2,048	1.1	0.5	12.7	-2.9	-7.9
France	1,648	1,669	1,699	1,901	0.5	0.5	1.8	11.9	2.1
Netherlands	1,205	1,307	1,437	1,561	0.4	0.4	9.9	8.6	3.8
Norway	874	1,250	1,242	1,300	0.3	0.3	-0.6	4.7	5.8
Denmark	2,525	1,448	1,152	1,035	0.8	0.3	-20.4	-10.2	-12.0
Austria	1,470	1,245	1,250	811	0.5	0.2	0.4	-35.1	-8.1
Spain	373	392	521	613	0.1	0.2	32.9	17.7	7.4
Belgium	298	304	336	420	0.1	0.1	10.5	25.0	5.0
Finland	528	417	324	333	0.2	0.1	-22.3	2.8	-6.4
Other Europe	325	625	717	932	0.1	0.2	14.7	30.0	16.2
Other World/Not specified	*1,352*	*1,586*	*2,136*	*2,505*	*0.4*	*0.6*	*34.7*	*17.3*	*9.2*

Source: World Tourism Organization (WTO) © (Data as collected by WTO September 2003)

Fiji

Nights of International Tourists in Hotels and Similar Establishments (by residence)

	1995	2000	2001	2002*	Market share (%) 1995	Market share (%) 2002*	Growth rate (%) 2001/00	Growth rate (%) 2002*/01	Average per year (%) 1995-2002*
Total	..	**1,519,030**	**1,463,062**	**1,871,003**		**100**	**-3.7**	**27.9**	
From Asia and the Pacific	..	*963,364*	*1,002,308*	*1,317,705*		*70.4*	*4.0*	*31.5*	
Australia	..	487,905	549,035	791,478		42.3	12.5	44.2	
New Zealand	..	318,241	317,318	366,598		19.6	-0.3	15.5	
Japan	..	111,230	93,907	109,531		5.9	-15.6	16.6	
Other Oceania	..	45,988	42,048	50,098		2.7	-8.6	19.1	
From other regions	..	*486,366*	*388,411*	*464,964*		*24.9*	*-20.1*	*19.7*	
United States	..	218,199	190,323	201,917		10.8	-12.8	6.1	
United Kingdom	..	116,049	88,368	135,626		7.2	-23.9	53.5	
Canada	..	44,618	29,789	36,171		1.9	-33.2	21.4	
Other Europe	..	107,500	79,931	91,250		4.9	-25.6	14.2	
Other World/Not specified	..	*69,300*	*72,343*	*88,334*		*4.7*	*4.4*	*22.1*	

Source: World Tourism Organization (WTO) © (Data as collected by WTO September 2003)

III.3.5 French Polynesia Oceania

Profile

French Polynesia

Capital	Papeete
Area (100 km²)	40
Population (2002, 1000)	258

East Asia and the Pacific
Oceania

	2000	2001	2002*	2001/2000	2002*/2001
International Arrivals					
Tourists (overnight visitors) (1000)	252	228	189	-9.8	-16.9
- per 100 of inhabitants	101	90	73		
Tourism accommodation					
Number of rooms	3,357	2,943	3,195	-12.3	8.6
Nights spent in collective establishments (1000)					
by non-residents (inbound tourism)	..	2,875	..		
Nights spent in hotels and similar establishments (1000)					
by non-residents (inbound tourism)	..	2,042	..		

Source: World Tourism Organization (WTO) (Data as collected by WTO September 2003)

See annex for methodological notes and reference of external sources used.

Survey

Contributed by *Ministère du Tourisme et des Transports, chargé de la sécurité routière*
www.tahiti-tourisme.pf ; www.tahiti-tourisme.com (promotional)
www.tourisme.gov.pf (institutional/corporate)

Tourism development and outlook

Most significant determinant

Positive factors:
- Development of our international airline company Air Tahiti Nui, serving Paris ;
- Growth in hotel capacity;
- Maintenance of hotel occupation rates;
- Reinforcing the promotion of the last 4 years in external markets;
- Return of the Wind Song ;
- Recovery in the cruise sector at the end of 2002.

Negative factors:
- Events of September 2000 ;
- End of Renaissances cruises, end of 2001 ;
- End of Air Lib, April 2002 ;
- Wind Song fire, end of 2002.

Tourism products

Beginning of the development of ecotourism.
Increase in accommodation capacity (+15%).
Air Tahiti Nui service to Paris.
Reinforcement of the main sectors: honeymoons, underwater diving.
Main attractions: Hawaiki Nui, Heiva, Billagong Pro.

Access

Air Tahiti Nui service to Paris.
Tahiti Faaa airport open 24/24.
Opening of airfields on the islands: 44 airfields open to date.

Generating markets

Main markets: United States, France, Japan.

Secondary markets: Italy, Great Britain, Germany, Spain, South America (Argentina, Brazil, Chile), Australia, New Zealand.

Emerging markets: Northern Europe, Central Europe, Russia.

North America: Unfavourable conditions: economic factors (reduction in purchasing power linked to the fall in the dollar), political factors (terrorism/war) and mainly the end of Renaissance cruises in French Polynesia.

Europe: inadequacy of the seat offer for the French Market and in the rest of Europe because of the end of Air Lib only partially compensated for by the spectacular development of Air Tahiti Nui.

Japan: increase of almost 20 per cent in this period as a direct consequence of the increase in offer of seats for this market.

Other Issues

Procedure for rating hotel establishments in progress: will enable a higher profile for offers to tourists.

Development of ecotourism: management of sites, footpaths and hiking.

Improvement of the quality ratio through tourist facilities, a policy of professional training and by raising awareness of tourism.

Development of tourist activities, notably through a redrafting of the regulatory framework in order to encourage sailing activity.

Outlook 2003

Air services:
The acquisition by Air Tahiti Nui of two new Airbuses will enable us to maintain our policy of tourism development by adding to the basic overall offer of seats after two successive years of reductions in flights and the withdrawals of Air France, Qantas, Hawaiian Airlines, Lan Chile, Air Lib and, in 2003, Corsair. However, the service from Paris remains inadequate even with the five weekly flights in high season by Air Tahiti Nui.

Cruises:
We are seeing the recovery of the cruise sector, largely marked by the coming into service of the Tahitian Princess thanks to the efforts made by the President of the government. In the first half of 2003, the number of cruise ships based in our islands should be 8 and the number of cabins 804.

Forecast fleet for the 1st half of 2003:
Tahitian Princess 345; Paul Gauguin 160; Aranui 3 84; Windstar 75; Tu Moana 37; Tia Moana 37; Haumana 19; Aggressor 12

Hotel capacity:
412 new international class hotel bedrooms are forecast in 2003 and around 140 for family hotels.

The overall increase in our accommodation capacity enables the destination to be sold in a better way. It is, however, necessary to avoid under-capacity in the seat offer which would adversely affect the occupation rate for tourist accommodation establishments.

The rating of hotel establishments and the quality control of products will be strengthened, enabling an improvement in the general quality of our part and a better profile for proposed tourist constructions and facilities.

Facilities:
After honeymoons and diving, ecotourism will be the 3rd sector to be developed for our destination.

The attraction for this sector is worldwide and represents a real social phenomenon. Today, tourists want to enjoy themselves in natural surroundings and it is advisable to make the most of the assets we have. We have numerous advantages in the area of ecotourism thanks to our many valleys and our young population willing to remain in their island of origin and developing existing employees. For this reason, we must develop activities linked to nature.

Tourism policy

Tourism development policy:

After many years, the territory has put in place, in close co-operation with the whole of the tourism profession, a range of measures intended to promote the development of tourism, focusing on 4 directions.

The first direction concerns the reinforcement and development of tourist infrastructures. So, the Territory is building airports, roads and harbours and private investors are constructing accommodation buildings.

The three legal provisions of metropolitan tax exemption, investment code and the Flosse Act have therefore enabled spectacular progress in hotel investment. Without the Flosse Act we would not have achieved this success.

The second direction involves promoting our destination through constant and unceasing effort with tour operators in target generating countries, coupled with the search for new emerging markets. These steps are completed through the use of international media and by a strengthening of training for travel agents.

The third direction is the acquisition of an international air service tool thanks to our airline Air Tahiti Nui, which enables us to adapt our offer of seats to demand and to reduce uncertainties due to the policies of certain international airlines.

The fourth direction operates in the area of improving the quality-price ratio of tourist sector facilities thanks to an accommodation classification policy linked to professional training programmes.

Recent activities:

Development of a unique tourist product with small family hotels. This type of accommodation is aimed at customers seeking authenticity.

This sector is in the process of development, is achieving clear success in terms of customers and enables the full integration of tourist expansion with the population. It is, in effect, local investors, in the islands, who are investing in this activity and who are managing these family organisations.

In order to maintain the inter-island cruise market, a regulatory framework initiative has been put in place and an extensive programme of harbour facilities aimed at cruise ships is in progress.

Concerning international air services, our company Air Tahiti Nui has brought its capacity up to 4 planes, with a standardised modern fleet built around the A340 Airbus, capable of responding to the demands of foreign markets.

Ongoing activities:

In the area of tourist activities, the diving sector is our second market segment after honeymoons. In 2003, the emphasis is notably being put on ecotourism and water sports.

Only mutual exchange serves to develop durable, harmonious and authentic tourism.

So, in the next few years, our tourist policy will be oriented in this direction.

The rating of all tourist accommodation will form one of our most important activities. Thanks to this, we will be able to offer our customers minimum quality standards and an easy-to-read table showing the standard of products and services offered by our establishments.

The same stocktaking, classification and rating job will be carried out for tourist activities in order to rationalise and streamline our range while improving the quality and safety of our facilities.

Measures will be taken to enliven the charter sailing sector in order to give it the place it deserves.

The improvement of service quality is also a priority. We are putting measures in place to enable hotel owners to recruit more staff, to strengthen their professional training and to increase manpower per room.

In the area of transport and road safety, the improvement of taxis and of the road network will also benefit tourists.

Finally the environment, an essential component for our tourism, has also been declared a priority sector by the President of the government. Waste management, sanitation, and municipal cleaning are among objectives that will benefit from the resources available so that the population and tourists can enjoy our exceptional surroundings.

Marketing & promotion

The 5 guiding principles making up the common strategic basis for promotion are the following:

- To promote the destination year-round in order to reduce high and low season;
- To promote the island of Tahiti as an entire destination;
- To promote Huahine, Raiatea, Tahaa, Tikehau, Fakarava, Manihi and the Marquises islands;
- To streamline press relations activities in the markets;
- To begin the co-ordination of hotel and airline seasons.

Concerning promotion and communication in the markets, the new directions taken are:

- Tiare Agent training programme: agents specialising in the destination Tahiti and its islands are trained and named Tiare Tahiti Agents;
- Web Strategy: result-oriented strategy: the central website which only distributes "free" information must give way on search engines to commercial sites where the architecture is much more sales oriented, particularly through pages dedicated to Business to Business and Business to Consumer. Our sales office sites enable visitors to obtain information but also and above all to discover current special offers (offers from partners in co-operation with the tour operators) and the list of Tiare Tahiti agents capable of showing them offers and selling them a product;

- Communication programmes: development of common standards. To encourage co-operation between Tahiti Tourisme and providers, specific tools will be developed, including promotional and advertising activities. Local professionals will therefore be able to see in which markets, when and for which activities they will be able to link their promotional budgets with the Tahiti Tourism organisation for joint operations (advertising campaigns) or for promotional support (brochures).

Cultural Tourism (CT)

Specific place for CT in tourism policy: yes.

Main objectives & instruments

Concerning culture, the policy undertaken by the government intends to make culture a living, dynamic thing that can be transmitted to more people. It considers culture as a factor in personal development and as an element of social cohesion contributing to development of the archipelagos which plays a part in expanding the number of places of tourist interest. So, numerous activities are carried out relating to the conservation and development of heritage and to the encouragement of culture: Heiva, historical reconstruction, dance, music, painting, traditional art, marae landscape developments, cultural remains.

The Heiva Nui statutory body has recently been set up with a mission to manage cultural events and attractions.

The Paul Gauguin year enables the holding of several events this year: original paintings in the Paul Gauguin museum, conferences at the University, events on the Marquises, reconstruction of the house at Tiki Village on Moorea.

Main focus of attention supply

Attraction for tourists and development.

Importance of combining authenticity and attraction

Main focus of attention demand

European markets, particularly the French one, have a strong demand for cultural tourism.

Specific place for CT in marketing & promotion plan: yes.

Main objectives & programmes

The cultural lever particularly serves the purpose of hitting targets for over-50s in the markets and for maintaining islands such as the Marquises and Tahiti.

Every year the schedule of events is transmitted to the various partners in the markets. The schedule in the promotional support from the Tahiti Tourisme organisation (Travel Guide, brochures) and distributed to travel agents, tour operators and consumers, promotes the main cultural events in the destination.

Special activities undertaken

Paul Gauguin Year
Heiva
Hawaiki Nui.

International Tourism by Origin

French Polynesia
International Tourist Arrivals at Frontiers

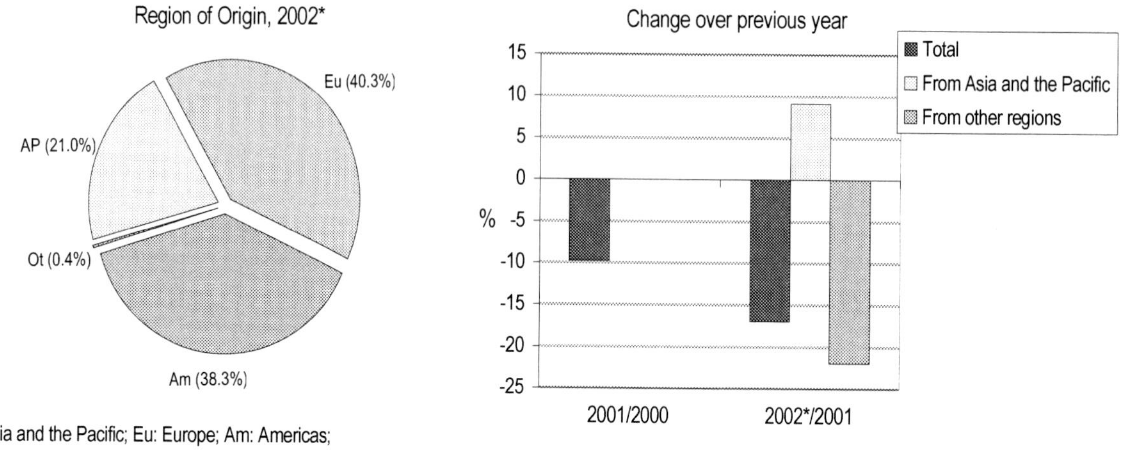

AP: Asia and the Pacific; Eu: Europe; Am: Americas;
Ot: Other;

Source: World Tourism Organization (WTO) ©

French Polynesia
Nights of International Tourists in All Accommodation Establishments

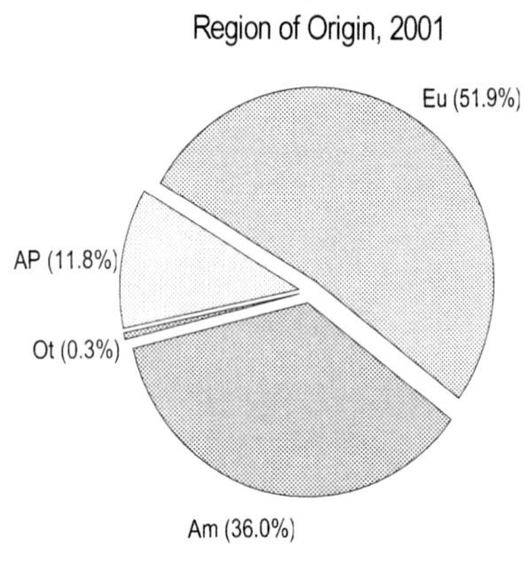

AP: Asia and the Pacific; Eu: Europe; Am: Americas;
Ot: Other;

Source: World Tourism Organization (WTO) ©

French Polynesia
International Tourist Arrivals at Frontiers (by residence)

					Market share (%)		Growth rate (%)		Average per year (%)
	1995	2000	2001	2002*	1995	2002*	2001/00	2002*/01	1995-2002*
Total	**172,129**	**252,200**	**227,547**	**188,998**	**100**	**100**	**-9.8**	**-16.9**	**1.3**
From Asia and the Pacific	*37,245*	..	*36,429*	*39,743*	*21.6*	*21.0*		*9.1*	*0.9*
Japan	19,297	..	19,031	23,632	11.2	12.5		24.2	2.9
Australia	5,878	..	6,420	5,346	3.4	2.8		-16.7	-1.3
New Zealand	4,646	..	5,435	5,282	2.7	2.8		-2.8	1.8
New Caledonia	3,671	..	3,238	3,225	2.1	1.7		-0.4	-1.8
Taiwan (Pr. of China)	21	..	121	266	0.0	0.1		119.8	43.7
Cook Is	665	..	268	252	0.4	0.1		-6.0	-12.9
Singapore	171	..	251	241	0.1	0.1		-4.0	5.0
Hong Kong (China)	125	..	191	192	0.1	0.1		0.5	6.3
Korea, Republic of	199	..	56	132	0.1	0.1		135.7	-5.7
Fiji	482	..	84	83	0.3	0.0		-1.2	-22.2
Malaysia	27	..	64	66	0.0	0.0		3.1	13.6
Philippines	51	..	81	65	0.0	0.0		-19.8	3.5
Thailand	38	..	71	47	0.0	0.0		-33.8	3.1
India	36	..	43	46	0.0	0.0		7.0	3.6
Other Asia	174	..	312	230	0.1	0.1		-26.3	4.1
Other Oceania	1,507	..	639	566	0.9	0.3		-11.4	-13.1
Other intraregional	257	..	124	72	0.1	0.0		-41.9	-16.6
From other regions	*134,495*	..	*190,902*	*149,003*	*78.1*	*78.8*		*-21.9*	*1.5*
United States	49,050	..	93,363	61,888	28.5	32.7		-33.7	3.4
France	43,719	..	50,466	46,602	25.4	24.7		-7.7	0.9
Italy	5,609	..	9,351	8,853	3.3	4.7		-5.3	6.7
United Kingdom	5,006	..	6,496	5,399	2.9	2.9		-16.9	1.1
Germany	9,531	..	5,448	4,190	5.5	2.2		-23.1	-11.1
Canada	2,738	..	3,648	2,793	1.6	1.5		-23.4	0.3
Switzerland	3,742	..	2,770	2,476	2.2	1.3		-10.6	-5.7
Spain	1,270	..	2,112	2,323	0.7	1.2		10.0	9.0
Hawaii (USA)	2,062	..	2,936	2,314	1.2	1.2		-21.2	1.7
Mexico	..	..	1,473	1,523		0.8		3.4	
Chile	1,941	..	1,454	1,452	1.1	0.8		-0.1	-4.1
Brazil	1,005	..	1,713	1,257	0.6	0.7		-26.6	3.2
Belgium	1,183	..	1,491	1,158	0.7	0.6		-22.3	-0.3
Austria	1,514	..	775	701	0.9	0.4		-9.5	-10.4
Argentina	1,994	..	1,635	680	1.2	0.4		-58.4	-14.2
Netherlands	445	..	618	609	0.3	0.3		-1.5	4.6
Portugal	253	..	743	576	0.1	0.3		-22.5	12.5
Sweden	448	..	581	484	0.3	0.3		-16.7	1.1
Norway	204	..	405	357	0.1	0.2		-11.9	8.3
All Africa	268	..	280	253	0.2	0.1		-9.6	-0.8
Former U.S.S.R.	42	..	157	235	0.0	0.1		49.7	27.9
Denmark	310	..	269	212	0.2	0.1		-21.2	-5.3
All Middle East	137	..	191	182	0.1	0.1		-4.7	4.1
Finland	163	..	272	167	0.1	0.1		-38.6	0.3
Luxembourg	132	..	152	163	0.1	0.1		7.2	3.1
Other interregional	1,729	..	2,103	2,156	1.0	1.1		2.5	3.2
Other World/Not specified	*389*	*252,200*	*216*	*252*	*0.2*	*0.1*	*-99.9*	*16.7*	*-6.0*

Source: World Tourism Organization (WTO) © (Data as collected by WTO September 2003)

French Polynesia

Nights of International Tourists in All Accommodation Establishments (by residence)

					Market share (%)		Growth rate (%)		Average per year (%)
	1995	1999	2000	2001	1995	2001	2000/99	2001/00	1995-2001
Total	**2,066,630**	**2,492,520**	**..**	**2,875,094**	**100**	**100**			**5.7**
From Asia and the Pacific	*343,665*	*255,342*	*..*	*337,956*	*16.6*	*11.8*			*-0.3*
Japan	132,818	76,143	..	142,388	6.4	5.0			1.2
Australia	48,842	62,605	..	66,416	2.4	2.3			5.3
New Caledonia	70,959	44,482	..	52,363	3.4	1.8			-4.9
New Zealand	41,670	52,866	..	50,682	2.0	1.8			3.3
Singapore	1,443	1,501	..	2,807	0.1	0.1			11.7
Cook Is	8,870	2,994	..	2,688	0.4	0.1			-18.0
Hong Kong (China)	1,199	990	..	1,926	0.1	0.1			8.2
Taiwan (Pr. of China)	201	1,012	..	1,870	0.0	0.1			45.0
Philippines	398	501	..	1,776	0.0	0.1			28.3
Thailand	358	555	..	1,398	0.0	0.0			25.5
Indonesia	700	555	..	1,288	0.0	0.0			10.7
Malaysia	207	655	..	774	0.0	0.0			24.6
Fiji	7,271	2,191	..	719	0.4	0.0			-32.0
India	224	319	..	530	0.0	0.0			15.4
Korea, Republic of	1,512	834	..	425	0.1	0.0			-19.1
Tonga	1,988	382	..	147	0.1	0.0			-35.2
Samoa	187	221	..	140	0.0	0.0			-4.7
Other Asia	1,373	1,936	..	3,968	0.1	0.1			19.3
Other Oceania	23,445	4,600	..	5,651	1.1	0.2			-21.1
From other regions	*1,717,296*	*2,231,727*	*..*	*2,534,809*	*83.1*	*88.2*			*6.7*
France	934,505	1,209,189	..	1,093,719	45.2	38.0			2.7
United States	375,620	564,504	..	889,472	18.2	30.9			15.5
Italy	65,462	118,686	..	122,758	3.2	4.3			11.0
Germany	82,317	53,010	..	58,585	4.0	2.0			-5.5
All South America	51,566	67,546	..	57,120	2.5	2.0			1.7
United Kingdom	33,726	33,752	..	55,653	1.6	1.9			8.7
Switzerland	44,892	35,266	..	43,880	2.2	1.5			-0.4
Canada	23,402	26,224	..	41,092	1.1	1.4			9.8
Hawaii (USA)	24,035	28,638	..	31,954	1.2	1.1			4.9
Belgium	16,866	17,824	..	23,381	0.8	0.8			5.6
Spain	13,732	19,325	..	23,255	0.7	0.8			9.2
All Central America	4,809	8,571	..	14,780	0.2	0.5			20.6
Austria	17,483	7,507	..	10,250	0.8	0.4			-8.5
Portugal	2,821	6,630	..	9,242	0.1	0.3			21.9
Netherlands	4,251	5,238	..	7,570	0.2	0.3			10.1
Sweden	3,683	3,384	..	6,687	0.2	0.2			10.5
All Africa	2,794	2,289	..	5,082	0.1	0.2			10.5
Norway	2,061	2,820	..	4,850	0.1	0.2			15.3
Denmark	3,144	2,561	..	4,177	0.2	0.1			4.8
Luxembourg	1,449	1,824	..	2,954	0.1	0.1			12.6
All Middle East	1,122	2,687	..	2,220	0.1	0.1			12.0
Finland	801	1,930	..	1,952	0.0	0.1			16.0
Former U.S.S.R.	348	1,128	..	1,765	0.0	0.1			31.1
Other Europe	6,407	11,194	..	22,411	0.3	0.8			23.2
Other World/Not specified	*5,669*	*5,451*	*..*	*2,329*	*0.3*	*0.1*			*-13.8*

Source: World Tourism Organization (WTO) © (Data as collected by WTO September 2003)

III.3.6 Guam Oceania

Profile

Guam		
	Capital	Agana
	Area (10 km²)	55
	Population (2002, 1000)	161
East Asia and the Pacific		
Oceania		

	2000	2001	2002*	2001/2000	2002*/2001
International Arrivals					
Tourists (overnight visitors) (1000)	1,287	1,160	1,059	-9.9	-8.7
- per 100 of inhabitants	832	736	659		
Cruise passengers (1000)	8	36	28	350.0	-22.2
Tourism accommodation					
Number of rooms	10,110	9,002	..	-11.0	

Source: World Tourism Organization (WTO) (Data as collected by WTO September 2003)

See annex for methodological notes and reference of external sources used.

Survey

Contributed by *Guam Visitors Bureau*
www.i-loveguam.com (promotional)
www.visitguam.org (institutional/corporate)
www.visitguam.org (research and data)

Tourism development and outlook

Most significant determinant

The most significant factors were the following:
- Japan's economic downturn.
- The war against Iraq.
- Overseas travellers were preoccupied by the SARS outbreak.

Tourism products

Guam's infrastructure was damaged by two devastating typhoons in 2002.

Access

Airline seat capacity was reduced due to low demand.

Generating markets

Growth in outbound Korean travel.
Steady business in wedding groups.

Other Issues

More interest from China for tourism.

Outlook 2003	New tourism prospects include Korean visitors, military personnel and expatriates. Core target groups: the young, executive women, group travel and family travel from Japan.
Tourism policy	To brand Guam as a world class tourism destination. Promotion of regional tourism through a Visit Magnificent Micronesia campaign. To strengthen and improve the tourism product.

Cultural Tourism (CT)

Specific place for CT in tourism policy: yes.

Main objectives & instruments	Guam Visitors Bureau's mission statement includes the promotion and presentation of the Chamorro culture of Guan.
Main focus of attention supply	Cultural artifacts and performing arts.
Main focus of attention demand	To increase the number of tours and develop tour sites.

Specific place for CT in marketing & promotion plan: yes.

Main objectives & programmes	The promotion of Chamorro Village night market and a working tour of the famous capital city landmarks.
Special activities undertaken	In Guam's big Summer Festival, the Guam Visitors Bureau promotes street fairs and cultural performing arts fairs.

Importance of cultural tourism:

- in total tourism offer	Twenty per cent of total tour packages include a degree of cultural tourism.

International Tourism by Origin

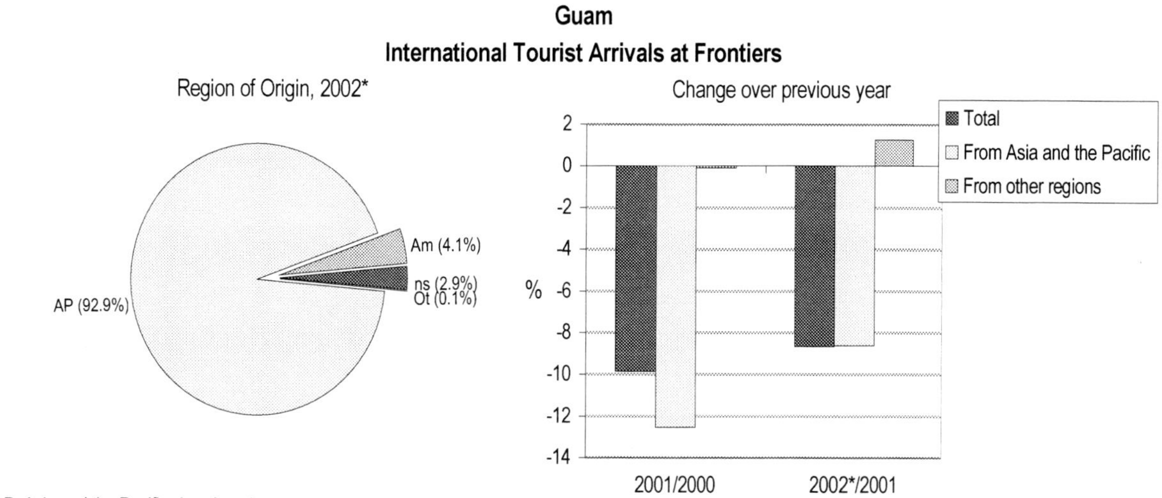

AP: Asia and the Pacific; Am: Americas;
ns: Not specified; Ot: Other;

Source: World Tourism Organization (WTO) ©

Guam
International Tourist Arrivals at Frontiers (by residence)

	1995	2000	2001	2002*	Market share (%) 1995	Market share (%) 2002*	Growth rate (%) 2001/00	Growth rate (%) 2002*/01	Average per year (%) 1995-2002*
Total	**1,361,830**	**1,286,807**	**1,159,895**	**1,059,377**	**100**	**100**	**-9.9**	**-8.7**	**-3.5**
From Asia and the Pacific	*1,275,948*	*1,231,413*	*1,077,140*	*984,373*	*93.7*	*92.9*	*-12.5*	*-8.6*	*-3.6*
Japan	996,219	1,048,813	901,536	786,947	73.2	74.3	-14.0	-12.7	-3.3
Korea, Republic of	186,264	87,070	89,655	128,307	13.7	12.1	3.0	43.1	-5.2
Taiwan (Pr. of China)	31,816	39,451	31,539	19,500	2.3	1.8	-20.1	-38.2	-6.8
N.Mariana Is	32,767	22,889	22,541	19,080	2.4	1.8	-1.5	-15.4	-7.4
Hong Kong (China)	..	9,050	9,174	8,444		0.8	1.4	-8.0	
Micronesia (Fed.St.of)	..	10,435	9,757	8,388		0.8	-6.5	-14.0	
Philippines	4,533	6,000	5,697	6,530	0.3	0.6	-5.1	14.6	5.4
Palau	..	3,846	3,392	3,190		0.3	-11.8	-6.0	
Australia	..	1,638	1,724	1,788		0.2	5.3	3.7	
China	..	787	868	1,236		0.1	10.3	42.4	
Thailand	..	184	272	229		0.0	47.8	-15.8	
Vietnam	..	52	26	51		0.0	-50.0	96.2	
Nauru	..	336	89	10		0.0	-73.5	-88.8	
Other East Asia/Pacific	24,349	862	870	673	1.8	0.1	0.9	-22.6	-40.1
From other regions	*56,626*	*43,902*	*43,857*	*44,411*	*4.2*	*4.2*	*-0.1*	*1.3*	*-3.4*
United States	56,626	41,664	41,875	41,521	4.2	3.9	0.5	-0.8	-4.3
Canada	..	620	670	1,454		0.1	8.1	117.0	
All Europe	..	1,618	1,312	1,436		0.1	-18.9	9.5	
Other World/Not specified	*29,256*	*11,492*	*38,898*	*30,593*	*2.1*	*2.9*	*238.5*	*-21.4*	*0.6*

Source: World Tourism Organization (WTO) © (Data as collected by WTO September 2003)

III.3.7 Kiribati Oceania

Profile

Kiribati

East Asia and the Pacific
Oceania

Capital	Tarawa
Area (10 km²)	73
Population (2002, 1000)	96
Gross Domestic Product (GDP) (2002, US$ million)	54
GDP per capita (2002, US$)	609
GDP growth (real, %)	

'-> 2001: 1.8; 2002: 1.0; 2003*: 2.5; 2004*: 1.8

	2000	2001	2002*	2001/2000	2002*/2001
International Arrivals					
Tourists (overnight visitors) (1000)	5	5	5	-5.9	18.2
- per 100 of inhabitants	5	5	6		
Tourism accommodation					
Number of rooms	158	158	..		
Receipts and Expenditure for International Tourism					
International Tourism Receipts (US$ million)	3	3	..	18.5	
- per Tourist Arrival (US$)	558	703	..	26.0	
- per capita (US$)	29	34	..		

Source: World Tourism Organization (WTO) (Data as collected by WTO September 2003)
See annex for methodological notes and reference of external sources used.

International Tourism by Origin

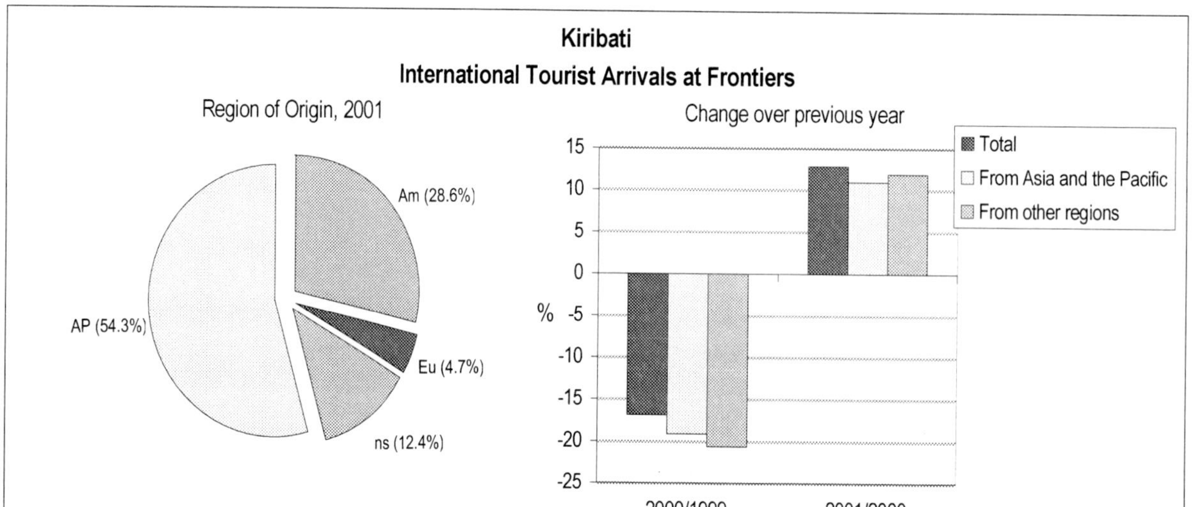

AP: Asia and the Pacific; Am: Americas; Eu: Europe;
ns: Not specified;

Source: World Tourism Organization (WTO) ©

Kiribati
International Tourist Arrivals at Frontiers (by nationality)

	1995	1999	2000	2001	Market share (%) 1995	Market share (%) 2001	Growth rate (%) 2000/99	Growth rate (%) 2001/00	Average per year (%) 1995-2001
Total	**3,942**	**4,854**	**4,035**	**4,555**	**100**	**100**	**-16.9**	**12.9**	**2.4**
From Asia and the Pacific	*2,377*	*2,756*	*2,229*	*2,474*	*60.3*	*54.3*	*-19.1*	*11.0*	*0.7*
Australia	496	754	555	739	12.6	16.2	-26.4	33.2	6.9
Nauru	452	717	378	423	11.5	9.3	-47.3	11.9	-1.1
Japan	291	363	365	345	7.4	7.6	0.6	-5.5	2.9
Fiji	173	227	264	335	4.4	7.4	16.3	26.9	11.6
New Zealand	216	223	192	255	5.5	5.6	-13.9	32.8	2.8
Tuvalu	516	240	75	174	13.1	3.8	-68.8	132.0	-16.6
Marshall Is	136	123	76	..	3.5		-38.2		
Solomon Is	41	28	12	..	1.0		-57.1		
Other Oceania	56	81	312	203	1.4	4.5	285.2	-34.9	23.9
From other regions	*1,246*	*1,706*	*1,354*	*1,516*	*31.6*	*33.3*	*-20.6*	*12.0*	*3.3*
United States	973	1,452	1,202	1,303	24.7	28.6	-17.2	8.4	5.0
United Kingdom	199	214	123	177	5.0	3.9	-42.5	43.9	-1.9
Germany	74	40	29	36	1.9	0.8	-27.5	24.1	-11.3
Other World/Not specified	*319*	*392*	*452*	*565*	*8.1*	*12.4*	*15.3*	*25.0*	*10.0*

Source: World Tourism Organization (WTO) © (Data as collected by WTO September 2003)

III.3.8 Marshall Island Oceania

Profile

Marshall Island

East Asia and the Pacific
Oceania

Capital	Majuro
Area (10 km²)	18
Population (2002, 1000)	55

	2000	2001	2002*	2001/2000	2002*/2001
International Arrivals					
Tourists (overnight visitors) (1000)	5	5	6	3.8	10.2
- per 100 of inhabitants	10	10	11		
Cruise passengers (1000)	..	..	2		
Tourism accommodation					
Number of rooms	305	..	..		
Receipts and Expenditure for International Tourism					
International Tourism Receipts (US$ million)	4	..	4		
- per Tourist Arrival (US$)	762	..	667		
- per capita (US$)	75	..	73		

Source: World Tourism Organization (WTO) (Data as collected by WTO September 2003)
See annex for methodological notes and reference of external sources used.

Survey

Contributed by *Marshall Islands Visitors Authority*
www.visitmarshallislands.com (promotional)
www.rmiembassyus.org (institutional/corporate)

Tourism development and outlook

Most significant determinant

As in previous years, the geographic isolation of the Marshall Islands has been a constraint to tourism development. Increased global tensions have contributed as well to a 3 per cent decrease in 2002, especially from Japan. However, greater numbers from North American markets indicate destination resilience.

Tourism products

New 32-room luxury accommodation and extensions/renovations to existing tourist facilities gave increased capacity. Events such as fishing tournaments and sailing canoe races mature, and a new dive operator opened up for business. Price levels for international and domestic airfares remain relatively high.

Access

The addition of Air Kiribati reconnected the Nadi and Majuro hubs, once a week at the present time. Since 2000, there are 5 weekly flights from Honolulu and 3 weekly from Guam. The "Bottleneck" via Guam for Asian visitors to Majuro remains in effect, resulting in poor international access from Asian countries. Domestic transport

	capacity aboard Air Marshall Islands has improved with the acquisition of a 36-seater Dash-8 aircraft.
Generating markets	Japanese and Amercian divers continue to make up roughly 60 per cent of all holiday visitors to the Marshall Islands, with indications of growth in the sports fishing market (big game and fly fishing) and the cultural market. Taiwan is emerging as a general interest market.
Other Issues	Fostering the establishment of a land registry authority to, among other things, provide secure land access for both domestic and foreign investors remains a priority of the Marshallese government. There is also continued poor access to investment capital for domestic investors.
Outlook 2003	Similar decrease in tourist arrivals by 3 per cent counteracted by growth in overall visitor arrivals (business, VFR, etc.). Continued growth can be seen in the North American markets. Potentially significant growth in late 2003 due to promotional campaigns in September/October.
Tourism policy	Priority is being given to placing secure land on the market, making it easier for foreign and domestic investors. Tourism identified by the National Training Council Labour Market Survey to be the number four priority for human resource development in the nation. A review of current tax structure for the country is being undertaken, with streamlining and predictability. Greater attention will be given to private sector development, e.g. tourism, in the new Compact of Free Association with the United States. The long-term Tourism Master Plan is expected for no later than 2005.
Marketing & promotion	Continued focus on niche markets of diving and sports fishing, and to a lesser extent nautical and World War II tourism. New website launched, with upcoming e-newsletter. Updated brochures in both English and Japanese languages. CSPro software installed for broader tabulations of data gathered through in-flight arrival forms. Continued representation in major source markets via travel trade shows, such as DEMA, Diving Festival, Marine Diving Fair, International Travel Fair Taipei, etc. Special promotion campaigns in geographically closer source markets such as the Hawaiian Islands and Kwajalein Atoll United States of America military base, focusing on cultural tours.

Cultural Tourism (CT)

Specific place for CT in tourism policy: no.

Main focus of attention supply	Traditional sailing canoes, handicrafts, and cuisine and to a lesser extent pearl farm tours and World War II heritage tours, Bikini Atoll, World Heritage listing, etc.
Main focus of attention demand	The Japanese market and the United States of America nautical tourism market (canoes).

Specific place for CT in marketing & promotion plan: yes.

Main objectives & programmes	Using Marshallese sailing canoes and handicraft uniqueness to cultivate a unique "Marshallese cultural experience". Women's handicraft center and association, plus Waan Aelon in Majol canoe project both are examples of the objectives realized. Translation of these efforts into tourism promotion has primarily been implemented through local annual events, overseas trade show participation, and visiting media and familiarization trips.
Special activities undertaken	Yes.

Importance of cultural tourism:

- in total tourism offer	Ten per cent of tours offered.
- in intern. arrivals	Ten per cent of tourist arrivals.

International Tourism by Origin

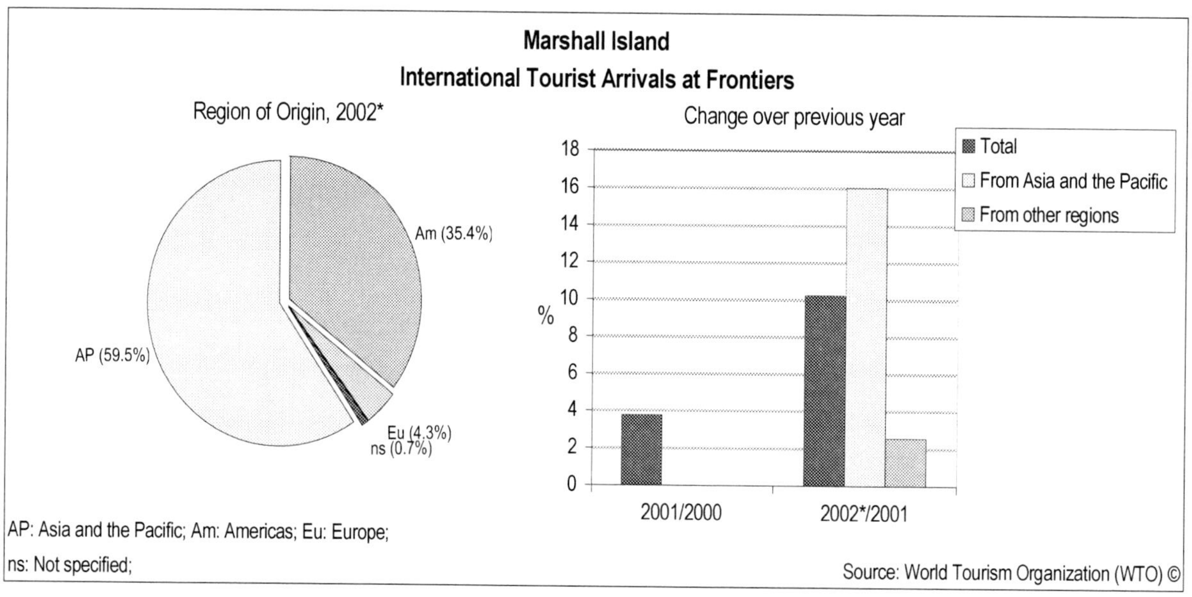

Marshall Island
International Tourist Arrivals at Frontiers (by nationality)

	1995	2000	2001	2002*	Market share (%) 1995	Market share (%) 2002*	Growth rate (%) 2001/00	Growth rate (%) 2002*/01	Average per year (%) 1995-2002*
Total	**5,504**	**5,246**	**5,444**	**6,002**	**100**	**100**	**3.8**	**10.2**	**1.2**
From Asia and the Pacific	*3,262*	*2,673*	*3,076*	*3,569*	*59.3*	*59.5*	*15.1*	*16.0*	*1.3*
Japan	506	856	996	892	9.2	14.9	16.4	-10.4	8.4
Taiwan (Pr. of China)	..	..	412	402		6.7		-2.4	
Kiribati	978	321	283	269	17.8	4.5	-11.8	-4.9	-16.8
Philippines	237	170	222	258	4.3	4.3	30.6	16.2	1.2
Micronesia (Fed.St.of)	212	420	203	245	3.9	4.1	-51.7	20.7	2.1
Australia	250	140	190	191	4.5	3.2	35.7	0.5	-3.8
China	261	83	114	189	4.7	3.1	37.3	65.8	-4.5
Korea, Republic of	109	72	91	171	2.0	2.8	26.4	87.9	6.6
New Zealand	113	62	101	134	2.1	2.2	62.9	32.7	2.5
Nauru	13	18	66	130	0.2	2.2	266.7	97.0	38.9
Fiji	124	148	94	103	2.3	1.7	-36.5	9.6	-2.6
Palau	49	65	47	45	0.9	0.7	-27.7	-4.3	-1.2
Tuvalu	125	17	21	17	2.3	0.3	23.5	-19.0	-24.8
Other Asia	211	109	165	414	3.8	6.9	51.4	150.9	10.1
Other Oceania	74	192	71	109	1.3	1.8	-63.0	53.5	5.7
From other regions	*2,069*	*2,151*	*2,328*	*2,388*	*37.6*	*39.8*	*8.2*	*2.6*	*2.1*
United States	1,695	1,999	2,039	2,065	30.8	34.4	2.0	1.3	2.9
United Kingdom	72	31	102	133	1.3	2.2	229.0	30.4	9.2
Canada	58	20	61	59	1.1	1.0	205.0	-3.3	0.2
Germany	72	25	27	34	1.3	0.6	8.0	25.9	-10.2
Other Americas	17	3	7	3	0.3	0.0	133.3	-57.1	-21.9
Other Europe	155	73	92	94	2.8	1.6	26.0	2.2	-6.9
Nationals residing abroad	*23*	*181*	..	..	*0.4*				
Other World/Not specified	*150*	*241*	*40*	*45*	*2.7*	*0.7*	*-83.4*	*12.5*	*-15.8*

Source: World Tourism Organization (WTO) © (Data as collected by WTO September 2003)

III.3.9 Micronesia (Federated States of) Oceania

Profile

Micronesia, Federated States of

East Asia and the Pacific
Oceania

Capital	Palikir
Area (10 km²)	70
Population (2002, 1000)	136

	2000	2001	2002*	2001/2000	2002*/2001
International Arrivals					
Tourists (overnight visitors) (1000)	21	15	19	-25.5	24.8
- per 100 of inhabitants	15	11	14		
Receipts and Expenditure for International Tourism					
International Tourism Receipts (US$ million)	15	13	..	-13.3	
- per Tourist Arrival (US$)	732	852	..	16.4	
- per capita (US$)	113	97	..		

Source: World Tourism Organization (WTO) (Data as collected by WTO September 2003)

See annex for methodological notes and reference of external sources used.

International Tourism by Origin

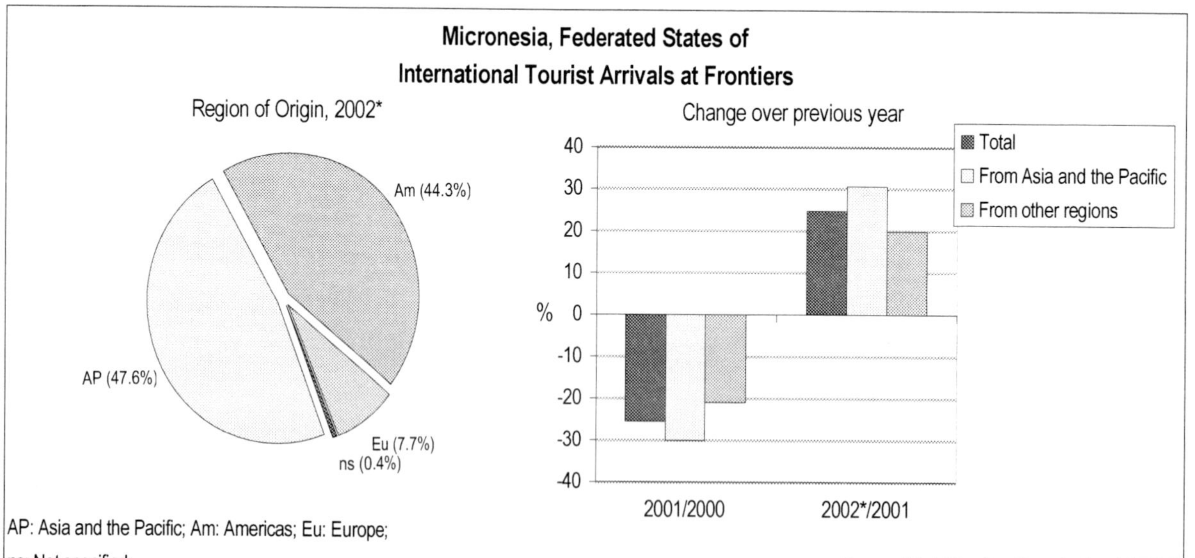

AP: Asia and the Pacific; Am: Americas; Eu: Europe;
ns: Not specified;

Source: World Tourism Organization (WTO) ©

Micronesia, Federated States of
International Tourist Arrivals at Frontiers (by residence)

	1995	2000	2001	2002*	Market share (%) 1995	Market share (%) 2002*	Growth rate (%) 2001/00	Growth rate (%) 2002*/01	Average per year (%) 1995-2002*
Total	..	**20,501**	**15,265**	**19,046**		**100**	**-25.5**	**24.8**	
From Asia and the Pacific	..	*9,925*	*6,936*	*9,062*		*47.6*	*-30.1*	*30.7*	
Japan	..	4,871	3,118	4,057		21.3	-36.0	30.1	
Australia	..	817	516	572		3.0	-36.8	10.9	
New Zealand	..	101	94	169		0.9	-6.9	79.8	
Other Asia	..	2,928	2,247	2,827		14.8	-23.3	25.8	
Other Oceania	..	1,208	961	1,437		7.5	-20.4	49.5	
From other regions	..	*10,452*	*8,262*	*9,909*		*52.0*	*-21.0*	*19.9*	
United States	..	8,779	6,903	8,215		43.1	-21.4	19.0	
All Europe	..	1,461	1,188	1,474		7.7	-18.7	24.1	
Canada	..	212	171	220		1.2	-19.3	28.7	
Other World/Not specified	..	*124*	*67*	*75*		*0.4*	*-46.0*	*11.9*	

Source: World Tourism Organization (WTO) © (Data as collected by WTO September 2003)

III.3.9.a Yap State Oceania

Survey

Contributed by *Yap Visitors Bureau*
www.visityap.com (promotional)
www.visityap.com (institutional/corporate)

Tourism development and outlook

Most significant determinant

During the past year there has been no drastic change. However, there were some donated infrastructure development projects that were implemented, which gave a boost to the foreign arrivals, mainly from Asian countries. There is an indication of slow recovery from the 11 September 2001 tragedy.

Tourism products

There are plans in place for the hotel operators to build additional rooms in the near future.

In terms of entertainment and activities, there are quite a number of potential operations being explored at the present time.

Traditional sea navigation (sailing) is being revived and explored to determine the viable options in which it can be utilized as one of our traditional attractions and whether this product could provide viable access to neighbouring sister states as well as countries within the Pacific.

Access

Continental is currently the main international and interstate transportation.

As for domestic access to the outer islands of Yap, Pacific Missionary Aviation (PMA) is running scheduled routes between Yap proper and those outer islands with smaller craft runways.

Access by sea is also available and running under the control of the Yap State Government.

Generating markets

The United States of America mainland is currently the leading market for Yap followed by Japan.
In recent years, the European market has emerged with a significant increase rate, particularly in diving.

Outlook 2003

With the increase in arrival numbers in 2002, specifically from the Philippines and China, arrivals reached 53 per cent more than the projected figure.

In the year 2003, the projected total of arrivals is expected to reach 7,860 arrivals.

Tourism policy

The Yap State Legislature passed a resolution to broaden the assessment of potential products to be developed and marketed alongside Yap's existing tourism attractions.

Marketing & promotion

The Yap Visitors Bureau's new website has been launched, which is a breakthrough as it was an important promotion objective. This site features hotels, dive shops and other information connected to the Yap tourism industry.

Cultural Tourism (CT)

Specific place for CT in tourism policy: yes.

Main objectives & instruments	Yes. The main island of Yap and the outer laying islands place priority on culture.The first attempt toward revival of traditional navigation recently took place.This trip aims to revive the traditional ties between the communities in Yap and Palau.This trial run was successful and future trips are being planned.
Main focus of attention supply	The heritage of traditional navigation is a recognized component of our culture.This type of navigation is uncommon among the Micronesian islands due to its nature and the way in which it has been transferred to the younger generations. Yap state has designated 1 March to be the "Yap Day", when communities throughout the Islands get together and perform as well as display numerous cultural activities and products..
Main focus of attention demand	We have still not determined the prime focus among the variety that Yap has to offer.

Specific place for CT in marketing & promotion plan: yes.

Main objectives & programmes	Yes. In terms of cultural tourism, Yap, for the past several years has been working with various entities to promote as well as revive the cultural heritage.
Special activities undertaken	The governing board of Yap Visitors Bureau has held discussions about available products and their options at hand to broaden and increase the number of cultural activities and events to enhance cultural tourism in Yap.

Importance of cultural tourism:

- in total tourism offer	Yap State is identified among all the sister states as the only island that stresses the importance of maintaining customs and cultural aspects of daily life. We receive a number of film groups annually that come to capture the cultural side of Yap.
- in intern. arrivals	In terms of foreign arrivals, Yap averages 4,000 visitors annually. The leading market for Yap is the dive market.

III.3.10 New Caledonia Oceania

Profile

New Caledonia

East Asia and the Pacific
Oceania

Capital	Nouméa
Area (100 km²)	186
Population (2002, 1000)	208

	2000	2001	2002*	2001/2000	2002*/2001
International Arrivals					
Visitors (1000)	161	152	158	-5.6	3.9
Tourists (overnight visitors) (1000)	110	101	104	-8.3	3.5
- per 100 of inhabitants	54	49	50		
Same-day visitors (1000)	2	1	..	-50.0	
Cruise passengers (1000)	49	51	54	4.1	5.9
Tourism accommodation					
Number of rooms	2,441	..	..		
Nights spent in hotels and similar establishments (1000)	553	562	545	1.6	-3.0
by non-residents (inbound tourism)	372	400	352	7.5	-11.9
by residents (domestic tourism)	181	162	193	-10.5	19.1
Outbound Tourism					
Trips abroad (1000)	69	68	72	-1.4	5.9
- per 100 of inhabitants	34	33	35		
Receipts and Expenditure for International Tourism					
International Tourism Receipts (US$ million)	110	93	..	-15.5	
- per Tourist Arrival (US$)	1,004	925	..	-7.8	
- per Visitor Arrival (US$)	683	612	..	-10.4	
- per capita (US$)	545	454	..		

Source: World Tourism Organization (WTO) (Data as collected by WTO September 2003)

See annex for methodological notes and reference of external sources used.

Survey

Contributed by *Nouvelle-Calédonie Tourisme Point Sud*
www.nouvellecaledonietourisme-sud.com ; www.new caledoniatourism-south.com (promotional)

Tourism development and outlook

Most significant determinant	Acquisition by Aircalin, a Caledonian airline, of two Airbus A330s in a low tax operational regime at the beginning of 2003 on the Nournéa-Osaka, Nournéa-Tokyo, Nournéa-Sydney and Nournéa-Auckland routes. Latent depressed world economic climate having a bad effect on international tourism. Japan's economic difficulties. Following the Bali bombings, security measures and controls on entering the territory have been reinforced.
Tourism products	Opening of Ouré Lodge on Ile des Pins (3-star rated establishment) and Casa del Sole, an apartment hotel on Citrons Bay at Nournéa (128 apartments). Closure of hotels for renovation: Tontoutel situated near Tontouta international airport, Parkroyal Escapade Island Resort at Nouméa and Evasion 130 at Sarraméa. The Pacific Princess, a luxury liner with capacity for 700 passengers, has been making a stop at New Caledonia since 2002.
Access	New Caledonia benefits from the following weekly air links: - 5 Air France flights to Tokyo (Japan) - 2 Aircalin flights to Osaka (Japan) - 7 code-sharing Aircalin/Qantas flights to Sydney and 3 to Brisbane in Australia. - 4 flights to Auckland (New Zealand), 2 operated by Aircalin and 2 by Air New Zealand.
Outlook 2003	Lack of visibility due to the war in Iraq.
Tourism policy	Removal from tax liability of tourism investments. Campaign to raise the local population's awareness of tourism.
Marketing & promotion	Strengthening of campaigns in Japan. Development of the congress and incentive market in Australia and New Zealand.

Cultural Tourism (CT)

Specific place for CT in tourism policy: yes.

Main objectives & instruments	Depending on the French and European markets.
Main focus of attention supply	Tjibaou Cultural Centre.
Main focus of attention demand	The French and European markets.

Specific place for CT in marketing & promotion plan: yes.

Main objectives & programmes	Slogan: "Terre, Mer et Culture" (Land, Sea and Culture).
Special activities undertaken	Systematic linking of the Tjibaou Cultural Centre with promotional operations.

International Tourism by Origin

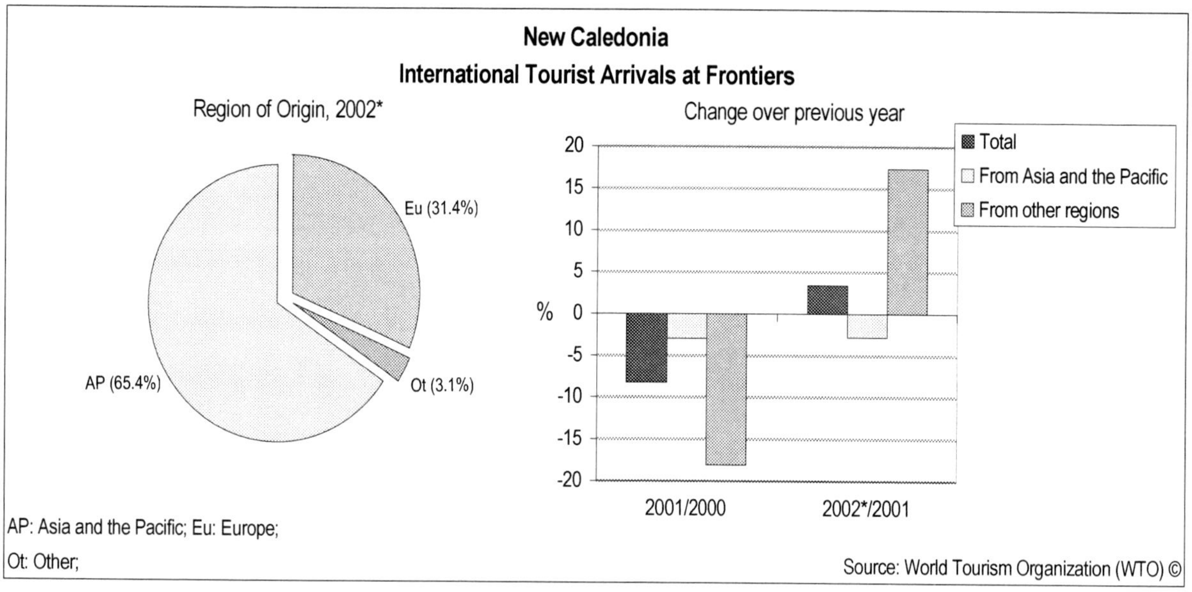

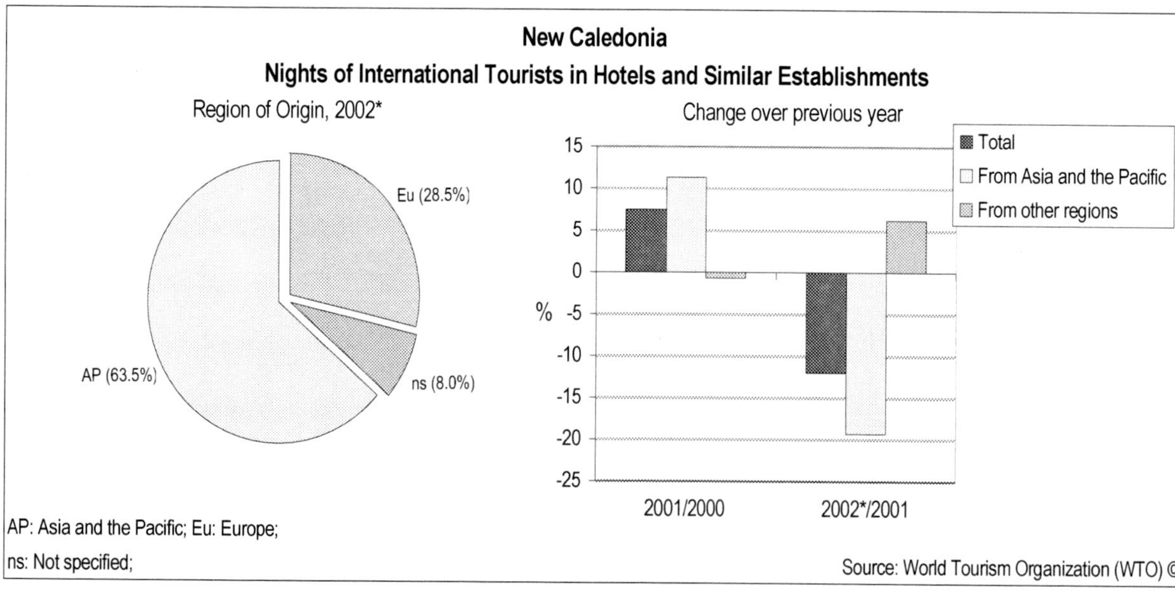

New Caledonia
International Tourist Arrivals at Frontiers (by residence)

	1995	2000	2001	2002*	Market share (%) 1995	Market share (%) 2002*	Growth rate (%) 2001/00	Growth rate (%) 2002*/01	Average per year (%) 1995-2002*
Total	**86,256**	**109,587**	**100,515**	**103,933**	**100**	**100**	**-8.3**	**3.4**	**2.7**
From Asia and the Pacific	*57,942*	*72,129*	*69,980*	*67,998*	*67.2*	*65.4*	*-3.0*	*-2.8*	*2.3*
Japan	25,066	31,051	27,954	27,202	29.1	26.2	-10.0	-2.7	1.2
Australia	15,325	18,012	19,200	19,216	17.8	18.5	6.6	0.1	3.3
Wallis Fut.I	3,775	4,420	6,582	7,559	4.4	7.3	48.9	14.8	10.4
New Zealand	7,168	9,576	8,049	5,935	8.3	5.7	-15.9	-26.3	-2.7
French Polynesia	2,646	3,676	3,840	3,706	3.1	3.6	4.5	-3.5	4.9
Vanuatu	2,258	2,606	2,492	2,538	2.6	2.4	-4.4	1.8	1.7
Hong Kong (China)	76	44	80	59	0.1	0.1	81.8	-26.3	-3.6
Korea, Republic of	37	57	90	51	0.0	0.0	57.9	-43.3	4.7
Taiwan (Pr. of China)	17	17	73	42	0.0	0.0	329.4	-42.5	13.8
Other Asia	930	945	824	1,081	1.1	1.0	-12.8	31.2	2.2
Other Oceania	644	1,725	796	609	0.7	0.6	-53.9	-23.5	-0.8
From other regions	*28,304*	*36,757*	*30,114*	*35,344*	*32.8*	*34.0*	*-18.1*	*17.4*	*3.2*
France	24,707	30,702	25,202	29,964	28.6	28.8	-17.9	18.9	2.8
United States	816	1,722	1,114	1,202	0.9	1.2	-35.3	7.9	5.7
United Kingdom	324	527	376	551	0.4	0.5	-28.7	46.5	7.9
Canada	215	453	424	522	0.2	0.5	-6.4	23.1	13.5
Italy	275	473	562	461	0.3	0.4	18.8	-18.0	7.7
Switzerland	304	444	390	395	0.4	0.4	-12.2	1.3	3.8
Reunion	235	367	392	363	0.3	0.3	6.8	-7.4	6.4
Germany	363	408	363	318	0.4	0.3	-11.0	-12.4	-1.9
All the Caribbean	96	168	191	226	0.1	0.2	13.7	18.3	13.0
Argentina	11	27	15	20	0.0	0.0	-44.4	33.3	8.9
Other Africa	258	216	200	157	0.3	0.2	-7.4	-21.5	-6.9
Other Americas	55	153	126	171	0.1	0.2	-17.6	35.7	17.6
Other Europe	645	1,097	759	994	0.7	1.0	-30.8	31.0	6.4
Other World/Not specified	*10*	*701*	*421*	*591*	*0.0*	*0.6*	*-39.9*	*40.4*	*79.1*

Source: World Tourism Organization (WTO) © (Data as collected by WTO September 2003)

New Caledonia
Nights of International Tourists in Hotels and Similar Establishments (by residence)

	1995	2000	2001	2002*	Market share (%) 1995	Market share (%) 2002*	Growth rate (%) 2001/00	Growth rate (%) 2002*/01	Average per year (%) 1995-2002*
Total	**313,452**	**371,904**	**399,668**	**351,765**	**100**	**100**	**7.5**	**-12.0**	**1.7**
From Asia and the Pacific	*212,005*	*248,701*	*276,813*	*223,328*	*67.6*	*63.5*	*11.3*	*-19.3*	*0.7*
Japan	101,176	113,421	123,594	109,490	32.3	31.1	9.0	-11.4	1.1
Australia	74,429	88,613	112,273	93,744	23.7	26.6	26.7	-16.5	3.4
New Zealand	36,400	46,667	40,946	20,094	11.6	5.7	-12.3	-50.9	-8.1
From other regions	*88,863*	*95,129*	*94,428*	*100,296*	*28.3*	*28.5*	*-0.7*	*6.2*	*1.7*
France	88,863	95,129	94,428	100,296	28.3	28.5	-0.7	6.2	1.7
Other World/Not specified	*12,584*	*28,074*	*28,427*	*28,141*	*4.0*	*8.0*	*1.3*	*-1.0*	*12.2*

Source: World Tourism Organization (WTO) © (Data as collected by WTO September 2003)

III.3.11 New Zealand — Oceania

Profile

New Zealand

East Asia and the Pacific
Oceania

Capital	Wellington
Area (1000 km²)	271
Population (2002, million)	3.9
Gross Domestic Product (GDP) (2002, US$ million)	58,157
GDP per capita (2002, US$)	14,804
GDP growth (real, %)	
'-> 2001: 2.6; 2002: 4.4; 2003*: 2.6; 2004*: 2.9	

	2000	2001	2002*	2001/2000	2002*/2001
International Arrivals					
Visitors (1000)	1,787	1,909	2,045	6.9	7.1
- per 100 of inhabitants	47	49	52		
Cruise passengers (1000)	7	9	19	28.6	111.1
Tourism accommodation					
Number of rooms	25,911	26,679	..	3.0	
Nights spent in collective establishments (1000)	25,497	27,149	28,919	6.5	6.5
by non-residents (inbound tourism)	9,115	10,452	11,625	14.7	11.2
by residents (domestic tourism)	16,382	16,697	17,294	1.9	3.6
Outbound Tourism					
Trips abroad (1000)	1,283	1,287	1,293	0.3	0.5
- per 100 of inhabitants	34	33	33		
Receipts and Expenditure for International Tourism					
International Tourism Receipts (US$ million)	2,240	2,334	2,918	4.2	25.0
- per Visitor Arrival (US$)	1,254	1,222	1,427	-2.5	16.7
- per capita (US$)	587	604	747		
International Tourism Expenditure (US$ million)	1,537	1,334	1,480	-13.2	11.0
- per trip (US$)	1,198	1,036	1,145	-13.5	10.5
- per capita (US$)	402	345	379		
△ International Tourism Balance (US$ million)	703	1,000	1,438		

Source: World Tourism Organization (WTO) (Data as collected by WTO September 2003)

See annex for methodological notes and reference of external sources used.

Survey

Contributed by *Ministry of Tourism*
www.newzealand.com (promotional)
www.tourism.govt.nz (institutional/corporate)
www.trcnz.govt.nz (research and data)

Tourism development and outlook

Most significant determinant

Two major events that showcased New Zealand were the release of the first film of the Lord of the Rings trilogy, and the America's Cup yachting regatta that have provided excellent opportunities for New Zealand to raise its profile in off-shore markets.

Tourism products

Little innovation has appeared in tourism products over the last five years with the majority of new experiences centred around accommodation (luxury lodges) set in spectacular natural settings and tours providing access to the natural environment.

Mainstream accommodation capacity has substantially increased but there has been little reinvestment in plant, therefore quality has dropped.

In looking at pricing issues we have little data available but can say that the hotel sector, while delivering one of the lowest revenues per available room (RevPar) in the world, it is increasing. Although this is not keeping pace with occupancy increases.

Quality has become a central issue for the New Zealand industry with the government funding through its National Tourism Organization (NTO) the further development of a national quality system. This is widely supported by international trade who cannot keep pace and monitor quality of the wide range of products in New Zealand. This system applies to all tourism experiences and services.

New Zealand has developed a significant understanding of its comparative international performance in regards to market share and is taking action to ensure that our share is maintained within our target audience. This is leading to increased investment in some markets (e.g. The United States of America).

Access

The New Zealand Government bought a majority share in Air New Zealand in 2002 when the airline was in financial difficulty.

Generating markets

In 2002, New Zealand's inbound travel increased by 7 per cent. The top ten markets provided 78 per cent of the inbound visitors. Strong growth was experienced from South Korea (26%), China (17%), Japan (16%), the United Kingdom (12%) and the United States of America (10%). A weak performance was noted from Australia (0.3%) and Germany (-7%).

Outlook 2003

International visitor arrivals are forecast to increase by 6 per cent to 2008.

Tourism policy

Policy development focused on the implementation of key recommendations of the New Zealand Tourism Strategy 2010 that provided leadership to the industry. These include addressing issues on quality (rebranding of Qualmark to set in place a national accreditation framework for tourism products and services), the relaunching of the Visitor Information Network with the fern and i-Site branding, to work better with the launch of the Business Builder CD-Rom, a new training course on customer service for tourism employees, consolidation of tourism statistical data in one organisation (the Ministry of Tourism) and environmental management.

Marketing & promotion

Key international marketing activities include Tourism New Zealand rolling out Phase Two of the 100 per cent "Pure New Zealand" campaign with a new suit of images; worked on with Discovery Channel to deliver New Zealand Week to audiences in over eleven countries; to increase the profile of the Maori culture and leverage on the two major events - the America's Cup yachting regatta and the release of the Lord of the Rings film.

Cultural Tourism (CT)

Specific place for CT in tourism policy: yes.

Main objectives & instruments

Tourism New Zealand has identified the importance of cultural tourism to our target market and has taken initial steps to understand the relative demand for experiences through an extensive research programme. In addition, Tourism New Zealand has developed its understanding of the importance and role of the New Zealand indigenous Maori culture in attracting visitors to New Zealand. This has led to the appointment of a Maori Tourism Development Manager within Tourism New Zealand.

The Ministry of Tourism has taken the lead in developing a government response to the two New Zealand Tourism Strategy recommendations related to cultural tourism. An informal inter-Government working group comprising government agencies representing tourism, cultural, Maori and economic development interests has been meeting regularly to develop proposals resulting in:

- Funding provided to Tourism New Zealand to manage a three-stage research project into the demand for cultural tourism experiences by domestic and international visitors. The first two stages have been completed with stage three due for delivery in July 2003. The results already show that the cultural experience, and in particular interaction with New Zealander people, is a strong driver of visits to New Zealand by international tourists;
- Funding to create demand for cultural tourism and to encourage and support the five regions that have established positions as cultural tourism providers to create a cultural tourism development programme focused on capacity and capability building.

Main focus of attention supply

The main focus is on the New Zealand Maori culture and visitor interaction with New Zealand's living culture.

Main focus of attention demand

Attention is being given to researching relative demand across the cultural tourism sector.

Specific place for CT in marketing & promotion plan: yes.

Main objectives & programmes

While New Zealand continues to play to its iconic strengths, Tourism New Zealand understands the importance of culture to our defined target audience. Cultural themes run through our marketing activity, not necessarily as the motivator for visiting, but as a vehicle for talking to our target audience. These aspects include film, food and wine and the Maori culture.

Special activities undertaken

Tourism New Zealand has been involved in leveraging extensively off New Zealand's status as the "Home of Middle Earth", promoting the existence of Maori tourism experiences and utilising cultural events internationally to raise New Zealand's profile and create awareness of cultural experiences. Examples include Food and Wine

Festivals where New Zealand wines have a strong presence or the launch of a New Zealand movie.

Importance of cultural tourism:

- in total tourism offer Tourism New Zealand is aware that cultural tourism experiences represent anywhere between 10 per cent and 35 per cent of visitor holidays in New Zealand.

International Tourism by Origin

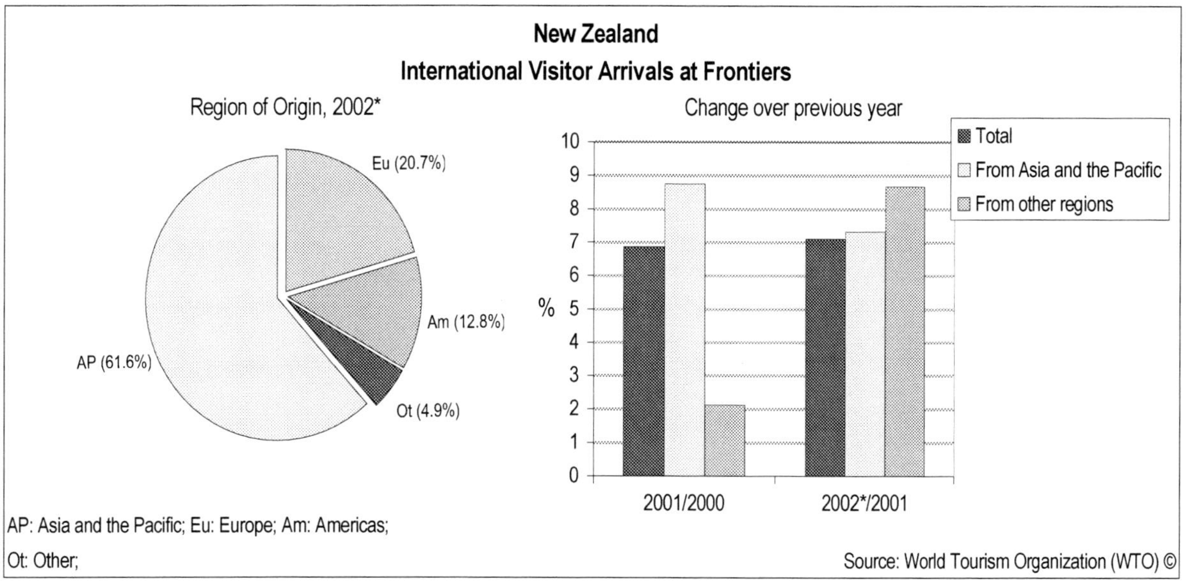

New Zealand

International Visitor Arrivals at Frontiers (by residence)

	1995	2000	2001	2002*	Market share (%) 1995	Market share (%) 2002*	Growth rate (%) 2001/00	Growth rate (%) 2002*/01	Average per year (%) 1995-2002*
Total	**1,408,826**	**1,786,765**	**1,909,381**	**2,045,064**	**100**	**100**	**6.9**	**7.1**	**5.5**
From Asia and the Pacific	*909,981*	*1,079,485*	*1,173,932*	*1,259,791*	*64.6*	*61.6*	*8.7*	*7.3*	*4.8*
Australia	402,657	573,862	630,549	632,470	28.6	30.9	9.9	0.3	6.7
Japan	151,543	151,373	149,085	173,567	10.8	8.5	-1.5	16.4	2.0
Korea, Republic of	104,389	66,581	87,167	109,936	7.4	5.4	30.9	26.1	0.7
China	8,918	33,502	53,174	76,534	0.6	3.7	58.7	43.9	35.9
Taiwan (Pr. of China)	64,971	40,848	36,188	38,358	4.6	1.9	-11.4	6.0	-7.3
Singapore	21,332	35,725	32,808	34,019	1.5	1.7	-8.2	3.7	6.9
Hong Kong (China)	31,447	29,942	30,439	28,873	2.2	1.4	1.7	-5.1	-1.2
Thailand	27,764	26,693	20,814	24,832	2.0	1.2	-22.0	19.3	-1.6
Malaysia	15,231	20,531	21,074	22,195	1.1	1.1	2.6	5.3	5.5
India	3,202	8,327	12,665	17,270	0.2	0.8	52.1	36.4	27.2
French Polynesia	6,699	11,792	15,799	17,046	0.5	0.8	34.0	7.9	14.3
Fiji	11,104	13,656	16,386	15,633	0.8	0.8	20.0	-4.6	5.0
Samoa	12,529	14,827	14,258	13,877	0.9	0.7	-3.8	-2.7	1.5
Tonga	6,991	8,515	9,507	9,854	0.5	0.5	11.7	3.6	5.0
New Caledonia	5,698	7,282	7,401	8,584	0.4	0.4	1.6	16.0	6.0
Indonesia	12,934	9,047	9,654	8,248	0.9	0.4	6.7	-14.6	-6.2
Cook Is	4,568	6,641	7,309	7,972	0.3	0.4	10.1	9.1	8.3
Philippines	4,306	5,066	4,788	5,150	0.3	0.3	-5.5	7.6	2.6
Other intraregional	13,698	15,275	14,867	15,373	1.0	0.8	-2.7	3.4	1.7
From other regions	*463,835*	*640,693*	*654,323*	*711,074*	*32.9*	*34.8*	*2.1*	*8.7*	*6.3*
United Kingdom	121,155	200,250	211,646	236,986	8.6	11.6	5.7	12.0	10.1
United States	152,203	195,781	187,381	205,289	10.8	10.0	-4.3	9.6	4.4
Germany	54,937	51,451	52,482	48,951	3.9	2.4	2.0	-6.7	-1.6
Canada	29,077	32,971	36,694	39,669	2.1	1.9	11.3	8.1	4.5
Netherlands	13,342	23,873	25,164	26,037	0.9	1.3	5.4	3.5	10.0
South Africa	8,545	16,200	17,229	15,790	0.6	0.8	6.4	-8.4	9.2
Switzerland	14,121	13,441	14,155	15,233	1.0	0.7	5.3	7.6	1.1
Ireland	3,153	9,559	11,252	13,489	0.2	0.7	17.7	19.9	23.1
France	6,290	10,716	10,934	13,239	0.4	0.6	2.0	21.1	11.2
Sweden	6,914	11,287	10,575	12,309	0.5	0.6	-6.3	16.4	8.6
Italy	5,440	7,885	6,632	8,379	0.4	0.4	-15.9	26.3	6.4
Denmark	7,021	7,371	7,426	8,001	0.5	0.4	0.7	7.7	1.9
Israel	2,402	5,430	7,149	7,481	0.2	0.4	31.7	4.6	17.6
Brazil	2,113	4,632	5,664	5,735	0.1	0.3	22.3	1.3	15.3
Spain	2,401	4,157	4,200	5,030	0.2	0.2	1.0	19.8	11.1
Austria	4,972	5,001	4,804	4,824	0.4	0.2	-3.9	0.4	-0.4
Norway	2,066	3,863	4,033	4,086	0.1	0.2	4.4	1.3	10.2
Belgium	1,764	3,688	3,623	3,962	0.1	0.2	-1.8	9.4	12.3
Mexico	1,021	2,066	2,020	3,035	0.1	0.1	-2.2	50.2	16.8
Zimbabwe	352	1,521	2,231	2,808	0.0	0.1	46.7	25.9	34.5
Argentina	3,250	5,271	4,680	2,603	0.2	0.1	-11.2	-44.4	-3.1
Untd Arab Emirates	978	1,814	2,184	2,574	0.1	0.1	20.4	17.9	14.8
Other interregional	20,318	22,465	22,165	25,564	1.4	1.3	-1.3	15.3	3.3
Nationals residing abroad	*9,732*	*18,534*	*22,014*	*15,174*	*0.7*	*0.7*	*18.8*	*-31.1*	*6.6*
Other World/Not specified	*25,278*	*48,053*	*59,112*	*59,025*	*1.8*	*2.9*	*23.0*	*-0.1*	*12.9*

Source: World Tourism Organization (WTO) © (Data as collected by WTO September 2003)

III.3.12 Niue Oceania

Profile

Niue

Capital	Alofi
Area (10 km²)	26

East Asia and the Pacific
Oceania

	2000	2001	2002*	2001/2000	2002*/2001
International Arrivals					
Visitors (1000)	..	..	3		
Tourists (overnight visitors) (1000)	2	2	2	2.9	0.7
Cruise passengers (1000)	..	..	0		
Tourism accommodation					
Number of rooms	..	72	72		

Source: World Tourism Organization (WTO) (Data as collected by WTO September 2003)

See annex for methodological notes and reference of external sources used.

International Tourism by Origin

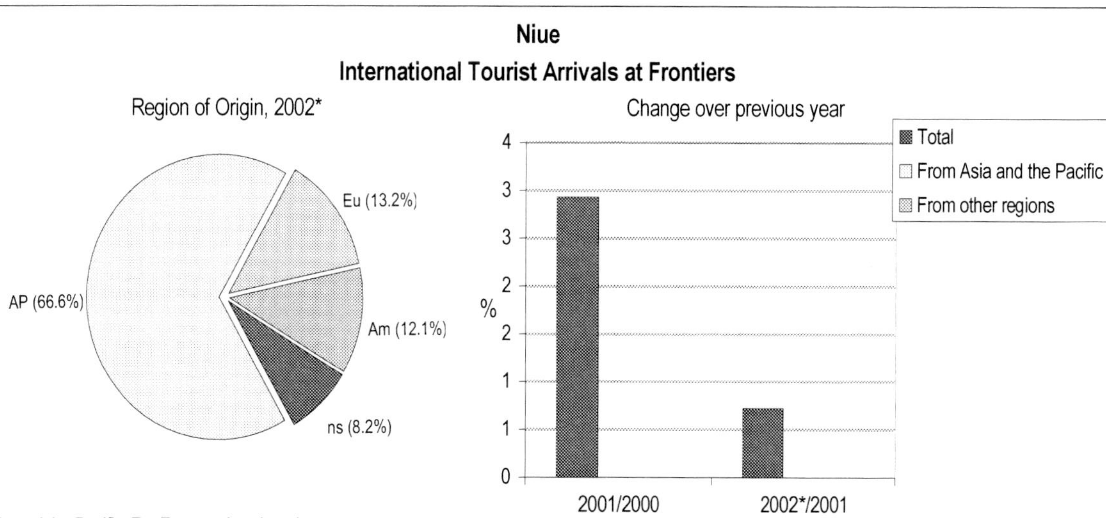

AP: Asia and the Pacific; Eu: Europe; Am: Americas;
ns: not specified

Source: World Tourism Organization (WTO) ©

Niue

International Tourist Arrivals at Frontiers (by residence)

					Market share (%)		Growth rate (%)		Average per year (%)
	1995	2000	2001	2002*	1995	2002*	2001/00	2002*/01	1995-2002*
Total	**2,161**	**2,010**	**2,069**	**2,084**	**100**	**100**	**2.9**	**0.7**	**-0.5**
From Asia and the Pacific	*2,048*	*1,416*	*1,679*	*1,387*	*94.8*	*66.6*	*18.6*	*-17.4*	*-5.4*
New Zealand	1,805	1,000	682	926	83.5	44.4	-31.8	35.8	-9.1
All Oceania	124	..	..	..	5.7				
Australia	108	172	143	180	5.0	8.6	-16.9	25.9	7.6
Tonga	..	58	..	71		3.4			
Samoa	..	16	..	69		3.3			
Fiji	..	58	..	63		3.0			
China	..	2	..	9		0.4			
Japan	8	16	21	9	0.4	0.4	31.3	-57.1	1.7
Cook Is	..	31	..	4		0.2			
Korea, Republic of	..	3	..	..					
Malaysia	..	1	..	..					
Singapore	..	1	..	..					
Other North-East Asia	..	3	..	8		0.4			
Other Asia	3	..	8	..	0.1				
Other Polynesia	..	55	..	48		2.3			
Other Oceania	..	..	825	..					
From other regions	*89*	*288*	*373*	*527*	*4.1*	*25.3*	*29.5*	*41.3*	*28.9*
United States	32	145	164	221	1.5	10.6	13.1	34.8	31.8
United Kingdom	5	32	61	93	0.2	4.5	90.6	52.5	51.8
Germany	18	21	39	42	0.8	2.0	85.7	7.7	12.9
Canada	..	12	29	31		1.5	141.7	6.9	
France	..	4	15	30		1.4	275.0	100.0	
Norway	..	21	..	..					
Denmark	..	10	..	..					
All Middle East	..	10	..	..					
Netherlands	..	5	..	..					
Sweden	..	5	..	..					
Belgium	..	4	..	..					
South Africa	..	3	..	..					
Switzerland	..	3	..	..					
All South America	..	3	..	..					
Finland	..	2	..	..					
Italy	..	1	..	..					
Portugal	..	1	..	..					
All North Africa	..	1	..	..					
Other North America	..	3	..	..					
Other Europe	34	2	65	110	1.6	5.3	3150.0	69.2	18.3
Other World/Not specified	*24*	*306*	*17*	*170*	*1.1*	*8.2*	*-94.4*	*900.0*	*32.3*

Source: World Tourism Organization (WTO) © (Data as collected by WTO September 2003)

III.3.13 Northern Mariana Islands — Oceania

Profile

Northern Mariana Islands		
	Capital	Saipan
	Area (10 km²)	46
	Population (2002, 1000)	77
East Asia and the Pacific		
Oceania		

	2000	2001	2002*	2001/2000	2002*/2001
International Arrivals					
Visitors (1000)	529	444	476	-16.0	7.1
Tourists (overnight visitors) (1000)	517	438	466	-15.3	6.4
- per 100 of inhabitants	719	587	603		
Cruise passengers (1000)	12	6	10	-50.0	66.7
Tourism accommodation					
Number of rooms	4,551	4,521	..	-0.7	

Source: World Tourism Organization (WTO) (Data as collected by WTO September 2003)

See annex for methodological notes and reference of external sources used.

International Tourism by Origin

Northern Mariana Islands
International Visitor Arrivals at Frontiers

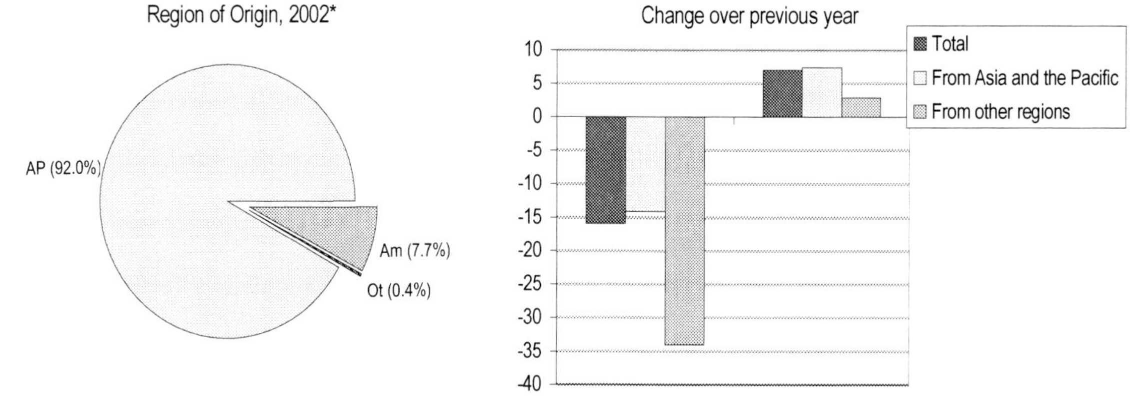

AP: Asia and the Pacific; Am: Americas;
Ot: Other;

Source: World Tourism Organization (WTO) ©

Northern Mariana Islands
International Visitor Arrivals at Frontiers (by nationality)

					Market share (%)		Growth rate (%)		Average per year (%)
	1995	2000	2001	2002*	1995	2002*	2001/00	2002*/01	1995-2002*
Total	**676,161**	**528,608**	**444,284**	**475,547**	**100**	**100**	**-16.0**	**7.0**	**-4.9**
From Asia and the Pacific	*574,803*	*473,976*	*407,104*	*437,322*	*85.0*	*92.0*	*-14.1*	*7.4*	*-3.8*
Japan	426,679	377,899	333,911	326,735	63.1	68.7	-11.6	-2.1	-3.7
Korea, Republic of	124,794	71,936	56,627	90,324	18.5	19.0	-21.3	59.5	-4.5
China	2,633	1,698	2,101	10,470	0.4	2.2	23.7	398.3	21.8
Hong Kong (China)	4,717	5,009	4,327	3,416	0.7	0.7	-13.6	-21.1	-4.5
Philippines	4,234	2,665	2,625	2,906	0.6	0.6	-1.5	10.7	-5.2
Taiwan (Pr. of China)	7,086	9,960	4,507	1,228	1.0	0.3	-54.7	-72.8	-22.2
Micronesia (Fed.St.of)	1,475	2,337	1,498	1,061	0.2	0.2	-35.9	-29.2	-4.6
Palau	958	1,011	739	748	0.1	0.2	-26.9	1.2	-3.5
Australia	828	643	384	316	0.1	0.1	-40.3	-17.7	-12.9
New Zealand	247	122	..	..	0.0				
Thailand	5	249	385	118	0.0	0.0	54.6	-69.4	57.1
Singapore	164	97	..	..	0.0				
India	178	80	..	..	0.0				
Malaysia	162	72	..	..	0.0				
Indonesia	29	49	..	..	0.0				
Fiji	11	41	..	..	0.0				
Macao (China)	6	22	..	..	0.0				
Samoa	25	21	..	..	0.0				
Vietnam	133	11	..	..	0.0				
Other intraregional	439	54	..	..	0.1				
From other regions	*101,278*	*54,582*	*36,026*	*37,049*	*15.0*	*7.8*	*-34.0*	*2.8*	*-13.4*
United States	98,593	51,240	35,142	35,858	14.6	7.5	-31.4	2.0	-13.5
United Kingdom	557	811	..	..	0.1				
All Europe	..	..	566	598		0.1		5.7	
Canada	470	721	307	593	0.1	0.1	-57.4	93.2	3.4
All South America	272	299	..	..	0.0				
France	267	279	..	..	0.0				
Germany	309	269	..	..	0.0				
Former U.S.S.R.	13	220	..	..	0.0				
Italy	114	68	..	..	0.0				
Sweden	43	66	..	..	0.0				
Denmark	43	63	..	..	0.0				
Portugal	82	57	..	..	0.0				
Switzerland	127	56	..	..	0.0				
All Middle East	28	49	..	..	0.0				
Mexico	17	40	..	..	0.0				
Netherlands	68	30	..	..	0.0				
Spain	23	29	..	..	0.0				
South Africa	19	22	..	..	0.0				
Norway	9	21	..	..	0.0				
All Central America	10	18	..	..	0.0				
Finland	23	4	..	..	0.0				
Other Africa	18	14	..	..	0.0				
Other Americas	11	13	11	..	0.0		-15.4		
Other interregional	162	193	..	..	0.0				
Other World/Not specified	*80*	*50*	*1,154*	*1,176*	*0.0*	*0.2*	*2208.0*	*1.9*	*46.8*

Source: World Tourism Organization (WTO) © (Data as collected by WTO September 2003)

III.3.14 Palau Oceania

Profile

Palau

Capital	Koror
Area (10 km²)	46
Population (2002, 1000)	19

East Asia and the Pacific
Oceania

	2000	2001	2002*	2001/2000	2002*/2001
International Arrivals					
Tourists (overnight visitors) (1000)	58	54	59	-6.9	9.3
- per 100 of inhabitants	309	283	304		
Cruise passengers (1000)	..	2	..		
Receipts and Expenditure for International Tourism					
International Tourism Receipts (US$ million)	53	59	59	9.9	0.8
- per Tourist Arrival (US$)	918	1,084	1,000	18.1	-7.7
- per capita (US$)	2,836	3,066	3,040		
International Tourism Expenditure (US$ million)	2	2	2	-4.3	3.4
- per capita (US$)	108	101	103		
△ International Tourism Balance (US$ million)	51	57	57		

Source: World Tourism Organization (WTO) (Data as collected by WTO September 2003)
See annex for methodological notes and reference of external sources used.

International Tourism by Origin

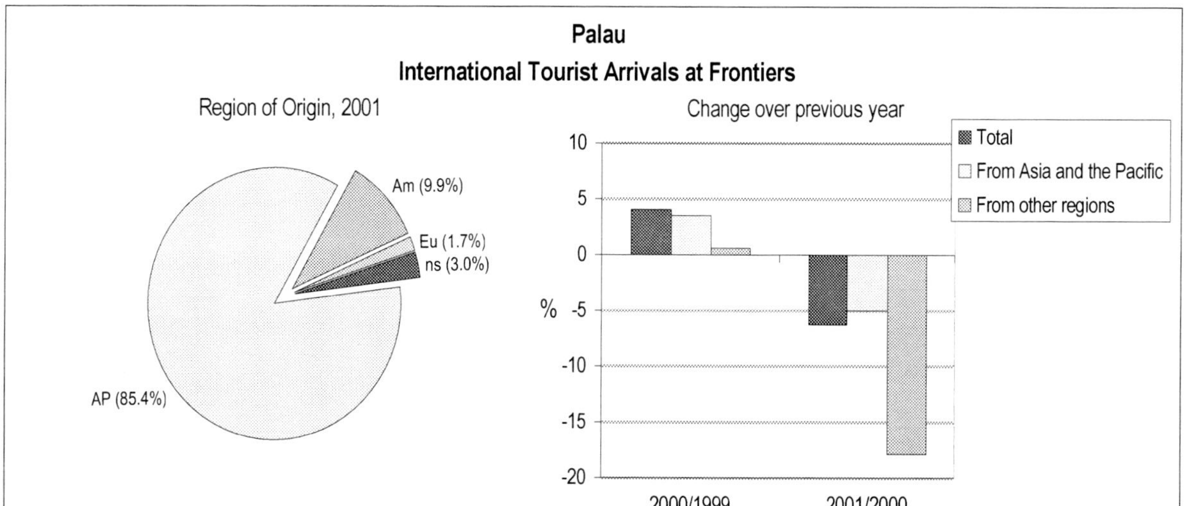

AP: Asia and the Pacific; Am: Americas; Eu: Europe;
ns: not specified

Source: World Tourism Organization (WTO) ©

Palau

International Tourist Arrivals at Frontiers (by residence)

					Market share (%)		Growth rate (%)		Average per year (%)
	1995	1999	2000	2001	1995	2001	2000/99	2001/00	1995-2001
Total	**..**	**55,493**	**57,732**	**54,111**		**100**	**4.0**	**-6.3**	
From Asia and the Pacific	*..*	*46,991*	*48,630*	*46,197*		*85.4*	*3.5*	*-5.0*	
Japan	..	22,087	21,708	22,399		41.4	-1.7	3.2	
Taiwan (Pr. of China)	..	10,936	14,122	12,476		23.1	29.1	-11.7	
Philippines	..	2,952	3,981	4,130		7.6	34.9	3.7	
Guam	..	5,594	4,331	2,967		5.5	-22.6	-31.5	
Micronesia (Fed.St.of)	..	1,284	1,179	934		1.7	-8.2	-20.8	
N.Mariana Is	..	913	1,036	914		1.7	13.5	-11.8	
China	..	868	889	867		1.6	2.4	-2.5	
Hong Kong (China)	..	344	355	663		1.2	3.2	86.8	
Australia	..	402	347	426		0.8	-13.7	22.8	
Korea, Republic of	..	539	586	350		0.6	8.7	-40.3	
Thailand	..	105	..	..					
Indonesia	..	89	..	..					
Fiji	..	75	..	..					
Singapore	..	129	96	71		0.1	-25.6	-26.0	
Malaysia	..	55	..	..					
India	..	50	..	..					
Solomon Is	..	33	..	..					
American Samoa	..	28	..	..					
Bangladesh	..	25	..	..					
Vanuatu	..	18	..	..					
Kiribati	..	17	..	..					
Pakistan	..	5	..	..					
Other intraregional	..	443	..	..					
From other regions	*..*	*7,632*	*7,678*	*6,305*		*11.7*	*0.6*	*-17.9*	
United States	..	5,587	6,704	5,375		9.9	20.0	-19.8	
Germany	..	796	372	296		0.5	-53.3	-20.4	
United Kingdom	..	300	311	288		0.5	3.7	-7.4	
Canada	..	190	..	..					
Netherlands	..	15	..	172		0.3			
Switzerland	..	135	150	..			11.1		
Italy	..	101	76	106		0.2	-24.8	39.5	
France	..	86	65	68		0.1	-24.4	4.6	
Austria	..	60	..	..					
Denmark	..	43	..	..					
Spain	..	33	..	..					
Finland	..	27	..	..					
All South America	..	27	..	..					
Belgium	..	26	..	..					
All Middle East	..	19	..	..					
South Africa	..	16	..	..					
Other interregional	..	171	..	..					
Other World/Not specified	*..*	*870*	*1,424*	*1,609*		*3.0*	*63.7*	*13.0*	

Source: World Tourism Organization (WTO) © (Data as collected by WTO September 2003)

III.3.15 Papua New Guinea Oceania

Profile

Papua New Guinea

East Asia and the Pacific
Oceania

Capital	Port Moresby
Area (1000 km²)	463
Population (2002, million)	5.2
Gross Domestic Product (GDP) (2002, US$ million)	2,931
GDP per capita (2002, US$)	541
GDP growth (real, %)	
> 2001: -3.4; 2002: -3.3; 2003*: 2.5; 2004*: 2.3	

	2000	2001	2002*	2001/2000	2002*/2001
International Arrivals					
Tourists (overnight visitors) (1000)	58	54	54	-7.2	-0.4
- per 100 of inhabitants	1	1	1		
Tourism accommodation					
Number of rooms	..	1,976	..		
Outbound Tourism					
Trips abroad (1000)	52	38	92	-26.9	142.1
- per 100 of inhabitants	1	1	2		
Receipts and Expenditure for International Tourism					
International Tourism Receipts (US$ million)	92	101	..	9.8	
- per Tourist Arrival (US$)	1,574	1,862	..	18.3	
- per capita (US$)	19	20	..		
International Tourism Expenditure (US$ million)	50	38	..	-24.0	
- per trip (US$)	962	1,000	..	4.0	
- per capita (US$)	10	8	..		
△ International Tourism Balance (US$ million)	42	63	..		

Source: World Tourism Organization (WTO) (Data as collected by WTO September 2003)

See annex for methodological notes and reference of external sources used.

Survey

Contributed by *Tourism Promotion Authority*
www.pngtourism.org.pg (promotional)
www.pngtourism.org.pg (institutional/corporate)

Tourism development and outlook

Most significant determinant

Tourism development in our country over the last two years has been very slow. This was due to the 11 September 2001 event in the United States of America that affected global tourism travel; our country's political instability and general election; depreciation of our country's currency against other major currencies and the bad image perception of PNG by other source countries.

Tourism products

Tourism in our country had a positive impact due to the development of new products; new accommodation establishments, capacity and facilities; entertainment and cultural events from time to time every year. However, the price increase of goods and services due to the fall of our country's currency is having and will have a negative impact.

Access

Holiday visitors from various source markets have increased due to the introduction of direct international flights, e.g. Port Moresby (PNG) - Narita (Japan).

Generating markets

Visitor arrivals from the Japanese market had a positive change due to the direct flight being introduced, the American market has also experienced a positive impact in the holiday visitor arrivals.

Other Issues

PNG is taking the advantage of tourism-restricting events that are taking place in other parts of the world. Our locals are more interested in the tourism business and are a contributing factor to tourism development.

Outlook 2003

The tourism trend this year and in the next few years is expected to improve due to major developments such as the introduction of direct international flights, regular cultural events (Mt. Hagen Cultural Show, Enga Cultural Show, Hiri Moale Festival, the Independence Celebrations etc), more promotions and awareness etc. The number of visitor arrivals is forecast to increase by an average annual rate of 4.1 per cent in the short term (five years) and 3.7 per cent in the long term (ten years), from 53,000 in 2002 to 66,000 in 2007 and 78,000 in 2012.

Tourism policy

The Tourism Promotion Authority (TPA) has been designated by the National Government of Papua New Guinea as the lead agency in the implementation of the Government's tourism policy. The policy of the National Government of Papua New Guinea establishes the cohesive, controlled and sensitive development, growth and maintenance of tourism as a national priority.

The Corporate Plan of TPA seeks to provide a framework to efficiently and effectively implement government policy for the year 2002-2006.

Fundamental principals of the formulation of this corporate plan are:
- Optimisation of impact within the context of limited resources;
- Prioritisation of implementation strategies; and
- Coordination and integration of focus and initiatives of both government and industry.

The development of the TPA Five-Year Corporate Plan ensures that the broadest policy objectives stipulated in the TPA Act are translated into practice. There is a vision on how TPA wants to shape the industry; the government's policy objectives which have bearings on the operations of TPA are clearly developed into strategies; these strategies are clearly defined with achievable measures; and to identify issues and concerns which are beyond the TPA's control but can be achieved if proper planning strategies are developed. In short, the TPA Five-Year Corporate Plan gives us the vision, direction and strategies to pursue in a coordinated effort to achieve the government's tourism policy objectives.

There is no National Tourism Master Plan in Papua New Guinea. However, TPA will take the lead role in developing a comprehensive and integrated tourism master plan in collaboration with governmental agencies and private sector organisations. This will take into consideration the private sector, government agencies, non-governmental agencies, groups and individuals who contribute to tourism development or that will be affected by tourism development in the country.

Marketing & promotion	Launching of the new logo and slogan in 2002 as a promotional campaign to lure more tourists into the country. Awareness campaigns in new markets such as the Russian and Scandinavian Markets. Engaging Travel Writers, Travel Agents, Film Crews, and Television Programs to visit Papua New Guinea. Aggressive campaigns in old or existing markets.

Cultural Tourism (CT)

Specific place for CT in tourism policy: yes.

Main objectives & instruments	Yes. The Tourism Promotion Authority (constituted by an Act of Parliament in 1993) has established specific guidelines for the promotion of cultural tourism and has also set down guidelines for the protection of cultural habits and traditions.
Main focus of attention supply	In all the provinces of the country, TPA's focus is to encourage locals to keep their cultural habits and traditions and to look after caves, war memorials, etc.
Main focus of attention demand	Our main focus is to attract more visitors from the major generating markets, especially in the holiday segments by organising more cultural events regularly, more promotional campaigns and developing more cultural tourism products, etc.

Specific place for CT in marketing & promotion plan: yes.

Main objectives & programmes	We promote cultural events as a tourism product. The National Cultural Commission is the office in charge and TPA works in liaison with them.They provide TPA with the Calendar of Events which TPA promotes.
Special activities undertaken	TPA does promote cultural tourism. TPA assists regional tourism in promoting cultural events in each province and also assists by sponsoring the events.

International Tourism by Origin

Papua New Guinea
International Tourist Arrivals at Frontiers

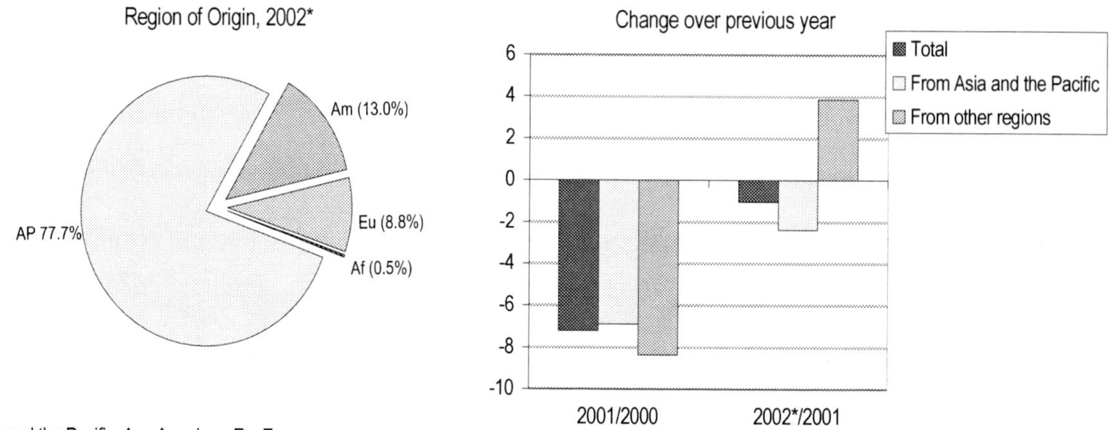

AP: Asia and the Pacific; Am: Americas; Eu: Europe;
Af: Africa; ns: not specified

Source: World Tourism Organization (WTO) ©

Papua New Guinea
International Tourist Arrivals at Frontiers (by residence)

	1995	2000	2001	2002*	Market share (%) 1995	Market share (%) 2002*	Growth rate (%) 2001/00	Growth rate (%) 2002*/01	Average per year (%) 1995-2002*
Total	**42,328**	**58,448**	**54,235**	**53,670**	**100**	**100**	**-7.2**	**-1.0**	**3.4**
From Asia and the Pacific	*29,894*	*45,847*	*42,688*	*41,677*	*70.6*	*77.7*	*-6.9*	*-2.4*	*4.9*
Australia	16,415	29,285	27,661	26,562	38.8	49.5	-5.5	-4.0	7.1
All South-East Asia	..	..	..	5,608		10.4			
Japan	3,443	3,244	2,686	3,804	8.1	7.1	-17.2	41.6	1.4
Philippines	..	2,656	2,540	..			-4.4		
New Zealand	2,109	2,648	2,731	2,351	5.0	4.4	3.1	-13.9	1.6
Malaysia	..	2,066	1,831	..			-11.4		
China	..	1,100	1,016	..			-7.6		
India	..	1,019	1,013	..			-0.6		
Other Asia	7,299	2,473	1,800	1,926	17.2	3.6	-27.2	7.0	-17.3
Other Oceania	628	1,356	1,410	1,426	1.5	2.7	4.0	1.1	12.4
From other regions	*12,034*	*12,601*	*11,547*	*11,992*	*28.4*	*22.3*	*-8.4*	*3.9*	*0.0*
United States	4,858	5,429	5,314	6,053	11.5	11.3	-2.1	13.9	3.2
United Kingdom	2,824	2,279	2,133	1,803	6.7	3.4	-6.4	-15.5	-6.2
Canada	611	719	705	848	1.4	1.6	-1.9	20.3	4.8
Germany	1,316	976	1,148	802	3.1	1.5	17.6	-30.1	-6.8
France	..	289	330	..			14.2		
All Africa	..	212	244	271		0.5	15.1	11.1	
Other Americas	..	1,043	123	89		0.2	-88.2	-27.6	
Other Europe	2,425	1,654	1,550	2,126	5.7	4.0	-6.3	37.2	-1.9
Other World/Not specified	*400*	..	..	*1*	*0.9*	*0.0*			*-57.5*

Source: World Tourism Organization (WTO) ©

(Data as collected by WTO September 2003)

III.3.16 Samoa Oceania

Profile

Samoa		
	Capital	Apia
	Area (100 km²)	28
	Population (2002, 1000)	179
	Gross Domestic Product (GDP) (2002, US$ million)	265
	GDP per capita (2002, US$)	1,509
East Asia and the Pacific	GDP growth (real, %)	
Oceania	'-> 2001: 6.2; 2002: 1.8; 2003*: 3.1; 2004*: 3.2	

	2000	2001	2002*	2001/2000	2002*/2001
International Arrivals					
Tourists (overnight visitors) (1000)	88	88	89	0.7	0.8
- per 100 of inhabitants	49	49	50		
Tourism accommodation					
Number of rooms	764	817	..	6.9	
Receipts and Expenditure for International Tourism					
International Tourism Receipts (US$ million)	41	40	45	-2.4	12.5
- per Tourist Arrival (US$)	468	453	506	-3.1	11.6
- per capita (US$)	228	223	252		

Source: World Tourism Organization (WTO) (Data as collected by WTO September 2003)

See annex for methodological notes and reference of external sources used.

Survey

Contributed by *Samoa Tourism Authority*
www.visitsamoa.ws (promotional)
www.visitsamoa.ws (institutional/corporate)

Tourism development and outlook

Most significant determinant	Strong living culture "fa'asamoa". Green, clean, natural environment. Friendly hospitable people. Political stability. Transparent policies for foreign investment in Samoa. More travellers seeking authentic and less touristy destination. Better infrastructural services in place e.g. road networks, telecommunications, water supply, education and health standards etc.
Tourism products	Diversifying and upgrading the products and services.

Access	Frequent flights to and from the major tourism markets of Australia and New Zealand. Airfares very expensive because we are only served by three major airlines. Fast and efficient facilitation of entry formalities.
Generating markets	Australian and New Zealand visitors are still increasing. Germany, the United Kingdom and the United States of America are other strong markets. However, the number of European and American visitors dropped due to the war and terrorist attacks for a short time, but have now picked up again.
Other Issues	Samoa is unique with its authentic cultural and natural environment. Most tourism operations are owned and run by the local Samoans. There are no 5-star chain hotels
Outlook 2003	According to the Samoa Tourism Development Plan 2002-2006, it is projected that there will be a 5-10 per cent annual increase over this period in visitor arrivals. This means, visitor numbers will be between 118,000 to 157,000 in 2006, from visitor numbers of 88,000 in 2002. The marketing campaign will be focused on New Zealand, Australia, and American Samoa, while the United States of America and Europe will be targeted using web-based marketing.
Tourism policy	The Samoan Government's Strategy for the Development of Samoa 2002-2004 has identified tourism as one of its nine key strategies and priorities. Tourism investment opportunities have been opened up to foreign investors in all areas and also offered to local investors. The government has also set up the Trade and Investment Promotion Unit to specifically facilitate foreign investorment in all areas including tourism. The government also offers special duty concessions for investors in hotels and other tourism operations for development. Samoa is in the process of joining the World Trade Organisation, and this will open up Samoa as an investment destination for other businesses from WTO member countries, which include tourism. A hospitality and tourism course at the Samoa Polytechnic was set up due to the government's commitment to improve and develop tourism in Samoa. The government has encouraged a partnership between the government and the private sector to ensure development of Samoa through all sectors.
Marketing & promotion	The Samoa Tourism Authority (formerly called 'Samoa Visitors Bureau'), had a change in name for a 'Focused Future of Tourism in Samoa'. It has now formulated the new "Tourism Development Plan 2002-2006" , identifying a new path forward for the Samoa Tourism Authority and a new direction for the tourism industry as a whole. Our website will be upgraded and targeting of long-haul markets will also be updated. Collateral material, e.g. posters, calendars, postcards, bookmarks, videos etc., is sold to travellers and travel agents, wholesalers, tour operators and individual customers overseas. We also attend travel exchanges and shows for promotions. We also utilise journalists who write stories about Samoa in overseas publications. Filming is also part of our promotional tools. We have our Teuila festivals every September, as well as Village Beautification Competitions to ensure villages are clean and beautiful. Our customer survey is undertaken to receive feedback from tourists on what their experiences of Samoa are as a tourist destination.

Cultural Tourism (CT)

Specific place for CT in tourism policy: yes.

Main objectives & instruments	In our Tourism Development Plan 2002-2006, it clearly supports and respects the fa'asamoa and the country's built and natural heritage and calls on the tourism industry to help conserve and enhance these valuable assets. Tourists are advised and educated about certain codes of dressing and protocols to be respected while in villages. They are also advised to seek permission from the village authority if they want to visit certain areas within a village. Tourism operators are also encouraged to use our culture and traditions as a basis for all their operations.
Main focus of attention supply	All the cultural sites and monuments are now in the process of being upgraded and protected. Legends and stories relating to these sites are being documented and researched in order to communicate those stories and legends to our visitors from overseas when they visit a particular site.
Main focus of attention demand	Culture is ranked fourth as the reason why visitors want to visit Samoa. So we are targeting a certain niche market that wants to experience our culture. Therefore, we are encouraging local operations that offer a combination of opportunities for culture, nature, adventure and coastal tourism, underpinned by the fa'asamoa (traditional Samoan way of life).

Specific place for CT in marketing & promotion plan: yes.

Main objectives & programmes	In our brochures and on our website, we are heavily focusing on our culture as another tourist attraction. Tourists will be able to experience traditional ceremonies such as the ava ceremony, traditional weddings and matai title bestowals etc.
Special activities undertaken	We have our annual Teuila Festival which features many traditional Samoan activities and entertainment. Overseas visitors are encouraged to come and participate in this festival for them to enjoy and learn the fa'asamoa. A group of cultural experts in the fa'asamoa and legends are now working on documenting legends associated with each cultural site to further enhance visitors' experience and appreciation of Samoa's cultural sites and values.

Importance of cultural tourism:

- in intern. arrivals	Cultural tourism - approximately 20 per cent of 88,000 in 2002 (estimate).

International Tourism by Origin

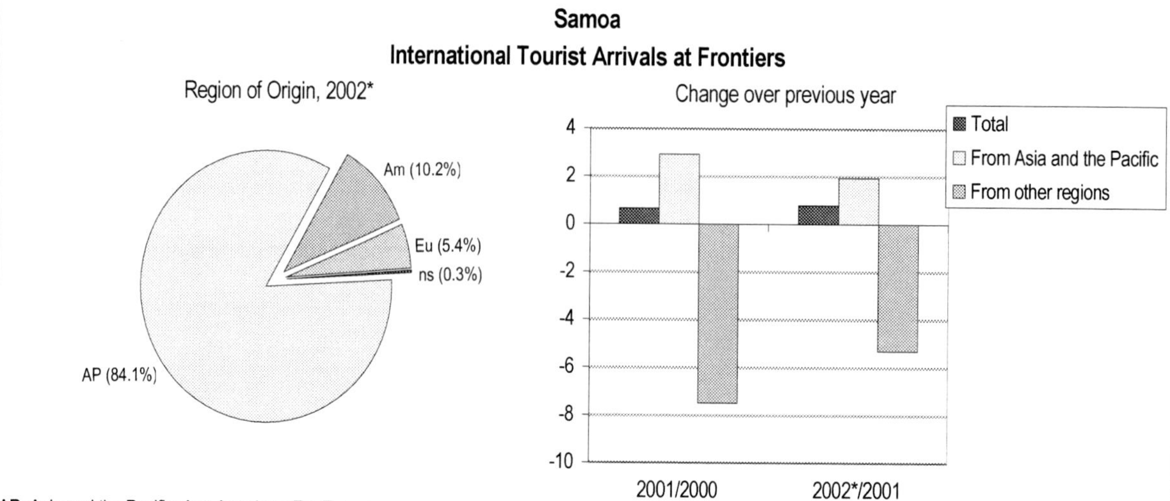

AP: Asia and the Pacific; Am: Americas; Eu: Europe;
ns: Not specified;

Source: World Tourism Organization (WTO) ©

Samoa
International Tourist Arrivals at Frontiers (by residence)

	1995	2000	2001	2002*	Market share (%) 1995	Market share (%) 2002*	Growth rate (%) 2001/00	Growth rate (%) 2002*/01	Average per year (%) 1995-2002*
Total	**68,392**	**87,688**	**88,263**	**88,960**	**100**	**100**	**0.7**	**0.8**	**3.8**
From Asia and the Pacific	*53,462*	*71,314*	*73,403*	*74,822*	*78.2*	*84.1*	*2.9*	*1.9*	*4.9*
American Samoa	23,817	30,063	31,016	31,803	34.8	35.7	3.2	2.5	4.2
New Zealand	17,709	22,818	23,337	23,790	25.9	26.7	2.3	1.9	4.3
Australia	6,816	10,954	11,224	11,438	10.0	12.9	2.5	1.9	7.7
Fiji	..	2,032	2,104	1,928		2.2	3.5	-8.4	
Japan	836	713	718	577	1.2	0.6	0.7	-19.6	-5.2
Cook Is	..	76	87	111		0.1	14.5	27.6	
Other Asia	..	1,263	1,753	1,310		1.5	38.8	-25.3	
Other Oceania	4,284	3,395	3,164	3,865	6.3	4.3	-6.8	22.2	-1.5
From other regions	*13,407*	*15,818*	*14,634*	*13,857*	*19.6*	*15.6*	*-7.5*	*-5.3*	*0.5*
United States	6,202	9,032	8,467	8,720	9.1	9.8	-6.3	3.0	5.0
United Kingdom	1,238	2,092	1,722	1,480	1.8	1.7	-17.7	-14.1	2.6
Germany	2,696	1,784	1,928	1,196	3.9	1.3	8.1	-38.0	-11.0
Scandinavia	..	713	880	803		0.9	23.4	-8.8	
Canada	254	390	370	375	0.4	0.4	-5.1	1.4	5.7
Benelux	..	262	201	185		0.2	-23.3	-8.0	
Other Europe	3,017	1,545	1,066	1,098	4.4	1.2	-31.0	3.0	-13.4
Other World/Not specified	*1,523*	*556*	*226*	*281*	*2.2*	*0.3*	*-59.4*	*24.3*	*-21.5*

Source: World Tourism Organization (WTO) ©

(Data as collected by WTO September 2003)

III.3.17 Solomon Islands Oceania

Profile

Solomon Islands

East Asia and the Pacific
Oceania

Capital	Honiara
Area (1000 km²)	29
Population (2002, 1000)	495
Gross Domestic Product (GDP) (2002, US$ million)	322
GDP per capita (2002, US$)	661
GDP growth (real, %)	
> 2001: -9.0; 2002: -2.0; 2003*: 1.9; 2004*: 3.1	

Source: World Tourism Organization (WTO) (Data as collected by WTO September 2003)

See annex for methodological notes and reference of external sources used.

International Tourism by Origin

Solomon Islands
International Tourist Arrivals at Frontiers

Region of Origin, 1999

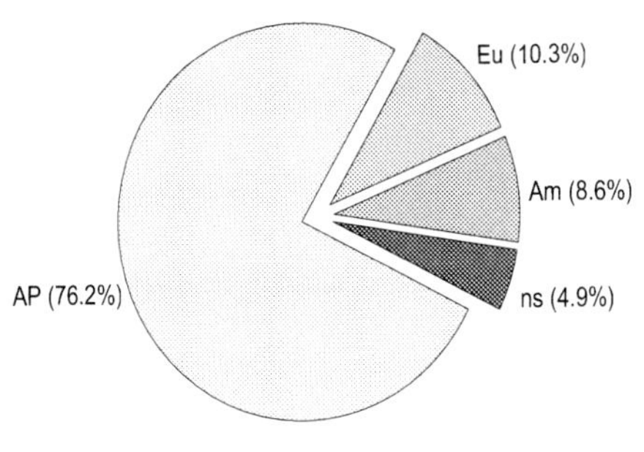

AP: Asia and the Pacific; Eu: Europe; Am: Americas;
ns: Not specified;

Source: World Tourism Organization (WTO) ©

Solomon Islands
International Tourist Arrivals at Frontiers (by residence)

					Market share (%)		Growth rate (%)		Average per year (%)
	1995	1999	2000	2001	1995	2001	2000/99	2001/00	1995-2001
Total	**11,795**	**21,318**	**..**	**..**	**100**				
From Asia and the Pacific	*9,158*	*16,247*	*..*	*..*	*77.6*				
Australia	4,268	4,979	..	..	36.2				
Philippines	..	2,102	..	..					
Papua New Guinea	739	1,457	..	..	6.3				
China	..	1,347	..	..					
Korea, Republic of	..	1,237	..	..					
New Zealand	1,581	925	..	..	13.4				
Japan	749	887	..	..	6.4				
Fiji	..	729	..	..					
Taiwan (Pr. of China)	..	478	..	..					
Vanuatu	..	372	..	..					
Malaysia	..	287	..	..					
Tuvalu	..	174	..	..					
Singapore	..	43	..	..					
Kiribati	..	22	..	..					
Nauru	..	20	..	..					
Other Asia	917	1,050	..	..	7.8				
Other Oceania	904	138	..	..	7.7				
From other regions	*2,593*	*4,017*	*..*	*..*	*22.0*				
United States	970	1,589	..	..	8.2				
United Kingdom	859	893	..	..	7.3				
Canada	119	235	..	..	1.0				
Germany	169	131	..	..	1.4				
Netherlands	..	86	..	..					
France	117	..	..	..	1.0				
Other Europe	359	1,083	..	..	3.0				
Other World/Not specified	*44*	*1,054*	*..*	*..*	*0.4*				

Source: World Tourism Organization (WTO) © (Data as collected by WTO September 2003)

III.3.18 Tonga Oceania

Profile

Tonga		
	Capital	Nuku'alofa
	Area (10 km²)	75
	Population (2002, 1000)	106
	Gross Domestic Product (GDP) (2002, US$ million)	136
	GDP per capita (2002, US$)	1,348
East Asia and the Pacific	GDP growth (real, %)	
Oceania	-> 2001: 0.5; 2002: 1.6; 2003*: 2.5; 2004*: -0.5	

	2000	2001	2002*	2001/2000	2002*/2001
International Arrivals					
Visitors (1000)	48	43	53	-10.4	23.3
Tourists (overnight visitors) (1000)	35	32	37	-6.7	14.2
- per 100 of inhabitants	34	31	35		
Cruise passengers (1000)	8	6	5	-25.0	-16.7
Receipts and Expenditure for International Tourism					
International Tourism Receipts (US$ million)	7	7	9		28.6
- per Tourist Arrival (US$)	202	216	243	7.1	12.5
- per Visitor Arrival (US$)	146	163	170	11.6	4.3
- per capita (US$)	68	67	85		
International Tourism Expenditure (US$ million)	..	3	..		
- per capita (US$)	..	29	..		
△ International Tourism Balance (US$ million)	..	4	..		

Source: World Tourism Organization (WTO) (Data as collected by WTO September 2003)

See annex for methodological notes and reference of external sources used.

Survey

Contributed by *Tonga Visitors Bureau*

Tourism development and outlook

Most significant determinant	Active promotion of ecotourism. Active public participation in tourism business. Huge increase in the number of tourism foreign exchange earnings that is totally due to the successful promotion and marketing.
Tourism products	New accommodation is now due to be completed and upgrading of current accommodation is underway.
Access	Air access is adequate.

Generating markets The United States of America market increased tremendously compared to recent years.

Other Issues Environmentally friendly products to be incorporated in the promotion and marketing of the tourism industry.

Outlook 2003 Tonga forecasts stable growth for 2003-2005 tourist arrivals. As such, actions have already been taken to achieve this target.

Tourism policy
Increase community participation.
Improved infrastructure.
Increase marketing and promotion.
Increase the number of proposed projects for the ourism business.
Increase interest in cultural festivals.

Marketing & promotion Promotion and marketing of quality products for tourism.

Cultural Tourism (CT)

Specific place for CT in tourism policy: yes.

Main focus of attention supply The focus is put on destinations, products and the people as well.

Specific place for CT in marketing & promotion plan: yes.

Special activities undertaken The Heilala week festival has been successfully undertaken every year and is now commonly known to be successful.

International Tourism by Origin

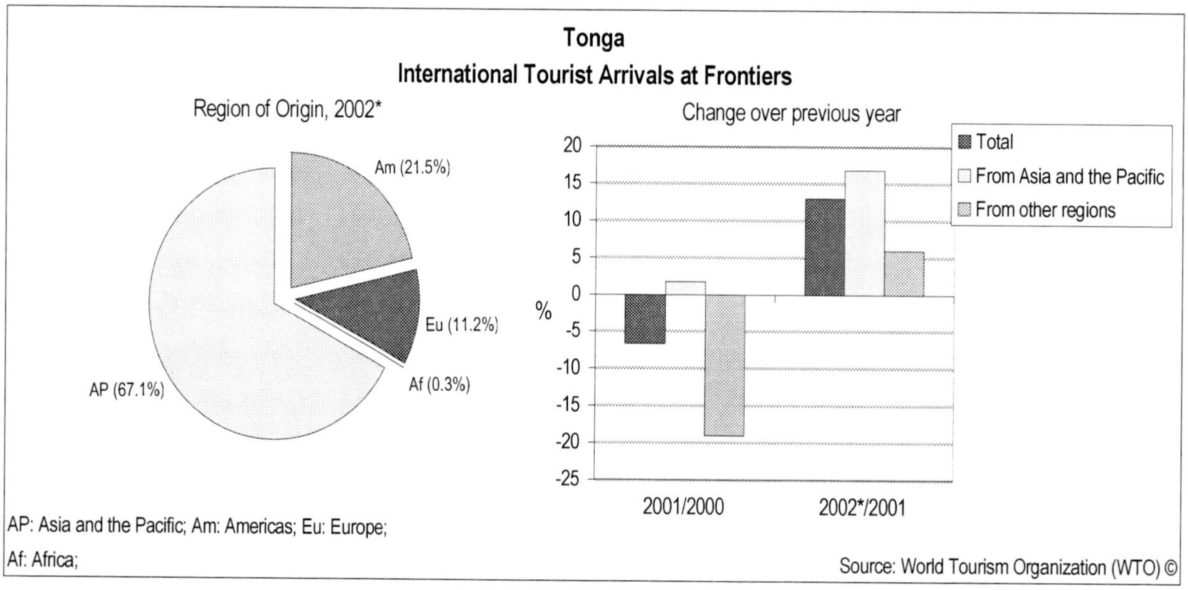

Tonga

International Tourist Arrivals at Frontiers (by residence)

	1995	2000	2001	2002*	Market share (%) 1995	Market share (%) 2002*	Growth rate (%) 2001/00	Growth rate (%) 2002*/01	Average per year (%) 1995-2002*
Total	**29,520**	**34,694**	**32,386**	**36,588**	**100**	**100**	**-6.7**	**13.0**	**3.1**
From Asia and the Pacific	*18,016*	*20,659*	*21,024*	*24,554*	*61.0*	*67.1*	*1.8*	*16.8*	*4.5*
New Zealand	9,542	10,464	11,064	12,938	32.3	35.4	5.7	16.9	4.4
Australia	4,715	5,662	5,416	6,261	16.0	17.1	-4.3	15.6	4.1
Fiji	1,498	1,782	1,696	2,112	5.1	5.8	-4.8	24.5	5.0
Japan	807	784	832	796	2.7	2.2	6.1	-4.3	-0.2
Samoa	443	527	657	784	1.5	2.1	24.7	19.3	8.5
Taiwan (Pr. of China)	278	468	269	414	0.9	1.1	-42.5	53.9	5.9
American Samoa	93	46	24	114	0.3	0.3	-47.8	375.0	3.0
India	71	102	104	77	0.2	0.2	2.0	-26.0	1.2
Hong Kong (China)	26	11	182	44	0.1	0.1	1554.5	-75.8	7.8
Other Asia	252	323	311	352	0.9	1.0	-3.7	13.2	4.9
Other Oceania	291	490	469	662	1.0	1.8	-4.3	41.2	12.5
From other regions	*11,445*	*14,035*	*11,362*	*12,034*	*38.8*	*32.9*	*-19.0*	*5.9*	*0.7*
United States	5,859	7,621	6,302	7,473	19.8	20.4	-17.3	18.6	3.5
United Kingdom	1,226	1,969	1,384	1,334	4.2	3.6	-29.7	-3.6	1.2
Germany	1,909	1,349	1,273	945	6.5	2.6	-5.6	-25.8	-9.6
Canada	337	359	370	328	1.1	0.9	3.1	-11.4	-0.4
Italy	402	540	350	322	1.4	0.9	-35.2	-8.0	-3.1
France	141	254	217	271	0.5	0.7	-14.6	24.9	9.8
Sweden	312	387	328	212	1.1	0.6	-15.2	-35.4	-5.4
Austria	196	176	126	137	0.7	0.4	-28.4	8.7	-5.0
Switzerland	290	262	142	127	1.0	0.3	-45.8	-10.6	-11.1
South Africa	..	43	30	59		0.2	-30.2	96.7	
Other Africa	..	10	25	33		0.1	150.0	32.0	
Other Americas	57	25	34	59	0.2	0.2	36.0	73.5	0.5
Other Europe	716	1,040	781	734	2.4	2.0	-24.9	-6.0	0.4
Other World/Not specified	*59*	..	..	..	*0.2*				

Source: World Tourism Organization (WTO) © (Data as collected by WTO September 2003)

III.3.19 Tuvalu — Oceania

Profile

Tuvalu		
East Asia and the Pacific	Capital	Funafuti
Oceania	Area (10 km²)	3
	Population (2002, 1000)	11

	2000	2001	2002*	2001/2000	2002*/2001
International Arrivals					
Tourists (overnight visitors) (1000)	1	1	1	-5.0	8.4
- per 100 of inhabitants	11	..	11		

Source: World Tourism Organization (WTO) (Data as collected by WTO September 2003)

See annex for methodological notes and reference of external sources used.

Survey

Contributed by *Ministry of Finance, Economic Planning and Industries*

Tourism development and outlook

Most significant determinant

Tourism in Tuvalu is still in its infant stage. In terms of significant factors, a boost in the development of tourism last year is not well demonstrated. However, tourists often come to Tuvalu as it is small and peaceful in comparison to other countries.

Tourism products

In terms of accommodation capacity, we have one hotel and four guesthouses and a Conservation Area run by native people. Another factor is that no more hotels or guesthouses have been built due to the very limited land available.

The tourism products fluctuate depending on the number of tourists visiting the country.

Entertainment: many entertainment events are organised within the country e.g. Beauty Pageants.

Access

We have limited access for overseas travellers. All flights to and from Tuvalu have to pass by Fiji and the airfares are very expensive for tourists travelling to Tuvalu.

Generating markets

Most visitors are business travellers and thus appears to be more a MICE market. This is not the targeted group that Tuvalu is aiming for, although it is mainly the business traveller who can afford to visit Tuvalu.

Tuvalu will be concentrating more on the ecotourism sector.

Outlook 2003	Tuvalu is now concentrating on ecotourism in order to preserve the environment naturally, culturally and economically. We have set up a Conservation Area and it has been successfully run for quite a few years now. At the present time, we are studying the options on activities that will generate income from tourists. As airfares are too high for travellers, we are now also concentrating on the yacht/cruise tourist and have increased the buoys for boats in the lagoon. It is planned to increase the number of tourism training courses and workshops for staff employed in the industry. More campaigns will be organised to Keep Tuvalu Clean. Personnel in the tourism office will be increased.
Tourism policy	There has been no tourism policy making and planning during previous years. Nevertheless, this is a field that is under study at the present time.
Marketing & promotion	At the present time, we are following the general marketing plan which is included in the Five Year Action Plan. However, focus is not being made on any particular area.

Cultural Tourism (CT)

Specific place for CT in tourism policy: no.

Main objectives & instruments	Owing to the lack of specific tourism policy making and planning up to the present time.
Main focus of attention supply	We will be mainly focusing on cultural products such as handicrafts, cultural lifestyles and sites and dance performances.
Main focus of attention demand	We will be targeting the specific segment in generating markets that bring in tourists interested in our cultural dances, performances and way of life.

Specific place for CT in marketing & promotion plan: yes.

Main objectives & programmes	Yes, although we have to do more research to identify the benefits and risks of this type of tourism and then we will commence marketing and promotion.
Special activities undertaken	The only promotion we have at the present time is the Miss South Pacific Beauty Pageant in which our Miss Tuvalu will be entering for the first time. This will be a good opportunity to publicize our cultural dances, performances and way of life.

Importance of cultural tourism:

- in total tourism offer	In our case we are, and will be, concentrating on ecotourism. If this is then linked to cultural tourism, we estimate approximately 50 per cent of arrivals will fall into this category.

International Tourism by Origin

Tuvalu
International Tourist Arrivals at Frontiers

Region of Origin, 2001

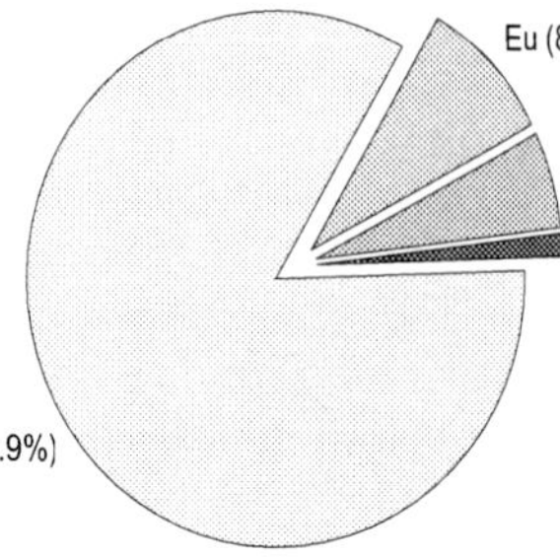

AP: Asia and the Pacific; Eu: Europe; Am: Americas;
ns: Not specified;

Source: World Tourism Organization (WTO) ©

Tuvalu
International Tourist Arrivals at Frontiers (by residence)

	1995	1999	2000	2001	Market share (%) 1995	Market share (%) 2001	Growth rate (%) 2000/99	Growth rate (%) 2001/00	Average per year (%) 1995-2001
Total	**922**	..	..	**1,140**	**100**	**100**			**3.6**
From Asia and the Pacific	*676*	..	..	*957*	*73.3*	*83.9*			*6.0*
All Oceania	274	..	..	416	29.7	36.5			7.2
Japan	76	..	..	189	8.2	16.6			16.4
Australia	179	..	..	165	19.4	14.5			-1.3
New Zealand	89	..	..	140	9.7	12.3			7.8
Other Asia	58	..	..	47	6.3	4.1			-3.4
From other regions	*238*	..	..	*167*	*25.8*	*14.6*			*-5.7*
United States	63	..	..	55	6.8	4.8			-2.2
United Kingdom	62	..	..	31	6.7	2.7			-10.9
France	8	..	..	21	0.9	1.8			17.5
Canada	7	..	..	10	0.8	0.9			6.1
Germany	44	..	..	4	4.8	0.4			-32.9
Other Europe	54	..	..	46	5.9	4.0			-2.6
Other World/Not specified	*8*	..	..	*16*	*0.9*	*1.4*			*12.2*

Source: World Tourism Organization (WTO) ©

(Data as collected by WTO September 2003)

III.3.20 Vanuatu Oceania

Profile

Vanuatu

East Asia and the Pacific
Oceania

Capital	Port-Vila
Area (100 km²)	122
Population (2002, 1000)	196
Gross Domestic Product (GDP) (2002, US$ million)	228
GDP per capita (2002, US$)	1,127
GDP growth (real, %)	
> 2001: -2.1; 2002: -2.8; 2003*: 1.0; 2004*: 2.2	

	2000	2001	2002*	2001/2000	2002*/2001
International Arrivals					
Visitors (1000)	106	107	99	0.9	-7.5
Tourists (overnight visitors) (1000)	58	53	49	-7.5	-7.4
- per 100 of inhabitants	30	28	25		
Same-day visitors (1000)	1	1	..		
Cruise passengers (1000)	47	53	50	12.8	-5.7
Tourism accommodation					
Number of rooms	1,060	..	..		
Nights spent in hotels and similar establishments (1000)					
by non-residents (inbound tourism)	438	471	..	7.5	
Outbound Tourism					
Trips abroad (1000)	12	12	..		
- per 100 of inhabitants	6	6	..		
Receipts and Expenditure for International Tourism					
International Tourism Receipts (US$ million)	58	46	..	-20.7	
- per Tourist Arrival (US$)	1,007	863	..	-14.3	
- per Visitor Arrival (US$)	547	430	..	-21.4	
- per capita (US$)	306	238	..		
International Fare Receipts (US$ million)	13	12	..	-7.7	
International Tourism Expenditure (US$ million)	9	8	..	-11.1	
- per trip (US$)	750	667	..	-11.1	
- per capita (US$)	47	41	..		
△ International Tourism Balance (US$ million)	49	38	..		

Source: World Tourism Organization (WTO) (Data as collected by WTO September 2003)

See annex for methodological notes and reference of external sources used.

Survey

Contributed by *National Tourism Office (NTO)*
www.vanuatutourism.com (promotional)
www.vanuatutourism.com (institutional/corporate)
www.vanuatutourism.com (research and data)

Tourism development and outlook

Most significant determinant	The friendliness of the people and their hospitality. The cultural heritage. Vanuatu remains a safer destination compared to other neighbouring island countries in the South Pacific.
Tourism products	To strongly promote the establishment and upgrading of the Vanuatu Island Bungalows Association (VIBA) through assistance from the European Union (EU). The promotion of events e.g. the Efate Round Island Relay.
Access	The upgrading of Pekoa Airport in Santo (second urban centre) to accommodate International carriers. Also upgrading of the air terminal in the capital Port Vila to cater for largerr aircraft. The current airline (Air Vanuatu) lacks carrying capacity for Vanuatu visitors, something the government is currently trying to address. The problem also applies to our only domestic airline.
Generating markets	Our traditional markets have been and will continue to be Australia and New Zealand and we do everything to protect these markets in terms of promotional campaigns. We are now also looking toward Japan as a potential market to work towards.
Other Issues	Political and economic stability.
Outlook 2003	Increasing tourism promotional activities and budget which will aim at doubling the current tourism figure of 50,000.
Tourism policy	Increase air visitor arrivals to 100,000. Increase tourism facilities. Promote tourism development in the outer islands. Improve overall quality of tourism services. Implementation of the revised version of the Tourism Master Plan which was conducted by the Commonwealth Secretariat in 2002.
Marketing & promotion	The government has increased the 2003 promotional budget for the National Tourism Office (NTO). The NTO is also currently implementing the 2003 Marketing and Promotion Plan approved by the NTO Board.

Cultural Tourism (CT)

Specific place for CT in tourism policy: yes.

Main objectives & instruments	Vanuatu is a Melanesian country with a unique culture or "customs", different from other Melanesian countries in the Pacific. An advantage Vanuatu has over its competitors is that of major positioning for Vanuatu.
Main focus of attention supply	We concentrate on our unique culture and products.
Main focus of attention demand	Both elements as above, but with more concentration on segments.

Specific place for CT in marketing & promotion plan: yes.

Main objectives & programmes	Promotion together with Vanuatu Island Bungalows Association (VIBA) as a package.
Special activities undertaken	Continuous promotional activities are being carried out for the destination and products including culture and events.

Importance of cultural tourism:

- in total tourism offer	Around 30 percent (those travelling to the outer islands).

International Tourism by Origin

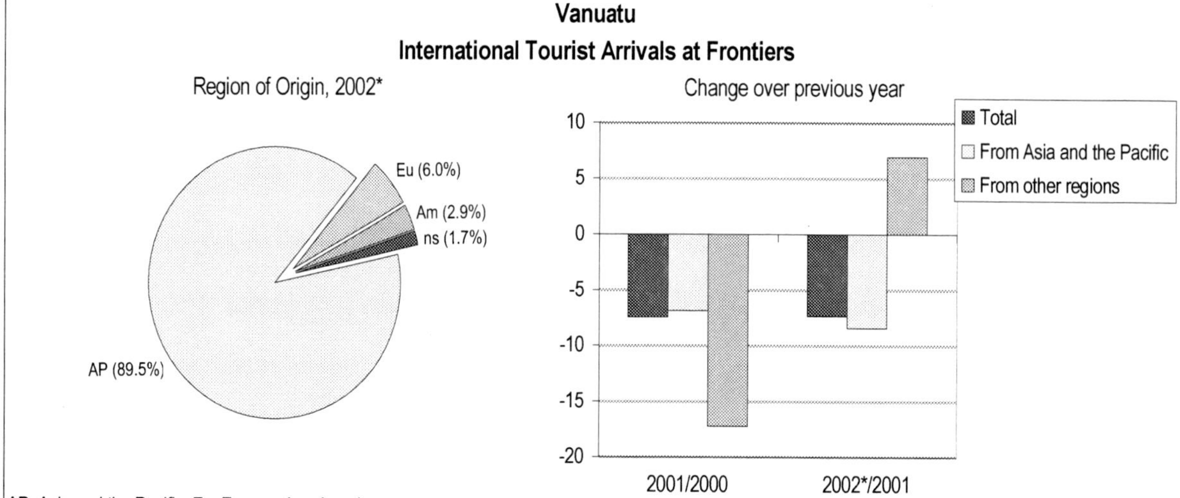

Vanuatu
International Tourist Arrivals at Frontiers (by residence)

	1995	2000	2001	2002*	Market share (%) 1995	Market share (%) 2002*	Growth rate (%) 2001/00	Growth rate (%) 2002*/01	Average per year (%) 1995-2002*
Total	**43,712**	**57,591**	**53,300**	**49,365**	**100**	**100**	**-7.5**	**-7.4**	**1.8**
From Asia and the Pacific	*39,993*	*51,803*	*48,234*	*44,165*	*91.5*	*89.5*	*-6.9*	*-8.4*	*1.4*
Australia	24,401	36,805	33,667	29,729	55.8	60.2	-8.5	-11.7	2.9
New Zealand	6,436	8,024	7,512	7,253	14.7	14.7	-6.4	-3.4	1.7
New Caledonia	4,962	4,124	4,039	4,625	11.4	9.4	-2.1	14.5	-1.0
Fiji	860	..	..	..	2.0				
Solomon Is	758	..	..	..	1.7				
Japan	981	811	834	730	2.2	1.5	2.8	-12.5	-4.1
Papua New Guinea	354	..	..	..	0.8				
French Polynesia	89	..	..	..	0.2				
Other Asia	796	..	..	..	1.8				
Other Oceania	356	2,039	2,182	1,828	0.8	3.7	7.0	-16.2	26.3
From other regions	*3,509*	*4,948*	*4,096*	*4,381*	*8.0*	*8.9*	*-17.2*	*7.0*	*3.2*
All Europe	..	3,401	2,683	2,943		6.0	-21.1	9.7	
All North America	..	1,547	1,413	1,438		2.9	-8.7	1.8	
France	1,030	..	..	..	2.4				
United States	977	..	..	..	2.2				
United Kingdom	515	..	..	..	1.2				
Germany	231	..	..	..	0.5				
Canada	180	..	..	..	0.4				
Other Europe	576	..	..	..	1.3				
Other World/Not specified	*210*	*840*	*970*	*819*	*0.5*	*1.7*	*15.5*	*-15.6*	*21.5*

Source: World Tourism Organization (WTO) © (Data as collected by WTO September 2003)

III.4 South Asia

III.4.1 Afghanistan South Asia

Profile

Afghanistan

South Asia

Capital	Kabul
Year of entry in WTO	1975
Area (1000 km²)	652
Population (2002, million)	27.8

Source: World Tourism Organization (WTO) (Data as collected by WTO September 2003)

See annex for methodological notes and reference of external sources used.

III.4.2 Bangladesh South Asia

Profile

Bangladesh

South Asia

Capital	Dhaka
Year of entry in WTO	1975
Area (1000 km²)	144
Population (2002, million)	136
Gross Domestic Product (GDP) (2002, US$ million)	49,551
GDP per capita (2002, US$)	347
GDP growth (real, %)	
'-> 2001: 4.8; 2002: 4.9; 2003*: 5.4; 2004*: 5.8	

	2000	2001	2002*	2001/2000	2002*/2001
International Arrivals					
Tourists (overnight visitors) (1000)	199	207	207	4.0	0.0
- per 100 of inhabitants	0	0	0		
Tourism accommodation					
Number of rooms	4,550	4,550	..		
Outbound Tourism					
Trips abroad (1000)	1,128	1,075	..	-4.7	
- per 100 of inhabitants	1	1	..		
Receipts and Expenditure for International Tourism					
International Tourism Receipts (US$ million)	50	48	..	-4.0	
- per Tourist Arrival (US$)	251	232	..	-7.7	
- per capita (US$)	0	0	..		
International Tourism Expenditure (US$ million)	301	166	..	-44.9	
- per trip (US$)	267	154	..	-42.1	
- per capita (US$)	2	1	..		
International Fare Expenditure (US$ million)	181	176	..	-3.0	
△ International Tourism Balance (US$ million)	-251	-118	..		

Source: World Tourism Organization (WTO) (Data as collected by WTO September 2003)

See annex for methodological notes and reference of external sources used.

International Tourism by Origin

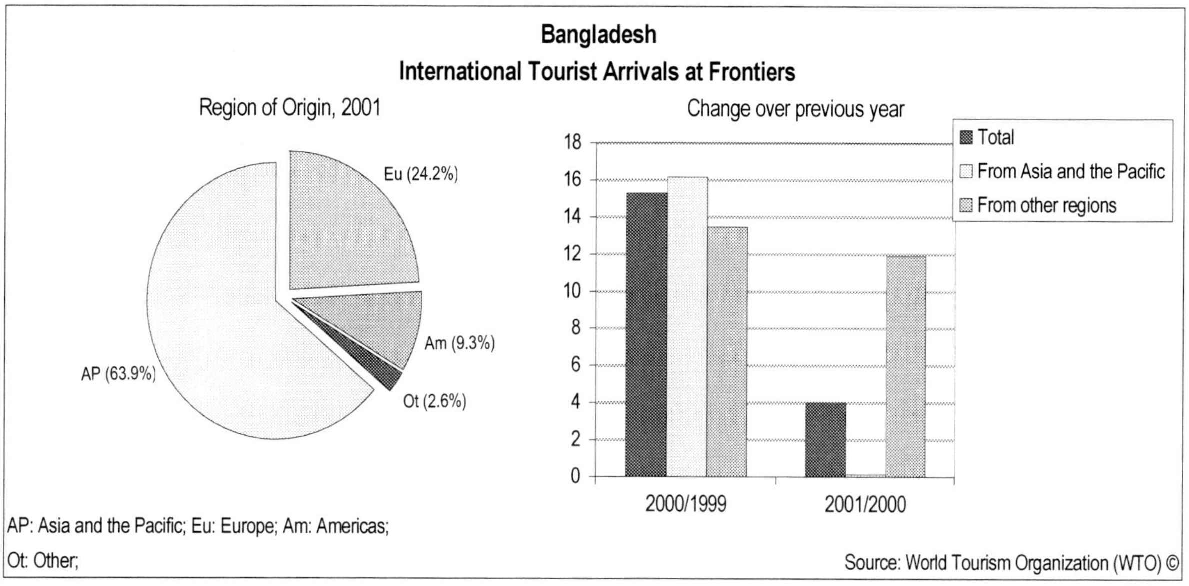

Bangladesh

International Tourist Arrivals at Frontiers (by nationality)

					Market share (%)		Growth rate (%)		Average per year (%)
	1995	1999	2000	2001	1995	2001	2000/99	2001/00	1995-2001
Total	**156,231**	**172,781**	**199,211**	**207,199**	**100**	**100**	**15.3**	**4.0**	**4.8**
From Asia and the Pacific	*89,921*	*113,743*	*132,138*	*132,319*	*57.6*	*63.9*	*16.2*	*0.1*	*6.6*
India	46,015	62,935	74,268	78,090	29.5	37.7	18.0	5.1	9.2
Japan	5,600	7,055	8,006	7,090	3.6	3.4	13.5	-11.4	4.0
Pakistan	12,903	7,894	10,637	7,010	8.3	3.4	34.7	-34.1	-9.7
Korea, Republic of	5,251	6,596	6,746	6,896	3.4	3.3	2.3	2.2	4.6
China	3,408	5,208	5,901	6,867	2.2	3.3	13.3	16.4	12.4
Nepal	2,995	4,733	4,481	4,280	1.9	2.1	-5.3	-4.5	6.1
Malaysia	2,209	2,890	3,827	3,204	1.4	1.5	32.4	-16.3	6.4
Sri Lanka	1,395	1,839	2,427	3,026	0.9	1.5	32.0	24.7	13.8
Thailand	1,519	2,159	2,492	2,881	1.0	1.4	15.4	15.6	11.3
Australia	2,076	2,091	2,377	2,722	1.3	1.3	13.7	14.5	4.6
Singapore	1,975	2,762	2,271	2,623	1.3	1.3	-17.8	15.5	4.8
Philippines	875	1,712	1,909	1,692	0.6	0.8	11.5	-11.4	11.6
Indonesia	505	1,067	1,250	1,379	0.3	0.7	17.2	10.3	18.2
Bhutan	417	730	1,010	1,263	0.3	0.6	38.4	25.0	20.3
Taiwan (Pr. of China)	767	1,603	1,649	1,028	0.5	0.5	2.9	-37.7	5.0
Iran	415	666	687	577	0.3	0.3	3.2	-16.0	5.6
Hong Kong (China)	308	472	739	551	0.2	0.3	56.6	-25.4	10.2
New Zealand	520	664	666	440	0.3	0.2	0.3	-33.9	-2.7
Myanmar	388	332	308	353	0.2	0.2	-7.2	14.6	-1.6
Other intraregional	380	335	487	347	0.2	0.2	45.4	-28.7	-1.5
From other regions	*66,310*	*58,887*	*66,826*	*74,786*	*42.4*	*36.1*	*13.5*	*11.9*	*2.0*
United Kingdom	31,984	22,510	29,106	34,087	20.5	16.5	29.3	17.1	1.1
United States	10,541	9,557	11,924	13,394	6.7	6.5	24.8	12.3	4.1
Canada	2,325	2,461	2,723	5,484	1.5	2.6	10.6	101.4	15.4
Germany	2,460	2,947	3,080	2,635	1.6	1.3	4.5	-14.4	1.2
Netherlands	3,279	2,767	2,951	2,508	2.1	1.2	6.6	-15.0	-4.4
France	2,258	2,457	2,336	2,289	1.4	1.1	-4.9	-2.0	0.2
Italy	1,753	1,789	2,118	1,780	1.1	0.9	18.4	-16.0	0.3
Saudi Arabia	1,537	2,509	2,049	1,642	1.0	0.8	-18.3	-19.9	1.1
Denmark	1,152	1,134	1,162	1,449	0.7	0.7	2.5	24.7	3.9
Sweden	1,575	1,075	1,455	1,350	1.0	0.7	35.3	-7.2	-2.5
Belgium	682	565	652	723	0.4	0.3	15.4	10.9	1.0
Switzerland	657	694	573	685	0.4	0.3	-17.4	19.5	0.7
Norway	549	766	714	650	0.4	0.3	-6.8	-9.0	2.9
Untd Arab Emirates	271	226	268	508	0.2	0.2	18.6	89.6	11.0
Turkey	98	326	254	443	0.1	0.2	-22.1	74.4	28.6
South Africa	92	429	459	432	0.1	0.2	7.0	-5.9	29.4
Spain	248	409	479	408	0.2	0.2	17.1	-14.8	8.7
Egypt	340	449	334	383	0.2	0.2	-25.6	14.7	2.0
Finland	246	492	312	304	0.2	0.1	-36.6	-2.6	3.6
Kenya	82	111	132	294	0.1	0.1	18.9	122.7	23.7
Ireland	281	234	257	268	0.2	0.1	9.8	4.3	-0.8
Austria	214	242	138	255	0.1	0.1	-43.0	84.8	3.0
Other interregional	3,686	4,738	3,350	2,815	2.4	1.4	-29.3	-16.0	-4.4
Other World/Not specified	..	*151*	*247*	*94*		*0.0*	*63.6*	*-61.9*	

Source: World Tourism Organization (WTO) © (Data as collected by WTO September 2003)

III.4.3 Bhutan South Asia

Profile

Bhutan

South Asia

Capital	Thimpu
Year of entry in WTO	2003
Area (1000 km²)	47
Population (2002, million)	2.1
Gross Domestic Product (GDP) (2002, US$ million)	566
GDP per capita (2002, US$)	700
GDP growth (real, %)	
'-> 2001: 6.6; 2002: 7.7; 2003*: 7.3; 2004*: 7.6	

	2000	2001	2002*	2001/2000	2002*/2001
International Arrivals					
Tourists (overnight visitors) (1000)	8	6	6	-15.7	-5.9
- per 100 of inhabitants	0	..	..		
Tourism accommodation					
Number of rooms	1,215	1,215	..		
Nights spent in hotels and similar establishments (1000)					
by non-residents (inbound tourism)	61	53	..	-13.1	
Receipts and Expenditure for International Tourism					
International Tourism Receipts (US$ million)	10	..	..		
- per Tourist Arrival (US$)	1,323	..	..		
- per capita (US$)	5	..	..		

Source: World Tourism Organization (WTO) (Data as collected by WTO September 2003)

See annex for methodological notes and reference of external sources used.

Survey

Contributed by *Ministry of Trade and Industry*
www.tourism.gov.bt (institutional/corporate)

Tourism development and outlook

Most significant determinant

Due to the regional disturbances, there has been a decrease in the number of tourist arrivals in the kingdom. Disruptions in flight schedules, landslides during the monsoon months and snow in the winter is a significant problem faced by the single national airline and for surface travel within the country.

Tourism products

A new Dzongkhag (district) Haa was opened to tourists for wider destination choice. The annual inspection of all hotels and restaurants was conducted and at the same time classification of the hotels was also done in order to keep in view the need to improve standards. The Department has initiated a feasibility study on the development of community-based tourism and the first phase is completed. When all the phases are completed, it will be one of the products that could be marketed and promoted.

Access

Access to the country is limited to a single national airline, Druk Air, with a fleet of just two planes with a carrying capacity of 72 passengers each. Druk Air has initiated measures to procure bigger aircraft e.g. the Airbus 318 with carrying capacity of more than 130 passengers per plane, which will increase the access capacity. For the present, they have increased frequency of flights especially to Bangkok, which is an important entry point for Bhutan. Druk Air also operates via Rangoon (Myanmar).

Generating markets

The work on the development of a new website has been initiated and it will be more interactive and informative to visitors.

Outlook 2003

In the 9th Plan, the Royal Government of Bhutan has placed great emphasis on the sustainable development of tourism and has accorded the sector a high priority as an employment generator, revenue/hard currency earner and a vehicle for promoting a positive image of Bhutan.

The establishment of the National Hotel and Tourism Management Training Institute is underway. With the establishment of the Institute, it will not only develop and provide adequate skilled manpower to the industry but will also raise the quality of services and increase the employment opportunities for youths in the sector.
Tourist arrivals are forecast at 16,000 by the year 2007.

Tourism policy

Tourism has been accorded a high priority in the 9th Five-Year Plan.

As a step towards developing tourism, the Department is in the process of reviewing the Master Plan and developing guidelines as well as legislation.

A series of meetings has been conducted with the relevant stakeholders to discuss issues relating to tax incentives, rules and regulations and human resource development etc.

Development of community-based tourism is also underway and the first phase has been completed.

The Department has also trained human resources in the field of tourism (cooks, guides, front office, etc).

Promotion and marketing of Bhutan as a tourist destination was also carried out at various fairs such as the ITB-Berlin, OTM-Delhi etc.

Marketing & promotion

The Department along with the Association of Bhutanese Tour Operators and the local tour operators participated in the ITB fair in Berlin. The ITB fair is attended yearly for marketing and promotion but greater efforts were made to improve the participation qualitatively. In the Outbound Travel Mart (OTM) held in India, Bhutan was declared and certified as the most promising new tourist destination for regional tourists. The work on the development of a new website has been initiated and it will be more interactive and informative to visitors.

Cultural Tourism (CT)

Specific place for CT in tourism policy: yes.

Main objectives & instruments

As culture and the people are the main center of attraction for tourists, most of the rules revolve around the conservation and preservation of culture and heritage while at the same time promoting tourism.

Main focus of attention supply

The main focus within cultural tourism are the festivals, which are held at different places. The other main product would include the Dzongs and monasteries, which are open to tourists.

Main focus of attention demand	One of the main focuses would be to enhance the marketing strategy to increase the number of tourist arrivals. Enhancing the visitor's experience will also be taken up as one of the activities. Feasibility studies on the development of products such as cultural tourism, religious/spiritual tourism, spa-tourism etc. will be carried out to generate markets outside Bhutan.

Specific place for CT in marketing & promotion plan: yes.

Main objectives & programmes	As stated earlier, most of the marketing and promotion also revolves around culture, festivals and the people. Mountains, flora and fauna are also included in promotion as trekking is also a major element of activities.
Special activities undertaken	Since the beginning of tourism promotion in the country, culture has been marketed as one of the main products. Festivals are one of the main attractions for tourists.

Importance of cultural tourism:

- in intern. arrivals	The total number of tourists for 2002 was 5,599. Approximately 90 per cent of the total visitors came as cultural tourists, and 10 per cent came for trekking, flora and fauna and others.

International Tourism by Origin

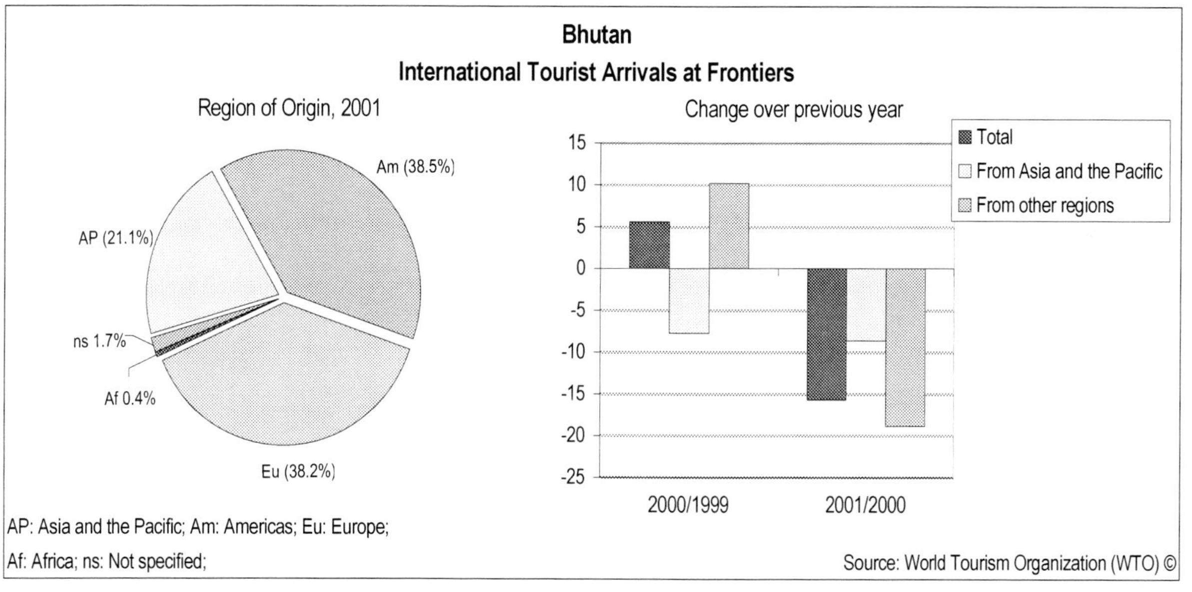

Bhutan

International Tourist Arrivals at Frontiers (by nationality)

	1995	1999	2000	2001	Market share (%) 1995	Market share (%) 2001	Growth rate (%) 2000/99	Growth rate (%) 2001/00	Average per year (%) 1995-2001
Total	**4,765**	**7,158**	**7,559**	**6,374**	**100**	**100**	**5.6**	**-15.7**	**5.0**
From Asia and the Pacific	*1,527*	*1,599*	*1,475*	*1,348*	*32.0*	*21.1*	*-7.8*	*-8.6*	*-2.1*
Japan	1,192	1,102	875	1,012	25.0	15.9	-20.6	15.7	-2.7
Australia	142	131	179	136	3.0	2.1	36.6	-24.0	-0.7
Taiwan (Pr. of China)	38	179	175	44	0.8	0.7	-2.2	-74.9	2.5
Thailand	57	71	92	36	1.2	0.6	29.6	-60.9	-7.4
Korea, Republic of	25	14	3	34	0.5	0.5	-78.6	1033.3	5.3
China	3	11	10	27	0.1	0.4	-9.1	170.0	44.2
New Zealand	37	22	31	25	0.8	0.4	40.9	-19.4	-6.3
Singapore	14	26	31	15	0.3	0.2	19.2	-51.6	1.2
Nepal	6	23	50	14	0.1	0.2	117.4	-72.0	15.2
Philippines	..	20	13	..			-35.0		
Malaysia	8	..	16	4	0.2	0.1		-75.0	-10.9
Indonesia	5	..	..	1	0.1	0.0			-23.5
From other regions	*3,231*	*5,498*	*6,060*	*4,918*	*67.8*	*77.2*	*10.2*	*-18.8*	*7.3*
United States	865	2,122	2,754	2,238	18.2	35.1	29.8	-18.7	17.2
United Kingdom	418	646	595	673	8.8	10.6	-7.9	13.1	8.3
Germany	500	574	662	411	10.5	6.4	15.3	-37.9	-3.2
France	338	236	399	287	7.1	4.5	69.1	-28.1	-2.7
Canada	55	149	194	196	1.2	3.1	30.2	1.0	23.6
Italy	202	276	156	194	4.2	3.0	-43.5	24.4	-0.7
Netherlands	100	362	359	180	2.1	2.8	-0.8	-49.9	10.3
Switzerland	218	296	137	146	4.6	2.3	-53.7	6.6	-6.5
Austria	200	197	131	129	4.2	2.0	-33.5	-1.5	-7.0
Israel	2	80	68	79	0.0	1.2	-15.0	16.2	84.5
Belgium	79	107	95	74	1.7	1.2	-11.2	-22.1	-1.1
Spain	22	118	141	70	0.5	1.1	19.5	-50.4	21.3
Portugal	4	43	19	43	0.1	0.7	-55.8	126.3	48.6
Poland	..	35	26	40		0.6	-25.7	53.8	
Turkey	..	49	34	..			-30.6		
Sweden	45	37	48	28	0.9	0.4	29.7	-41.7	-7.6
South Africa	..	12	7	26		0.4	-41.7	271.4	
Denmark	42	13	30	22	0.9	0.3	130.8	-26.7	-10.2
Russian Fed	2	17	13	19	0.0	0.3	-23.5	46.2	45.5
Finland	8	5	60	17	0.2	0.3	1100.0	-71.7	13.4
Czech Rep	..	..	12	..					
Greece	1	..	25	11	0.0	0.2		-56.0	49.1
Brazil	48	14	10	10	1.0	0.2	-28.6	0.0	-23.0
Ireland	6	16	10	10	0.1	0.2	-37.5	0.0	8.9
Mexico	13	49	37	7	0.3	0.1	-24.5	-81.1	-9.8
Other interregional	63	45	38	8	1.3	0.1	-15.6	-78.9	-29.1
Other World/Not specified	*7*	*61*	*24*	*108*	*0.1*	*1.7*	*-60.7*	*350.0*	*57.8*

Source: World Tourism Organization (WTO) ©

(Data as collected by WTO September 2003)

III.4.4 India South Asia

Profile

India

South Asia

Capital	New Delhi
Year of entry in WTO	1975
Area (1000 km²)	3,287
Population (2002, million)	1,034
Gross Domestic Product (GDP) (2002, US$ million)	494,821
GDP per capita (2002, US$)	471
GDP growth (real, %)	
'-> 2001: 4.2; 2002: 4.7; 2003*: 5.6; 2004*: 5.9	

	2000	2001	2002*	2001/2000	2002*/2001
International Arrivals					
Visitors (1000)	2,677	2,591	2,414	-3.2	-6.8
Tourists (overnight visitors) (1000)	2,649	2,537	2,370	-4.2	-6.6
- per 100 of inhabitants	0	0	0		
Cruise passengers (1000)	28	54	44	92.9	-18.5
Tourism accommodation					
Number of rooms	77,193	82,181	80,936	6.5	-1.5
Outbound Tourism					
Trips abroad (1000)	3,982	4,067	4,205	2.1	3.4
- per 100 of inhabitants	0	0	0		
Receipts and Expenditure for International Tourism					
International Tourism Receipts (US$ million)	3,168	3,042	2,923	-4.0	-3.9
- per Tourist Arrival (US$)	1,196	1,199	1,233	0.3	2.9
- per Visitor Arrival (US$)	1,183	1,174	1,211	-0.8	3.1
- per capita (US$)	3	3	3		
International Tourism Expenditure (US$ million)	2,567	2,571	2,942	0.2	14.4
- per trip (US$)	645	632	700	-1.9	10.7
- per capita (US$)	3	3	3		
△ International Tourism Balance (US$ million)	601	471	-19		

Source: World Tourism Organization (WTO) (Data as collected by WTO September 2003)

See annex for methodological notes and reference of external sources used.

Survey

Contributed by *Ministry of Tourism and Culture*
www.tourismofindia.com (promotional)
www.tourismofindia.com (institutional/corporate)

Tourism development and outlook

Most significant determinant

The international tourist arrivals in the country in the year 2002 is estimated to be 2.36 million as compared to 2.54 million in the year 2001, thus showing a decline of 6.9 per cent against a decline of 4.2 per cent observed in 2001.

After the 11 September 2001 incident at the World Trade Centre, New York and the subsequent developments leading to the Afghan war, Indo-Pakistan border tension and terrorist attacks in some places in India, foreign tourist arrivals in India were setback in the sense that there was a consistent negative growth rate in each month starting from September 2001 till September 2002. However, a revival trend has been observed from October 2002 onwards. While a growth rate of 16.8 per cent was recorded for the month of October 2002, positive growth rates of 16.2 per cent and 10.4 per cent were witnessed during November and December 2002. With the increase in the arrivals to the country, the foreign exchange earnings position also improved in October, November and December 2002 with an estimated growth rate of 24.4 per cent, 20.2 per cent and 13.7 per cent respectively.

Tourism products

Accommodation capacity as at the end of October, 2002:

Star category	No. of hotels	No. of Rooms
5-Star Deluxe	65	15,229
5-Star	72	9,367
4-Star	107	7,766
Heritage	70	1,810
3-Star	435	20,584
2-Star	460	15,470
1-Star	186	6,205
To be classified	95	4,505
Total	1,490	80,936

Human Resource Development:
As a result of vast expansion and modernization of the country's hospitality industry, hotel management and catering education rograms gained tremendous popularity and the profile of the students seeking admission to these courses also underwent transformation. At present, there are 21 Institutes of Hotel Management and 9 Food Craft Institutes.

Tourism Product:
There is a vast bounty of nature and also great treasures of art and architecture. There are opportunities for hill, adventure, rural and wild life tourism and unique techniques of Yoga, Siddha, Ayurveda and Unani systems of dealing with physical and mental illnesses.There are 572 nature endowed areas - 89 National Parks and 483 wildlife sanctuaries and 3,606 protected monuments. One of the new initiatives taken recently in the arena of tourism and culture is to synthesize the elements of tourism, culture and clear civil life and to create new hubs of tourism and culture.

Access

National Highways Development Project:
The National Highways Development Project (NHDP), was launched three years ago and is promising to achieve a turnaround in the road sector hardly imaginable at the start of the Ninth Plan. NHDP comprises the 6,000 km. Long Golden Quadrilateral (GQ) connecting the four metros of Delhi, Mumbai, Chennai and Kolkata and the 7,000 km. long North-South, East-West corridors connecting Srinagar-Kanyakumari and Silichar-Porbandar respectively. There are 4/6 lanes working on all but 700 km. The GQ have been awarded. The GQ is expected to be completed by 2003 and the two corridors by 2007.

Roads:
The 'Golden Quadrilateral' is expected to be substantially completed by December 2003.

Civil Aviation:
The international airports at Delhi, Mumbai, Chennai and Kolkota are proposed to be upgraded to the standards of world class airports.

Railways:
Seventeen inter-city train services called Jan Shatabdi have been introduced.

Generating markets

Following are the 15 major generating markets:

Nationality	Arrivals	% Share
United Kingdom	390,762	16.5
United States of America	333,382	14.1
Sri Lanka	107,729	4.6
Canada	87,440	3.7
France	82,044	3.5
Germany	67,125	2.8
Japan	58,721	2.5
Malaysia	54,943	2.3
Nepal	46,277	2.0
Australia	44,556	1.9
Singapore	41,918	1.8
The Netherlands	32,055	1.4
Italy	32,042	1.4
Korea (South)	31,519	1.3
The United Arab Emirates	27,126	1.1

Outlook 2003

Tourism Budget:
The Tourism Budget has been increased from 150.00 crores during 2001-2002 to 225.00 crores during 2002-2003 showing an increase in the budget by 50 per cent. The Tourism Budget estimates for the year 2003-2004 is 325.00 crores.

The Approach of the 10th Plan:
The approach of the 10th Plan will stimulate investment and encourage the state governments to develop unique tourism products suited to the genus. It will strive to remove the bottlenecks by ensuring better policy integration and co-ordination among all the relevant stakeholders in the development of state-of-the art tourism facilities. The development approach, however, will be equally concerned with the environment substantially.

Tourism policy

A new Tourism Policy which is government led, private-sector driven and community-welfare oriented was announced by the government in May 2002. The policy gives the direction to position India as a global brand to take advantage of the burgeoning global travel and trade, and the vast untapped potential of India as a destination. It envisages improvement and expansion of product development in (i) Cultural

Tourism; (ii) Beach and Coastal Tourism; (iii) Cruise/River Tourism; (iv) Rural/Village Tourism; (v) Adventure Tourism; (vi) Ecotourism; (vii) Cuisine Tourism; (viii) MICE Tourism; (ix) Health Tourism; and (x) Festival/Shopping Tourism. It also envisages creation and development of integrated tourism circuits based on India's unique civilisation, heritage and culture in partnership with the states, private sector and other agencies.

Following the new Tourism Policy, the Department of Tourism, Government of India, has adopted a new approach towards infrastructure and product development. The policy document seeks to enhance employment potential within the tourism sector as well as foster economic integration through developing linkages with other sectors. Broadly, the policy paper aims to:

- Position tourism as a major engine of economic growth;
- Harness the direct and multiplier effects of tourism for employment generation, economic development and providing impetus to rural tourism;
- Focus on domestic tourism as a major driver of tourism growth;
- Position India as a global brand to take advantage of the burgeoning global travel and trade and the vast untapped potential of India as a destination;
- Acknowledge the critical role of the private sector with the government working as a pro-active facilitator and catalyst;
- Create and develop integrated tourism circuits based on India's unique civilisation, heritage, and culture in partnership with the states, private sector and other agencies;
- Ensure that tourists to India become physically invigorated, mentally rejuvenated, culturally enriched, spiritually elevated and "feel India from within".

The policy document takes into consideration seven key areas that will provide the thrust for tourism development. These are:Swagat (Welcome), Soochana (Information), Suvidha (Facilitation), Suraksha (Safety), Sahyog (Co-operation), Samrachna (Infrastructure Development) and Safai (Cleanliness).

Marketing & promotion

India is a multi-destination country with a variety of tourist attractions and facilities. Its product range encompasses mountains, beaches, adventure sports, culture, heritage monuments, etc. The Department of Tourism has 13 offices in the overseas markets and through these it endeavors to fulfil the following marketing objectives:

- To position India in the tourism generating markets as a desirable tourism destination;
- To promote various Indian tourism products vis-à-vis competition faced from various destinations;
- To mitigate the effects of negative publicity in the foreign media, and to restore confidence amongst prospective tourists to India;
- To increase India's share of the global tourism market.

Tourism Generating Markets - Primary and Secondary Markets
From a marketing point of view the global market for India has been categoriesed into primary, secondary and tertiary markets.

The primary markets receive major attention in terms of a total marketing package, including advertising, public relations and other activities such as consumer and trade shows.

Secondary markets are given limited support.

The tertiary markets are provided with servicing and some promotion.

Promotional Strategy:
The Department has earmarked an aggressive Action Plan to position India as an attractive destination in various markets and to increase India's share in tourist

arrivals. An integrated electronic campaign on the leading television channels across the globe is being undertaken centrally. This is being supplemented by a print advertising campaign in the leading print media publications overseas. In view of the fact that world tourism trends indicate growth in intraregional tourism, due focus is being given to aggressive promotion in East Asia and the ASEAN countries.

Cultural Tourism (CT)

Specific place for CT in tourism policy: yes.

Main objectives & instruments	Yes. India has a unique cultural heritage. It has a vast array of protected monuments spread throughout the length and breadth of the country. India has 22 World Heritage sites (16 are monuments). The conservation, preservation and integrated development of the area around these monuments provides a rare opportunity for growth and expansion of cultural tourism in India.
Main focus of attention supply	The same as above.

Specific place for CT in marketing & promotion plan: yes.

Special activities undertaken	The Bodhgaya-Rajgir-Nalanda-Varansi Buddhist Circuit has been identified to promote the cultural tourism product:

Importance of cultural tourism:

- in total tourism offer	According to the International Passenger Survey Report conducted during 1996-1997, 42 per cent of tourists were motivated by cultural activities and resorts.

International Tourism by Origin

India

International Tourist Arrivals at Frontiers

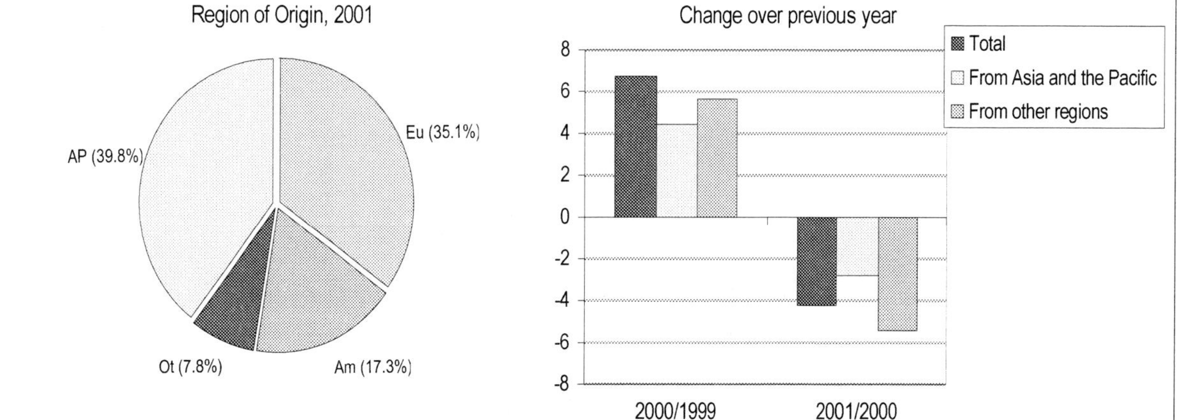

AP: Asia and the Pacific; Eu: Europe; Am: Americas;

Ot: Other;

Source: World Tourism Organization (WTO) ©

India

International Tourist Arrivals at Frontiers (by nationality)

					Market share (%)		Growth rate (%)		Average per year (%)
	1995	1999	2000	2001	1995	2001	2000/99	2001/00	1995-2001
Total	**2,123,683**	**2,481,928**	**2,649,378**	**2,537,282**	**100**	**100**	**6.7**	**-4.2**	**3.0**
From Asia and the Pacific	*829,557*	*993,648*	*1,037,671*	*1,008,676*	*39.1*	*39.8*	*4.4*	*-2.8*	*3.3*
Bangladesh	318,474	414,359	414,437	431,312	15.0	17.0	0.0	4.1	5.2
Sri Lanka	114,157	120,072	129,193	112,813	5.4	4.4	7.6	-12.7	-0.2
Japan	76,042	79,373	98,159	80,634	3.6	3.2	23.7	-17.9	1.0
Malaysia	50,039	52,613	60,513	57,869	2.4	2.3	15.0	-4.4	2.5
Pakistan	42,981	42,538	54,902	52,762	2.0	2.1	29.1	-3.9	3.5
Australia	36,150	73,041	53,995	52,691	1.7	2.1	-26.1	-2.4	6.5
Singapore	48,632	53,310	46,612	42,824	2.3	1.7	-12.6	-8.1	-2.1
Nepal	34,562	25,859	38,801	41,135	1.6	1.6	50.0	6.0	2.9
Korea, Republic of	9,831	19,188	23,411	27,150	0.5	1.1	22.0	16.0	18.4
Thailand	14,462	13,475	18,607	18,623	0.7	0.7	38.1	0.1	4.3
Maldives	..	3,312	21,633	17,564		0.7	553.2	-18.8	
China	5,111	6,487	14,420	13,901	0.2	0.5	122.3	-3.6	18.1
Iran	12,337	11,655	10,577	11,728	0.6	0.5	-9.2	10.9	-0.8
New Zealand	10,700	18,324	11,551	11,700	0.5	0.5	-37.0	1.3	1.5
Indonesia	7,795	9,452	8,659	7,767	0.4	0.3	-8.4	-10.3	-0.1
Philippines	5,580	6,640	7,521	7,199	0.3	0.3	13.3	-4.3	4.3
Other intraregional	42,704	43,950	24,680	21,004	2.0	0.8	-43.8	-14.9	-11.2
From other regions	*1,293,303*	*1,488,036*	*1,571,932*	*1,486,608*	*60.9*	*58.6*	*5.6*	*-5.4*	*2.3*
United Kingdom	334,827	345,080	432,624	405,472	15.8	16.0	25.4	-6.3	3.2
United States	203,343	251,926	348,292	329,147	9.6	13.0	38.3	-5.5	8.4
France	82,349	85,891	100,022	102,434	3.9	4.0	16.5	2.4	3.7
Canada	63,821	82,892	84,013	88,600	3.0	3.5	1.4	5.5	5.6
Germany	89,040	85,031	83,881	80,011	4.2	3.2	-1.4	-4.6	-1.8
Netherlands	40,147	48,820	46,370	42,368	1.9	1.7	-5.0	-8.6	0.9
Italy	53,015	50,677	50,419	41,351	2.5	1.6	-0.5	-18.0	-4.1
Former U.S.S.R.	40,665	..	..	..	1.9				
Israel	14,806	23,417	25,631	28,774	0.7	1.1	9.5	12.3	11.7
Switzerland	29,388	34,824	27,432	25,308	1.4	1.0	-21.2	-7.7	-2.5
Spain	24,411	23,688	26,050	23,073	1.1	0.9	10.0	-11.4	-0.9
Untd Arab Emirates	19,749	16,780	22,559	21,483	0.9	0.8	34.4	-4.8	1.4
South Africa	18,750	23,909	21,919	21,162	0.9	0.8	-8.3	-3.5	2.0
Belgium	18,732	25,328	20,230	18,851	0.9	0.7	-20.1	-6.8	0.1
Austria	13,114	19,051	19,185	17,787	0.6	0.7	0.7	-7.3	5.2
Mauritius	11,353	16,478	14,358	16,039	0.5	0.6	-12.9	11.7	5.9
Kenya	17,389	21,231	16,386	15,973	0.8	0.6	-22.8	-2.5	-1.4
Russian Fed	..	14,896	16,545	15,154		0.6	11.1	-8.4	
Denmark	14,128	16,127	16,272	14,531	0.7	0.6	0.9	-10.7	0.5
Sweden	19,013	22,738	14,717	14,446	0.9	0.6	-35.3	-1.8	-4.5
Oman	17,060	14,878	12,616	13,114	0.8	0.5	-15.2	3.9	-4.3
Saudi Arabia	16,252	14,424	10,739	9,851	0.8	0.4	-25.5	-8.3	-8.0
Finland	10,659	10,849	10,553	8,186	0.5	0.3	-2.7	-22.4	-4.3
Yemen	16,777	7,494	7,980	7,773	0.8	0.3	6.5	-2.6	-12.0
Norway	6,803	9,392	7,997	7,667	0.3	0.3	-14.9	-4.1	2.0
Other interregional	117,712	222,215	135,142	118,053	5.5	4.7	-39.2	-12.6	0.0
Other World/Not specified	*823*	*244*	*39,775*	*41,998*	*0.0*	*1.7*	*#####*	*5.6*	*92.6*

Source: World Tourism Organization (WTO) ©

(Data as collected by WTO September 2003)

III.4.5 Iran (Islamic Republic of) South Asia

Profile

Iran (Islamic Republic of)

South Asia

Capital	Tehran
Year of entry in WTO	1975
Area (1000 km²)	1,648
Population (2002, million)	67.5
Gross Domestic Product (GDP) (2002, US$ million)	108,134
GDP per capita (2002, US$)	1,637
GDP growth (real, %)	
'-> 2001: 5.9; 2002: 6.7; 2003*: 6.1; 2004*: 5.7	

	2000	2001	2002*	2001/2000	2002*/2001
International Arrivals					
Tourists (overnight visitors) (1000)	1,342	1,402	..	4.5	
- per 100 of inhabitants	2	2	..		
Tourism accommodation					
Number of rooms	22,665	27,889	..	23.0	
Nights spent in hotels and similar establishments (1000)	5,584	5,026		-10.0	
by non-residents (inbound tourism)	907	854	..	-5.8	
by residents (domestic tourism)	4,677	4,172	..	-10.8	
Outbound Tourism					
Trips abroad (1000)	2,286	2,400	..	5.0	
- per 100 of inhabitants	3	4	..		
Receipts and Expenditure for International Tourism					
International Tourism Receipts (US$ million)	671	1,122	..	67.2	
- per Tourist Arrival (US$)	500	800	..	60.1	
- per capita (US$)	10	17	..		
International Fare Receipts (US$ million)	210	231	..	10.0	
International Tourism Expenditure (US$ million)	631	238	..	-62.3	
- per trip (US$)	276	99	..	-64.1	
- per capita (US$)	10	4	..		
International Fare Expenditure (US$ million)	3	6	..	100.0	
△ International Tourism Balance (US$ million)	40	884	..		
△ International Fare Balance (US$ million)	207	225	..		

Source: World Tourism Organization (WTO) (Data as collected by WTO September 2003)

See annex for methodological notes and reference of external sources used.

Survey

Contributed by *Iran Touring & Tourism Organization (ITTO)*
www.irantourism.org (promotional)

Tourism development and outlook

Most significant determinant	The formulation of the Tourism Development and Management Master Plan for Iran helped in: - changing the negative image of tourism and generating awareness about the contribution of tourism to national development and; - devolving more responsibility to the provinces for developing their tourism and; - initiating plans and programs in relevant stakeholder ministries, organisations and local government for tourism development.
Tourism products	Due to Iran's special socio-political environment ecotourism has become the byword for tourism development and new ecotourism products are being planned. Tourism destinations have organized International festivals (Shiraz for the first time) The Iran Cultural Heritage Organization has shown initiative in starting a department for revitalisation of historic city cores and forming a council with the Ministry of the Interior and the Ministry of Housing and Urban Development: 60 cities have been identified for revitalisation of historic cores. A Christian site of importance to Korean Christians was introduced for the first time. No changes in the areas of facilities, competitiveness or price levels. The results of the ongoing product improvement and expansion plans will be visible by early 2005.
Access	The Civil Aviation Organization is purchasing aircraft in a fleet expansion program. Seven International Airports have been announced for upgradation and expansion into international airports Plans are underway for privatisation of airports. The Imam Khomeini Airport will be inaugurated in December. Rail routes are being developed as planned. No changes in Sea Access or Road Access infrastructure. No significant change in visa facilitation and formalities.
Generating markets	There have been no significant changes. Since there is no data on domestic tourism it is difficult to provide statistics on the impact of increased awareness on travel patterns or expenditure. International inbound markets have shown no significant change.
Other Issues	It is interesting to note that provincial and local government ministries and organisations other than the tourism office have initiated programs of their own in developing tourism resources and access infrastructure. Private Sector initiative is on the increase but the relative inexperience in tourism development is a deterrent in quality.
Outlook 2003	For the next couple of years, until end of 2005 no significant change in international arrivals is anticipated. The Regional international markets will see a small rise. Domestic Tourism will expand seeing the current trends in promotion of travel on national state television, the ongoing programs of the Iran Touring and Tourism Organization and the Provincial Governments. Plans and programs for product development will be underway at provincial and local levels.

Tourism policy

The planned merger between the Iran Cultural Heritage Organization and the National Tourism Office under the President is awaiting the approval of the parliament. On an ad-hoc basis some attempts to improve service standards, training, promotion of tourism among the domestic markets are being planned by the national tourism office. While small loans have been disbursed for establishing travel agencies or tour guide training no clear program for human resource development, improvement and expansion of services and facilities or promoting investment in the above mentioned areas has been implemented. Most of the current regulations continue.

Comments

It is important to remember that Iran was practically closed to International tourists since the Islamic Revolution. The 10 year long war with Iraq had several social, economic and environmental impacts and affected even domestic tourism patterns. Since the inception of the Iran Tourism Master Plan in September 2000, and its completion in September 2002 there has been a new surge of interest in tourism and its development and income opportunity generating potential. While there is sufficient political support for tourism development, a national budget of 3000 million Rials for tourism development in the Provinces, and a lot of enthusiasm among provincial government, there is a dearth of tourism planning and marketing professionals/consultants with enough international experience.

International Companies are not yet prepared to invest in Iran, while there is interest for a nominal presence – a sure indication that in spite of the potential regulations have to be streamlined and the system be made more transparent. The active presence of a quasi private sector has not helped the national objectives of privatisation.

Cultural Tourism (CT)

Specific place for CT in tourism policy: yes.

Main objectives & instruments

The National Tourism office is supporting and encouraging rural tourism and cultural eco-tourism to the nomadic tribes for its income opportunity generating potential. The Iran Cultural Heritage Organization (in view of the anticipated merger and the economic returns of tourist visits to heritage sites) has launched plans and programs for introducing Iran's cultural heritage and developing cultural products. They have a fairly good web-site :www. Icho.org . Religious tourism including non-islamic religions is being encouraged in a limited way.

Main focus of attention supply

The opportunities are in both destination development at city, town or rural level and cultural products – such as historic sites, attractions on the silk road, nomadic tribes, promotion of traditions, religious sites –both Islamic and non Islamic with provincial and local government organizations and municipalities and the cultural heritage organisation.

Main focus of attention demand

In the near future domestic generating markets can be seen as a sustainable source for cultural tourism, within the current political framework. The religious segment will see growth in international tourist arrivals – both Islamic and non Islamic. The regional international market interest is in nature based tourism with resort facilities.

Specific place for CT in marketing & promotion plan: yes.

Main objectives & programmes

The National Tourism Office has been an active promoter of Religious Tourism with a Hajj and Pilgrimage Organization operating alongside the Iran Tourism Organization. The Iran Cultural Heritage Organization, as indicated earlier has plans and programs for promoting cultural tourism. The Organization for Nomadic Affairs is promoting tourism among the Nomads. A tribal visitor center is being planned in Shiraz city on a 10 hectare land.

Special activities undertaken

A tourism festival was organised in Mashhad City – a religious destination for Shia Muslims. A conference was held at Hamedan for Korean Christians. The Yazd Province lead a delegation to India for promotion of trade and tourism.

Importance of cultural tourism:

- in total tourism offer

Reliable statistics on International arrivals by destination are not available. However, statistics provided by the Imam Reza shrine authorities indicate a high volume of both domestic and international visits. Of the total arrivals figure, the province accounts for 25 per cent of total domestic travel in Iran, and 9 per cent of total international arrivals at hotels in Iran.

International Tourism by Origin

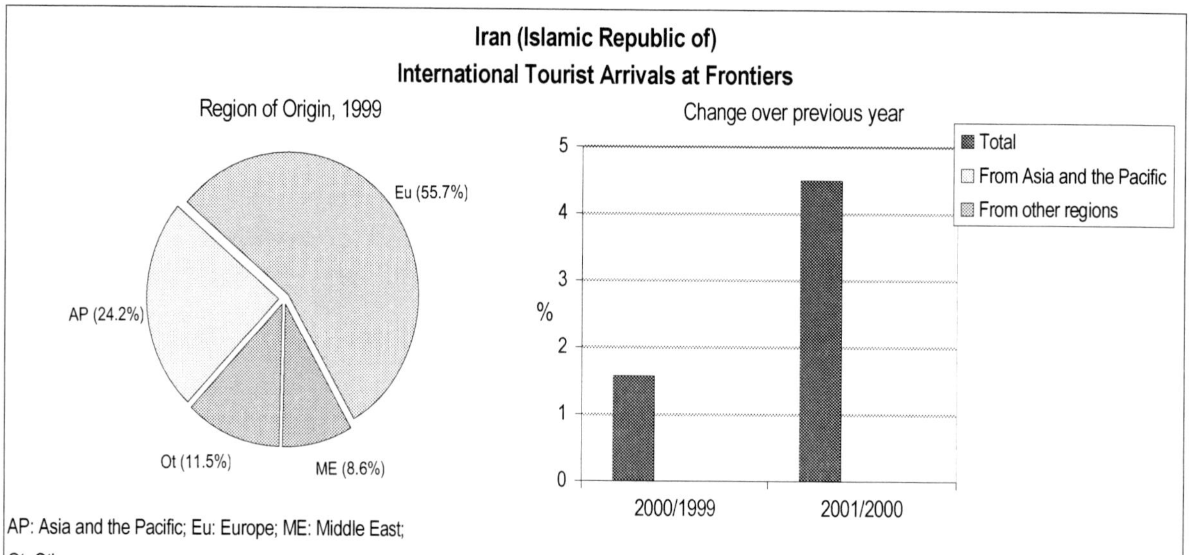

Source: World Tourism Organization (WTO) ©

Iran (Islamic Republic of)
International Tourist Arrivals at Frontiers (by nationality)

					Market share (%)		Growth rate (%)		Average per year (%)
	1995	1999	2000	2001	1995	2001	2000/99	2001/00	1995-2001
Total	**489,000**	**1,320,905**	**1,341,762**	**1,402,160**	**100**	**100**	**1.6**	**4.5**	**19.2**
From Asia and the Pacific	*170,600*	*319,759*	..	..	*34.9*				
Afghanistan	32,917	146,322	..	..	6.7				
Pakistan	105,823	134,917	..	..	21.6				
India	14,710	14,817	..	..	3.0				
Japan	6,035	8,668	..	..	1.2				
China	2,395	3,004	..	..	0.5				
Australia	1,119	2,187	..	..	0.2				
Indonesia	464	1,874	..	..	0.1				
Bangladesh	750	1,814	..	..	0.2				
Philippines	996	1,253	..	..	0.2				
Korea, Republic of	..	1,248	..	..					
Sri Lanka	349	1,029	..	..	0.1				
Malaysia	824	843	..	..	0.2				
Thailand	245	541	..	..	0.1				
Singapore	340	484	..	..	0.1				
Korea, D P Rp	3,246	326	..	..	0.7				
Other East Asia/Pacific	..	2	..	..					
Other intraregional	387	430	..	..	0.1				
From other regions	*281,319*	*853,931*	..	..	*57.5*				
Azerbaijan	52,799	447,797	..	..	10.8				
Turkey	6,881	188,130	..	..	1.4				
Kuwait	13,653	30,941	..	..	2.8				
Saudi Arabia	14,419	24,654	..	..	2.9				
Untd Arab Emirates	8,525	18,671	..	..	1.7				
Bahrain	8,904	16,740	..	..	1.8				
Germany	10,024	15,247	..	..	2.0				
Armenia	16,158	13,743	..	..	3.3				
Russian Fed	85,116	11,911	..	..	17.4				
Italy	4,563	9,590	..	..	0.9				
Kazakhstan	3,261	8,346	..	..	0.7				
Turkmenistan	682	7,473	..	..	0.1				
Lebanon	6,374	7,328	..	..	1.3				
Syrian Arab Republic	2,194	5,585	..	..	0.4				
Austria	3,106	4,362	..	..	0.6				
France	3,692	4,176	..	..	0.8				
Switzerland	1,163	3,624	..	..	0.2				
Uzbekistan	2,027	3,235	..	..	0.4				
Iraq	2,072	2,887	..	..	0.4				
Oman	2,217	2,494	..	..	0.5				
Qatar	1,879	2,315	..	..	0.4				
Ukraine	2,051	2,260	..	..	0.4				
Czech Rep	801	1,900	..	..	0.2				
Netherlands	776	1,569	..	..	0.2				
United Kingdom	3,826	1,483	..	..	0.8				
Other interregional	24,156	17,470	..	..	4.9				
Other World/Not specified	*37,081*	*147,215*	*1,341,762*	*1,402,160*	*7.6*	*100.0*	*811.4*	*4.5*	*83.2*

Source: World Tourism Organization (WTO) © (Data as collected by WTO September 2003)

III.4.6 Maldives South Asia

Profile

Maldives

South Asia

Capital	Male
Year of entry in WTO	1981
Area (10 km²)	30
Population (2002, 1000)	320
Gross Domestic Product (GDP) (2002, US$ million)	639
GDP per capita (2002, US$)	2,091
GDP growth (real, %)	
'-> 2001: 3.5; 2002: 6.0; 2003*: 6.2; 2004*: 4.0	

	2000	2001	2002*	2001/2000	2002*/2001
International Arrivals					
Tourists (overnight visitors) (1000)	467	461	485	-1.3	5.2
- per 100 of inhabitants	155	148	151		
Cruise passengers (1000)	7	5	3	-28.6	-40.0
Tourism accommodation					
Number of rooms	8,329	8,503	..	2.1	
Nights spent in hotels and similar establishments (1000)					
by non-residents (inbound tourism)	3,937	3,933	4,066	-0.1	3.4
Outbound Tourism					
Trips abroad (1000)	42	41	42	-2.4	2.4
- per 100 of inhabitants	14	13	13		
Receipts and Expenditure for International Tourism					
International Tourism Receipts (US$ million)	321	327	318	1.9	-2.8
- per Tourist Arrival (US$)	687	709	656	3.2	-7.6
- per capita (US$)	1,065	1,052	993		
International Tourism Expenditure (US$ million)	46	45	..	-2.2	
- per trip (US$)	1,095	1,098	..	0.2	
- per capita (US$)	153	145	..		
International Fare Expenditure (US$ million)	14	14	..		
△ International Tourism Balance (US$ million)	275	282	..		

Source: World Tourism Organization (WTO) (Data as collected by WTO September 2003)

See annex for methodological notes and reference of external sources used.

Survey

Contributed by *Ministry of Tourism*
www.visitmaldives.com (promotional)
www.maldivestourism.gov.mv (institutional/corporate)
www.maldivestourism.gov.mv (research and data)

Tourism development and outlook

Most significant determinant

The most significant determinant of the tourism development in the country is that Maldives continues to be a safe destination with a politically stable government. Maldives is also popularly known as a warm tropical destination which caters for upmarket products.

Tourism products

At the end of the year 2002, there were a total of 208 accommodation establishments with a bed capacity of 18,827 in the Maldives. These include 16,400 beds in the 87 Island Resorts, 670 beds in 8 Hotels, 282 beds in 17 Guest Houses and 1,475 beds in 96 Safari Boats. Every island opened for tourism has one resort with modern facilities.

As studies indicated the viability of developing a yacht marina in a northern atoll in the Maldives, the submission of bidding proposals to develop the Yacht Marina was opened on 15 September 2002. Five parties submitted proposals for this project. The proposals were evaluated by a committee from the government and the development of the Yacht Marina project to be constructed in Thiladunmathi Uthuruburi atoll Dhonakulhi was awarded to Turquoise Private Limited on 2nd March 2003.

Villingili Island will be a product with a different theme from that of the existing resorts owing to its isolation from other resorts, its size and landscape. These factors coupled with the need to provide better economic opportunities to the people in Addu Atoll, makes the island an ideal place to be developed into a resort. The island was leased to a joint venture company, Villingili Investment Pty. Ltd., on 31 August 2000. The plans for the resort have been approved and construction permission was given for two years as of 6 June 2001. According to Villingili Investment Pty. Ltd, the estimated completion date will be the end of 2003 or January 2004. Iit is expected to commence its initial operation with 500 beds.

Access

Male' International Airport is capable of handling all types of aircraft including the wide bodied B747. In addition there are 4 regional airports catering for domestic aircraft operations. A 30-day tourist visa will be granted to any tourist coming into Maldives with valid travel documents.

Generating markets

The total number of tourist arrivals in 2002 was 484,680, with a 5.1 per cent growth compared to 2001.

In 2002, the French, Japanese, Dutch, Swiss, British and American markets showed positive growth. However, the Italian market, which is the largest market to the Maldives, declined by -0.7 per cent and the German market, which used to be the second major market generator before 2002, declined by -4.4 per cent. The Australian market also declined by -21.3 per cent.

Other Issues

A programme to install recreational mooring buoys was commenced in 2002.The programme aims to minimize damage to the reefs and the marine environment from safari boats anchoring on popular sites.

A Shark-Watch Program was organized by the Ministry of Tourism, Maldives, to create awareness of the importance of sharks for the tourism industry in the Maldives through marine tourism promotion.

Outlook 2003

Growth level: it is hard to predict the growth level for 2003, as it highly depends on the world political and economic situation.
Promotional activities for 2003:

- Familiarization trips will be arranged with the following markets - China, France, Germany, Netherlands, India, Japan, Switzerland, Spain and the United Kingdom;
- Advertising Maldives in leading magazines/newspapers on a worldwide basis;
- Global advertising will be carried out on the following television networks - BBC, Star World, Discovery and Star Plus;
- Activities at ITB such as the initiation of interviews for the Minister, distribution of press kits and invitations to Maldivian Night, organizing a Press Brunch, follow up activities etc.;
- Regular press mailings to daily newspapers, trade and consumer press;
- Lokalpresse - print ready newspaper pages on a main topic to be transferred to about 3000 regional newspapers and supplements;
- Press Journey - consisting of journalists from highly published newspapers and magazines;
- Press lunch - invitation to editors and journalists of travel and vacation, leisure and lifestyle magazines;
- Shark Watching Programme - Exhibition of sharks, problems in protecting them and solutions. This will be a long term project;
- Press Ball - Invitation to guests from media, politics, and society - Maldives will sponsor a trip for 2 persons;
- Evaluation - based on the number of publications, types of media, quality of publication and success/effect of measures taken;
- Attendance at all the leading world Tourism Fairs in 2003 with participation by the NTO in Germany in the important Fairs to be held in Germany, Italy, Switzerland and the Czech Republic.

Tourism policy

Maldives tourism is a planned tourism.The second Tourism Master Plan (1996-2005) is being implemented now.Planning and Implementation of the Plan is carried out with the cooperation of the government and the private sector. Human resource development and environment issues are important for the sustainable development of tourism.

As the government has decided that tourism will be introduced to all the regions with an airport, a survey of some atolls was carried out to identify areas/islands that are suitable for resort/hotel development.

Marketing & promotion

The main issue facing the future growth of the tourism industry in the Maldives is to create a unique image for the destination.There is a need to create an identity, a brand image for the destination that projects uniqueness, quality, safety and the sun, sand and sea of island life in a beautiful environment.
Marketing objectives for 2003 include:

- Strengthening the image of the destination as a unique, safe, high-quality destination. An idyllic world of small tropical islands set in a superb marine environment where the pressures of life are far away;
- Maintain existing European markets and tap into new European markets;

- Promote Maldives strongly in other markets;
- Diversify market segments.

The Maldives Tourism Promotion Board (MTPB) is also working to develop the following market segments particularly in Japan:

- Working women's market;
- The senior market;
- Honeymooners;
- Special interest segments (e.g. water sports activities).

Cultural Tourism (CT)

Specific place for CT in tourism policy: no.

Specific place for CT in marketing & promotion plan: no.

International Tourism by Origin

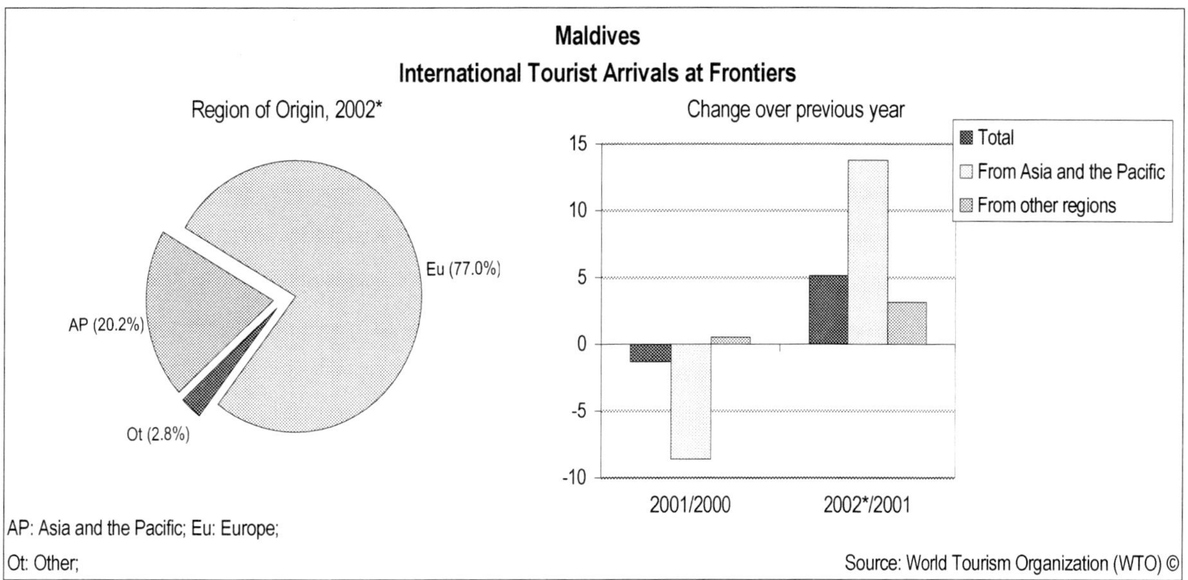

Maldives

International Tourist Arrivals at Frontiers (by nationality)

	1995	2000	2001	2002*	Market share (%) 1995	Market share (%) 2002*	Growth rate (%) 2001/00	Growth rate (%) 2002*/01	Average per year (%) 1995-2002*
Total	**314,869**	**467,154**	**460,984**	**484,680**	**100**	**100**	**-1.3**	**5.1**	**6.4**
From Asia and the Pacific	*74,971*	*94,059*	*85,974*	*97,822*	*23.8*	*20.2*	*-8.6*	*13.8*	*3.9*
Japan	30,089	47,180	41,895	43,705	9.6	9.0	-11.2	4.3	5.5
China	8,457	5,380	7,342	12,092	2.7	2.5	36.5	64.7	5.2
India	12,653	10,616	8,511	11,377	4.0	2.3	-19.8	33.7	-1.5
Korea, Republic of	810	5,771	6,708	7,696	0.3	1.6	16.2	14.7	37.9
Sri Lanka	11,127	8,413	6,902	6,909	3.5	1.4	-18.0	0.1	-6.6
Australia	3,673	8,090	6,435	5,063	1.2	1.0	-20.5	-21.3	4.7
Singapore	1,770	2,530	2,227	2,520	0.6	0.5	-12.0	13.2	5.2
Malaysia	1,585	1,829	1,478	2,240	0.5	0.5	-19.2	51.6	5.1
Thailand	583	1,007	1,350	2,002	0.2	0.4	34.1	48.3	19.3
Pakistan	1,148	1,049	1,017	1,329	0.4	0.3	-3.1	30.7	2.1
New Zealand	378	910	672	633	0.1	0.1	-26.2	-5.8	7.6
Iran	82	101	142	556	0.0	0.1	40.6	291.5	31.4
Indonesia	199	325	328	460	0.1	0.1	0.9	40.2	12.7
Philippines	277	317	346	405	0.1	0.1	9.1	17.1	5.6
Hong Kong (China)	799	1	..	291	0.3	0.1			-13.4
Bangladesh	1,053	321	321	241	0.3	0.0	0.0	-24.9	-19.0
Other intraregional	288	219	300	303	0.1	0.1	37.0	1.0	0.7
From other regions	*239,893*	*373,095*	*375,010*	*386,858*	*76.2*	*79.8*	*0.5*	*3.2*	*7.1*
Italy	52,105	106,323	115,740	114,955	16.5	23.7	8.9	-0.7	12.0
United Kingdom	37,666	71,440	77,151	80,377	12.0	16.6	8.0	4.2	11.4
Germany	72,326	77,642	66,149	63,212	23.0	13.0	-14.8	-4.4	-1.9
Switzerland	19,373	24,528	28,313	31,707	6.2	6.5	15.4	12.0	7.3
France	16,047	27,517	30,542	31,228	5.1	6.4	11.0	2.2	10.0
Austria	10,000	11,725	10,494	10,480	3.2	2.2	-10.5	-0.1	0.7
Russian Fed	2,700	3,608	3,983	7,550	0.9	1.6	10.4	89.6	15.8
Spain	2,766	5,322	4,203	5,160	0.9	1.1	-21.0	22.8	9.3
United States	1,984	4,795	4,435	5,030	0.6	1.0	-7.5	13.4	14.2
Netherlands	3,170	7,275	4,097	4,662	1.0	1.0	-43.7	13.8	5.7
Portugal	896	4,276	3,526	2,785	0.3	0.6	-17.5	-21.0	17.6
Belgium	1,890	5,071	3,719	2,606	0.6	0.5	-26.7	-29.9	4.7
Greece	578	1,776	1,775	2,446	0.2	0.5	-0.1	37.8	22.9
South Africa	7,715	1,767	1,368	1,914	2.5	0.4	-22.6	39.9	-18.1
Sweden	2,576	2,236	2,112	1,749	0.8	0.4	-5.5	-17.2	-5.4
Hungary	275	1,120	1,281	1,589	0.1	0.3	14.4	24.0	28.5
Canada	688	1,316	1,442	1,569	0.2	0.3	9.6	8.8	12.5
Czech Rep	205	1,091	1,054	1,493	0.1	0.3	-3.4	41.7	32.8
Turkey	372	1,419	998	1,321	0.1	0.3	-29.7	32.4	19.8
Ireland	551	1,486	1,211	1,303	0.2	0.3	-18.5	7.6	13.1
Poland	360	1,264	1,311	1,116	0.1	0.2	3.7	-14.9	17.5
Saudi Arabia	149	413	542	975	0.0	0.2	31.2	79.9	30.8
Denmark	889	772	891	938	0.3	0.2	15.4	5.3	0.8
Norway	412	945	577	772	0.1	0.2	-38.9	33.8	9.4
Ukraine	89	442	456	720	0.0	0.1	3.2	57.9	34.8
Other interregional	4,111	7,526	7,640	9,201	1.3	1.9	1.5	20.4	12.2
Other World/Not specified	*5*	..	..	..	*0.0*				

Source: World Tourism Organization (WTO) © (Data as collected by WTO September 2003)

III.4.7 Nepal South Asia

Profile

Nepal

Capital	Kathmandu
Year of entry in WTO	1975
Area (1000 km²)	147
Population (2002, million)	25.9
Gross Domestic Product (GDP) (2002, US$ million)	5,800
GDP per capita (2002, US$)	230
GDP growth (real, %)	

South Asia

-> 2001: 4.8; 2002: -0.5; 2003*: 2.3; 2004*: 4.0

	2000	2001	2002*	2001/2000	2002*/2001
International Arrivals					
Tourists (overnight visitors) (1000)	464	361	..	-22.1	
- per 100 of inhabitants	2	1	..		
Tourism accommodation					
Number of rooms	18,203	18,880	..	3.7	
Outbound Tourism					
Trips abroad (1000)	155	200	..	29.0	
- per 100 of inhabitants	1	1	..		
Receipts and Expenditure for International Tourism					
International Tourism Receipts (US$ million)	167	140	..	-16.2	
- per Tourist Arrival (US$)	360	388	..	7.6	
- per capita (US$)	7	6	..		
International Fare Receipts (US$ million)	61	47	..	-23.0	
International Tourism Expenditure (US$ million)	73	80	..	9.6	
- per trip (US$)	471	400	..	-15.1	
- per capita (US$)	3	3	..		
International Fare Expenditure (US$ million)	36	48	..	33.3	
△ International Tourism Balance (US$ million)	94	60	..		
△ International Fare Balance (US$ million)	25	-1	..		

Source: World Tourism Organization (WTO) (Data as collected by WTO September 2003)

See annex for methodological notes and reference of external sources used.

Survey

Contributed by *Nepal Tourism Board*
www.welcomenepal.com (promotional)
www.welcomenepal.com (institutional/corporate)
www.welcomenepal.com (research and data)

Tourism development and outlook

Most significant determinant

The internal security situation has deteriorated Nepal's image for quite sometime because of Maoist insurgency. Although after the ceasefire was announced, tourism has been slowly picking up.The external causes were poor economic conditions in major markets (Japan, the United States of America, Canada and Germany) as well as degrading security conditions internationally.The Bali and Mombasa terrorist attacks and recently the Iraq war have had a great influence.Tourism from India is increasing as the Indian economy continues to grow.

Tourism products

Positive factors:
- The fall in hotel room rates;
- One hundred and three new peaks have been opened up for climbing and five new rivers have been opened up for rafting purposes.

Access

Positive factors:
- A new airline Martin Air will start to operate this year connecting the Netherlands to Nepal, replacing Transavia which was formerly operating this route;
- Improvement in visa and frontier formalities.

Negative factor:
Singapore Airlines pulled out from the Nepal sector and there has been a reduction in some international airline frequencies.

Generating markets

Positive factor:
The effect of growth in the Indian economy and its impact on outbound traffic has created growth in Indian arrivals.

Negative factor:
Poor economic conditions in Japan, the United States of America and other major tourist generating markets of Nepal.

Other Issues

The government led Destination Nepal Campaign 2002-2003 has contributed greatly to retaining Nepal's tourism image in the international markets. It has helped to maintain the marketing exercises and various product development programs have been created. Nepal is also gaining good attention from international media due to the International Year of Ecotourism and the celebration of the Mount Everest Golden Jubilee to mark the 50 years since the first ascent of Mount Everest.

Outlook 2003

Year 2003 looks cautiously optimistic but much depends on the continuation of the ceasefire in Nepal and the agreement of a peaceful solution.

The length of the Iraq war will also be one of the determinant factors in shaping up tourism.

To a large extent, improvement in the economies of Japan, Canada, the United States of America and Germany willl also be a deciding factor.

Tourism policy	The Nepal Tourism Board will possibly undertake a tourism recovery strategy in 2003 and in the meantime is working towards a Tourism Master Plan for 2003. There is also a possibility of setting up the Tourism Satellite Account.
Marketing & promotion	Apart from regular marketing efforts through participation in travel trade fairs, advertising, organizing familiarisation trips and production of promotional collateral, Destination Nepal Campaign 2002/03 and Celebration of International Year of Ecotourism as well as Mount Everest Golden Jubilee have added to the major marketing promotion efforts of the Nepal Tourism Board. A special campaign was also launched in North India to attract border city traffic to Nepal. A sales mission to China was among the major activities carried out last year.

Cultural Tourism (CT)

Specific place for CT in tourism policy: yes.

Main objectives & instruments	The major objectives of cultural tourism are: - To showcase the rich, diverse and complex cultural make-up of Nepal; - To allow pilgrims easy access to visit the sites; - To allow international assistance in improvements for tourism purposes (restoration, documentation etc.,).
Main focus of attention supply	Cultural heritage. Cultural history. Cultural monuments and sites emphasized.
Main focus of attention demand	The Indian market segment as well as the Buddhist segment from around the world.

Specific place for CT in marketing & promotion plan: yes.

Main objectives & programmes	To use the cultural heritage as a key distinguishing feature and a key point of attraction apart from the adventure/nature-based tourism.
Special activities undertaken	A special task force has been set up to document and investigate the potentiality of the Buddhist circuit in Nepal.

Importance of cultural tourism:

- in total tourism offer	About 5 per cent of tourists visiting Nepal come on a pilgrimage as their major purpose. However participating in cultural attractions goes hand in hand with most of the market segments. About 60 per cent of tourists take part in cultural activities one way or another.

International Tourism by Origin

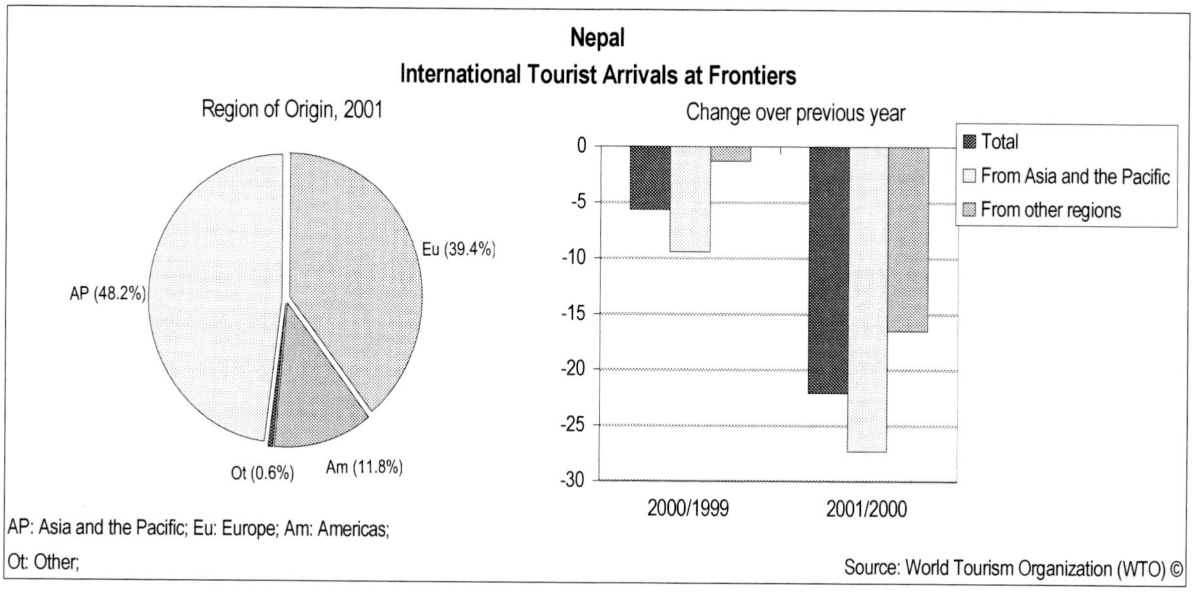

Nepal

International Tourist Arrivals at Frontiers (by residence)

	1995	1999	2000	2001	Market share (%) 1995	Market share (%) 2001	Growth rate (%) 2000/99	Growth rate (%) 2001/00	Average per year (%) 1995-2001
Total	**363,395**	**491,504**	**463,646**	**361,237**	**100**	**100**	**-5.7**	**-22.1**	**-0.1**
From Asia and the Pacific	*192,528*	*264,214*	*239,269*	*173,965*	*53.0*	*48.2*	*-9.4*	*-27.3*	*-1.7*
India	117,996	140,672	96,995	63,722	32.5	17.6	-31.0	-34.3	-9.8
Japan	25,402	38,566	40,841	28,554	7.0	7.9	5.9	-30.1	2.0
Korea, Republic of	2,770	5,098	8,581	11,380	0.8	3.2	68.3	32.6	26.6
Australia	9,395	11,997	12,138	10,711	2.6	3.0	1.2	-11.8	2.2
Sri Lanka	1,238	12,413	16,628	9,874	0.3	2.7	34.0	-40.6	41.3
China	4,587	5,160	6,627	8,564	1.3	2.4	28.4	29.2	11.0
Bangladesh	4,898	10,003	9,365	8,108	1.3	2.2	-6.4	-13.4	8.8
Taiwan (Pr. of China)	3,935	..	..	..	1.1				
Thailand	3,164	5,917	9,587	5,768	0.9	1.6	62.0	-39.8	10.5
Malaysia	1,663	2,835	3,310	3,734	0.5	1.0	16.8	12.8	14.4
Singapore	4,061	6,500	7,021	3,600	1.1	1.0	8.0	-48.7	-2.0
Hong Kong (China)	3,542	3,381	3,724	2,906	1.0	0.8	10.1	-22.0	-3.2
Other North-East Asia	63	..	..	..	0.0				
Other South-East Asia	660	..	..	..	0.2				
Other Asia	1,005	11,653	14,882	9,208	0.3	2.5	27.7	-38.1	44.7
Other Oceania	81	34	97	53	0.0	0.0	185.3	-45.4	-6.8
Other intraregional	8,068	9,985	9,473	7,783	2.2	2.2	-5.1	-17.8	-0.6
From other regions	*170,841*	*227,289*	*224,369*	*187,272*	*47.0*	*51.8*	*-1.3*	*-16.5*	*1.5*
United Kingdom	23,728	34,281	35,080	31,897	6.5	8.8	2.3	-9.1	5.1
United States	23,999	38,681	39,377	31,440	6.6	8.7	1.8	-20.2	4.6
Germany	32,484	25,990	25,907	21,809	8.9	6.0	-0.3	-15.8	-6.4
France	19,170	23,942	24,028	20,788	5.3	5.8	0.4	-13.5	1.4
Netherlands	8,487	16,872	15,878	13,049	2.3	3.6	-5.9	-17.8	7.4
Italy	10,214	12,656	11,384	8,503	2.8	2.4	-10.1	-25.3	-3.0
Israel	5,368	7,335	7,933	7,343	1.5	2.0	8.2	-7.4	5.4
Canada	4,788	6,834	7,764	6,373	1.3	1.8	13.6	-17.9	4.9
Spain	7,104	9,401	8,949	5,857	2.0	1.6	-4.8	-34.6	-3.2
Switzerland	6,247	8,666	6,526	5,747	1.7	1.6	-24.7	-11.9	-1.4
Belgium	5,214	5,513	5,427	4,824	1.4	1.3	-1.6	-11.1	-1.3
Austria	3,820	6,303	5,074	3,964	1.1	1.1	-19.5	-21.9	0.6
Denmark	4,417	4,447	4,721	3,642	1.2	1.0	6.2	-22.9	-3.2
Sweden	2,236	3,607	3,208	2,341	0.6	0.6	-11.1	-27.0	0.8
All Africa	1,147	1,891	2,038	2,038	0.3	0.6	7.8	0.0	10.1
Norway	1,665	2,183	2,171	1,766	0.5	0.5	-0.5	-18.7	1.0
Russian Fed	992	1,583	1,770	1,745	0.3	0.5	11.8	-1.4	9.9
Poland	870	1,620	1,738	1,486	0.2	0.4	7.3	-14.5	9.3
Mexico	366	1,386	1,370	1,400	0.1	0.4	-1.2	2.2	25.1
Ireland	1,068	1,922	2,035	1,298	0.3	0.4	5.9	-36.2	3.3
Argentina	644	1,039	1,068	1,297	0.2	0.4	2.8	21.4	12.4
Portugal	490	..	..	..	0.1				
Greece	757	1,194	1,156	1,057	0.2	0.3	-3.2	-8.6	5.7
Czech Rep	732	1,197	1,123	867	0.2	0.2	-6.2	-22.8	2.9
Finland	1,111	1,280	1,354	763	0.3	0.2	5.8	-43.6	-6.1
Other interregional	3,723	7,466	7,290	5,978	1.0	1.7	-2.4	-18.0	8.2
Other World/Not specified	*26*	*1*	*8*	..	*0.0*		*700.0*		

Source: World Tourism Organization (WTO) © (Data as collected by WTO September 2003)

III.4.8 Pakistan — South Asia

Profile

Pakistan

South Asia

Capital	Islamabad
Year of entry in WTO	1975
Area (1000 km²)	796
Population (2002, million)	148
Gross Domestic Product (GDP) (2002, US$ million)	63,649
GDP per capita (2002, US$)	436
GDP growth (real, %)	
'-> 2001: 2.7; 2002: 4.4; 2003*: 5.4; 2004*: 5.1	

	2000	2001	2002*	2001/2000	2002*/2001
International Arrivals					
Tourists (overnight visitors) (1000)	557	500	498	-10.3	-0.3
- per 100 of inhabitants	0	0	0		
Tourism accommodation					
Number of rooms	35,524	36,483	..	2.7	
Nights spent in hotels and similar establishments (1000)	4,194	4,494	4,494	7.2	
by non-residents (inbound tourism)	620	634	634	2.3	
by residents (domestic tourism)	3,574	3,860	3,860	8.0	
Receipts and Expenditure for International Tourism					
International Tourism Receipts (US$ million)	84	92	105	9.5	14.1
- per Tourist Arrival (US$)	151	184	211	22.0	14.5
- per capita (US$)	1	1	1		
International Fare Receipts (US$ million)	470	445	..	-5.3	
International Tourism Expenditure (US$ million)	252	255	179	1.2	-29.8
- per capita (US$)	2	2	1		
International Fare Expenditure (US$ million)	324	303	..	-6.5	
△ International Tourism Balance (US$ million)	-168	-163	-74		
△ International Fare Balance (US$ million)	146	142	..		

Source: World Tourism Organization (WTO) (Data as collected by WTO September 2003)

See annex for methodological notes and reference of external sources used.

Survey 1

Contributed by *Ministry of Culture, Sports, Tourism & Youth Affairs*
www.tourism.gov.pk (promotional)

Tourism development and outlook

Most significant determinant

Pakistan's foreign tourist arrivals during the last three years showed a declining trend as is evident from the following data:
2000: 556,707
2001: 499,719
2002: 498,059

The cause of above quoted decline in Pakistan's foreign tourist arrivals is mainly due to tension mounted between India and Pakistan during the year 2002 when the tourist arrivals from India declined by 95.5 per cent from 58,378 to 2,618. However, this decline is also attributed to the situation developed after September 11and due to the travel advisories issued by almost all the major tourist generating countries to Pakistan advising their citizens to cancel their avoidable visits to Pakistan. Moreover, around 40 per cent to 50 per cent tours operators were involved in handling the mountaineering expeditions and trekking parties. Around 60 per cent decline in the mountaineering expeditions (72 in 2001 and 29 in 2002) and 82 per cent in the trekking parties (245 in 2001 and 43 in 2002) have obliged these tour operators to shift their focus from foreign to domestic tourism, which is constantly increasing as is evident from the fact that 38.2 million in 2001 and 39.2 million in 2002 domestic tourists were estimated to have traveled within the country, showing an increase of 2.6 per cent. So the most significant determents in Pakistan were:

- Changing of focus from west to east for attracting more tourists. Made special efforts to attract tourists from Middle East, Arab Countries, China and Far eastern countries.
- Changing of focus on the promotion of domestic tourism in the country by extending special concessional packages both by tour operators and hoteliers.

Tourism products

Basant Festival (a kite flying festival) was developed as a National festival and now held every year under the patronage of the government of Pakistan during the months of February-March, in addition to the other National Festivals like Lok Virsa Islamabad (a folk festival), Shandur Polo Festival, Chitral, held every year at the world's highest Polo Ground from 7-9 July.

The total number of hotels and hotel rooms during 2001 and 2002 are given hereunder showing change in accommodation capacity:

- Year 2001: Hotels: 1,400
  Hotels Rooms: 35,524
- Year 2002: Hotels: 1,507 (5.3 per cent up)
  Hotels Rooms: 36.483 (2.62 per cent up)

Standard of service and condition of the Coaches of Pakistan Railways were up-graded.

50 per cent reduction in Royalty charged from mountaineering expeditions was allowed during the years 2002 being the International Year of Mountains (IYM), 2003 being the year of 50th Anniversary of scaling Nanga Parbat and 2004 for being the year of 50th Anniversary of scaling K-2.

- In order to complete in quality and price levels, special packages were offered both by the tour operators and hoteliers.

- A Car Rally is tentatively proposed to be held in October, 2003
- Golden Jubilee celebrations of Nanga Parbat to be held during the second half of 2003 in Islambad and Gilgit.

A "Seminar on tourism in Pakistan" is to be held in Yokohama (near Tokyo), Japan in the first week of October, 2003 besides participating there in the JATA International Travel Fair.

Golden Jubilee celebrations of K-2 is proposed to be held tentatively in January, 2004.

During the year 2002, Pakistan was got represented in 17 international tourism promotional events held in Germany, United Arab Emirates, Ireland, Bhutan, Malaysia, Egypt, Philippines, Chine, Uzbekistan, Singapore, India, England.

Access

Despite availability of reasonable infrastructure, the Access to Pakistan remained slightly difficult during the year 2002 because of:

- Closure of operation by a number of foreign airlines to Pakistan
- Ban on entering each others air space by the PIA and Air India
- Discontinuation of regular train service between Quetta (Pakistan) and Zahidian (Iran)
- Discontinuation of Lahore-Delhi Bus Service and Lahore-Delhi Rail Service in January, 2002.
- None use of road links with Afghanistan for tourist traffic in view of the situation developed there after September 11 and specially with the American led war against terrorism.
- Restrictive via policy, the Pakistan was obliged to adopt after September 11.

However, entry into Pakistan by road and by air from China and by air from all over the world remained easily available for all kind of travelers intended to visit Pakistan.

Generating markets

United Kingdom, Afghanistan, United states of America, Canada, Germany, Japan, Netherlands, China, Norway and France appeared as the major top 10 tourist generating countries to Pakistan. India which used to be in the top 3 tourist generating countries to Pakistan was not even included in the top 15 tourist generating countries to Pakistan during 2002. Since we are focusing on Middle East, Far East, China, South Asian Region etc. Therefore, our target groups were slightly different from those targeted in 2001.

Other Issues

It was noticed that a reasonable percentage of students approached us for completion of their thesis and different kind of papers on tourism. Similarly the journalists frequently visited this office for getting information on different segments of tourism besides the fact that domestic tourism increased as usual at the growth rate of 2.6 per cent. This all showed that awareness about tourism in Pakistan is gradually increasing.

Outlook 2003

Pakistan, China and Lahore-Delhi Bus Services are being resumed soon besides Rail Service from Lahore to Delhi. Moreover, PIA/Air India flights will also start their flights to each other country shortly. With these steps the tourist arrivals towards Pakistan is thus likely to receive 550,000 tourists in 2003 and 6000,000 tourists in 2004. Our focus is to attract and explore new markets in United Arab Emirates, China plus Far East countries. We intend to participate International tourism fairs in these countries to project Pakistan's friendly image. Moreover, relations with India to be improved.

Tourism policy

The Ministry of tourism is revising tourism Policy in consultation with other Ministries/Divisions and provincial governments. The recommendations made in the Tourism Development Master Plan 2000 prepared by the WTO/UNDP will be inserted in the new National Tourism Policy.

Marketing & promotion	Special Media Action Plan has been prepared for projection of Pakistan through National and International press and electronic media.

Cultural Tourism (CT)

Specific place for CT in tourism policy: yes.

Main objectives & instruments	Pakistan is concentrating to promote round the year tourism, with special focus on cultural varieties instead of continue depending on adventure or seasonal tourism.
Main focus of attention supply	Folk song, folk dances at historical places and promotion of the oldest games like Polo in Chitral and Basant (kite flying) in Lahore are mainly focused.
Main focus of attention demand	Up-Gradation of cultural centers, promotion of more cultural institutions, encouragement of artists, folk singers, dancers and entertainers are focused for promotion of cultural tourism.

Specific place for CT in marketing & promotion plan: yes.

Main objectives & programmes	A comprehensive list of Cultural Tourism Sites and museums in Pakistan is available
Special activities undertaken	We have held Basant Festival in Lahore during February-March, 2003 which contributed a lot in promoting cultural tourism in the country. Similarly Shandur Polo Festival held every year from 7-9 July which specifically promotes oldest living cultural of Kalash and Polo played in the oldest style at the world's highest Polo Ground in District Chitral of Pakistan.

Importance of cultural tourism:

- in total tourism offer	58,800 were the total foreign tourists who visited different cultural events/archaeological/Historical places in Pakistan representing 11.8 per cent of our total tourist arrivals during 2002.

Survey 2

Contributed by *Pakistan Tourism Development Corporation*
www.tourism.gov.pk (promotional)
www.tourism.gov.pk (institutional/corporate)

Tourism development and outlook

Most significant determinant

Geopolitical and security conditions are the prime factor affecting tourism promotion and development.
The second important factor is the weather (uncertain weather blocking roads) and economic conditions.
We are also not investing enough on marketing of our product.

Tourism products

Positive factors:
- Price levels;
- New products;
- Change in accommodation capacity.

Negative factors:
- Lack of proper planning for events;
- Lack of evening entertainment;
- Negative image portrayed by foreign media.

Access

We have built new terminals at Karachi and Lahore International Airports and a plan is underway for Islamabad. With new motorways and highways, road access has improved.
Entry/visa formalities remain rigid after 11 September 2001 events.

Generating markets

We have a sharp decline in arrivals from the United States of America, the United Kingdom and Europe due to the after affects of 11 September 2001.
Emerging markets are Japan, Korea, the Far East and the Middle East. Another emerging market segment is expatriate Pakistanis.

Other Issues

Domestic tourism is on the rise, mainly originating from industrial cities like Karachi, Lahore, Faisalabad, Sialkot etc. Pakistan families go on holidays to the mountains during the Summer.

Outlook 2003

The year 2003 will bring further decline in foreign tourist arrivals to Pakistan. Although owing to the improvement of the relationship with India and the security situation in Afghanistan, the year 2004 will see the recovery of the decline accumulating after 11 September 2001. Our average annual arrivals remained between 450,000 and 480,000 over the previous 5-10 years.

Tourism policy

We carried out a study for a Master Plan in collaboration with WTO/UNDP in 1998-1999 but implementation of these recommendations has been slow.
Marketing efforts are being concentrated on the Middle East, the Far East and South Asia, instead of Europe, America, Australia etc. Motorways and highway projects (Lahore-Islamabad, Islamabad-Peshawar, Karachi-Gawadar and the Indus Highway) and development of the Gawadar Port/Coastal Highway will contribute to the promotion of tourism by 2004 and 2005.

Marketing & promotion	The Promotion and Publicity Department of the Pakistan Tourism Development Corporation has be converted into a fully fledged marketing department. The six most important travel trade events (WTM London and ITB Berlin being the most important) have been identified for regular participation. New promotional documentaries are planned and 2003 is being celebrated as the Year of Nanga Parbat Mountain and 2004 as the year of the K2 Mountain.

Cultural Tourism (CT)

Specific place for CT in tourism policy: yes.

Main objectives & instruments	A calendar of cultural events has been planned and is being followed. Our thrust is on the Annual Shandur Polo Festival and Kalash Festivals (Chitral), The Silk Route Festival (Gilgit/Hunza/Skardu), Basant Festival (Lahore) and a Folk Festival (Islamabad).
Main focus of attention supply	Our main focus is the holding of Folk and Cultural Festivals as described above. Other cultural destinations are Lahore, Peshawar, Swat, Multan, Moenjodaro and Karachi.
Main focus of attention demand	We are focusing on young people who will enjoy culture and adventure together for mountain areas and mature/seniors for cities.

Specific place for CT in marketing & promotion plan: yes.

Main objectives & programmes	For the domestic market, we wish to create cultural harmony and tolerance among different people. For foreign tourists, we are presenting a positive picture of Pakistani culture, people and society.
Special activities undertaken	The Silk Route Festival and the Karakoram Car Rally were introduced in 2001 by our organisation to promote cultural tourism in Pakistan. These festivals are now an annual feature. The Basant (Kit Flying Festival) is also now being celebrated with new vigour. We have plans to arrange food/cultural festivals in the Middle East and China.

Importance of cultural tourism:

- in intern. arrivals	We estimate that those who come for cultural tourism account for approximately 10 per cent of the total arrivals.

International Tourism by Origin

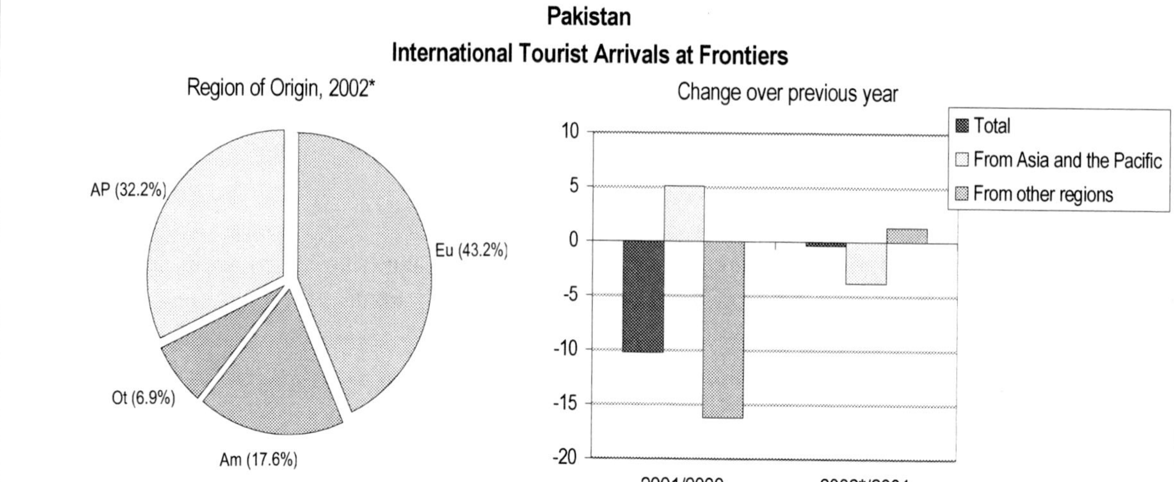

AP: Asia and the Pacific; Eu: Europe; Am: Americas;
Ot: Other;

Source: World Tourism Organization (WTO) ©

Pakistan
International Tourist Arrivals at Frontiers (by nationality)

					Market share (%)		Growth rate (%)		Average per year (%)
	1995	2000	2001	2002*	1995	2002*	2001/00	2002*/01	1995-2002*
Total	**378,400**	**556,805**	**499,719**	**498,059**	**100**	**100**	**-10.3**	**-0.3**	**4.0**
From Asia and the Pacific	*124,191*	*158,614*	*166,668*	*160,369*	*32.8*	*32.2*	*5.1*	*-3.8*	*3.7*
Afghanistan	24,975	27,913	46,994	98,498	6.6	19.8	68.4	109.6	21.7
Japan	10,880	12,794	7,580	9,975	2.9	2.0	-40.8	31.6	-1.2
China	9,105	6,191	5,704	8,896	2.4	1.8	-7.9	56.0	-0.3
Iran	12,105	5,365	6,366	6,394	3.2	1.3	18.7	0.4	-8.7
Australia	4,568	7,697	7,435	5,740	1.2	1.2	-3.4	-22.8	3.3
Bangladesh	7,748	1,389	6,233	5,581	2.0	1.1	348.7	-10.5	-4.6
Korea, Republic of	..	4,078	4,487	4,158		0.8	10.0	-7.3	
Malaysia	3,305	4,317	5,114	4,095	0.9	0.8	18.5	-19.9	3.1
India	31,589	66,061	58,378	2,618	8.3	0.5	-11.6	-95.5	-29.9
Thailand	1,525	2,001	2,134	2,363	0.4	0.5	6.6	10.7	6.5
Philippines	1,723	2,160	1,679	2,079	0.5	0.4	-22.3	23.8	2.7
Sri Lanka	4,151	4,113	3,063	1,960	1.1	0.4	-25.5	-36.0	-10.2
Singapore	..	2,323	2,639	1,772		0.4	13.6	-32.9	
Indonesia	933	2,580	1,756	1,692	0.2	0.3	-31.9	-3.6	8.9
New Zealand	1,292	1,905	2,425	1,339	0.3	0.3	27.3	-44.8	0.5
Other South-East Asia	..	1,302	194	64		0.0	-85.1	-67.0	
Other South Asia	3,092	638	103	11	0.8	0.0	-83.9	-89.3	-55.3
Other East Asia/Pacific	7,200	..	..	..	1.9				
Other intraregional	..	5,787	4,384	3,134		0.6	-24.2	-28.5	
From other regions	*254,120*	*396,893*	*332,642*	*337,113*	*67.2*	*67.7*	*-16.2*	*1.3*	*4.1*
United Kingdom	88,690	179,758	144,408	151,341	23.4	30.4	-19.7	4.8	7.9
United States	49,971	71,518	69,067	69,030	13.2	13.9	-3.4	-0.1	4.7
Canada	7,039	12,956	11,813	18,150	1.9	3.6	-8.8	53.6	14.5
Germany	11,835	14,121	9,047	12,243	3.1	2.5	-35.9	35.3	0.5
Netherlands	6,865	9,794	7,277	9,751	1.8	2.0	-25.7	34.0	5.1
Norway	3,589	7,947	4,183	7,075	0.9	1.4	-47.4	69.1	10.2
France	6,981	517	7,159	6,892	1.8	1.4	1284.7	-3.7	-0.2
Denmark	3,315	4,887	4,400	4,846	0.9	1.0	-10.0	10.1	5.6
Oman	3,153	6,223	5,207	4,702	0.8	0.9	-16.3	-9.7	5.9
Untd Arab Emirates	3,587	7,548	7,090	4,563	0.9	0.9	-6.1	-35.6	3.5
Saudi Arabia	4,103	6,344	5,831	4,220	1.1	0.8	-8.1	-27.6	0.4
South Africa	1,658	3,777	3,694	3,667	0.4	0.7	-2.2	-0.7	12.0
Italy	3,723	3,775	3,046	3,036	1.0	0.6	-19.3	-0.3	-2.9
Sweden	2,566	4,107	3,228	2,902	0.7	0.6	-21.4	-10.1	1.8
Turkey	3,144	3,486	3,036	2,777	0.8	0.6	-12.9	-8.5	-1.8
Switzerland	2,159	4,673	3,282	2,314	0.6	0.5	-29.8	-29.5	1.0
Former U.S.S.R.	9,244	..	..	..	2.4				
Qatar	..	953	2,012	1,971		0.4	111.1	-2.0	
Nigeria	..	2,044	2,684	1,830		0.4	31.3	-31.8	
Belgium	1,283	2,556	2,015	1,694	0.3	0.3	-21.2	-15.9	4.0
Austria	1,108	2,068	1,439	1,667	0.3	0.3	-30.4	15.8	6.0
Kenya	1,574	2,388	1,588	1,597	0.4	0.3	-33.5	0.6	0.2
Egypt	1,125	2,552	1,915	1,589	0.3	0.3	-25.0	-17.0	5.1
Other interregional	37,408	42,901	29,221	19,256	9.9	3.9	-31.9	-34.1	-9.1
Other World/Not specified	*89*	*1,298*	*409*	*577*	*0.0*	*0.1*	*-68.5*	*41.1*	*30.6*

Source: World Tourism Organization (WTO) © (Data as collected by WTO September 2003)

III.4.9 Sri Lanka South Asia

Profile

Sri Lanka

South Asia

Capital	Sri Jayawardhanapura-Kotte
Year of entry in WTO	1975
Area (1000 km²)	66
Population (2002, million)	19.6
Gross Domestic Product (GDP) (2002, US$ million)	16,423
GDP per capita (2002, US$)	822
GDP growth (real, %)	
-> 2001: -1.5; 2002: 4.0; 2003*: 5.5; 2004*: 6.5	

	2000	2001	2002*	2001/2000	2002*/2001
International Arrivals					
Visitors (1000)	445	397	457	-10.8	15.1
Tourists (overnight visitors) (1000)	400	337	393	-15.9	16.7
- per 100 of inhabitants	2	2	2		
Same-day visitors (1000)	45	60	64	33.3	6.7
Tourism accommodation					
Number of rooms	15,860	15,637	16,318	-1.4	4.4
Nights spent in collective establishments (1000)					
by non-residents (inbound tourism)	4,056	3,342	3,989	-17.6	19.4
Nights spent in hotels and similar establishments (1000)	4,687	3,939	4,423	-16.0	12.3
by non-residents (inbound tourism)	3,735	2,876	3,180	-23.0	10.6
by residents (domestic tourism)	952	1,063	1,243	11.7	16.9
Outbound Tourism					
Trips abroad (1000)	524	505	553	-3.6	9.5
- per 100 of inhabitants	3	3	3		
Receipts and Expenditure for International Tourism					
International Tourism Receipts (US$ million)	253	211	253	-16.6	19.9
- per Tourist Arrival (US$)	632	626	643	-0.8	2.7
- per Visitor Arrival (US$)	569	531	554	-6.5	4.2
- per capita (US$)	13	11	13		
International Fare Receipts (US$ million)	140	136	..	-2.9	
International Tourism Expenditure (US$ million)	244	245	253	0.4	3.3
- per trip (US$)	466	485	458	4.2	-5.7
- per capita (US$)	13	13	13		
International Fare Expenditure (US$ million)	143	152	..	6.3	
△ International Tourism Balance (US$ million)	9	-34			
△ International Fare Balance (US$ million)	-3	-16	..		

Source: World Tourism Organization (WTO) (Data as collected by WTO September 2003)

See annex for methodological notes and reference of external sources used.

Survey

Contributed by *Sri Lanka Tourist Board*
www.srilankatourism.org (promotional)

Tourism development and outlook

Most significant determinant	Improved security situation in the country due to the commencement of the peace process. New airline commenced operations, national carrier, Srilankan airlines increased the number of frequencies.
Tourism products	Visa on arrivals to South Asian Regional Cooperation (SARRC) countries. Formulated plans to improve the infrastructure and transport facilities in the coastal area. Quality enhancement in the accommodation sector. Events such as Miss Tourism International and Asian cup international cricket match were held.
Access	Positive: Resumed flights, increased frequencies, promotion on emerging markets on China, Malaysia etc., launched "buy one get one free" promotional programme for Indian market. Relaxation of travel advisories from Japan and other countries.
Generating markets	Major markets: India 106.2 per cent, United Kingdom 0.4 per cent and Germany 8.7 per cent. Emerging markets: China 16.6 per cent, Malaysia 146.8 per cent.
Other Issues	Approved destination status for Sri Lanka from Chinese government. Information technology.
Outlook 2003	Year 2003: Arrivals 500,000 Year 2004: Arrivals 650,000 Year 2005: Arrivals 850,000
Tourism policy	Open sky policy. Tax incentives for foreign investments. Proposed restructure of the National Tourism Organization with private sector participation. Creation of a cess fund for promotional purposes.
Marketing & promotion	Successful participation in fairs (WTM, ITB etc.). Prominent media were invited for publicity through FAM tours. Advertising and Public Relations activities. Distribution of promotional materials.

Cultural Tourism (CT)

Specific place for CT in tourism policy: yes.

Main objectives & instruments	Product diversification beyond traditional beach products. Focused more on European markets. VFR – Indian and other markets.
Main focus of attention supply	Products: cultural triangle archaeological areas, festivals, traditional dances, people living style etc.
Main focus of attention demand	United Kingdom, Germany, Italy, Netherlands, Japan, China, Singapore etc.

Specific place for CT in marketing & promotion plan: yes.

Main objectives & programmes	Cultural products promote through brochures, posters, advertisements, internet, Educational tours and through overseas offices.
Special activities undertaken	Arranged cultural programmes including cultural shows, folk dances, food festivals etc.

Importance of cultural tourism:

- in total tourism offer	34 per cent tourists visited to cultural triangle area in 2002.

International Tourism by Origin

Sri Lanka

International Tourist Arrivals at Frontiers

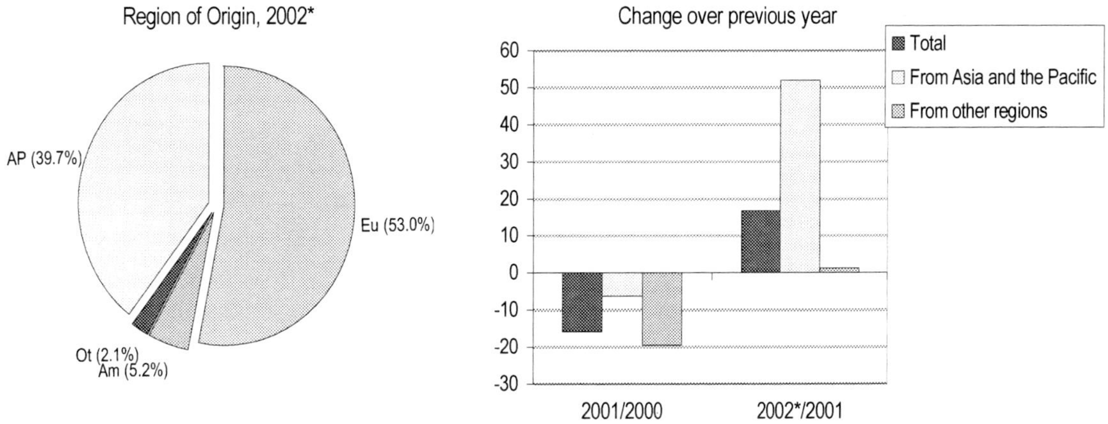

AP: Asia and the Pacific; Eu: Europe; Am: Americas;
Ot: Other;

Source: World Tourism Organization (WTO) ©

Sri Lanka

Nights of International Tourists in All Accommodation Establishments

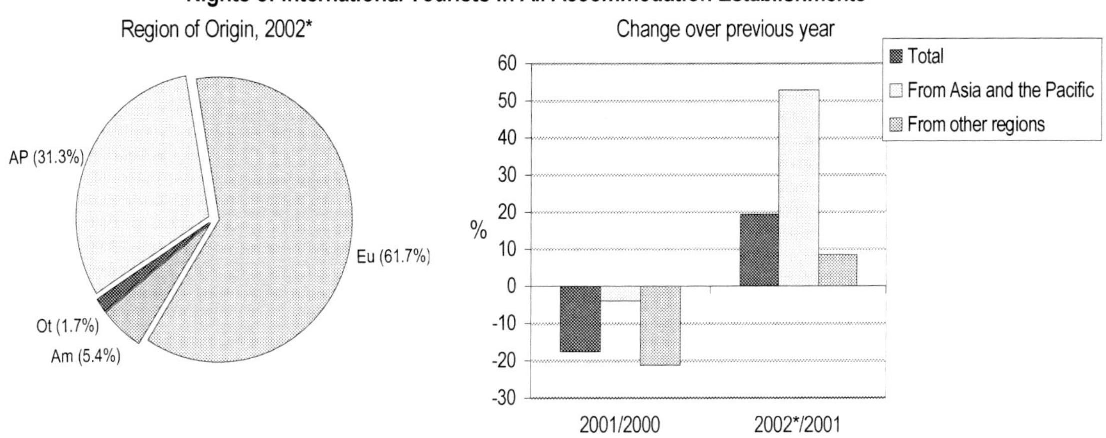

AP: Asia and the Pacific; Eu: Europe; Am: Americas;
Ot: Other;

Source: World Tourism Organization (WTO) ©

Sri Lanka

International Tourist Arrivals at Frontiers (by residence)

	1995	2000	2001	2002*	Market share (%) 1995	Market share (%) 2002*	Growth rate (%) 2001/00	Growth rate (%) 2002*/01	Average per year (%) 1995-2002*
Total	**403,101**	**400,414**	**336,794**	**393,171**	**100**	**100**	**-15.9**	**16.7**	**-0.4**
From Asia and the Pacific	*128,577*	*109,749*	*102,837*	*156,273*	*31.9*	*39.7*	*-6.3*	*52.0*	*2.8*
India	47,448	31,860	33,924	69,960	11.8	17.8	6.5	106.2	5.7
Japan	18,180	10,266	9,237	13,602	4.5	3.5	-10.0	47.3	-4.1
Australia	9,066	16,443	11,457	11,217	2.2	2.9	-30.3	-2.1	3.1
Maldives	6,558	7,935	9,019	9,861	1.6	2.5	13.7	9.3	6.0
Malaysia	4,305	4,833	3,910	9,651	1.1	2.5	-19.1	146.8	12.2
Singapore	5,643	5,019	4,641	7,599	1.4	1.9	-7.5	63.7	4.3
Pakistan	11,325	10,005	8,562	6,756	2.8	1.7	-14.4	-21.1	-7.1
China	1,437	2,208	3,721	4,338	0.4	1.1	68.5	16.6	17.1
Thailand	5,073	3,408	2,956	3,945	1.3	1.0	-13.3	33.5	-3.5
Hong Kong (China)	7,194	3,348	2,319	3,759	1.8	1.0	-30.7	62.1	-8.9
Taiwan (Pr. of China)	3,534	3,543	2,834	3,432	0.9	0.9	-20.0	21.1	-0.4
Korea, Republic of	2,553	2,613	2,778	2,616	0.6	0.7	6.3	-5.8	0.3
New Zealand	1,104	1,737	1,528	1,920	0.3	0.5	-12.0	25.7	8.2
Philippines	1,389	1,428	1,427	1,641	0.3	0.4	-0.1	15.0	2.4
Bangladesh	1,257	1,218	1,745	1,521	0.3	0.4	43.3	-12.8	2.8
Indonesia	996	2,604	1,081	1,476	0.2	0.4	-58.5	36.5	5.8
Nepal	453	534	508	789	0.1	0.2	-4.9	55.3	8.2
Other South Asia	..	..	..	1,302		0.3			
Other Asia	978	699	1,070	816	0.2	0.2	53.1	-23.7	-2.6
Other Oceania	84	48	120	72	0.0	0.0	150.0	-40.0	-2.2
From other regions	*274,524*	*290,665*	*233,957*	*236,898*	*68.1*	*60.3*	*-19.5*	*1.3*	*-2.1*
United Kingdom	63,582	84,693	67,830	67,533	15.8	17.2	-19.9	-0.4	0.9
Germany	79,698	70,584	60,405	55,170	19.8	14.0	-14.4	-8.7	-5.1
France	30,996	25,992	20,949	19,989	7.7	5.1	-19.4	-4.6	-6.1
Italy	18,378	16,883	12,074	12,177	4.6	3.1	-28.5	0.9	-5.7
Netherlands	14,274	22,618	12,569	11,748	3.5	3.0	-44.4	-6.5	-2.7
United States	9,096	9,816	8,374	11,565	2.3	2.9	-14.7	38.1	3.5
Switzerland	8,334	8,490	6,228	9,375	2.1	2.4	-26.6	50.5	1.7
Canada	5,469	7,503	7,609	8,301	1.4	2.1	1.4	9.1	6.1
All Middle East	3,819	4,341	5,544	6,492	0.9	1.7	27.7	17.1	7.9
Austria	6,930	6,294	5,968	6,117	1.7	1.6	-5.2	2.5	-1.8
Belgium	7,347	10,224	5,250	4,767	1.8	1.2	-48.7	-9.2	-6.0
Russian Fed	2,466	3,552	2,542	2,946	0.6	0.7	-28.4	15.9	2.6
Norway	1,062	2,010	2,261	2,889	0.3	0.7	12.5	27.8	15.4
Sweden	7,563	4,344	4,265	2,487	1.9	0.6	-1.8	-41.7	-14.7
Spain	2,949	1,848	1,529	2,328	0.7	0.6	-17.3	52.3	-3.3
Denmark	2,982	1,653	1,628	1,968	0.7	0.5	-1.5	20.9	-5.8
Finland	3,225	2,316	535	729	0.8	0.2	-76.9	36.3	-19.1
South Africa	279	372	341	660	0.1	0.2	-8.3	93.5	13.1
Other Africa	519	522	611	951	0.1	0.2	17.0	55.6	9.0
Other Americas	612	447	429	555	0.2	0.1	-4.0	29.4	-1.4
Other Central/Eastern Europe	2,112	3,288	4,523	5,133	0.5	1.3	37.6	13.5	13.5
Other Europe	2,832	2,875	2,493	3,018	0.7	0.8	-13.3	21.1	0.9

Source: World Tourism Organization (WTO) ©

(Data as collected by WTO September 2003)

Sri Lanka
Nights of International Tourists in All Accommodation Establishments (by nationality)

	1995	2000	2001	2002*	Market share (%) 1995	Market share (%) 2002*	Growth rate (%) 2001/00	Growth rate (%) 2002*/01	Average per year (%) 1995-2002*
Total	**4,023,795**	**4,056,306**	**3,342,233**	**3,989,058**	**100**	**100**	**-17.6**	**19.4**	**-0.1**
From Asia and the Pacific	*951,699*	*849,375*	*815,957*	*1,247,265*	*23.7*	*31.3*	*-3.9*	*52.9*	*3.9*
India	322,646	239,201	251,097	531,970	8.0	13.3	5.0	111.9	7.4
Australia	117,804	157,009	120,108	140,542	2.9	3.5	-23.5	17.0	2.6
Japan	125,442	90,320	80,027	120,737	3.1	3.0	-11.4	50.9	-0.5
Maldives	53,776	56,937	61,838	69,971	1.3	1.8	8.6	13.2	3.8
Singapore	38,372	47,545	34,148	59,336	1.0	1.5	-28.2	73.8	6.4
Malaysia	27,122	4,830	24,599	58,962	0.7	1.5	409.3	139.7	11.7
Pakistan	77,010	78,834	69,028	57,507	1.9	1.4	-12.4	-16.7	-4.1
China	8,766	19,159	31,183	30,015	0.2	0.8	62.8	-3.7	19.2
Thailand	41,091	29,009	25,265	29,728	1.0	0.7	-12.9	17.7	-4.5
New Zealand	12,806	17,323	15,642	24,384	0.3	0.6	-9.7	55.9	9.6
Korea, Republic of	13,020	25,104	22,248	24,375	0.3	0.6	-11.4	9.6	9.4
Hong Kong (China)	41,006	18,453	14,086	23,856	1.0	0.6	-23.7	69.4	-7.4
Taiwan (Pr. of China)	39,934	28,368	23,753	23,724	1.0	0.6	-16.3	-0.1	-7.2
Bangladesh	..	6,577	11,297	10,778		0.3	71.8	-4.6	
Philippines	8,751	14,537	14,647	9,984	0.2	0.3	0.8	-31.8	1.9
Indonesia	6,076	7,482	4,343	8,617	0.2	0.2	-42.0	98.4	5.1
Other Asia	17,472	8,519	12,207	22,089	0.4	0.6	43.3	81.0	3.4
Other Oceania	605	168	441	690	0.0	0.0	162.5	56.5	1.9
From other regions	*3,072,096*	*3,206,931*	*2,526,276*	*2,741,793*	*76.3*	*68.7*	*-21.2*	*8.5*	*-1.6*
Germany	1,042,707	845,294	724,387	750,130	25.9	18.8	-14.3	3.6	-4.6
United Kingdom	697,143	904,946	690,479	740,025	17.3	18.6	-23.7	7.2	0.9
France	297,682	271,452	222,988	213,898	7.4	5.4	-17.9	-4.1	-4.6
Netherlands	165,516	278,871	142,562	152,116	4.1	3.8	-48.9	6.7	-1.2
United States	80,965	95,660	94,353	124,254	2.0	3.1	-1.4	31.7	6.3
Italy	172,928	154,730	122,933	123,206	4.3	3.1	-20.5	0.2	-4.7
Switzerland	87,805	95,725	69,708	117,917	2.2	3.0	-27.2	69.2	4.3
Canada	57,365	69,553	79,627	82,700	1.4	2.1	14.5	3.9	5.4
Austria	82,530	94,728	72,101	81,233	2.1	2.0	-23.9	12.7	-0.2
Belgium	70,673	137,417	60,087	52,484	1.8	1.3	-56.3	-12.7	-4.2
All Middle East	30,170	41,383	42,966	51,050	0.7	1.3	3.8	18.8	7.8
Russian Fed	21,219	24,884	20,938	32,648	0.5	0.8	-15.9	55.9	6.3
Norway	13,145	19,650	24,568	31,260	0.3	0.8	25.0	27.2	13.2
Sweden	88,678	45,604	47,734	28,225	2.2	0.7	4.7	-40.9	-15.1
Denmark	35,515	17,868	20,290	24,923	0.9	0.6	13.6	22.8	-4.9
Spain	29,857	19,542	13,095	22,785	0.7	0.6	-33.0	74.0	-3.8
All Africa	5,804	8,999	8,648	14,987	0.1	0.4	-3.9	73.3	14.5
Finland	37,876	31,111	5,391	8,579	0.9	0.2	-82.7	59.1	-19.1
Other Americas	8,835	3,560	4,024	7,358	0.2	0.2	13.0	82.9	-2.6
Other Central/Eastern Europe	18,064	12,693	32,739	49,179	0.4	1.2	157.9	50.2	15.4
Other Europe	27,619	33,261	26,658	32,836	0.7	0.8	-19.9	23.2	2.5

Source: World Tourism Organization (WTO) © (Data as collected by WTO September 2003)

Annex

1. International Tourist Arrivals

International Tourist Arrivals, 1950-2002*

	World	Africa	Americas	Asia and the Pacific	Europe	Middle East	World	Africa	Americas	Asia and the Pacific	Europe	Middle East
	International Tourist Arrivals (million)						Change over previous year (%)[1]					
1950	25.3	0.5	7.5	0.2	16.8	0.2						
1960	69.3	0.8	16.7	0.9	50.4	0.6						
1965	112.9	1.4	23.2	2.1	83.7	2.4						
1970	165.8	2.4	42.3	6.2	113.0	1.9						
1975	222.3	4.7	50.0	10.2	153.9	3.5						
1980	286.5	7.4	61.4	24.3	186.0	7.5	2.0	22.3	3.5	38.9	-3.6	46.1
1981	287.6	8.2	61.5	26.3	183.8	7.9	0.4	11.0	0.1	8.4	-1.1	5.3
1982	286.5	7.6	58.6	27.5	184.7	8.0	-0.4	-6.6	-4.6	4.6	0.5	2.4
1983	288.3	8.1	58.9	27.5	185.9	7.7	0.6	6.5	0.5	0.1	0.7	-3.9
1984	318.4	8.8	67.9	30.4	203.8	7.6	10.4	7.9	15.2	10.3	9.6	-2.3
1985	328.8	9.6	64.4	33.6	213.4	7.8	3.3	9.3	-5.2	10.7	4.7	3.3
1986	340.5	9.4	71.5	37.6	215.2	6.8	3.6	-2.4	11.1	11.7	0.9	-12.5
1987	360.1	9.8	76.3	34.1	232.8	7.1	5.7	4.9	6.7	-9.2	8.1	4.2
1988	384.8	12.7	83.2	39.4	240.8	8.7	6.9	29.1	9.1	15.3	3.4	23.0
1989	425.5	13.8	87.2	50.8	264.9	8.9	10.6	8.7	4.7	29.1	10.0	1.2
1990	455.9	15.0	93.0	57.7	280.6	9.7	7.2	8.4	6.7	13.6	5.9	9.4
1991	461.1	16.2	95.5	59.7	280.6	9.1	1.1	8.1	2.7	3.4	0.0	-6.0
1992	502.2	18.1	102.3	67.8	302.7	11.3	8.9	11.6	7.0	13.6	7.9	24.6
1993	515.3	18.4	102.2	74.7	308.5	11.4	2.6	2.1	-0.1	10.1	1.9	0.8
1994	535.8	18.9	104.8	80.6	319.3	12.1	4.0	2.4	2.6	8.0	3.5	5.9
1995	550.4	20.0	108.8	85.6	322.3	13.6	2.7	6.0	3.8	6.1	0.9	12.6
1996	580.2	21.6	114.4	94.1	334.7	15.4	5.4	7.9	5.1	10.0	3.9	12.9
1997	601.5	22.4	116.1	93.2	353.2	16.5	3.7	3.8	1.5	-1.0	5.5	7.4
1998	621.4	24.9	119.2	92.7	366.9	17.8	3.3	10.8	2.6	-0.5	3.9	7.5
1999	643.3	26.4	122.0	102.6	371.2	21.2	3.5	6.1	2.3	10.7	1.2	19.5
2000	687.3	27.4	128.0	115.3	392.7	24.0	6.8	4.1	4.9	12.3	5.8	13.0
2001	684.1	28.3	120.2	121.1	390.8	23.6	-0.5	3.2	-6.1	5.1	-0.5	-1.3
2002*	702.6	29.1	114.9	131.3	399.8	27.6	2.7	2.8	-4.4	8.4	2.3	16.7

Average annual growth (%)	World	Africa	Americas	Asia and the Pacific	Europe	Middle East
1950-2000	6.8	8.2	5.8	13.2	6.5	10.1
1950-2002*	6.6	8.0	5.4	12.9	6.3	10.0
1950-1960	10.6	3.7	8.4	14.1	11.6	12.3
1960-1970	9.1	12.4	9.7	21.6	8.4	11.5
1970-1980	5.6	11.8	3.8	14.5	5.1	14.9
1980-1990	4.8	7.3	4.2	9.1	4.2	2.6
1980-1985	2.8	5.4	0.9	6.7	2.8	0.9
1985-1990	6.8	9.3	7.6	11.4	5.6	4.4
1990-2000	4.2	6.3	3.2	7.2	3.4	9.5
1990-1995	3.8	6.0	3.2	8.2	2.8	7.1
1995-2000	4.5	6.5	3.3	6.1	4.0	11.9
2000-2002*	1.1	3.0	-5.3	6.7	0.9	7.3

Source: World Tourism Organization (WTO) © (Data as collected by WTO September 2003)

[1] Before 1995, data are simple aggregates of country results and are not corrected for changes in series, so changes on previous year might not be in all cases correct.

International Tourist Arrivals by Country of Destination

		International Tourist Arrivals (1000)					Market share in the region (%)		Change (%)		Average annual growth (%)	
	Series	1990	1995	2000	2001	2002*	1995	2002*	001/00	02*/01	90-95	95-00
Africa		***14,963***	***20,030***	***27,445***	***28,330***	***29,136***	***100***	***100***	***3.2***	***2.8***	***6.0***	***6.5***
North Africa		**8,398**	**7,304**	**10,075**	**10,562**	**10,307**	**36.5**	**35.4**	**4.8**	**-2.4**	**-2.8**	**6.6**
Algeria	VF	1,137	520	866	901	998	2.6	3.4	4.1	10.7	-14.5	10.8
Morocco	TF	4,024	2,602	4,113	4,223	4,193	13.0	14.4	2.7	-0.7	-8.4	9.6
Sudan	TF	33	63	38	50	52	0.3	0.2	32.9	4.0	13.8	-9.8
Tunisia	TF	3,204	4,120	5,058	5,387	5,064	20.6	17.4	6.5	-6.0	5.2	4.2
West Africa		**1,352**	**1,889**	**2,596**	**2,723**	**2,945**	**9.4**	**10.1**	**4.9**	**8.2**	**6.9**	**6.6**
Benin	TF	110	138	96	88	72	0.7	0.2	-8.8	-17.4	4.6	-7.0
Burkina Faso	THS	74	124	126	128	149	0.6	0.5	2.2	16.0	10.9	0.2
Cape Verde	TF	24	28	83	115	126	0.1	0.4	38.5	9.3	3.0	24.5
Côte d'Ivoire	TF	196	188	..	..	..	0.9				-0.8	
Gambia	TF	100	45	79	75	..	0.2		-4.4		-14.6	11.6
Ghana	TF	146	286	399	439	483	1.4	1.7	10.0	10.1	14.4	6.9
Guinea	TF	..	..	33	38	43		0.1	16.6	13.5		
Guinea-Bissau	TF	..	..	..	8	..						
Mali	TF	44	42	86	89	96	0.2	0.3	2.5	8.3	-0.9	15.5
Mauritania	TF	..	..	30	..	..						
Niger	TF	21	35	50	52	..	0.2		3.5		10.8	7.4
Nigeria	TF	190	656	813	831	..	3.3		2.2		28.1	4.4
Senegal	THS	246	280	389	396	427	1.4	1.5	1.8	7.7	2.6	6.8
Sierra Leone	TF	98	14	16	24	28	0.1	0.1	53.2	18.3	-32.5	2.7
Togo	THS	103	53	60	57	..	0.3		-4.9		-12.4	2.3
Central Africa		**371**	**358**	**666**	**660**	**739**	**1.8**	**2.5**	**-0.9**	**12.0**	**-0.7**	**13.2**
Angola	TF	67	9	51	67	91	0.0	0.3	31.4	35.8	-33.1	41.5
Cameroon	THS	89	100	277	221	..	0.5		-20.4		2.3	22.7
Cent.Afr.Rep.	TF	..	26	..	..	..	0.1					
Chad	THS	9	19	43	57	..	0.1		32.1		15.9	18.0
Congo	THS	33	37	19	..	..	0.2				2.6	-12.9
Dem.R.Congo	TF	55	36	103	..	..	0.2				-8.3	23.5
Gabon	TF	109	125	155	169	212	0.6	0.7	8.9	25.3	2.7	4.5
Sao Tome Prn	TF	3	6	7	8	..	0.0		6.1		15.5	3.0
East Africa		**2,836**	**4,488**	**5,877**	**6,228**	**6,291**	**22.4**	**21.6**	**6.0**	**1.0**	**9.6**	**5.5**
Burundi	TF	109	34	29	36	..	0.2		24.1		-20.7	-3.2
Comoros	TF	8	23	24	..	..	0.1				23.3	0.9
Djibouti	TF	33	21	..	..	..	0.1				-8.6	
Eritrea	VF	..	315	70	113	101	1.6	0.3	60.6	-10.6		-25.9
Ethiopia	TF	79	103	136	148	156	0.5	0.5	9.2	5.1	5.5	5.6
Kenya	TF	814	896	899	841	838	4.5	2.9	-6.5	-0.4	1.9	0.1
Madagascar	TF	53	75	160	170	..	0.4		6.3		7.1	16.5
Malawi	TF	130	192	228	266	285	1.0	1.0	16.7	6.9	8.1	3.5
Mauritius	TF	292	422	656	660	682	2.1	2.3	0.6	3.2	7.7	9.2
Reunion	TF	200	304	430	424	426	1.5	1.5	-1.4	0.5	8.7	7.2
Rwanda	TF	..	..	104	113	..			8.6			
Seychelles	TF	104	121	130	130	132	0.6	0.5	-0.2	1.9	3.0	1.5
Tanzania	TF	..	285	459	501	550	1.4	1.9	9.2	9.8		10.0
Uganda	TF	69	160	193	205	254	0.8	0.9	6.5	23.7	18.3	3.8
Zambia	TF	141	163	457	492	565	0.8	1.9	7.6	14.8	2.9	22.9
Zimbabwe	TF	605	1,363	1,868	2,068	..	6.8		10.7		17.6	6.5
Southern Africa		**2,006**	**5,991**	**8,232**	**8,158**	**8,852**	**29.9**	**30.4**	**-0.9**	**8.5**	**24.5**	**6.6**
Botswana	TF	543	521	1,104	1,049	1,037	2.6	3.6	-5.0	-1.1	-0.8	16.2
Lesotho	TF	171	87	..	..	..	0.4				-12.6	
Namibia	TF	..	399	..	670	..	2.0					
South Africa	VF	1,029	4,684	6,001	5,908	6,550	23.4	22.5	-1.5	10.9	35.4	5.1
Swaziland	THS	263	300	284	341	332	1.5	1.1	20.1	-2.6	2.7	-1.1

Source: World Tourism Organization (WTO) ©

(Data as collected by WTO September 2003)

International Tourist Arrivals by Country of Destination

		International Tourist Arrivals (1000)					Market share in the region (%)		Change (%)		Average annual growth (%)	
	Series	1990	1995	2000	2001	2002*	1995	2002*	001/00	02*/01	90-95	95-00
Americas		***92,984***	***108,822***	***127,952***	***120,156***	***114,853***	***100***	***100***	***-6.1***	***-4.4***	***3.2***	***3.3***
North America		**71,747**	**80,491**	**91,213**	**84,388**	**81,616**	**74.0**	**71.1**	**-7.5**	**-3.3**	**2.3**	**2.5**
Canada	TF	15,209	16,932	19,627	19,679	20,057	15.6	17.5	0.3	1.9	2.2	3.0
Mexico	TF	17,176	20,241	20,641	19,810	19,667	18.6	17.1	-4.0	-0.7	3.3	0.4
United States	TF	39,362	43,318	50,945	44,898	41,892	39.8	36.5	-11.9	-6.7	1.9	3.3
Caribbean		**11,400**	**14,025**	**17,180**	**16,902**	**16,058**	**12.9**	**14.0**	**-1.6**	**-5.0**	**4.2**	**4.1**
Anguilla	TF	31	39	44	48	44	0.0	0.0	9.5	-8.3	4.4	2.6
Antigua,Barb	TF	206	220	237	..	..	0.2				1.3	1.5
Aruba	TF	433	619	721	691	643	0.6	0.6	-4.1	-7.0	7.4	3.1
Bahamas	TF	1,562	1,598	1,544	1,538	..	1.5		-0.4		0.5	-0.7
Barbados	TF	432	442	545	507	498	0.4	0.4	-6.9	-1.8	0.5	4.3
Bermuda	TF	435	387	332	278	284	0.4	0.2	-16.3	2.1	-2.3	-3.0
Bonaire	TF	37	59	51	50	52	0.1	0.0	-1.7	3.2	9.9	-2.9
Br.Virgin Is	TF	160	219	281	296	285	0.2	0.2	5.2	-3.7	6.5	5.1
Cayman Islands	TF	253	361	354	334	303	0.3	0.3	-5.6	-9.3	7.4	-0.4
Cuba	TF	327	742	1,741	1,736	1,656	0.7	1.4	-0.3	-4.6	17.8	18.6
Curaçao	TF	219	224	191	205	218	0.2	0.2	7.3	6.3	0.5	-3.1
Dominica	TF	45	60	70	66	67	0.1	0.1	-4.6	1.1	6.1	2.9
Dominican Rp	TF	1,305	1,776	2,973	2,882	2,811	1.6	2.4	-3.0	-2.5	6.4	10.9
Grenada	TF	76	108	129	123	132	0.1	0.1	-4.3	7.3	7.3	3.6
Guadeloupe	TCE	331	640	603	521	..	0.6		-13.6		14.1	-1.2
Haiti	TF	144	145	140	142	140	0.1	0.1	0.8	-1.1	0.2	-0.7
Jamaica	TF	989	1,147	1,323	1,277	1,266	1.1	1.1	-3.5	-0.8	3.0	2.9
Martinique	TF	282	457	526	460	448	0.4	0.4	-12.5	-2.7	10.1	2.9
Montserrat	TF	13	19	10	10	10	0.0	0.0	-5.2	-1.9	7.9	-11.5
Puerto Rico	TF	2,560	3,131	3,341	3,551	3,087	2.9	2.7	6.3	-13.1	4.1	1.3
Saba	TF	..	10	9	9	11	0.0	0.0	-1.3	19.7		-1.8
Saint Lucia	TF	141	231	270	250	253	0.2	0.2	-7.3	1.3	10.4	3.1
St.Eustatius	TF	..	9	9	10	10	0.0	0.0	5.8	4.2		0.5
St.Kitts-Nev	TF	73	79	73	71	68	0.1	0.1	-3.5	-4.3	1.6	-1.5
St.Maarten	TF	545	449	432	403	381	0.4	0.3	-6.9	-5.4	-3.8	-0.7
St.Vincent,Grenadines	TF	54	60	73	71	78	0.1	0.1	-2.7	9.3	2.1	4.0
Trinidad Tbg	TF	195	260	399	383	379	0.2	0.3	-3.9	-1.1	5.9	8.9
Turks,Caicos	TF	49	79	152	165	155	0.1	0.1	8.6	-6.3	10.0	14.0
US.Virgin Is	TF	463	454	607	592	553	0.4	0.5	-2.5	-6.6	-0.4	6.0
Central America		**1,945**	**2,611**	**4,345**	**4,417**	**4,701**	**2.4**	**4.1**	**1.7**	**6.4**	**6.1**	**10.7**
Belize	TF	197	131	196	196	200	0.1	0.2	0.1	1.8	-7.8	8.4
Costa Rica	TF	435	785	1,088	1,131	1,113	0.7	1.0	4.0	-1.6	12.5	6.8
El Salvador	TF	194	235	795	735	951	0.2	0.8	-7.6	29.5	3.9	27.6
Guatemala	TF	509	563	826	835	881	0.5	0.8	1.1	5.4	2.1	8.0
Honduras	TF	290	271	471	518	550	0.2	0.5	10.0	6.2	-1.4	11.7
Nicaragua	TF	106	281	486	483	472	0.3	0.4	-0.6	-2.3	21.6	11.6
Panama	TF	214	345	484	519	534	0.3	0.5	7.2	2.9	10.0	7.0
South America		**7,892**	**11,695**	**15,213**	**14,449**	**12,479**	**10.7**	**10.9**	**-5.0**	**-13.6**	**8.2**	**5.4**
Argentina	TF	1,930	2,289	2,909	2,620	2,820	2.1	2.5	-9.9	7.6	3.5	4.9
Bolivia	TF	254	284	306	308	..	0.3		0.7		2.3	1.5
Brazil	TF	1,091	1,991	5,313	4,773	3,783	1.8	3.3	-10.2	-20.7	12.8	21.7
Chile	TF	943	1,540	1,742	1,723	1,412	1.4	1.2	-1.1	-18.0	10.3	2.5
Colombia	TF	813	1,399	557	616	541	1.3	0.5	10.6	-12.2	11.5	-16.8
Ecuador	VF	362	440	627	641	654	0.4	0.6	2.1	2.1	4.0	7.4
French Guiana	TF	..	..	..	65	65		0.1		0.0		
Guyana	TF	64	106	105	95	104	0.1	0.1	-9.5	9.8	10.6	-0.2
Paraguay	TF	280	438	289	279	250	0.4	0.2	-3.4	-10.1	9.3	-8.0
Peru	TF	317	444	797	798	846	0.4	0.7	0.1	6.0	7.0	12.4
Suriname	TF	46	43	58	..	..	0.0				-1.2	6.0
Uruguay	TF	..	2,022	1,968	1,892	1,258	1.9	1.1	-3.9	-33.5		-0.5
Venezuela	TF	525	700	469	584	432	0.6	0.4	24.6	-26.1	5.9	-7.7

Source: World Tourism Organization (WTO) © (Data as collected by WTO September 2003)

International Tourist Arrivals by Country of Destination

		International Tourist Arrivals (1000)					Market share in the region (%)		Change (%)		Average annual growth (%)	
	Series	1990	1995	2000	2001	2002*	1995	2002*	001/00	02*/01	90-95	95-00
Asia and the Pacific		*57,748*	*85,599*	*115,252*	*121,147*	*131,294*	*100*	*100*	*5.1*	*8.4*	*8.2*	*6.1*
North-East Asia		**27,969**	**44,102**	**62,507**	**65,604**	**73,634**	**51.5**	**56.1**	**5.0**	**12.2**	**9.5**	**7.2**
China	TF	..	20,034	31,229	33,167	36,803	23.4	28.0	6.2	11.0		9.3
Hong Kong (China)	VF	6,581	10,200	13,059	13,725	16,566	11.9	12.6	5.1	20.7	9.2	5.1
Japan	TF	3,236	3,345	4,757	4,772	5,239	3.9	4.0	0.3	9.8	0.7	7.3
Korea, D P Rp	*	115	..	..	..	..						
Korea, Republic of	VF	2,959	3,753	5,322	5,147	5,347	4.4	4.1	-3.3	3.9	4.9	7.2
Macao (China)	TF	2,513	4,202	5,197	5,842	6,565	4.9	5.0	12.4	12.4	10.8	4.3
Mongolia	TF	147	108	158	166	198	0.1	0.2	5.0	19.4	-6.0	7.9
Taiwan (Pr. of China)	VF	..	2,332	2,624	2,617	2,726	2.7	2.1	-0.3	4.2		2.4
South-East Asia		**21,469**	**29,173**	**37,006**	**40,236**	**42,228**	**34.1**	**32.2**	**8.7**	**4.9**	**6.3**	**4.9**
Brunei Darussalam	VF	377	498	984	..	..	0.6				5.7	14.6
Cambodia	TF	17	220	466	605	787	0.3	0.6	29.8	30.1	66.9	16.2
Indonesia	TF	2,178	4,324	5,064	5,154	5,033	5.1	3.8	1.8	-2.3	14.7	3.2
Lao P.D.R.	TF	14	60	191	173	215	0.1	0.2	-9.4	24.3	33.8	26.1
Malaysia	TF	7,446	7,469	10,222	12,775	13,292	8.7	10.1	25.0	4.0	0.1	6.5
Myanmar	TF	21	117	208	205	217	0.1	0.2	-1.3	6.0	41.0	12.2
Philippines	TF	1,025	1,760	1,992	1,797	1,933	2.1	1.5	-9.8	7.6	11.4	2.5
Singapore	TF	4,842	6,422	6,917	6,726	6,996	7.5	5.3	-2.8	4.0	5.8	1.5
Thailand	TF	5,299	6,952	9,579	10,133	10,873	8.1	8.3	5.8	7.3	5.6	6.6
Vietnam	TF	250	..	1,383	1,599	..			15.6			
Oceania		**5,152**	**8,086**	**9,648**	**9,491**	**9,564**	**9.4**	**7.3**	**-1.6**	**0.8**	**9.4**	**3.6**
American Samoa	TF	26	34	44	..	..	0.0				5.5	5.4
Australia	VF	2,215	3,726	4,931	4,856	4,841	4.4	3.7	-1.5	-0.3	11.0	5.8
Cook Is	TF	34	48	73	75	73	0.1	0.1	2.2	-2.1	7.1	8.8
Fiji	TF	279	318	294	348	398	0.4	0.3	18.3	14.4	2.7	-1.6
French Polynesia	TF	132	172	252	228	189	0.2	0.1	-9.8	-16.9	5.5	7.9
Guam	TF	780	1,362	1,287	1,160	1,059	1.6	0.8	-9.9	-8.7	11.8	-1.1
Kiribati	TF	3	4	5	5	5	0.0	0.0	-5.9	18.2	5.6	4.2
Marshall Is	TF	5	6	5	5	6	0.0	0.0	3.8	10.2	1.9	-1.0
Micronesia (Fed.St.of)	TF	..	..	21	15	19		0.0	-25.5	24.8		
N.Mariana Is	TF	426	669	517	438	466	0.8	0.4	-15.3	6.4	9.4	-5.0
New Caledonia	TF	87	86	110	101	104	0.1	0.1	-8.3	3.5	-0.2	4.9
New Zealand	VF	..	1,409	1,787	1,909	2,045	1.6	1.6	6.9	7.1		4.9
Niue	TF	1	2	2	2	2	0.0	0.0	2.9	0.7	16.7	-1.4
Palau	TF	33	53	58	54	59	0.1	0.0	-6.9	9.3	9.9	1.8
Papua New Guinea	TF	41	42	58	54	54	0.0	0.0	-7.2	-0.4	0.6	6.7
Samoa	TF	48	68	88	88	89	0.1	0.1	0.7	0.8	7.3	5.1
Solomon Is	TF	9	12	..	..	..	0.0				5.6	
Tonga	TF	21	30	35	32	37	0.0	0.0	-6.7	14.2	7.0	3.3
Tuvalu	TF	1	1	1	1	1	0.0	0.0	-5.0	8.4	-1.6	5.4
Vanuatu	TF	35	44	58	53	49	0.1	0.0	-7.5	-7.4	4.5	5.7
South Asia		**3,158**	**4,238**	**6,090**	**5,816**	**5,869**	**4.9**	**4.5**	**-4.5**	**0.9**	**6.1**	**7.5**
Bangladesh	TF	115	156	199	207	207	0.2	0.2	4.0	0.0	6.3	5.0
Bhutan	TF	2	5	8	6	6	0.0	0.0	-15.7	-5.9	19.0	9.7
India	TF	1,707	2,124	2,649	2,537	2,370	2.5	1.8	-4.2	-6.6	4.5	4.5
Iran	TF	154	489	1,342	1,402	..	0.6		4.5		26.0	22.4
Maldives	TF	195	315	467	461	485	0.4	0.4	-1.3	5.2	10.1	8.2
Nepal	TF	255	363	464	361	..	0.4		-22.1		7.3	5.0
Pakistan	TF	424	378	557	500	498	0.4	0.4	-10.3	-0.3	-2.2	8.0
Sri Lanka	TF	298	403	400	337	393	0.5	0.3	-15.9	16.7	6.2	-0.1

Source: World Tourism Organization (WTO) ©

(Data as collected by WTO September 2003)

International Tourist Arrivals by Country of Destination

		International Tourist Arrivals (1000)					Market share in the region (%)		Change (%)		Average annual growth (%)	
	Series	1990	1995	2000	2001	2002*	1995	2002*	001/00	02*/01	90-95	95-00
Europe		*280,562*	*322,270*	*392,663*	*390,829*	*399,759*	*100*	*100*	*-0.5*	*2.3*	*2.8*	*4.0*
Northern Europe		**32,269**	**41,405**	**46,753**	**44,567**	**46,385**	**12.8**	**11.6**	**-4.7**	**4.1**	**5.1**	**2.5**
Denmark	TCE	..	..	2,088	2,028	2,010		0.5	-2.8	-0.9		
Finland	TF	..	1,779	2,714	2,826	2,875	0.6	0.7	4.1	1.7		8.8
Iceland	TF	142	190	303	..	278	0.1	0.1			6.0	9.8
Ireland	TF	3,666	4,818	6,646	6,353	6,476	1.5	1.6	-4.4	1.9	5.6	6.6
Norway	TCE	1,955	2,880	3,103	3,073	3,107	0.9	0.8	-1.0	1.1	8.1	1.5
Sweden	TCE	..	2,310	2,746|	7,154	7,459	0.7	1.9		4.3		3.5
United Kingdom	VF	18,013	23,537	25,209	22,835	24,180	7.3	6.0	-9.4	5.9	5.5	1.4
Western Europe		**113,838**	**116,746**	**142,829**	**139,150**	**141,099**	**36.2**	**35.3**	**-2.6**	**1.4**	**0.5**	**4.1**
Austria	TCE	19,011	17,173	17,982	18,180	18,611	5.3	4.7	1.1	2.4	-2.0	0.9
Belgium	TCE	..	5,560	6,457	6,452	6,724	1.7	1.7	-0.1	4.2		3.0
France	TF	52,497	60,033	77,190	75,202	77,012	18.6	19.3	-2.6	2.4	2.7	5.2
Germany	TCE	17,045	14,847	18,983	17,861	17,969	4.6	4.5	-5.9	0.6	-2.7	5.0
Liechtenstein	THS	78	59	62	56	49	0.0	0.0	-8.2	-13.2	-5.3	0.7
Luxembourg	TCE	820	768	852	829	876	0.2	0.2	-2.6	5.6	-1.3	2.1
Monaco	THS	245	233	300	270	263	0.1	0.1	-10.1	-2.6	-1.0	5.2
Netherlands	TCE	5,795	6,574	10,003	9,500	9,595	2.0	2.4	-5.0	1.0	2.6	8.8
Switzerland	TF	13,200	11,500	11,000	10,800	10,000	3.6	2.5	-1.8	-7.4	-2.7	-0.9
Central/Eastern Europe		**38,981**	**61,445**	**62,327**	**63,424**	**65,241**	**19.1**	**16.3**	**1.8**	**2.9**	**9.5**	**0.3**
Armenia	TCE	..	12	45	123	..	0.0		172.6			30.3
Azerbaijan	TF	..	93	681	767	834	0.0	0.2	12.6	8.8		48.9
Belarus	TF	..	161	60	61	..	0.1		2.3			-18.0
Bulgaria	TF	..	3,466	2,785	3,186	3,433	1.1	0.9	14.4	7.8		-4.3
Czech Rep	TCE	..	3,381	4,666	5,194	4,579	1.0	1.1	11.3	-11.8		6.7
Estonia	TF	..	530	1,240	1,320	1,360	0.2	0.3	6.5	3.0		18.5
Former U.S.S.R.	TF	2,286	..	..	..	..						
Georgia	TF	..	85	387	302	298	0.0	0.1	-22.0	-1.2		35.3
Hungary	VF/2	20,510	20,690	15,571	15,340	15,870	6.4	4.0	-1.5	3.5	0.2	-5.5
Kazakhstan	TF	..	..	1,471	1,845	2,832		0.7	25.4	53.5		
Kyrgyzstan	TF	..	36	..	..	..	0.0					
Latvia	TF	..	539	509	591	848	0.2	0.2	16.1	43.5		-1.1
Lithuania	TF	..	650	1,083	1,271	1,433	0.2	0.4	17.4	12.7		10.7
Poland	TF	..	19,215	17,400	15,000	13,980	6.0	3.5	-13.8	-6.8		-2.0
Rep Moldova	TF	..	32	18	16	18	0.0	0.0	-11.1	12.5		-10.9
Romania	TF	3,099	2,757	3,274	3,300	3,204	0.9	0.8	0.8	-2.9	-2.3	3.5
Russian Fed	TF	..	..	7,030	7,400	7,943		2.0	5.3	7.3		
Slovakia	TCE	822	903	1,053	1,219	1,399	0.3	0.3	15.8	14.8	1.9	3.1
Tajikistan	TF	..	..	4	4	..			-7.9			
Turkmenistan	TF	..	218	..	..	..	0.1					
Ukraine	TF	..	3,716	4,406	5,791	6,326	1.2	1.6	31.4	9.2		3.5
Uzbekistan	TF	..	92	302	345	332	0.0	0.1	14.2	-3.7		26.8
Southern Europe		**88,051**	**91,275**	**126,065**	**129,012**	**130,971**	**28.3**	**32.8**	**2.3**	**1.5**	**0.7**	**6.7**
Albania	THS	30	40	32	34	..	0.0		6.3		5.9	-4.4
Andorra	TF	..	..	2,949	3,516	3,388			19.2	-3.6		
Bosnia Herzg	TCE	..	37	171	139	160	0.0	0.0	-19.0	15.3		35.8
Croatia	TCE	7,049	1,485	5,831	6,544	6,944	0.5	1.7	12.2	6.1	-26.8	31.5
F.Yug.Rp.Macedonia	TCE	562	147	224	99	123	0.0	0.0	-55.8	24.3	-23.5	8.8
Greece	TF	8,873	10,130	13,096	14,057	14,180	3.1	3.5	7.3	0.9	2.7	5.3
Italy	TF	26,679	31,052	41,181	39,563	39,799	9.6	10.0	-3.9	0.6	3.1	5.8
Malta	TF	872	1,116	1,216	1,180	1,134	0.3	0.3	-2.9	-3.9	5.1	1.7
Portugal	TF	8,020	9,511	12,097	12,167	11,666	3.0	2.9	0.6	-4.1	3.5	4.9
San Marino	THS	45	28	43	49	45	0.0	0.0	14.0	-8.2	-9.1	9.0
Serbia & Montenegro	TCE	1,186	228	239	351	448	0.1	0.1	47.0	27.5	-28.1	1.0
Slovenia	TC	..	732	1,090	1,219	1,302	0.2	0.3	11.9	6.8		8.3
Spain	TF	34,085|	34,920	47,898	50,094	51,748	10.8	12.9	4.6	3.3		6.5
East Mediterranean Eu.		**7,423**	**11,398**	**14,689**	**14,677**	**16,062**	**3.5**	**4.0**	**-0.1**	**9.4**	**9.0**	**5.2**
Cyprus	TF	1,561	2,100	2,686	2,697	2,418	0.7	0.6	0.4	-10.3	6.1	5.0
Israel	TF	1,063	2,215	2,417	1,196	862	0.7	0.2	-50.5	-27.9	15.8	1.8
Turkey	TF	4,799	7,083	9,586	10,784	12,782	2.2	3.2	12.5	18.5	8.1	6.2

Source: World Tourism Organization (WTO) © (Data as collected by WTO September 2003)

International Tourist Arrivals by Country of Destination

		International Tourist Arrivals (1000)					Market share in the region (%)		Change (%)		Average annual growth (%)	
	Series	1990	1995	2000	2001	2002*	1995	2002*	001/00	02*/01	90-95	95-00
Middle East		***9,689***	***13,633***	***23,969***	***23,646***	***27,594***	***96***	***100***	***-1.3***	***16.7***	***7.1***	***11.9***
Bahrain	TF	1,376	1,396	2,420	2,789	3,167	10.2	11.5	15.2	13.6	0.3	11.6
Egypt	TF	2,411	2,871	5,116	4,357	4,906	21.1	17.8	-14.8	12.6	3.6	12.2
Iraq	VF	748	61	78	127	..	0.4		61.4		-39.5	5.3
Jordan	TF	572	1,074	1,427	1,478	1,622	7.9	5.9	3.6	9.8	13.4	5.9
Kuwait	THS	15	72	78	73	..	0.5		-6.4		36.9	1.6
Lebanon	TF	..	450	742	837	956	3.3	3.5	12.9	14.2		10.5
Libyan Arab Jamahiriya	TF	96	56	174	..	..	0.4				-10.2	25.5
Oman	THS	149	279	571	562	602	2.0	2.2	-1.6	7.1	13.4	15.4
Palestine	TF	..	..	330	7	..			-97.9			
Qatar	TF	136	294			..	2.2		13.4		16.7	-25.6
Saudi Arabia	TF	2,209	3,325 |	6,585	6,727	7,511	24.4	27.2	2.1	11.7	8.5	14.6
Syrian Arab Republic	TCE	562	815	1,416	1,318 |	2,809	6.0	10.2	-6.9		7.7	11.7
Untd Arab Emirates	THS	973	2,315	3,907	4,134	5,445	17.0	19.7	5.8	31.7	18.9	11.0
Yemen	THS	52	61	75	76	89	0.4	0.3	0.8	17.8	3.2	4.2

Source: World Tourism Organization (WTO) © (Data as collected by WTO September 2003)

| : change of series.

2. International Tourism Receipts

International Tourism Receipts, World

	International Tourism Receipts				(billion)	Change current prices		(%)	Change constant prices		(%)
	1990	1995	2000	2001	2002*	00/99	01/00	02*/01	00/99	01/00	02*/01
Local currencies						14.2	3.1	3.7	9.7	-1.0	0.3
US$	264.1	404.6	473.4	459.5	474.2	4.1	-2.9	3.2	0.6	-5.6	1.6
Euro	207.4	309.3	512.5	513.0	501.5	20.1	0.1	-2.2	17.4	-2.4	-4.4

Source: World Tourism Organization (WTO) © (Data as collected by WTO September 2003)

International Tourism Receipts by (Sub)region

	US$	(billion)	Receipts per arrival	euro	(billion)	Receipts per arrival	Change[1]		(%)	Market share (%)
	2001	2002*	2002*	2001	2002*	2002*	00/99	01/00	02*/01	2002*
World	**459.5**	**474.2**	**675**	**513.0**	**501.5**	**714**	**9.7**	**-1.0**	**0.3**	**100**
Africa	***11.7***	***11.8***	***404***	***13.0***	***12.5***	***428***	***9.1***	***14.8***	***2.0***	***2.5***
North Africa	4.3	3.8	365	4.8	4.0	386	12.5	22.2	-16.2	0.8
West Africa	1.2	1.3	454	1.3	1.4	480	28.5	9.8	9.0	0.3
Central Africa	0.1	0.1	163	0.1	0.1	172	5.7	5.8	1.3	0.0
East Africa	2.8	3.0	485	3.2	3.2	513	0.7	5.4	6.0	0.6
Southern Africa	3.3	3.5	397	3.6	3.7	420	6.1	16.1	20.0	0.7
Americas	***122.2***	***114.3***	***995***	***136.5***	***120.8***	***1,052***	***6.1***	***-9.9***	***-4.8***	***24.1***
North America	91.1	85.1	1,043	101.7	90.0	1,103	6.0	-12.6	-8.0	17.9
Caribbean	17.1	16.6	1,035	19.1	17.6	1,094	5.1	-1.1	-3.2	3.5
Central America	3.0	3.4	718	3.3	3.6	759	16.3	-7.7	12.3	0.7
South America	11.1	9.2	734	12.4	9.7	776	5.8	0.4	14.2	1.9
Asia and the Pacific	***88.0***	***94.7***	***721***	***98.2***	***100.1***	***763***	***9.9***	***5.1***	***5.1***	***20.0***
North-East Asia	43.5	47.9	651	48.6	50.7	688	8.0	8.9	11.1	10.1
South-East Asia	26.3	27.4	648	29.3	28.9	685	13.8	4.4	-1.5	5.8
Oceania	13.2	14.3	1,498	14.7	15.2	1,585	9.9	-4.2	1.2	3.0
South Asia	5.0	5.1	865	5.6	5.4	915	4.4	4.5	-2.6	1.1
Europe	***225.8***	***240.5***	***602***	***252.1***	***254.3***	***636***	***9.6***	***-1.1***	***-1.8***	***50.7***
Northern Europe	31.7	35.5	766	35.4	37.6	810	4.0	-3.9	4.1	7.5
Western Europe	81.4	87.1	618	90.9	92.2	653	12.4	-0.5	-0.6	18.4
Central/Eastern Europe	22.7	23.5	359	25.3	24.8	380	0.2	-6.8	-4.4	4.9
Southern Europe	79.1	82.3	628	88.3	87.0	665	10.8	0.9	-4.6	17.4
East Mediterranean Eu.	10.9	12.1	751	12.2	12.8	795	18.2	0.9	-2.7	2.5
Middle East	***11.8***	***13.0***	***470***	***13.2***	***13.7***	***497***	***9.0***	***-1.6***	***13.3***	***2.7***

Source: World Tourism Organization (WTO) © (Data as collected by WTO September 2003)

[1] Local currencies, constant prices

International Tourism Receipts, 1950-2002*

	World	Africa	Americas	Asia and the Pacific	Europe	Middle East	World	Africa	Americas	Asia and the Pacific	Europe	Middle East
	International Tourism Receipts (US$, billion)						International Tourism Receipts (euro/ECU, billion)					
1950	2.1	0.1	1.1	0.04	0.9	0.03						
1960	6.9	0.2	2.5	0.2	3.9	0.1						
1965	11.6	0.3	3.4	0.5	7.2	0.3						
1970	17.9	0.5	4.8	1.2	11.0	0.4						
1975	40.7	1.3	10.2	2.5	25.9	0.9	32.8	1.0	8.2	2.0	20.8	0.7
1980	105.4	2.6	25.4	10.3	63.6	3.5	75.7	1.9	18.3	7.4	45.7	2.5
1981	107.5	2.9	29.2	12.1	59.2	4.1	96.3	2.6	26.2	10.8	53.0	3.7
1982	101.8	2.7	25.1	12.2	57.8	3.9	103.9	2.8	25.7	12.5	59.0	3.9
1983	101.1	2.7	24.7	12.8	56.6	4.3	113.5	3.0	27.7	14.4	63.5	4.9
1984	111.2	2.5	31.9	13.7	58.5	4.6	140.9	3.2	40.5	17.3	74.1	5.8
1985	118.0	2.5	33.3	14.6	63.4	4.2	154.6	3.3	43.6	19.1	83.0	5.5
1986	143.3	2.9	38.4	18.8	79.8	3.4	145.6	3.0	39.0	19.1	81.0	3.4
1987	176.5	3.8	43.0	24.8	100.3	4.5	152.9	3.3	37.3	21.5	86.9	3.9
1988	204.0	4.6	51.3	32.4	111.4	4.3	172.5	3.9	43.4	27.4	94.2	3.7
1989	220.8	4.5	60.1	36.3	115.4	4.5	200.4	4.1	54.6	32.9	104.8	4.1
1990	264.1	5.3	69.2	41.3	143.8	4.5	207.4	4.2	54.3	32.4	113.0	3.6
1991	277.9	5.1	76.8	42.8	149.3	4.0	224.2	4.1	61.9	34.5	120.5	3.2
1992	317.1	6.8	83.8	50.7	170.5	5.3	244.3	5.2	64.6	39.1	131.3	4.0
1993	322.9	6.8	89.1	56.5	164.5	5.9	275.7	5.8	76.1	48.3	140.5	5.0
1994	356.0	7.5	93.2	66.9	181.7	6.6	299.3	6.3	78.4	56.3	152.7	5.6
1995	404.6	8.2	99.6	77.7	210.2	8.9	309.3	6.2	76.2	59.4	160.7	6.8
1996	438.8	9.3	109.9	87.9	221.9	9.8	345.6	7.4	86.5	69.2	174.8	7.8
1997	442.9	9.5	116.3	81.6	224.7	10.9	390.6	8.4	102.5	72.0	198.1	9.6
1998	445.2	10.1	116.4	75.1	233.2	10.3	397.1	9.0	103.8	67.0	208.0	9.2
1999	455.0	10.7	122.2	80.0	230.6	11.4	426.9	10.0	114.7	75.1	216.4	10.7
2000	473.4	10.8	133.5	86.9	229.7	12.4	512.5	11.7	144.5	94.1	248.7	13.5
2001	459.5	11.7	122.2	88.0	225.8	11.8	513.0	13.0	136.5	98.2	252.1	13.2
2002*	474.2	11.8	114.3	94.7	240.5	13.0	501.5	12.5	120.8	100.1	254.3	13.7

Source: World Tourism Organization (WTO) © (Data as collected by WTO September 2003)

[1] Receipts data are in current US$ and euro (based on the average annual exchange rate for euro or ECU to US$) and can be strongly influenced by exchange rate fluctuations.

See for tables in euro values pages Annex - 16 to Annex - 20

International Tourism Receipts by Country of Destination

	International Tourism Receipts (US$ million)					Market share in the region (%)		Change (%)		Average annual growth (%)	
	1990	1995	2000	2001	2002*	1995	2002*	001/00	02*/01	90-95	95-00
Africa	*5,325*	*8,169*	*10,819*	*11,665*	*11,785*	*100*	*100*	*7.8*	*1.0*	*8.9*	*5.8*
North Africa	**2,292**	**2,748**	**3,662**	**4,287**	**3,760**	**33.6**	**31.9**	**17.1**	**-12.3**	**3.7**	**5.9**
Algeria	64	32	96	100	133	0.4	1.1	4.2	33.0	-12.9	24.6
Morocco	1,259	1,304	2,040	2,526	2,152	16.0	18.3	23.8	-14.8	0.7	9.4
Sudan	21	19	30	56	..	0.2		86.7		-2.0	9.6
Tunisia	948	1,393	1,496	1,605	1,422	17.1	12.1	7.3	-11.4	8.0	1.4
West Africa	**602**	**751**	**1,063**	**1,179**	**1,338**	**9.2**	**11.4**	**11.0**	**13.5**	**4.5**	**7.2**
Benin	55	85	77	73	60	1.0	0.5	-5.2	-17.8	9.1	-2.0
Burkina Faso	11	25	..	34	..	0.3				17.8	
Cape Verde	6	10	..	..	..	0.1				10.8	
Côte d'Ivoire	51	89	49	48	..	1.1		-2.0		11.8	-11.3
Gambia	26	23	..	..	..	0.3				-2.4	
Ghana	81	233	386	448	520	2.9	4.4	16.1	16.1	23.5	10.6
Guinea	30	1	12	14	31	0.0	0.3	16.7	118.6	-49.4	64.4
Mali	47	25	71	..	..	0.3				-11.9	23.2
Mauritania	9	11	..	..	..	0.1				4.1	
Niger	17	15	..	..	..	0.2				-2.5	
Nigeria	25	54	148	156	..	0.7		5.4		16.7	22.3
Senegal	167	161	140	..	..	2.0				-0.7	-2.8
Sierra Leone	19	6	..	..	..	0.1				-20.6	
Togo	58	13	5	11	..	0.2		120.0		-25.9	-17.4
Central Africa	**98**	**91**	**105**	**111**	**120**	**1.1**	**1.0**	**5.2**	**8.5**	**-1.5**	**3.0**
Angola	13	10	18	22	..	0.1		22.2		-5.1	12.5
Cameroon	53	36	39	..	..	0.4				-7.4	1.6
Cent.Afr.Rep.	3	..	..	..	..						
Chad	8	..	..	..	..						
Congo	8	14	..	..	..	0.2				11.8	
Dem.R.Congo	7	..	..	..	..						
Equatorial Guinea	1	..	..	..	..						
Gabon	3	7	7	7	..	0.1		0.0		18.5	0.0
Sao Tome Prn	2	..	..	8	..						
East Africa	**1,092**	**1,938**	**2,738**	**2,832**	**3,049**	**23.7**	**25.9**	**3.4**	**7.7**	**12.2**	**7.2**
Burundi	4	1	1	1	..	0.0		50.0		-24.2	-4.4
Comoros	2	21	15	..	..	0.3				60.0	-6.5
Djibouti	..	4	..	..	..	0.0					
Eritrea	..	58	36	74	73	0.7	0.6	105.6	-1.4		-9.1
Ethiopia	25	26	68	75	..	0.3		10.3		0.8	21.2
Kenya	443	486	276	308	297	5.9	2.5	11.6	-3.6	1.9	-10.7
Madagascar	40	58	121	115	..	0.7		-5.0		7.7	15.8
Malawi	16	9	27	28	125	0.1	1.1	3.7	346.4	-10.9	24.6
Mauritius	244	430	542	624	612	5.3	5.2	15.1	-1.9	12.0	4.7
Mozambique	..	..	186	134	144		1.2	-27.9	7.4		
Reunion	..	216	255	244	284	2.6	2.4	-4.3	16.4		3.4
Rwanda	10	2	4	9	..	0.0		125.0		-27.5	14.9
Seychelles	126	98	115	113	130	1.2	1.1	-1.7	15.0	-4.9	3.3
Tanzania	65	259	739	725	730	3.2	6.2	-1.9	0.7	31.8	23.3
Uganda	10	78	113	163	185	1.0	1.6	44.2	13.5	50.8	7.7
Zambia	41	47	111	117	..	0.6		5.4		2.8	18.8
Zimbabwe	60	145	125	81	76	1.8	0.6	-35.2	-6.2	19.3	-2.9
Southern Africa	**1,241**	**2,641**	**3,250**	**3,256**	**3,517**	**32.3**	**29.8**	**0.2**	**8.0**	**16.3**	**4.2**
Botswana	117	162	313	300	309	2.0	2.6	-4.2	3.0	6.7	14.1
Lesotho	17	27	24	23	..	0.3		-4.2		9.7	-2.3
Namibia	85	278	..	404	..	3.4				26.7	
South Africa	992	2,126	2,513	2,501	2,719	26.0	23.1	-0.5	8.7	16.5	3.4
Swaziland	30	48	35	28	28	0.6	0.2	-20.0	0.0	9.9	-6.1

Source: World Tourism Organization (WTO) © (Data as collected by WTO September 2003)

International Tourism Receipts by Country of Destination

	International Tourism Receipts (US$ million)					Market share in the region (%)		Change (%)		Average annual growth (%)	
	1990	1995	2000	2001	2002*	1995	2002*	001/00	02*/01	90-95	95-00
Americas	***69,167***	***99,649***	***133,479***	***122,247***	***114,255***	***100***	***100***	***-8.4***	***-6.5***	***7.6***	***6.0***
North America	**54,813**	**77,456**	**101,534**	**91,068**	**85,105**	**77.7**	**74.5**	**-10.3**	**-6.5**	**7.2**	**5.6**
Canada	6,339	7,882	10,839	10,774	9,700	7.9	8.5	-0.6	-10.0	4.5	6.6
Mexico	5,467	6,179	8,295	8,401	8,858	6.2	7.8	1.3	5.4	2.5	6.1
United States	43,007	63,395	82,400	71,893	66,547	63.6	58.2	-12.8	-7.4	8.1	5.4
Caribbean	**8,712**	**12,185**	**16,993**	**17,125**	**16,616**	**12.2**	**14.5**	**0.8**	**-3.0**	**6.9**	**6.9**
Anguilla	35	49	55	61	55	0.0	0.0	10.9	-9.8	7.0	2.3
Antigua,Barb	298	247	290	272	..	0.2		-6.2		-3.7	3.3
Aruba	350	521	638	890	898	0.5	0.8	39.5	0.9	8.3	4.1
Bahamas	1,324	1,346	1,719	1,636	..	1.4		-4.8		0.3	5.0
Barbados	494	612	711	687	..	0.6		-3.4		4.4	3.0
Bermuda	490	488	431	351	..	0.5		-18.6		-0.1	-2.5
Bonaire	18	37	87	75	..	0.0		-13.8		15.5	18.6
Br.Virgin Is	132	211	315	337	..	0.2		7.0		9.8	8.3
Cayman Islands	236	394	559	585	..	0.4		4.7		10.8	7.2
Cuba	243	963	1,737	1,692	1,633	1.0	1.4	-2.6	-3.5	31.7	12.5
Curaçao	120	175	227	253	273	0.2	0.2	11.5	7.9	7.8	5.3
Dominica	25	34	48	39	36	0.0	0.0	-19.1	-7.7	6.3	7.2
Dominican Rp	900	1,568	2,860	2,798	2,736	1.6	2.4	-2.2	-2.2	11.7	12.8
Grenada	38	54	93	83	84	0.1	0.1	-9.8	0.7	7.3	11.4
Guadeloupe	197	458	418	..	..	0.5				18.4	-1.8
Haiti	46	56	54	54	..	0.1		0.0		4.0	-0.7
Jamaica	740	1,069	1,333	1,233	1,209	1.1	1.1	-7.5	-1.9	7.6	4.5
Martinique	240	384	302	245	..	0.4		-18.9		9.9	-4.7
Montserrat	7	20	9	8	..	0.0		-5.8		23.4	-14.8
Puerto Rico	1,366	1,828	2,388	2,728	2,486	1.8	2.2	14.2	-8.9	6.0	5.5
Saint Lucia	154	268	297	258	256	0.3	0.2	-13.1	-0.9	11.7	2.1
St.Kitts-Nev	58	65	58	60	57	0.1	0.0	2.7	-5.0	2.3	-2.1
St.Maarten	316	349	498	493	..	0.4		-1.0		2.0	7.4
St.Vincent,Grenadines	56	41	75	80	81	0.0	0.1	6.7	1.3	-6.0	12.8
Trinidad Tbg	95	73	213	201	224	0.1	0.2	-5.6	11.4	-5.1	23.9
Turks,Caicos	37	53	285	311	292	0.1	0.3	9.1	-6.1	7.5	40.0
US.Virgin Is	697	822	1,292	1,323	1,240	0.8	1.1	2.4	-6.3	3.4	9.5
Central America	**735**	**1,579**	**3,085**	**2,954**	**3,375**	**1.6**	**3.0**	**-4.2**	**14.2**	**16.5**	**14.3**
Belize	44	77	120	121	133	0.1	0.1	0.8	9.9	11.8	9.3
Costa Rica	275	660	1,229	1,096	1,078	0.7	0.9	-10.9	-1.6	19.1	13.2
El Salvador	18	41	254	235	342	0.0	0.3	-7.5	45.5	17.9	44.0
Guatemala	185	277	535	493	695	0.3	0.6	-7.9	41.0	8.4	14.1
Honduras	29	107	260	275	342	0.1	0.3	5.7	24.5	29.8	19.4
Nicaragua	12	50	111	109	106	0.1	0.1	-2.1	-2.8	33.0	17.4
Panama	172	367	576	626	679	0.4	0.6	8.7	8.5	16.4	9.4
South America	**4,907**	**8,429**	**11,867**	**11,100**	**9,159**	**8.5**	**8.0**	**-6.5**	**-17.5**	**11.4**	**7.1**
Argentina	1,131	2,144	2,817	2,547	..	2.2		-9.6		13.6	5.6
Bolivia	91	139	160	156	..	0.1		-2.5		8.8	2.9
Brazil	1,444	2,097	4,228	3,701	3,120	2.1	2.7	-12.5	-15.7	7.7	15.1
Chile	540	911	819	799	733	0.9	0.6	-2.6	-8.2	11.0	-2.1
Colombia	406	657	1,026	1,209	962	0.7	0.8	17.8	-20.4	10.1	9.3
Ecuador	188	255	402	430	447	0.3	0.4	7.0	4.0	6.3	9.5
French Guiana	..	..	..	42	45		0.0		7.1		
Guyana	27	78	..	..	..	0.1				23.6	
Paraguay	128	137	73	69	62	0.1	0.1	-5.5	-10.1	1.4	-11.8
Peru	217	428	911	817	841	0.4	0.7	-10.3	2.9	14.6	16.3
Suriname	1	21	16	14	..	0.0		-12.5		83.8	-5.3
Uruguay	238	611	652	561	318	0.6	0.3	-14.0	-43.3	20.8	1.3
Venezuela	496	951	634	682	468	1.0	0.4	7.6	-31.4	13.9	-7.8

Source: World Tourism Organization (WTO) ©

(Data as collected by WTO September 2003)

International Tourism Receipts by Country of Destination

	International Tourism Receipts (US$ million)					Market share in the region (%)		Change (%)		Average annual growth (%)	
	1990	1995	2000	2001	2002*	1995	2002*	001/00	02*/01	90-95	95-00
Asia and the Pacific	***39,226***	***74,215***	***86,921***	***87,967***	***94,697***	***100***	***95***	***1.2***	***7.7***	***13.6***	***3.2***
North-East Asia	**17,634**	**33,690**	**41,276**	**43,523**	**47,936**	**45.4**	**50.6**	**5.4**	**10.1**	**13.8**	**4.1**
China	2,218	8,733	16,224	17,792	20,385	11.8	21.5	9.7	14.6	31.5	13.2
Hong Kong (China)	5,032	9,604	7,886	8,282	10,117	12.9	10.7	5.0	22.2	13.8	-3.9
Japan	3,578	3,226	3,373	3,301	3,499	4.3	3.7	-2.1	6.0	-2.0	0.9
Korea, D P Rp	29	..	..	..	..						
Korea, Republic of	3,559	5,587	6,811	6,373	5,277	7.5	5.6	-6.4	-17.2	9.4	4.0
Macao (China)	1,473	3,233	3,205	3,745	4,415	4.4	4.7	16.8	17.9	17.0	-0.2
Mongolia	5	21	36	39	..	0.0		8.3		33.2	11.4
Taiwan (Pr. of China)	1,740	3,286	3,741	3,991	4,197	4.4	4.4	6.7	5.2	13.6	2.6
South-East Asia	**14,473**	**28,311**	**26,490**	**26,280**	**27,353**	**38.1**	**28.9**	**-0.8**	**4.1**	**14.4**	**-1.3**
Cambodia	..	100	228	304	379	0.1	0.4	33.3	24.7		17.9
Indonesia	2,105	5,229	5,749	5,411	..	7.0		-5.9		20.0	1.9
Lao P.D.R.	3	25	114	104	113	0.0	0.1	-8.8	8.7	52.8	35.5
Malaysia	1,667	3,909	4,562	6,374	6,785	5.3	7.2	39.7	6.4	18.6	3.1
Myanmar	9	38	42	45	..	0.1		7.1		33.4	2.0
Philippines	1,306	2,454	2,134	1,723	1,741	3.3	1.8	-19.3	1.0	13.4	-2.8
Singapore	4,937	8,390	6,018	5,081	4,932	11.3	5.2	-15.6	-2.9	11.2	-6.4
Thailand	4,326	8,043	7,489	7,077	7,902	10.8	8.3	-5.5	11.7	13.2	-1.4
Vietnam	85	..	..	..	..						
Oceania	**7,119**	**12,214**	**14,430**	**13,172**	**14,329**	**16.5**	**15.1**	**-8.7**	**8.8**	**11.4**	**3.4**
American Samoa	10	..	..	..	..						
Australia	4,088	7,857	8,451	7,624	8,087	10.6	8.5	-9.8	6.1	14.0	1.5
Cook Is	16	28	36	38	46	0.0	0.0	5.6	21.1	11.8	5.2
Fiji	202	283	181	217	267	0.4	0.3	19.9	23.0	7.0	-8.6
French Polynesia	171	326	..	..	..	0.4				13.8	
Guam	936	..	..	..	..						
Kiribati	1	2	3	3	..	0.0		18.5		12.5	8.4
Marshall Is	..	3	4	..	4	0.0	0.0				9.9
Micronesia (Fed.St.of)	..	..	15	13	..			-13.3			
N.Mariana Is	455	655	..	..	..	0.9				7.6	
New Caledonia	94	108	110	93	..	0.1		-15.5		2.8	0.4
New Zealand	1,030	1,488	2,240	2,334	2,918	2.0	3.1	4.2	25.0	7.6	8.5
Niue	..	2	..	..	..	0.0					
Palau	..	..	53	59	59		0.1	9.9	0.8		
Papua New Guinea	41	60	92	101	..	0.1		9.8		7.9	8.9
Samoa	20	34	41	40	45	0.0	0.0	-2.4	12.5	11.2	3.8
Solomon Is	7	16	..	..	..	0.0				18.0	
Tonga	9	10	7	7	9	0.0	0.0	0.0	28.6	2.1	-6.9
Tuvalu	..	0	..	..	..	0.0					
Vanuatu	39	58	58	46	..	0.1		-20.7		8.3	0.0
South Asia	**2,029**	**3,484**	**4,725**	**4,993**	**5,078**	**100.0**	**70.9**	**5.7**	**1.7**	**11.4**	**6.3**
Bangladesh	11	23	50	48	..	0.7		-4.0		15.9	16.8
Bhutan	2	5	10	..	..	0.1				20.1	14.9
India	1,513	2,583	3,168	3,042	2,923	74.1	57.6	-4.0	-3.9	11.3	4.2
Iran	61	205	671	1,122	..	5.9		67.2		27.4	26.8
Maldives	89	211	321	327	318	6.1	6.3	1.9	-2.8	18.8	8.8
Nepal	64	117	167	140	..	3.4		-16.2		12.8	7.4
Pakistan	156	114	84	92	105	3.3	2.1	9.5	14.1	-6.1	-5.9
Sri Lanka	132	225	253	211	253	6.5	5.0	-16.6	19.9	11.3	2.4

Source: World Tourism Organization (WTO) © (Data as collected by WTO September 2003)

International Tourism Receipts by Country of Destination

	International Tourism Receipts (US$ million)					Market share in the region (%)		Change (%)		Average annual growth (%)	
	1990	1995	2000	2001	2002*	1995	2002*	001/00	02*/01	90-95	95-00
Europe	***143,847***	***210,165***	***229,726***	***225,787***	***240,490***	***100***	***100***	***-1.7***	***6.5***	***7.9***	***1.8***
Northern Europe	**24,325**	**32,045**	**33,901**	**31,661**	**35,522**	**15.2**	**14.8**	**-6.6**	**12.2**	**5.7**	**1.1**
Denmark	3,322	3,728	4,038	4,600	5,785	1.8	2.4	13.9	25.8	2.3	1.6
Finland	1,167	1,570	1,412	1,441	1,573	0.7	0.7	2.1	9.2	6.1	-2.1
Iceland	139	186	228	235	250	0.1	0.1	3.1	6.4	6.0	4.2
Ireland	1,459	2,211	2,608	2,790	3,089	1.1	1.3	7.0	10.7	8.7	3.4
Norway	1,570	2,362	1,992	2,037	2,738	1.1	1.1	2.3	34.4	8.5	-3.3
Sweden	2,906	3,434	4,079	4,275	4,496	1.6	1.9	4.8	5.2	3.4	3.5
United Kingdom	13,762	18,554	19,544	16,283	17,591	8.8	7.3	-16.7	8.0	6.2	1.0
Western Europe	**64,631**	**79,584**	**82,355**	**81,370**	**87,136**	**37.9**	**36.2**	**-1.2**	**7.1**	**4.3**	**0.7**
Austria	13,417	12,927	9,931	10,118	11,237	6.2	4.7	1.9	11.1	-0.7	-5.1
Belgium	3,721	4,548	6,592	6,903	6,892	2.2	2.9	4.7	-0.2	4.1	7.7
France	20,184	27,527	30,754	29,979	32,329	13.1	13.4	-2.5	7.8	6.4	2.2
Germany	14,288	17,243	18,479	18,422	19,158	8.2	8.0	-0.3	4.0	3.8	1.4
Luxembourg	..	1,721	1,807	1,915	2,186	0.8	0.9	6.0	14.2		1.0
Netherlands	4,155	6,252	7,217	6,723	7,706	3.0	3.2	-6.8	14.6	8.5	2.9
Switzerland	7,411	9,365	7,576	7,310	7,628	4.5	3.2	-3.5	4.4	4.8	-4.2
Central/Eastern Europe	**4,849**	**23,010**	**22,290**	**22,696**	**23,450**	**10.9**	**9.8**	**1.8**	**3.3**	**36.5**	**-0.6**
Armenia	..	5	45	123	..	0.0		173.3			55.2
Azerbaijan	228	70	63	43	..	0.0		-31.7		-21.0	-2.1
Belarus	..	23	93	82	..	0.0		-11.8			32.2
Bulgaria	320	473	1,074	1,201	1,344	0.2	0.6	11.8	11.9	8.1	17.8
Czech Rep	419	2,875	2,982	3,106	2,941	1.4	1.2	4.2	-5.3	47.0	0.7
Estonia	..	353	506	507	555	0.2	0.2	0.2	9.5		7.5
Georgia	..	..	413	442	472		0.2	7.0	6.8		
Hungary	824	2,929	3,445	3,770	3,273	1.4	1.4	9.4	-13.2	28.9	3.3
Kazakhstan	..	122	356	396	621	0.1	0.3	11.2	56.8		23.9
Kyrgyzstan	..	5	15	24	..	0.0		60.0			24.6
Latvia	..	20	131	120	161	0.0	0.1	-8.4	34.4		45.6
Lithuania	..	77	391	383	513	0.0	0.2	-2.0	33.9		38.4
Poland	358	6,614	6,100	4,815	4,500	3.1	1.9	-21.1	-6.5	79.2	-1.6
Rep Moldova	..	57	46	46	55	0.0	0.0	0.0	19.6		-4.2
Romania	106	590	359	500	612	0.3	0.3	39.3	22.4	41.0	-9.5
Russian Fed	..	4,312	3,429	3,560	4,188	2.1	1.7	3.8	17.6		-4.5
Slovakia	70	620	432	639	724	0.3	0.3	47.9	13.3	54.7	-7.0
Tajikistan	..	..	0	0	..			0.0			
Ukraine	..	3,865	2,207	2,725	2,992	1.8	1.2	23.5	9.8		-10.6
Uzbekistan	..	..	63	72	68		0.0	14.3	-5.6		
Southern Europe	**44,163**	**65,817**	**78,312**	**79,123**	**82,311**	**31.3**	**34.2**	**1.0**	**4.0**	**8.3**	**3.5**
Albania	4	65	389	446	..	0.0		14.7		74.7	43.0
Bosnia Herzg	..	7	69	73	..	0.0		5.8			58.0
Croatia	1,704	1,349	2,758	3,335	3,811	0.6	1.6	20.9	14.3	-4.6	15.4
F.Yug.Rp.Macedonia	45	19	37	25	39	0.0	0.0	-32.4	56.0	-15.8	14.3
Greece	2,587	4,136	9,221	9,447	9,741	2.0	4.1	2.4	3.1	9.8	17.4
Italy	16,458	28,729	27,500	25,796	26,915	13.7	11.2	-6.2	4.3	11.8	-0.9
Malta	496	659	613	579	568	0.3	0.2	-5.4	-2.0	5.9	-1.5
Portugal	3,555	4,339	5,282	5,505	5,919	2.1	2.5	4.2	7.5	4.1	4.0
Serbia & Montenegro	..	42	28	43	77	0.0	0.0	53.6	79.1		-7.8
Slovenia	..	1,084	961	1,001	1,083	0.5	0.5	4.2	8.2		-2.4
Spain	18,593	25,388	31,454	32,873	33,609	12.1	14.0	4.5	2.2	6.4	4.4
East Mediterranean Eu.	**5,879**	**9,709**	**12,868**	**10,937**	**12,070**	**4.6**	**5.0**	**-15.0**	**10.4**	**10.6**	**5.8**
Cyprus	1,258	1,788	1,894	1,981	1,863	0.9	0.8	4.6	-6.0	7.3	1.2
Israel	1,396	2,964	3,338	1,570	1,197	1.4	0.5	-53.0	-23.8	16.3	2.4
Turkey	3,225	4,957	7,636	7,386	9,010	2.4	3.7	-3.3	22.0	9.0	9.0

Source: World Tourism Organization (WTO) © (Data as collected by WTO September 2003)

International Tourism Receipts by Country of Destination

	International Tourism Receipts (US$ million)					Market share in the region (%)		Change (%)		Average annual growth (%)	
	1990	1995	2000	2001	2002*	1995	2002*	001/00	02*/01	90-95	95-00
Middle East	***4,548***	***8,943***	***12,438***	***11,785***	***12,963***	***73***	***100***	***-5.2***	***10.0***	***14.5***	***6.8***
Bahrain	135	247	573	630	..	2.8		9.9		12.8	18.3
Egypt	1,100	2,684	4,345	3,800	3,764	30.0	29.0	-12.5	-0.9	19.5	10.1
Jordan	512	652	722	700	786	7.3	6.1	-3.0	12.3	5.0	2.1
Kuwait	132	121	98	104	118	1.4	0.9	6.1	13.9	-1.7	-4.1
Lebanon	..	710	742	837	956	7.9	7.4	12.8	14.2		0.9
Libyan Arab Jamahiriya	6	..	..	..	..						
Oman	69	92	120	118	116	1.0	0.9	-1.7	-1.7	5.9	5.5
Palestine	..	..	155	9	..			-94.2			
Saudi Arabia	..	..	..	3,420	..						
Syrian Arab Republic	320	1,338	1,082	..	1,366	15.0	10.5			33.1	-4.2
Untd Arab Emirates	315	632	1,012	1,064	1,328	7.1	10.2	5.1	24.8	14.9	9.9
Yemen	20	50	76	38	..	0.6		-50.0		20.1	8.7

Source: World Tourism Organization (WTO) © (Data as collected by WTO September 2003)

See for tables in US$ values pages Annex – 11 to Annex - 15

International Tourism Receipts by Country of Destination

	International Tourism Receipts (euro million)					Market share in the region (%)		Change (%)		Average annual growth (%)	
	1990	1995	2000	2001	2002*	1995	2002*	001/00	02*/01	90-95	95-00
Africa	*4,182*	*6,245*	*11,714*	*13,024*	*12,463*	*100*	*100*	*11.2*	*-4.3*	*8.4*	*13.4*
North Africa	**1,800**	**2,101**	**3,965**	**4,787**	**3,976**	**33.6**	**31.9**	**20.7**	**-16.9**	**3.1**	**13.5**
Algeria	50	24	104	112	141	0.4	1.1	7.4	26.0	-13.4	33.6
Morocco	989	997	2,209	2,820	2,276	16.0	18.3	27.7	-19.3	0.2	17.2
Sudan	16	15	32	63	..	0.2		92.5		-2.5	17.5
Tunisia	744	1,065	1,620	1,792	1,504	17.1	12.1	10.6	-16.1	7.4	8.7
West Africa	**473**	**574**	**1,151**	**1,317**	**1,415**	**9.2**	**11.4**	**14.4**	**7.5**	**4.0**	**14.9**
Benin	43	65	83	82	63	1.0	0.5	-2.2	-22.1	8.5	5.1
Burkina Faso	9	19	..	38	..	0.3				17.2	
Cape Verde	5	8	..	..	..	0.1				10.2	
Côte d'Ivoire	40	68	53	54	..	1.1		1.0		11.2	-4.9
Gambia	20	18	..	..	..	0.3				-2.9	
Ghana	64	178	418	500	550	2.9	4.4	19.7	9.9	22.9	18.6
Guinea	24	1	13	16	32	0.0	0.3	20.3	107.0	-49.6	76.2
Mali	37	19	77	..	..	0.3				-12.3	32.1
Mauritania	7	8	..	..	..	0.1				3.5	
Niger	13	11	..	..	..	0.2				-3.0	
Nigeria	20	41	160	174	..	0.7		8.7		16.0	31.2
Senegal	131	123	152	..	..	2.0				-1.3	4.3
Sierra Leone	15	5	..	..	..	0.1				-21.0	
Togo	46	10	5	12	..	0.2		126.9		-26.2	-11.4
Central Africa	**77**	**70**	**114**	**124**	**127**	**1.1**	**1.0**	**8.5**	**2.8**	**-2.0**	**10.4**
Angola	10	8	19	25	..	0.1		26.0		-5.6	20.6
Cameroon	42	28	42	..	..	0.4				-7.9	8.9
Cent.Afr.Rep.	2	..	..	..	..						
Chad	6	..	..	..	..						
Congo	6	11	..	..	..	0.2				11.2	
Dem.R.Congo	5	..	..	..	..						
Equatorial Guinea	1	..	..	..	..						
Gabon	2	5	8	8	..	0.1		3.1		17.8	7.2
Sao Tome Prn	2	..	..	9	..						
East Africa	**858**	**1,482**	**2,965**	**3,162**	**3,225**	**23.7**	**25.9**	**6.6**	**2.0**	**11.6**	**14.9**
Burundi	3	1	1	1	..	0.0		54.7		-24.6	2.5
Comoros	2	16	16	..	..	0.3				59.2	0.2
Djibouti	..	3	..	..	..	0.0					
Eritrea	..	44	39	83	77	0.7	0.6	112.0	-6.6		-2.5
Ethiopia	20	20	74	84	..	0.3		13.7		0.2	29.9
Kenya	348	372	299	344	314	5.9	2.5	15.1	-8.7	1.3	-4.3
Madagascar	31	44	131	128	..	0.7		-2.0		7.1	24.2
Malawi	13	7	29	31	132	0.1	1.1	6.9	322.8	-11.3	33.6
Mauritius	192	329	587	697	647	5.3	5.2	18.7	-7.1	11.4	12.3
Mozambique	..	..	202	150	153		1.2	-25.6	1.8		
Reunion	..	165	276	272	300	2.6	2.4	-1.3	10.2		10.8
Rwanda	8	2	4	10	..	0.0		132.0		-27.9	23.1
Seychelles	99	75	125	126	137	1.2	1.1	1.3	9.0	-5.4	10.7
Tanzania	51	198	800	809	772	3.2	6.2	1.2	-4.6	31.1	32.2
Uganda	8	60	122	182	196	1.0	1.6	48.8	7.5	50.0	15.5
Zambia	32	36	120	131	..	0.6		8.7		2.2	27.3
Zimbabwe	47	111	135	90	80	1.8	0.6	-33.2	-11.1	18.7	4.1
Southern Africa	**975**	**2,019**	**3,519**	**3,635**	**3,720**	**32.3**	**29.8**	**3.3**	**2.3**	**15.7**	**11.8**
Botswana	92	124	339	335	327	2.0	2.6	-1.2	-2.4	6.2	22.3
Lesotho	13	21	26	26	..	0.3		-1.2		9.1	4.7
Namibia	67	213	..	451	..	3.4				26.1	
South Africa	779	1,625	2,721	2,792	2,876	26.0	23.1	2.6	3.0	15.8	10.9
Swaziland	24	37	38	31	30	0.6	0.2	-17.5	-5.3	9.3	0.6

Source: World Tourism Organization (WTO) ©

(Data as collected by WTO September 2003)

International Tourism Receipts by Country of Destination

	International Tourism Receipts (euro million)					Market share in the region (%)		Change (%)		Average annual growth (%)	
	1990	1995	2000	2001	2002*	1995	2002*	001/00	02*/01	90-95	95-00
Americas	***54,316***	***76,183***	***144,518***	***136,493***	***120,831***	***100***	***100***	***-5.6***	***-11.5***	***7.0***	***13.7***
North America	**43,044**	**59,217**	**109,931**	**101,680**	**90,004**	**77.7**	**74.5**	**-7.5**	**-11.5**	**6.6**	**13.2**
Canada	4,978	6,026	11,735	12,030	10,258	7.9	8.5	2.5	-14.7	3.9	14.3
Mexico	4,293	4,724	8,981	9,380	9,368	6.2	7.8	4.4	-0.1	1.9	13.7
United States	33,773	48,467	89,215	80,271	70,377	63.6	58.2	-10.0	-12.3	7.5	13.0
Caribbean	**6,841**	**9,316**	**18,398**	**19,120**	**17,572**	**12.2**	**14.5**	**3.9**	**-8.1**	**6.4**	**14.6**
Anguilla	27	37	60	68	58	0.0	0.0	14.4	-14.6	6.4	9.7
Antigua,Barb	234	189	314	304	..	0.2		-3.3		-4.2	10.7
Aruba	275	398	691	994	950	0.5	0.8	43.9	-4.4	7.7	11.6
Bahamas	1,040	1,029	1,861	1,827	..	1.4		-1.8		-0.2	12.6
Barbados	388	468	770	767	..	0.6		-0.4		3.8	10.5
Bermuda	385	373	467	392	..	0.5		-16.0		-0.6	4.6
Bonaire	14	28	94	84	..	0.0		-11.1		14.9	27.2
Br.Virgin Is	104	161	341	376	..	0.2		10.3		9.2	16.2
Cayman Islands	185	301	605	653	..	0.4		7.9		10.2	15.0
Cuba	191	736	1,881	1,889	1,727	1.0	1.4	0.5	-8.6	31.0	20.6
Curaçao	94	134	246	282	289	0.2	0.2	14.9	2.2	7.3	12.9
Dominica	20	26	52	44	38	0.0	0.0	-16.5	-12.6	5.8	15.0
Dominican Rp	707	1,199	3,097	3,124	2,893	1.6	2.4	0.9	-7.4	11.1	20.9
Grenada	30	41	100	93	89	0.1	0.1	-7.0	-4.7	6.7	19.4
Guadeloupe	155	350	453	..	..	0.5				17.7	5.3
Haiti	36	43	58	60	..	0.1		3.1		3.5	6.4
Jamaica	581	817	1,443	1,377	1,279	1.1	1.1	-4.6	-7.1	7.1	12.0
Martinique	188	294	327	274	..	0.4		-16.3		9.3	2.2
Montserrat	5	15	10	9	..	0.0		-2.9		22.7	-8.6
Puerto Rico	1,073	1,398	2,585	3,046	2,629	1.8	2.2	17.8	-13.7	5.4	13.1
Saint Lucia	121	205	322	289	271	0.3	0.2	-10.4	-6.1	11.1	9.5
St.Kitts-Nev	46	50	63	67	60	0.1	0.0	5.9	-10.0	1.8	5.0
St.Maarten	248	267	539	550	..	0.4		2.1		1.5	15.1
St.Vincent,Grenadines	44	31	81	89	86	0.0	0.1	10.0	-4.1	-6.5	21.0
Trinidad Tbg	75	56	231	224	237	0.1	0.2	-2.7	5.6	-5.6	32.8
Turks,Caicos	29	41	309	347	309	0.1	0.3	12.5	-11.1	6.9	50.1
US.Virgin Is	547	628	1,399	1,477	1,311	0.8	1.1	5.6	-11.2	2.8	17.4
Central America	**577**	**1,207**	**3,340**	**3,298**	**3,569**	**1.6**	**3.0**	**-1.3**	**8.2**	**15.9**	**22.6**
Belize	35	59	130	135	141	0.1	0.1	4.0	4.1	11.2	17.2
Costa Rica	216	505	1,331	1,223	1,140	0.7	0.9	-8.1	-6.8	18.5	21.4
El Salvador	14	31	275	262	362	0.0	0.3	-4.6	37.8	17.3	54.4
Guatemala	145	212	579	550	735	0.3	0.6	-5.0	33.5	7.8	22.3
Honduras	23	82	281	307	362	0.1	0.3	9.0	18.0	29.1	28.0
Nicaragua	9	38	121	122	112	0.1	0.1	1.0	-7.9	32.3	25.8
Panama	135	281	624	699	718	0.4	0.6	12.1	2.7	15.7	17.3
South America	**3,853**	**6,444**	**12,849**	**12,394**	**9,686**	**8.5**	**8.0**	**-3.5**	**-21.8**	**10.8**	**14.8**
Argentina	888	1,639	3,050	2,844	..	2.2		-6.8		13.0	13.2
Bolivia	71	106	173	174	..	0.1		0.5		8.3	10.3
Brazil	1,134	1,603	4,578	4,132	3,300	2.1	2.7	-9.7	-20.2	7.2	23.3
Chile	424	696	887	892	776	0.9	0.6	0.5	-13.0	10.4	5.0
Colombia	319	502	1,111	1,350	1,017	0.7	0.8	21.5	-24.6	9.5	17.2
Ecuador	148	195	435	480	473	0.3	0.4	10.3	-1.5	5.7	17.4
French Guiana	..	..	..	47	48		0.0		1.5		
Guyana	21	60	..	..	..	0.1				23.0	
Paraguay	101	105	79	77	66	0.1	0.1	-2.5	-14.9	0.8	-5.5
Peru	170	327	986	912	889	0.4	0.7	-7.5	-2.5	13.9	24.7
Suriname	1	16	17	16	..	0.0		-9.8		82.9	1.5
Uruguay	187	467	706	626	336	0.6	0.3	-11.3	-46.3	20.1	8.6
Venezuela	389	727	686	761	495	1.0	0.4	10.9	-35.0	13.3	-1.1

Source: World Tourism Organization (WTO) © (Data as collected by WTO September 2003)

International Tourism Receipts by Country of Destination

	International Tourism Receipts (euro million)					Market share in the region (%)		Change (%)		Average annual growth (%)	
	1990	1995	2000	2001	2002*	1995	2002*	001/00	02*/01	90-95	95-00
Asia and the Pacific	***30,803***	***56,739***	***94,110***	***98,218***	***100,147***	***100***	***95***	***4.4***	***2.0***	***13.0***	***10.6***
North-East Asia	**13,848**	**25,757**	**44,690**	**48,595**	**50,695**	**45.4**	**50.6**	**8.7**	**4.3**	**13.2**	**11.7**
China	1,742	6,677	17,566	19,865	21,558	11.8	21.5	13.1	8.5	30.8	21.3
Hong Kong (China)	3,952	7,342	8,538	9,247	10,699	12.9	10.7	8.3	15.7	13.2	3.1
Japan	2,810	2,466	3,652	3,686	3,700	4.3	3.7	0.9	0.4	-2.6	8.2
Korea, D P Rp	23	..	..	..	..						
Korea, Republic of	2,795	4,271	7,374	7,116	5,581	7.5	5.6	-3.5	-21.6	8.9	11.5
Macao (China)	1,157	2,472	3,470	4,181	4,669	4.4	4.7	20.5	11.7	16.4	7.0
Mongolia	4	16	39	44	..	0.0		11.7		32.5	19.4
Taiwan (Pr. of China)	1,366	2,512	4,050	4,456	4,439	4.4	4.4	10.0	-0.4	13.0	10.0
South-East Asia	**11,365**	**21,644**	**28,681**	**29,342**	**28,928**	**38.1**	**28.9**	**2.3**	**-1.4**	**13.8**	**5.8**
Cambodia	..	76	247	339	401	0.1	0.4	37.5	18.1		26.4
Indonesia	1,653	3,998	6,224	6,042	..	7.0		-2.9		19.3	9.3
Lao P.D.R.	2	19	123	116	120	0.0	0.1	-5.9	2.9	52.0	45.2
Malaysia	1,309	2,989	4,939	7,117	7,176	5.3	7.2	44.1	0.8	18.0	10.6
Myanmar	7	29	45	50	..	0.1		10.5		32.7	9.4
Philippines	1,026	1,876	2,310	1,924	1,841	3.3	1.8	-16.7	-4.3	12.8	4.3
Singapore	3,877	6,414	6,516	5,673	5,216	11.3	5.2	-12.9	-8.1	10.6	0.3
Thailand	3,397	6,149	8,108	7,902	8,357	10.8	8.3	-2.5	5.8	12.6	5.7
Vietnam	67	..	..	..	..						
Oceania	**5,590**	**9,338**	**15,623**	**14,707**	**15,154**	**16.5**	**15.1**	**-5.9**	**3.0**	**10.8**	**10.8**
American Samoa	8	..	..	..	..						
Australia	3,210	6,007	9,150	8,512	8,552	10.6	8.5	-7.0	0.5	13.4	8.8
Cook Is	13	21	39	42	49	0.0	0.0	8.9	14.7	11.2	12.7
Fiji	159	216	196	242	282	0.4	0.3	23.6	16.5	6.4	-2.0
French Polynesia	134	249	..	..	..	0.4				13.2	
Guam	735	..	..	..	..						
Kiribati	1	1	3	4	..	0.0		22.2		11.9	16.3
Marshall Is	..	2	4	..	4	0.0	0.0				17.8
Micronesia (Fed.St.of)	..	..	16	15	..			-10.6			
N.Mariana Is	357	501	..	..	..	0.9				7.0	
New Caledonia	74	83	119	104	..	0.1		-12.8		2.3	7.6
New Zealand	809	1,138	2,426	2,606	3,086	2.0	3.1	7.4	18.4	7.1	16.3
Niue	..	1	..	..	..	0.0					
Palau	..	..	58	65	62		0.1	13.4	-4.5		
Papua New Guinea	32	46	100	113	..	0.1		13.2		7.3	16.8
Samoa	16	26	44	45	48	0.0	0.0	0.6	6.6	10.6	11.3
Solomon Is	5	12	..	..	..	0.0				17.3	
Tonga	7	8	8	8	10	0.0	0.0	3.1	21.8	1.6	-0.2
Tuvalu	..	0	..	..	..	0.0					
Vanuatu	31	44	63	51	..	0.1		-18.2		7.7	7.2
South Asia	**1,593**	**2,664**	**5,116**	**5,574**	**5,371**	**100.0**	**70.9**	**9.0**	**-3.7**	**10.8**	**13.9**
Bangladesh	9	18	54	54	..	0.7		-1.0		15.3	25.2
Bhutan	2	4	11	..	..	0.1				19.5	23.1
India	1,188	1,975	3,430	3,396	3,091	74.1	57.6	-1.0	-9.0	10.7	11.7
Iran	48	157	726	1,253	..	5.9		72.4		26.8	35.9
Maldives	70	161	348	365	336	6.1	6.3	5.1	-7.9	18.2	16.6
Nepal	50	89	181	156	..	3.4		-13.5		12.2	15.1
Pakistan	123	87	91	103	111	3.3	2.1	12.9	8.1	-6.6	0.9
Sri Lanka	104	172	274	236	268	6.5	5.0	-14.0	13.6	10.7	9.8

Source: World Tourism Organization (WTO) ©

(Data as collected by WTO September 2003)

International Tourism Receipts by Country of Destination

	International Tourism Receipts (euro million)					Market share in the region (%)		Change (%)		Average annual growth (%)	
	1990	1995	2000	2001	2002*	1995	2002*	001/00	02*/01	90-95	95-00
Europe	***112,960***	***160,676***	***248,725***	***252,099***	***254,332***	***100***	***100***	***1.4***	***0.9***	***7.3***	***9.1***
Northern Europe	**19,102**	**24,499**	**36,705**	**35,350**	**37,566**	**15.2**	**14.8**	**-3.7**	**6.3**	**5.1**	**8.4**
Denmark	2,609	2,850	4,372	5,136	6,118	1.8	2.4	17.5	19.1	1.8	8.9
Finland	916	1,200	1,529	1,609	1,664	0.7	0.7	5.2	3.4	5.5	5.0
Iceland	109	142	247	262	264	0.1	0.1	6.3	0.8	5.4	11.7
Ireland	1,146	1,690	2,824	3,115	3,267	1.1	1.3	10.3	4.9	8.1	10.8
Norway	1,233	1,806	2,157	2,274	2,896	1.1	1.1	5.5	27.3	7.9	3.6
Sweden	2,282	2,625	4,417	4,773	4,755	1.6	1.9	8.1	-0.4	2.8	11.0
United Kingdom	10,807	14,185	21,160	18,180	18,603	8.8	7.3	-14.1	2.3	5.6	8.3
Western Europe	**50,753**	**60,843**	**89,166**	**90,852**	**92,152**	**37.9**	**36.2**	**1.9**	**1.4**	**3.7**	**7.9**
Austria	10,536	9,883	10,752	11,297	11,884	6.2	4.7	5.1	5.2	-1.3	1.7
Belgium	2,922	3,477	7,137	7,707	7,289	2.2	2.9	8.0	-5.4	3.5	15.5
France	15,850	21,045	33,297	33,473	34,190	13.1	13.4	0.5	2.1	5.8	9.6
Germany	11,220	13,183	20,007	20,569	20,261	8.2	8.0	2.8	-1.5	3.3	8.7
Luxembourg	..	1,316	1,956	2,138	2,312	0.8	0.9	9.3	8.1		8.2
Netherlands	3,263	4,780	7,814	7,506	8,150	3.0	3.2	-3.9	8.6	7.9	10.3
Switzerland	5,820	7,160	8,203	8,162	8,067	4.5	3.2	-0.5	-1.2	4.2	2.8
Central/Eastern Europe	**3,808**	**17,592**	**24,133**	**25,341**	**24,800**	**10.9**	**9.8**	**5.0**	**-2.1**	**35.8**	**6.5**
Armenia	..	4	49	137	..	0.0		181.9			66.4
Azerbaijan	179	54	68	48	..	0.0		-29.6		-21.5	5.0
Belarus	..	18	101	92	..	0.0		-9.1			41.8
Bulgaria	251	362	1,163	1,341	1,421	0.2	0.6	15.3	6.0	7.6	26.3
Czech Rep	329	2,198	3,229	3,468	3,110	1.4	1.2	7.4	-10.3	46.2	8.0
Estonia	..	270	548	566	587	0.2	0.2	3.3	3.7		15.2
Georgia	..	..	447	494	499		0.2	10.4	1.1		
Hungary	647	2,239	3,730	4,209	3,461	1.4	1.4	12.9	-17.8	28.2	10.7
Kazakhstan	..	93	385	442	657	0.1	0.3	14.7	48.5		32.8
Kyrgyzstan	..	4	16	27	..	0.0		65.0			33.6
Latvia	..	15	142	134	170	0.0	0.1	-5.5	27.3		56.1
Lithuania	..	59	423	428	543	0.0	0.2	1.0	26.9		48.4
Poland	281	5,057	6,604	5,376	4,759	3.1	1.9	-18.6	-11.5	78.2	5.5
Rep Moldova	..	44	50	51	58	0.0	0.0	3.1	13.2		2.7
Romania	83	451	389	558	647	0.3	0.3	43.6	15.9	40.2	-2.9
Russian Fed	..	3,297	3,713	3,975	4,429	2.1	1.7	7.1	11.4		2.4
Slovakia	55	474	468	713	766	0.3	0.3	52.5	7.3	53.9	-0.3
Tajikistan	..	..	0	0	..			3.1			
Ukraine	..	2,955	2,390	3,043	3,164	1.8	1.2	27.3	4.0		-4.2
Uzbekistan	..	..	68	80	72		0.0	17.9	-10.5		
Southern Europe	**34,680**	**50,319**	**84,788**	**88,344**	**87,049**	**31.3**	**34.2**	**4.2**	**-1.5**	**7.7**	**11.0**
Albania	3	50	421	498	..	0.0		18.2		73.7	53.3
Bosnia Herzg	..	5	75	82	..	0.0		9.1			69.4
Croatia	1,338	1,031	2,986	3,724	4,030	0.6	1.6	24.7	8.2	-5.1	23.7
F.Yug.Rp.Macedonia	35	15	40	28	41	0.0	0.0	-30.3	47.8	-16.3	22.5
Greece	2,032	3,162	9,984	10,548	10,302	2.0	4.1	5.7	-2.3	9.3	25.9
Italy	12,924	21,964	29,774	28,802	28,464	13.7	11.2	-3.3	-1.2	11.2	6.3
Malta	389	504	663	647	601	0.3	0.2	-2.5	-7.2	5.3	5.6
Portugal	2,792	3,317	5,719	6,147	6,260	2.1	2.5	7.5	1.8	3.5	11.5
Serbia & Montenegro	..	32	30	48	81	0.0	0.0	58.4	69.6		-1.1
Slovenia	..	829	1,040	1,118	1,145	0.5	0.5	7.4	2.5		4.7
Spain	14,601	19,410	34,055	36,704	35,543	12.1	14.0	7.8	-3.2	5.9	11.9
East Mediterranean Eu.	**4,617**	**7,423**	**13,932**	**12,212**	**12,765**	**4.6**	**5.0**	**-12.4**	**4.5**	**10.0**	**13.4**
Cyprus	988	1,367	2,051	2,212	1,970	0.9	0.8	7.9	-10.9	6.7	8.4
Israel	1,096	2,266	3,614	1,753	1,266	1.4	0.5	-51.5	-27.8	15.6	9.8
Turkey	2,533	3,790	8,268	8,247	9,529	2.4	3.7	-0.3	15.5	8.4	16.9

Source: World Tourism Organization (WTO) © (Data as collected by WTO September 2003)

International Tourism Receipts by Country of Destination

	International Tourism Receipts (euro million)					Market share in the region (%)		Change (%)		Average annual growth (%)	
	1990	1995	2000	2001	2002*	1995	2002*	001/00	02*/01	90-95	95-00
Middle East	***3,571***	***6,837***	***13,467***	***13,159***	***13,709***	***73***	***100***	***-2.3***	***4.2***	***13.9***	***14.5***
Bahrain	106	189	620	703	..	2.8		13.4		12.2	26.9
Egypt	864	2,052	4,704	4,243	3,981	30.0	29.0	-9.8	-6.2	18.9	18.0
Jordan	402	498	782	782	831	7.3	6.1	0.0	6.4	4.4	9.4
Kuwait	104	93	106	116	125	1.4	0.9	9.4	7.9	-2.3	2.8
Lebanon	..	543	803	935	1,011	7.9	7.4	16.3	8.2		8.2
Libyan Arab Jamahiriya	5	..	..	..	..						
Oman	54	70	130	132	123	1.0	0.9	1.4	-6.9	5.4	13.1
Palestine	..	..	168	10	..			-94.0			
Saudi Arabia	..	..	..	3,819	..						
Syrian Arab Republic	251	1,023	1,171	..	1,445	15.0	10.5			32.4	2.7
Untd Arab Emirates	247	483	1,096	1,188	1,404	7.1	10.2	8.4	18.2	14.3	17.8
Yemen	16	38	82	42	..	0.6		-48.4		19.5	16.6

Source: World Tourism Organization (WTO) ©

(Data as collected by WTO September 2003)

3. Methodological Notes

3.1 Concepts and Definitions

According to the WTO/United Nations *Recommendations on Tourism Statistics*, Tourism comprises *the activities of persons travelling to and staying in places outside their usual environment for not more than one consecutive year for leisure, business and other purposes.*

This concept can be applied to different forms of tourism. Depending upon whether a person is travelling to, from or within a certain country the following forms can be distinguished:

- **Inbound Tourism**, involving the non-residents received by a destination country from the point of view of that destination;
- **Outbound Tourism**, involving residents travelling to another country from the point of view of the country of origin;
- **Domestic tourism**, involving residents of a given country travelling within that country.

All types of travellers engaged in tourism are described as visitors. Visitors can be distinguished as same-day visitors or tourists (overnight visitors).
There are various units of measure to quantify the volume of tourism. An overview is set out below:

Unit of measurement			Comment
Visitors	*Arrivals*	*- at frontiers*	or at a specific place in case of domestic tourism
Tourists (overnight visitors)	*Arrivals*	*- at frontiers*	
		- at collective tourism establishments (e.g. hotels and other, such as campings etc.) *- at hotels and similar establishments*	- excludes tourism in private accommodation; - arrivals are counted in every new accommodation visited
	Nights	*- at collective tourism establishments (e.g. hotels and other)* *- at hotels and similar establishments*	

Inbound Tourism

Unless otherwise stated, this report concentrates on **International Tourism** as measured from an **Inbound Tourism** perspective, i.e. the tourism received by any given destination country (and in a few cases territories) from non-residents travelling to that destination.

The most common unit of measure used to quantify the volume of International Tourism for statistical purposes is the number of International Tourist Arrivals. For a proper understanding of this unit, two considerations should be taken into account:

- Data refer exclusively to tourists (overnight visitors): 'a visitor who stays at least one night in a collective or private accommodation in the country visited'. Same-day visitors are not included.
- Data refer to the number of arrivals and not to the number of persons. The same person who makes several trips to a given country during a given period will be counted as a new arrival each time, as well as a person who travels through several countries on one trip is counted as a new arrival each time.

Figures on the volume of international tourism presented in the regional and subregional tables, preferably relate to the concept of *international tourist arrivals at frontiers*. However, as not all countries are collecting data according to this concept, another series may be used instead. In the tables, the series are indicated as follows:

TF: International tourist arrivals at frontiers (excluding same-day visitors);
VF: International visitor arrivals at frontiers (including tourists and same-day visitors);
TCE: International tourist arrivals at collective tourism establishments;
THS: International tourist arrivals at hotels and similar establishments.

With respect to the inbound tourism volume, if available, in the Profile tables for individual countries in Chapter III, except for data on International Tourist Arrivals, furthermore, data is included on International Visitor Arrivals, Same-day Visitor Arrivals, Cruise passengers (considered as a special category of same-day visitors) and Nights spent in collective establishments or in hotels and similar establishments.

Outbound Tourism

Data on outbound tourism volume in this series of reports originate from two different sources and likewise relate to two dissimilar concepts:

- On one hand, many countries are reporting the number of outbound trips of their residents. Data availability and comparability, however, is still limited and it is often not clear whether the reported figures refer only to tourists or to visitors in general.
- On the other hand, data are synthesised from the data on inbound tourism to destination countries (an arrival received in a destination can also be taken as an arrival generated by the generating country). Data on arrivals to destinations broken down by region of origin are taken to estimate and aggregate the number of arrivals originating from each region. The unit of measurement is the number of international tourist arrivals generated by the region of origin concerned. For a proper understanding, it should be borne in mind that these figures do not correspond to the number of trips, as one trip taken might result in various arrivals in destinations.

Domestic Tourism

International comparable data on domestic tourism is unfortunately still rather scarce. If available for a certain country, this series is represented in the Profile tables for countries in Chapter III of the regional volumes in the form of the number of nights spent by residents at hotels and similar establishments or at all collective tourism establishments.

Accommodation

As a measure for the capacity of accommodation, data is included on the number of rooms or the number of bed places in the country. When expressed in bed places, the number of rooms roughly will be half, as rooms on average count two bed places. The actual capacity of a country might eventually be larger, as some countries exclude hotels below a certain category or less than a certain size.

International Tourism Receipts and Expenditure

International Tourism Receipts are the receipts earned by a destination country from inbound tourism and cover all tourism receipts resulting from expenditure made by visitors from abroad, on for instance lodging, food and drinks, fuel, transport in the country, entertainment, shopping, etc. This concept includes receipts generated by overnight as well as by same-day trips, which can be substantial, as will be the case with countries where a lot of shopping for goods and services takes place by visitors from neighbouring countries. It excludes, however, the receipts related to international transport contracted by residents of other countries (for instance ticket receipts from foreigners travelling with a national company). These receipts are covered in the separate category ***International Fare Receipts***, which for most recent years is estimated at about 18 per cent of total tourism and fare receipts.

International Tourism Expenditure is the expenditure on tourism outside their country of residence made by visitors (same-day visitors and tourists) from a given country of origin.

Data on receipts and expenditure related to international tourism are generally gathered in the framework of the Balance of Payments under the items 'Services, Travel, Credit and Debit' (International Tourism Receipts and Expenditure) and 'Transportation, Passenger Services, Credit and Debit' (International Fare Receipts and Expenditure). See the *Balance of Payments Statistics Yearbook, Part 2 and Part 3* of the International Monetary Fund (IMF) for details on methodologies, compilation practices and data sources.

The International Tourism Balance and International Fare Balance as included in the Profile tables in Chapter III of the regional volumes, correspond to the net receipts or expenditure of a given country on respectively international tourism or international fares, i.e. receipts less expenditure.

Further information

More detailed information on concepts, definitions, classifications, indicators, methods of compiling and units of measure can be obtained from:

- the *Basic References on Tourism Statistics* on the WTO website under the link <www.world-tourism.org/statistics/tsa_project/basic_references/index-en.htm> setting out the main components that make up the System of Tourism Statistics (STS);

or from the following WTO publications:

- *Recommendations on tourism statistics* (WTO 1994),
- *Technical Manual No. 1: Concepts Definitions, and Classifications for Tourism Statistics* (WTO 1995);
- *Technical Manual No. 2: Collection for Tourism Expenditure Statistics* (WTO 1995);
- *Technical Manual No. 3: Collection of Domestic Tourism Statistics* (WTO 1995);
- *Technical Manual No. 4: Collection and Compilation of Tourism Statistics* (WTO 1995);
- *Data Collection & Analysis for Tourism Management, Marketing & Planning* (WTO 2000).

3.2 Sources, Data Treatment and Acknowledgement

General

Quantitative tourism-related data in this report is based on a selection of data included in the WTO database on World Tourism Statistics. This database contains a variety of series for over 200 countries and territories covering data for most countries from the 1980's on. The database is maintained by the WTO Secretariat and is updated on a continuous base.

Except where otherwise indicated, statistical data has been collected by the WTO Secretariat from the official institutions of the countries and territories (WTO member as well as non-member countries) or from official international bodies, e.g. the Caribbean Tourism Organization (CTO), International Monetary Fund (IMF).

The data for individual countries corresponding to 2002 are based on full year results, or projections, as communicated to the WTO Secretariat by the authorities of the countries and territories or disseminated through a news release, publication or on the Internet. Data collection for this series of reports closed in September 2003. For many countries 2002 figures are still preliminary and subject to revision.

In the world and (sub)regional aggregates, estimates are included for countries and territories with data still missing based upon data available for a part of the year or the general trend for the region. In particular for the Middle East and Africa the regional and subregional aggregates for 2002 should be treated with caution as estimations are based on a relatively small number of countries and territories that supplied data for the entire year. In the tables, provisional figures are marked with an asterisk (*).

WTO tourism statistics generally refer to figures for a country as a whole. In the collection of statistics, however, except for independent states, there are also a number of dependencies or territories of special sovereignty included (for instance Hong Kong (China) or French Polynesia). These territories report tourism figures independently and are for the sake of tourism statistics considered as an entity in itself. Because of this, where reference is made to "countries" the term generally should be taken to mean "countries and territories". In a few other cases, dependencies are not separately listed but included in the total for the country they depend upon (for instance Guernsey, Jersey and the Isle of Man in United Kingdom).

In general WTO does not collect data on the level of regions, states, provinces or specific destinations within a country (Hawaii is one of the few exceptions made because of its relevance for Asian outbound travel; in the overview tables, however, Hawaii is included in the United States figure). Most countries will have a further regional breakdown available as well as other series not included in the WTO database on World Tourism Statistics. Please refer to national sources for this data.

The regional country groupings are according to the WTO regional commissions. See the tables by country in the annex for the countries and territories included in the various regions and subregions.

The World Tourism Organization is aware of the limitations of the available statistical information on tourism. Despite the considerable progress made in recent decades, international tourism statistics are often not uniform, because definitions and methods of data collection tend to differ. Every user of this information should bear in mind that the international comparability of statistical data is still not optimal.

The qualitative information in the country sections of the reports was gathered by means of the survey on tourism development in 2002, as completed in the first eight months of 2003 by the NTAs, NTOs or Statistical Offices of the various countries and territories. See Annex 5 for the questionnaire used.

The World Tourism Organization wishes to express its gratitude to the correspondents of the various countries and territories for their indispensable cooperation.

Tourism series in this report

The tourism data series in Chapter II and in the Profile tables of countries in Chapter III correspond to the basic indicators included in the WTO *Compendium of Tourism Statistics*. Please refer to the latest publication for additional series, methodological references and notes on the series for specific countries.

A number of derived series are included relating tourism volume to the size of the population or tourism receipts and expenditure to tourism volume. In the Profile tables in Chapter III, those series are marked with '-'. Ratios are based on simple divisions of the concept in question by the population or of the receipts or expenditure by the corresponding concepts:

International Tourist Arrivals per 100 of inhabitants = International Tourist Arrivals / population * 100.

Trips abroad per 100 of inhabitants = Trips abroad / population * 100.

International Tourism Receipts per International Tourist Arrival = International Tourism Receipts / International Tourist Arrivals.

International Tourism Receipts per International Visitor Arrival = International Tourism Receipts / International Visitor Arrivals.

International Tourism Receipts per capita = International Tourism Receipts / population.

International Tourism Expenditure per trip abroad = International Tourism Expenditure / Trips abroad.

International Tourism Expenditure per capita = International Tourism Expenditure / population.

Financial data is generally collected and kept in the WTO database in US$ values. In the cases where countries report in local currency, values are transferred by WTO into US$ applying the average exchange rate for the corresponding year. However, part of the tables are also published in euros. These euro values are in general derived from the US$ values using the corresponding average annual exchange rates for the two currencies. The following exchange rates have been applied:

Exchange rates US$ versus euro (ECU for the years before 1999) annual averages

	€/ECU per US$	Change (%)	US$ per €/ECU	Change (%)
1995	0.76452		1.30801	
1996	0.78756	3.0	1.26975	-2.9
1997	0.88180	12.0	1.13404	-10.7
1998	0.89199	1.2	1.12109	-1.1
1999	0.93828	5.2	1.06578	-4.9
2000	1.08270	15.4	0.92361	-13.3
2001	1.11653	3.1	0.89563	-3.0
2002	1.05756	-5.3	0.94557	5.6

Source : Eurostat

As exchange rates fluctuate substantially over time, for the first time this year the evolution of International Tourism Receipts was also estimated in (weighted) local currencies. For this, receipts in US$ have been recomputed in local currencies using an exchange rate table provided by IMF. In order to take care of inflation, receipts have been put in constant prices using country data on inflation from IMF as deflator.

The data in the tables on international tourist or visitor arrivals and nights of international tourists by country of origin included in Chapter III correspond to the series as included in the WTO *Yearbook of Tourism Statistics*. Please refer to the latter publication for additional series, metrological references and notes on the series for specific countries.

Series from external sources
Information included, but not referring to tourism indicators, are in general taken from specialised international organisations and not collected by the WTO Secretariat from the individual countries and territories. Data are meant as indicators, providing a context for tourism performance and do not necessarily coincide fully with national data. The following series are included:

Population
Data refer to total midyear population as included in the International Database (IDB) of the International Programs Center (IPC) of the Population Division of the U.S. Bureau of the Census, <www.census.gov/ipc/www>. The IDB combines data from country sources (especially censuses and surveys) with IPC's estimates and projections to provide information dating back as far as 1950 and as far ahead as 2050. The IDB can be considered as a practically complete and consistent set of population data covering 227 countries and areas with 1998 populations of 5,000 or more.

Area
Data on the dimension of the area of countries and territories are taken from the Statistical database of the Food and Agriculture Organization of the United Nations (FAO) <www.fao.org> and refer to the total area of the country, including area under inland water bodies for the year 2000. In the case of Belgium and Luxembourg data is taken from national sources.

Economic Indicators
The series on Gross Domestic Product (GDP), Gross Domestic Product per capita and economic growth (annual per cent change of Real Gross Domestic Product) are based on the World Economic Outlook (WEO) Database of September 2003 of the International Monetary Fund (IMF). See <www.imf.org/external/pubs/ft/weo/2003/02/data/index.htm>.

4. Sources of Information

A. **WTO web site** <www.world-tourism.org>

The WTO has a comprehensive website available with news and information on its programme activities, members, regional activities, publications, special projects etc. in English, French and Spanish with a growing section in Russian.

- A qualitative and quantitative overview of world tourism and selected statistical country data is available under the *Facts & Figures* link, including the most updated tourism trends and data in the *"WTO World Tourism Barometer"*
- Information on the activities of the WTO Market Intelligence and Promotion section can be found under the *Market Intelligence and Promotion* link (forthcoming).
- Information on the activities, outputs and meeting of the WTO Tourism Recovery Committee is available under the *Tourism Recovery Committee* link.
- An overview of available publications and electronic products with detailed information on each item including contents and sample chapters, can be found in the WTO Infoshop: <www.world-tourism.org/infoshop>.

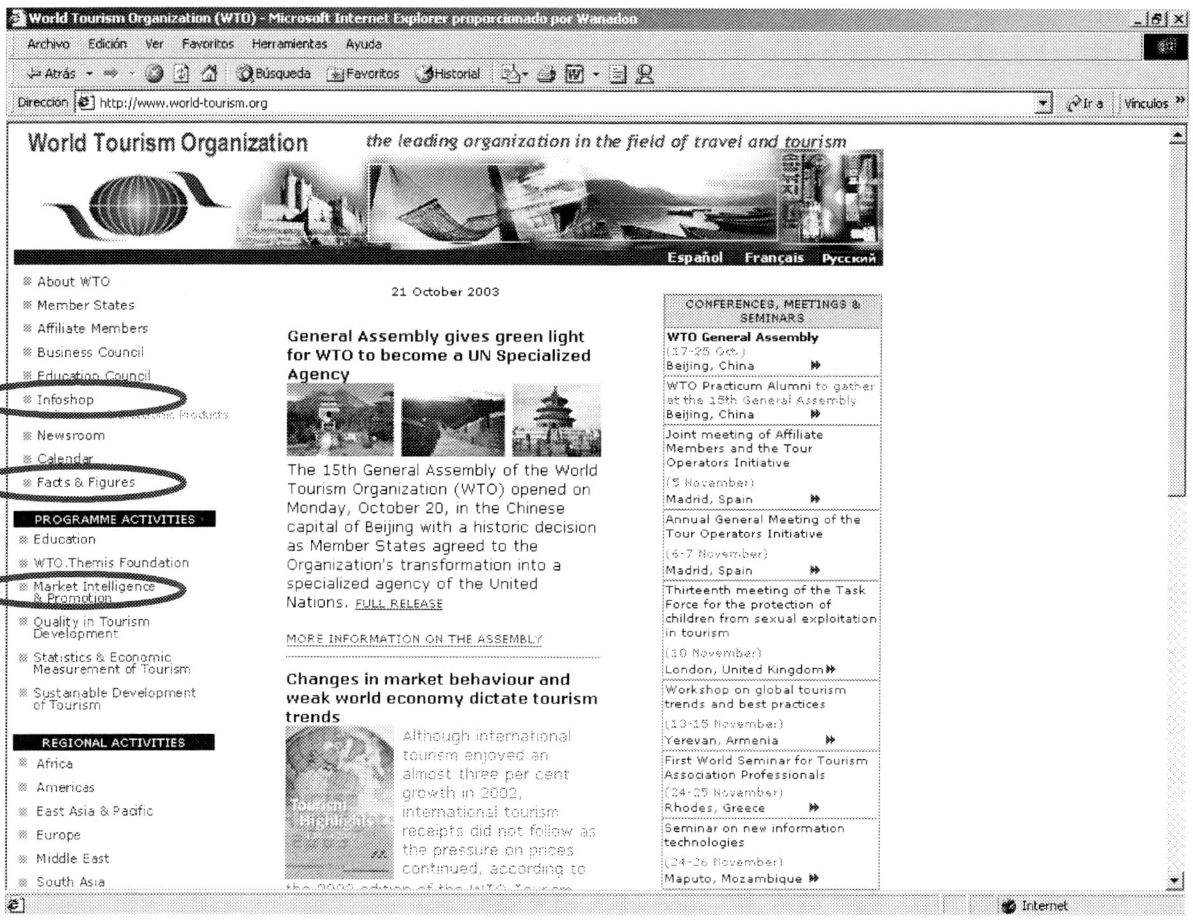

B. *Related Publications of the World Tourism Organization*

Inbound Tourism

This report is part of the *Tourism Market Trends, 2003 Edition* series consisting of 6 volumes published in English and partly in French and Spanish:

- World Overview and Tourism Topics (in English, French and Spanish)
- Africa (in English and French)
- Americas (in English and Spanish)
- Asia and the Pacific (in English)
- Europe (in English and French)
- Middle East (in English)

Excerpts of this series is included in:

- *Tourism Highlights 2003* (in English, French and Spanish). The electronic version in PDF-format can be downloaded free of charge from the Facts & Figures section of the WTO website at www.world-tourism.org/market_research/facts/menu.html.

- *Special report No 23:* Inbound Tourism to the Middle East and North Africa (WTO 2003; in English)

Outbound Tourism

- *Tourism Generating Markets: Overview and Country Profiles* (WTO 1999; in English, French and Spanish)
- *Special Reports* on specific markets:
  - No. 4: Outbound Tourism of Korea (WTO 2001; in English)
  - No. 5: Outbound Tourism of Australia (WTO 2001; in English)
  - No. 6: Outbound Tourism of Japan (WTO 2001; in English)
  - No. 7: Outbound Tourism of Belgium (WTO 2001; in English)
  - No. 8: Outbound Tourism of Spain (WTO 2001; in English and Spanish).
  - No. 9: Outbound Tourism of Japan & Korea, Results 2000 (WTO 2001; in English)
  - No. 21: Outbound Tourism of Scandinavia, Market Profile (WTO 2002; in English)
- Youth Outbound Travel of the Germans, the British & the French (WTO 2002, in English, French and Spanish)
- Chinese Outbound Tourism (WTO 2003; in English)
- Outbound Tourism from Saudi Arabia (WTO 2003; in English)

Short-term Indicators

- *WTO World Tourism Barometer* (WTO, 3 times a year since June 2003; in electronic format (PDF) and print, in English, French and Spanish)

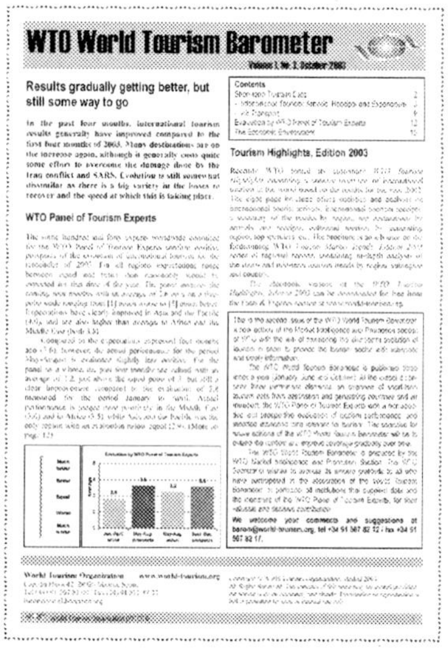
WTO World Tourism Barometer
Results gradually getting better, but still some way to go
Tourism Highlights, Edition 2003
WTO Panel of Tourism Experts

The WTO World Tourism Barometer monitors the short-term evolution of tourism and aims at providing adequate and timely information on the state of the sector. The Barometer is published three times a year (January, June, and October). It contains an overview of short-term tourism data from destination countries and tourism sectors such as air transport, a retrospective and prospective evaluation of tourism performance by the WTO Panel of Tourism Experts and selected economic data relevant for tourism.

A sample copy of the WTO World Tourism Barometer is available for download in the "Facts & Figures" section of the WTO website www.world-tourism.org.

Forecasting

WTO's long-term forecast *Tourism 2020 Vision* has been published in a series of 7 reports consisting of one summary volume and six regional volumes (WTO 2000, 2001):

- Global Forecasts and Profiles of Market Segments (in English, French and Spanish)
- Africa (in English and French)
- Americas (in English and Spanish)
- East Asia and the Pacific (in English)
- Europe (in English and French)
- Middle East (in English)
- South Asia (in English)

Tourism Products

- Tourism and Sport
  - *Sport and Tourism. 1st World Conference* (in English, French and Spanish; forthcoming). Excerpts of the presentations and the conference results of the World Conference on Sport and Tourism held February 2001 in Barcelona, Spain
  - *Introductory Report on Sport & Tourism* (WTO 2001);
  - *Sport Activities during the outbound holidays of the Germans, the Dutch and the French* (WTO 2001);
  - *Deporte Y Turismo: Destino América Latina* (WTO 2003; in Spanish)
- Ecotourism
  - Special report No. 10: The German Ecotourism Market (WTO 2001)
  - Special report No. 11: The British Ecotourism Market (WTO 2001)
  - Special report No. 12: The U.S. Ecotourism Market (WTO 2002)
  - Special report No. 13: The Italian Ecotourism Market (WTO 2002)
  - Special report No. 14: The Spanish Ecotourism Market (WTO 2002)
  - Special report No. 15: The Canadian Ecotourism Market (WTO 2002)
  - Special report No. 16: The French Ecotourism Market (WTO 2002)
- MICE
  - *MICE Outbound Tourism 2000* (WTO 2003;in English)
- Cruises
  - *Worldwide Cruise Ship Activity* (WTO 2003; in English, French and Spanish)

WTO Tourism Recovery Committee

- Special report No. 17: *The impact of the attacks in the United States on international tourism: An initial analysis* (included in the Annex of Special report No. 18, not available separately)
- Special report No. 18: *Tourism after 11 September 2001: Analysis, remedial actions and prospects* (WTO 2001; in English, French and Spanish)
- Special report No. 19: *Tourism Recovery Committee for the Mediterranean Region* (WTO 2002; in English, French and Spanish)
- Special report No. 20: *The impact of the September 11th attacks on tourism: The light at the end of the tunnel* (WTO 2002; in English, French and Spanish)
- Special report No. 21: 2002: Climbing Towards Recovery? (WTO 2002; in English)
- Special report No. 22: Fourth Meeting of the Tourism Recovery Committee - ITB Berlin 2003 (WTO 2003;in English)

Basic Statistical Reference

- *Compendium of Tourism Statistics* (WTO 2003; tri-lingual edition in English, French and Spanish and table descriptions in Arabic and Russian)
- *Yearbook of Tourism Statistics* (WTO 2003; tri-lingual edition in English, French and Spanish)

Statistical Methodology

- *Recommendations on Tourism Statistics* (WTO 1994; in English, French and Spanish)
- *Technical Manuals* (WTO 1995; in English, French and Spanish):
  - *No. 1: Concepts, Definitions and Classifications for Tourism Statistics*
  - *No. 2: Collection of Tourism Expenditure Statistics*
  - *No. 3: Collection of Domestic Tourism Statistics*
  - *No. 4: Collection and Compilation of Tourism Statistics*
- *Data Collection and Analysis for Tourism Management, Marketing and Planning* (WTO 2000; in English)

See for detailed information on concepts, definitions, classifications, indicators, methods of compiling and units of measure also the *Basic References on Tourism Statistics*, setting out the main components that make up the System of Tourism Statistics (STS), on the WTO website at: <www.world-tourism.org/statistics/tsa_project/basic_references/index-en.htm>.
See for documentation on the Tourism Satellite Account methodology the WTO website at: www.world-tourism.org/frameset/frame_statistics.html

Other

- *Tourism in the Age of Alliances, Mergers and Acquisitions* (WTO 2002)
- *Apuntes de la Metodología de la Investigación en Turismo* (WTO 2001, only in Spanish)
- *Marketing Papers No.1* (WTO 2002)

C. References

International Organizations

- United Nations; <www.un.org>
- United Nations Development Programme; <www.undp.org>
- International Monetary Fund (IMF); <www.imf.org>
- World Bank; <www.worldbank.org>
- Organisation for Economic Co-operation and Development (OECD); <www.oecd.org>
- World Trade Organization (WTO); <www.wto.org>

Research Companies / Consultants

- Tim Bartlett, TRI Hospitality Consulting Spain, <www.trihospitality.com>

Country Sources

References for information on the Internet of National Tourism Administrations (NTA), National Tourism Organisations (NTO) and / or web directions for research and data are included in the country contributions of Chapter III of the regional volumes of the *Tourism Market Trends 2003* series.

5. Questionnaire on Tourism Development 2002

Country:			
Institution:			
Department:			
Street:		**P.O. Box:**	
City:		**Post/Zip Code:**	
Tel:		**Fax:**	
Contact person:			
Job title:			
Email:			
Please indicate in what format you would like to receive the complimentary copy of the report on your region			Electronic (PDF) [.] paper [ ]

Web site(s) for promotional use (aimed at visitors to your country)**:**	
Web site(s) for institutional/corporate use (providing information on tourism policy, research, etc)**:**	
Web site(s) supplying research and data (providing research and timely information on evolution of tourism, statistical data on tourism volume, receipts, etc):	

Please feel free to use as much space as necessary for your answers to the following questions (but try not to exceed 5 pages for the total of your reply to all questions).

if you wish you can use a separate document making reference to the number of the question

Evaluation 2002 Tourism Results 2002	
1) What has/have been on the whole the most significant determinant(s) in the tourism development in your country last year? This can be both with respect to supply and demand as well as to external conditions such as the political and economic situation, weather, health and security, etc.	
Please indicate the most decisive ***positive*** *or* ***negative*** *factors for each of the following (if applicable).*	
2) Tourism Products For example: new products, changes in accommodation capacity, facilities, entertainment, events, quality, price level, competitiveness, quality, new products, niche markets, etc.	
3) Access For example: international and domestic transport infrastructure, capacity offered (routes and frequency)and competitiveness, facilitation of entry formalities, etc.	
4) Major generating markets For example: significant changes in performance of existing markets, emerging markets, niche markets, differentiation of target groups, etc.	
5) Other Other factors you deem of interest with respect to tourism development in your country. For example: political and economic situation, weather, health and security, other external conditions, etc.	

Outlook 2003	
6) What are your tourism prospects and forecasts for the current year / and for the next few years? Please include information on forecasts, upcoming special events, promotional campaigns, etc.	

Tourism development in recent past, present and near future	
7) What have been the major developments in the area of Tourism Policy For example: policy-making and planning, Tourism Master Plans, investment and tax incentives, deregulation, human resource development, public-private partnership, etc.	
8) What have been the major developments in the area of Marketing and Promotion For example: Marketing Plan (strategic and operational), distribution channels, special promotional campaigns and activities, events, contents and tools, use of new technologies, resources, research, etc.	

Cultural tourism *In this year's edition of the Tourism Market Trends we would like to pay special attention to cultural tourism. This type of tourism encompass cultural activities and experiences that attract visitors and enhance their visit. In this respect cultural tourism is linked to the discovery of monuments and sites, the local area, the lifestyle of the local people, history, archaeology, architecture, art, festivals of music and other performing arts, gastronomy, etc.*	
9) Does cultural tourism have a specific place within the tourism policy of your administration and/or tourism board? If yes, please provide a brief description of the main objectives identified and instruments applied. *(Please attach any relevant information or document to your reply of this questionnaire.)*	yes [ ] / no [ ]
10) With respect to supply, on which elements of cultural tourism is the main focus of your attention? E.g. destinations, products, etc.	
11) What is the main focus of your attention with respect to the demand for cultural tourism? E.g. generating markets, segments, etc.	
12) Does cultural tourism have a specific place in your marketing and promotion plan? If yes, please provide a brief description of the main objectives identified and related programmes or actions. *(Please attach any relevant information or document to your reply of this questionnaire.)*	yes [ ] / no [ ]
13) Has your tourism administration and/or tourism board undertaken special activities or campaigns to promote cultural tourism products lately? For example: specific promotion and marketing of destinations or products in the field of cultural tourism, themes, festivals, etc.	
14) Could you please provide an estimate of the importance/ size of cultural tourism in your country: - total tourism offer (for instance % of incoming tour operators) - international tourist arrivals	